The English Connection

The Puritan Roots of Seventh-day Adventist Belief

B. W. Ball

JAMES CLARKE
Cambridge

ISBN 0 227 67844 3

Published by:
JAMES CLARKE & Co,
7 All Saints' Passage,
Cambridge, CB2 3LS,
England

Printed in England by Biddles Ltd

TABLE OF CONTENTS

Introduction   1

1. The Sufficiency of Scripture   15

2. This Incomparable Jesus   31

3. The Lord our Righteousness   49

4. The New Man   67

5. Believer's Baptism   83

6. A High Priest in Heaven   102

7. Gospel Obedience   120

8. The Seventh-Day Sabbath   138

9. The Whole Man   159

10. The Return of Christ   178

11. That Great Almanack of Prophecy   193

12. The World to Come   213

References   229

Bibliography   244

Index of Biblical References   248

Index of Names   249

General Index   250

Truth indeed came once into the world with her divine Master, and was a perfect shape most glorious to look on: but when He ascended, and His Apostles after Him were laid asleep, then strait arose a wicked race of deceivers, who ... took the virgin Truth, hewd her lovely form into a thousand pieces, and scattered them to the four winds. From that time ever since, the sad friends of Truth, such as durst appear, ... went up and down gathering up limb by limb still as they could find them. We have not yet found them all, Lords and Commons, nor ever shall do, till her Master's second coming; He shall bring together every joint and member, and shall mould them into an immortal feature of loveliness and perfection.

John Milton *Areopagitica*

INTRODUCTION

To the modern mind, judging hastily and with animus irrelevant to the facts, the sixteenth-century Puritan may seem a morbid, introspective, inhibited moral bigot and religious zealot. To the common man of the time this was not so.... In spite of the restrictions placed upon their activities, they incessantly preached the gospel and published books. Almost no one reads their writings now, but the people read them then, and no one can wisely ignore them who desires to understand what Puritanism was and what.it came to mean.

William Haller *The Rise of Puritanism* pp.5, 36

To neglect God's work in the past is to neglect his Word in the present, for throughout history God has raised up men and movements whose great work was to expound and apply that Word to their own generation, and by implication to ours also. Such men were the Puritans and such a movement was Puritanism.

Peter Lewis *The Genius of Puritanism* p.11

It is not unreasonable to assume that William Ings and John Loughborough, when they arrived in England late in 1878 to proclaim Seventh-day Adventist beliefs, gave little thought to their Puritan forbears who, two hundred years or more previously, had advocated similar views. Ellen White's *Great Controversy Between Christ and Satan* would number among the outstanding religious leaders of the past three Puritan divines, Richard Baxter, John Flavel, and Joseph Alleine. But *Great Controversy* had not yet been published, and there is little reason to think that Ings, Loughborough, or any early Seventh-day Adventist had undertaken a detailed study of Puritanism, or, indeed, that to any appreciable extent they had read English religious history in its broader aspects. The study of the Puritan era as a seed-bed for the religious and political ideas which later would profoundly affect the course of Western civilisation was yet in the future. Consequently this fascinating, and fundamental, background to the emergence of later Protestant denominations, Seventh-day Adventists among them, was to assume much greater significance in the years that followed the arrival of Ings and Loughborough and their first tentative attempts to establish Seventh-day Adventism in the land where most of its major tenets had appeared some two centuries earlier.

It will hardly be disputed that every religious movement has roots in the soil of the past. That being so, the purpose of this book is to examine specific doctrines which flourished in England between the end of the sixteenth century and the beginning of the eighteenth century and which now, a hundred years after the first official representatives of the nascent Seventh-day Adventist Church began their work,[1] make it clear that, in its essentials, Seventh-day Adventist belief had been preached and practised in England during the Puritan era. This is not to quarrel with those who would point out that the Seventh-day Adventist movement as it now exists arose in North America during the first half of the nineteenth century. That is an indisputable historical fact, rooted in the Great Advent Awakening — itself by no means a uniquely American phenomenon — and linked to such specific events as the emergence of the name Seventh-day Adventist in 1860, and the official organisation of the Church in 1863. Neither is it to ignore other historical antecedents in the British Isles. Strands in the present doctrinal stance of Seventh-day Adventism appeared in the beliefs of the Celtic Church, as Dr. Leslie Hardinge's study, *The Celtic Church in Britain*, demonstrates. Emphases in the teachings of Wycliffe and Lollardism, and in Wesley, are also evident in the Adventist position. A careful analysis of all these, as well as of certain Continental movements, would be necessary to give a complete account of Adventism's theological background. We are only concerned here, however, to portray the characteristically Puritan historico-theological roots of those beliefs which coalesced in North America during the nineteenth century and which have, in the intervening years, if we may refer to a more recent study of Adventism, produced a religious movement unique in modern times.[2]

One notable feature of the Seventh-day Adventist Church is its rapid growth-rate on a world scale, and it is this which provides justification for a serious study of Adventist backgrounds. In 1981 membership of the Church passed the 3,500,000 mark, with adherents in 189 countries. Yet at the turn of the century total membership stood at merely 66,000, after more than half a century of determined evangelistic activity. The first million mark was attained in 1955, and this was doubled by 1970. While it took fifteen years to add a second million to the Church's world membership, it took only eight years to add the third million. Latest reports suggest that the Church's growth-rate is still increasing.[3] On the basis of these figures it seems that Adventism may be poised for a phenomenal expansion. This study is presented from the standpoint that, in order to understand completely the contemporary world-wide appeal of this biblically conservative Church, it is desirable to see it in the context of its theological ancestry and not merely as a late occurrence in the development of Christian thought. While the Puritan strain may not be the only hereditary line to trace back, it may in the end prove to be the dominant one.

Further justification for a study of this nature may be drawn from the character of Adventism vis-à-vis other religious movements which appeared in the nineteenth century. Misunderstanding has persisted at this point, as no less a voice than that of David Edwards indicates when classifying Seventh-day Adventists, together with the Jehovah's Witness organisation,[4] as 'Churches for the disinherited', both teaching that at Christ's second coming 'only 144,000 persons will then be saved out of the human race'.[5] To maintain, after duly considering the evidence appearing in the first chapters of this study, that Adventism is deviant from basic Christianity, would be to misread or misunderstand that evidence. Puritanism was nothing if it was not thoroughly Protestant, and the links in Seventh-day Adventist theology with Puritan thought are so many and so fundamental that it is only remarkable that they have not previously been examined at length. This study in its entirety hopefully will demonstrate Adventism's essential affinity with historic, biblical Protestantism as opposed to any superficial relationship to nineteenth-century pseudo-Christian sectarianism.

Theologically, then, Seventh-day Adventism may be regarded from one standpoint as a synthesis of certain doctrines which re-appeared in the Reformation and which matured largely, if not entirely, in seventeenth-century English Puritanism. Some of those doctrines were common to Protestantism as a whole. Some, inevitably, were controversial in their day, and have remained so since. Some were professed at the time only by a minority. Some, such as the baptism of believers, have been debated again more recently and have been judged worthy of further consideration. Together these doctrines, perpetuated through the intervening centuries by various groups large and small, were to become the substance of Seventh-day Adventist belief. Of course, it is only fair to point out that many Puritans did not hold any of the doctrines which would later become distinctive tenets of Adventism, with the exception perhaps of belief in the literal second coming of Christ at the end of the age. For all that, the evidence is strong that Puritan religious thought, in its broadest sense, gave to the English-speaking world all the essentials of contemporary Adventist belief.

Given that this book attempts to trace those essentials in Puritan theology, it must at the same time be recognised that no claim is made that the mere existence of certain beliefs in the seventeenth century establishes their truthfulness. The presence of such doctrines within Puritanism authenticates them no more than the absence of other ideas then, or at any time in Christian history, of itself excludes them from the true body of faith. The validity of Puritanism's beliefs can only be assessed ultimately in the light of the approach used by Puritan expositors to the divine revelation in Scripture and in the light of the conclusions they reached. It is almost certainly true that Adventism would wish to be judged by the same criteria. Such assessments must be left until the evidence is before us. We merely wish to emphasise at this point that the existence of a particular belief at any time in the past or present cannot of itself be taken as evidence of its authenticity.

The chapters that follow, therefore, examine certain beliefs which became established in the religious thinking of Christians in seventeenth-century England. Some of them in their day were, as we have said, more widely accepted than others, many of them were of the very essence of Protestantism as such, and all of them are to be found indelibly recorded in the pages of innumerable works of theology and devotion which characterised the Puritan era as a whole. It might be argued that a more thorough presentation of official Adventist doctrine is desirable in a work which sets out to establish the affinity between it and its seventeenth-century antecedents. That approach has its attractions, but it would have necessitated a reduced and inevitably superficial treatment of the original source material. Access is readily available to the large annual output of books and periodicals from the Church's publishing programme for those who wish to compare current Adventist belief.[6] More to the point, of course, is that what appears here, albeit in the form and style of Puritan theologians, represents the Adventist position on the doctrines examined, at least as far as the present author understands it. Also, while it is recognised that final conclusions cannot be drawn from isolated references, the quotations which appear at the heads of chapters have been selected from representative Adventist authors and have been placed together with typical statements from Puritan spokesmen in order to illustrate succinctly the fundamental relationship which it is the main purpose of this book to demonstrate.

Since doctrinal statements and theological ideas in isolation tend to appear rather nebulous, even irrelevant to contemporary thought at times, it may be helpful to begin by calling to mind, if only briefly, some of the more prominent events and trends which marked the rise and growth of the English Puritan movement. This will provide a more meaningful factual background for the doctrinal viewpoints which will occupy the main part of the book. Those whose acquaintance with the historical context needs no refreshing may wish to pass over the section which follows, and turn immediately to the concluding section of the introduction, or to the first chapter.

Who precisely were Puritans? And what exactly was Puritanism? These are questions which are still debated by historians, and although the answers given vary according to viewpoint, one thing is beyond question. The word Puritan has been persistently misunderstood and misused. Even after the careful efforts of scholars to provide a more objective understanding of Puritanism, it is difficult to dissociate the term in the popular mind from Ben Jonson's Zeal-of-the-Land-Busy, or from the implications of John Pym's neat phrase 'that odious and factious name of Puritan'. The concept of narrowness, bigotry, even hypocrisy, is far from the true character of Puritanism, as those who are familiar with Puritan thought in its wholeness continue to point out. Inevitably, this jaundiced view owes something to the origin of the term, which it will not be amiss to recall. Like many names which have come to have a lasting religious significance, Quaker and Methodist among them, the term Puritan arose as a derisive comment on the attitudes and actions of a small group in the Anglican Church during the latter part of the sixteenth century. It was initially applied to those within the Church of England who were dissatisfied with the extent to which the Reformation had been carried, and who wanted a more thorough-going reform of the national Church. Their chief concern appears to have been with the structure and liturgy of the Anglican Church and with the desire that it should be remodelled according to the Presbyterian pattern of the Reformed Church at Geneva. Few historians would now insist on such a narrow definition of Puritanism, although it is true that at this early stage the concern of the Puritan faction was less with Christian life and doctrine than it was with the organisation of the Church.

This early emphasis was soon to give way to something more fundamental, and as the sixteenth century ended and the seventeenth century began, it is clear that there existed in England a much wider body of opinion, both within and without the Anglican Church, whose chief concern was for purity of doctrine and holiness of life. A concern over the nature of the Church remained, as we shall have occasion to observe, but with this larger group it was not an end in itself, but rather a means for the recovery of true doctrine and the preservation of the true Christian life. As such, Puritanism came into its own early in the seventeenth century and continued with remarkable vigour through many vicissitudes for a hundred years or thereabouts, thereafter to be disseminated in various channels, of which some would persist until the present time. William Haller, whose *Rise of Puritanism* is indispensable for all who would truly understand the Puritan impetus, points out with discernment that Puritanism 'was nothing new or totally unrelated to the past but something old, deep-seated, and English, with roots reaching far back into mediaeval life'.[7] That comment must be allowed its due place in our thinking if we are to understand Puritanism in its essence, grasp its fundamentally English character, and sense its significance to the later development of religious thought in the Western world. Indeed, the main thesis of this present volume is that one of the later manifestations of the Puritan spirit is itself neither intrinsically new nor totally unrelated to the past, but that in its own nature it partakes of something that is old and deep-seated in the English religious tradition.

If a date is required for the formal beginnings of Puritanism, it will not be inappropriate to suggest 1570, when Thomas Cartwright, Lady Margaret Professor of Divinity at the University of Cambridge, was removed from his chair for advocating the abolition of the Episcopal system of government in the Church of England in favour of Presbyterianism. What may appear on the surface as a technical matter of little consequence was, in fact, a matter of some considerable significance at the time, particularly for those whose main court of appeal was the Bible. In Puritan eyes it was a question of whether the Anglican Church was willing to accept a more scriptural form of Church organisation, or persist with a system which could not be supported from the Word of God and which savoured too strongly of Rome and Antichrist. Matters of worship and liturgy were also far from satisfactory to the Puritan mind, since they retained too many features of the Roman system. Again, it was a question of origin and authority. If Scripture supported such practices, let them be retained. If not, they should be rejected and replaced by practices more in harmony with the Bible. The debate over organisation and worship was to continue for a good many years into the future, and although it was always fraught with the question of national sovereignty, it would always come back in the end to the more basic question of authority.

These issues went back to the earliest days of the English Reformation. Henry VIII had finally broken with Rome in 1534, although many historians feel that this was essentially a political and personal move,[8] and that compared with what would transpire later, it scarcely affected the doctrine of the Church or the life of the individual believer. There were changes, of course, and research has shown that there were evidences of genuine reformation during Henry's reign and earlier. A.G. Dickens describes the work of Wycliffe and the Lollards as 'the abortive reformation', and demonstrates that Lollard influence persisted well into the sixteenth century. For all that, it is probably true that the formal reformation which took place in the reign of Henry VIII was largely political, and that the religious life of the age saw little practical improvement. The reigns of Edward VI and Mary were accompanied by more definite changes, with a move towards more thorough-going Protestantism under Edward and a violent return to Rome under Mary. By the time that Elizabeth I came to the throne in 1558 the country was bewildered and torn. Some preferred the old way and wanted to retain the Catholic faith and its manner of worship. Others wanted reformation, and wanted it to be as thorough as that which had taken place at Geneva under John Calvin. Here, from the Puritan viewpoint, was a true Utopia, a practical demonstration of godly rule in action. Many, perhaps the majority, had no strong convictions, except that they be left in peace to live a life of their own choosing. Elizabeth's religious policy was to follow the *via media* between these two extremes, with the object of maintaining a united kingdom at the expense of returning to Rome or going on to a more thorough form of Protestantism. The Elizabethan Settlement, as it has come to be known, was her attempt to establish a national Church which would appeal to the majority of her subjects and keep in subjection the extremists on either wing.

It was with this compromise that Thomas Cartwright and his followers in 1570 showed their dissatisfaction. They had waited impatiently for ten years or more for the changes which they believed necessary. When it became clear that such changes were not going to materialise, they took matters into their own hands and began in earnest a war of words which manifested itself in sermons, tracts and other forms of literature calculated to demonstrate the strength of their arguments and the need for true reformation. Increasingly thereafter the call for reformation in England was heard in pulpit and press. Although time revealed that it would not be until 1643, with the calling of the Westminster Assembly, that Presbyterianism would be seriously considered, albeit briefly, as an alternative to the Anglican Church, seeds had been sown which would take firm root and which would grow and bear fruit of a kind which even Cartwright could not have foreseen. Before the turn of the century, advocates of total separation from the Anglican Church had arisen, and little groups of Separatists met secretly for worship, or emigrated to Holland where they were able to meet freely to pursue their religion according to the dictates of conscience. By the time Elizabeth came to the end of her illustrious reign, the Puritan tide was well on its way in.

What had taken place under the Tudor monarchs in the sixteenth century, momentous as it undoubtedly was, served merely as a prelude to what would transpire under the Stuarts in the century which followed. Now the nation was to witness civil war, the execution of an archbishop and a king, a republican government, the Protectorate under Cromwell, the Restoration of the Monarchy, and severe religious persecution, all to some extent as a consequence of religious convictions, to say nothing at this stage of the nature of those convictions themselves. Not without reason may the seventeenth century be regarded as the most momentous in the history of England, and as seminal to the subsequent development of Western society as a whole. The accession of James I in 1603 was an event which Puritans had in general heralded with some expectation. In Scotland, James had presided over the establishment of a Presbyterian system, in theory at least, and many hoped that he would be favourably disposed to the Puritan cause in England. On his journey south to take residence in London, he was met by a large delegation of Puritan clergymen who petitioned him to press on at once with the re-organisation of the English Church. But, as Haller says, although James continued to champion Calvinistic theology,[9] 'he had had more than enough of Presbyterianism'.[10] Those who had clung to hopes of a Puritan breakthrough were soon to be disillusioned, and we are left with the unhappy record of James threatening to harry Puritans out of the land. From then until 1640 the Puritan impetus was driven to seek expression in less conspicuous ways. It did so through preaching, and notably through the production of a vast corpus of literature which grew in quantity, and generally in quality, as the seventeenth century continued to unfold. It is to this body of literature that we shall turn in the chapters which follow, and which, if nothing else, will surely convince us of the essentially spiritual and irenic nature of mainstream Puritan thought.

With the events which began in 1640, it seemed as though an avalanche had been precipitated which no man or group of men could contain. In that year, Parliament impeached the Archbishop of Canterbury, William Laud, for high treason, and committed him to the Tower from which, five years later, he was led out and beheaded. A similar fate awaited Charles I, whose execution in 1649, following the verdict of a court constituted by the

Commons, was an event of unprecedented boldness. Charles had declared war on the Parliamentary armies in 1642, and for some six years civil conflict was waged up and down the land. It was a traumatic time for Englishmen. In 1643 a summoned body of Puritan divines, mostly Presbyterians by conviction, met at Westminster for the purpose of advising Parliament in the matter of reforming the Church. They produced the famous Westminster Confession of Faith and two catechisms, all of which in their own way influenced Puritan doctrine and devotion in succeeding years. Before they met for the last time in 1649, they also produced a Presbyterian directory for worship, which, though approved by Parliament, was never put into practice. That all this could transpire whilst Royalist and Parliamentary forces confronted each other on the battlefield is some indication of the religious nature of the age and of the undertones which ran through the conflict itself.

With the cessation of armed hostilities, the imprisonment of the king, and the demise of high churchmanship, the way was opened for a unique experience in English history. For twelve years from 1648, with no ruler claiming as his authority the divine right of kings, the government of the land proceeded by a succession of experiments, which Oliver Cromwell, to give him his due, attempted to guide for the good of the nation as a whole. From the broad Puritan position, the experiment reached its high-point in July 1653 when the Nominated Parliament met for the first time. It consisted solely of members appointed by Cromwell and his advisors for their religious convictions and evident godliness, 'saints' to use the contemporary word. It was known more generally as the 'Barbones' Parliament, after 'Praise-God' Barbones, one of its members. Cromwell addressed the new Parliament in significant terms as they began their work: 'Truly you are called by God to rule with Him, and for Him, ... I confess I never looked to see such a day as this ... when Jesus Christ should be so owned as He is, at this day.'[11] It was, they felt, the beginning of the long-awaited reign of the saints on earth, prior to the glorious coming of Christ and the promised millennium. But, alas, it was not to be. For reasons which it is not possible to examine here, the experiment ended in failure, the Nominated Parliament lasting less than six months and giving way to Cromwell's Protectorate, itself a form of government which, in principle, was less than ideal and which, in practice, proved less than popular. By 1660 most Englishmen were ready for Anglicanism and the monarchy to be restored and a return to stable government. Perhaps the greatest lesson which these years re-emphasise is that the kingdoms of this world are not to be confused with the Kingdom of God. It was a lesson, nonetheless, that many at the time were unwilling, or unable, to learn.

Many of the specifically religious developments of these years were of equal significance to the subsequent growth of Protestantism in England and in America as they were to the Church in their own day. This is particularly true of the years between 1640 and 1660, which beyond question were the high-watermark of pre-Restoration Puritanism. From the beginning of the seventeenth century, Puritanism, in both senses in which it has been defined, became a powerful and growing force in the religious life of the nation. The ecclesiastical Puritans, intent as always on reforming the structure of the national Church, pressed on with their aims until, as we have observed, they formed a majority in the Westminster Assembly called to advise Parliament on the reform of the Church. Only with the Restoration of the Monarchy in 1660 did it finally become clear that there was not to be a Presbyterian Church in place of the Episcopal Anglican Church. The more spiritual Puritans, both inside the established Church and among the independent, separatist groups which sprang up throughout the land, while not ignoring the importance of correct discipline and order, were chiefly concerned fo find the way of salvation for themselves and for their families, and to lead a godly life while on earth. Although prior to 1640, due to the repressive measures of Archbishops Bancroft and Laud, and the antipathy of James I and Charles I, both streams of the Puritan movement were held in check, Puritan preachers, as they were permitted, continued to make use of the pulpit and the press to propagate their ideas, so laying a foundation for the tumultuous years which lay just ahead.

Between 1640 and 1660 this outwardly stable situation changed almost beyond recognition, not only in the political arena but, more significantly for our purpose, in the realm of religion and religious activity. Ideas which had lain dormant for decades, or which had been discussed in secret, suddenly burst forth with amazing vitality. Mention must be made in this respect of the eschatological convictions which came to play such an important role in the religio-political events of the 1640s and the 1650s. From the earliest days of the English Reformation men had looked forward to the second coming of Christ and the Kingdom of God on earth. An increasing interest, during the latter part of the sixteenth century, in the books of Daniel and Revelation, which grew to intensive study during the seventeenth century, provided new understanding and gave fresh hope for the future. That many of the interpretations were incorrect and many of the conclusions reached unfounded, particularly among the less qualified expositors, it is hardly necessary to point out. What is beyond doubt is that eschatological expectation ran high for much of the first half of the seventeenth century, reaching its zenith between 1640 and 1660, and affecting during those years not only the religious views of the population but also the political activity of men in high office. Combined with these hopes of a coming Millennium and the Kingdom of God were revived fears and convictions concerning the Papacy and the Antichrist. Few doctrines had been more calculated to propel Englishmen in the direction of Protestantism than those which identified the Papacy with the Antichrist, particularly at times when the sovereignty of the state was threatened by papal decrees and intrigue. With Foxe's *Book of Martyrs* ever before them, and with the reported Romanizing tendencies of Laud and Charles I realities with potentially serious consequences, it is not surprising that, in the years we are considering, those who studied Scripture carefully found justification for a renewed preoccupation with the dreaded Antichrist.

These years also saw the emergence of religious groups hitherto unheard of, manv of which were to pass into obscurity almost as rapidly as they had arisen, but some of which, containing elements of a more enduring nature, were destined to influence the religious scene of later centuries. From the beginning of the seventeenth century the Independents had begun to withdraw from formal Anglican services, believing that Church membership should be limited to the regenerate, and to meet independently for worship, often in the parish Church itself, but not according to its ritual. The Independents grew in strength as the century developed, and although never numerically as strong as the Presbyterian party, nonetheless counted among their adherents some of the most influential clergy of the day. These early years had also seen the beginnings of a movement towards complete separation from the national Church. Guided by bold spirits who saw an irreducible connection between Rome, the Church of England, and Antichrist, little groups of believers, impatient with the slow progress towards reform, sought to make a thorough break with the establishment by instituting a Church and pattern of worship totally divorced from that of the Church of England. These were the Separatists, and from them and their Independent brethren religious communions such as Congregationalists, Presbyterians and Baptists were to arise, reaching down to the twentieth century and out into the whole Christian world.

It is quite impossible, in the limited space available, to give an account which would be less than confused of the bewildering number of sects which mushroomed almost overnight from 1640 onwards, to say nothing of their equally bewildering beliefs. If we mention only the Fifth Monarchy Men, who were in their own day, and have since been recognised as, one of the extreme religio-political groups of the time, and say that judged by the views of some of the other sects their opinions were comparatively sane, we have said much. The beliefs of the Fifth Monarchists, who held that the four kingdoms of Daniel chapters ii and vii had been fulfilled in history, and that the kingdom of the stone, the fifth kingdom of prophecy, was about to be established on earth, and that they had been called by God to bring that kingdom into existence by political activism, even by the use of the sword, should that prove necessary, may seem bizarre, but, in comparison with groups such as Muggletonians, Behmenists, Ranters, Diggers and the Family of Love, their ideas were not extreme. The existence of these groups serves as a reminder of the new freedom which now prevailed, and which was equally appreciated and exploited by the wider and more sober body of Puritanism.

For our immediate purposes the most significant religious development after 1640 was, perhaps, in the area of literature. When William Laud succeeded to the archbishopric of Canterbury in 1633, he set himself the task, among others, of rectifying the laxity which had crept into the regulations controlling printing and publishing, especially those concerning censorship. It was too late to prevent the dissemination of Puritan ideas by the press, but not too late to make a determined stand against anything which savoured of heresy or of an attack on the existing order. As one writer points out, Laud — like most of his contemporaries — did not distinguish words which merely expressed ideas from words which actually incited rebellion or violence. To Laud and his contemporaries words were words, whether spoken or written, and, if the need was such, should be punished for what they were.[12] It was this understanding, or lack of it, which prompted Laud to direct his keenest attention to the Puritan preachers and pamphleteers, who ever sought to go into print. As a consequence, the years immediately preceding 1640 are noticeably lacking in printed material other than strictly devotional works by established Puritan preachers, and similar works by Anglican authors. This should not be taken to suggest that prior to 1640 religious works were infrequently published. Any representative bibliography, including that which appears at the end of this book, will prove that this was not the case. It is intended to suggest that there was a prodigious increase in the output of literature of all kinds, and of Puritan literature in particular, after Laud's removal from the scene in 1640. That, too, will be evident from the publication dates in the bibliography.

With the accession of Charles II and the Restoration of the Monarchy in 1660, the course of English history took another sharp turn. From the Puritan viewpoint it was decidedly a turn for the worse. The heady days of Cromwell's England were now past, and Puritans were soon to learn the harsh realities of a system intolerant of nonconformity, to say nothing of open dissent. In 1662 Parliament passed the Act of Uniformity, which required all clergymen to take an oath of loyalty and non-resistance, and to declare their total assent to the Book of Common Prayer. It was a cruel dilemma for hundreds of clergymen throughout the land who had espoused Puritan ideals, particularly as the date for compliance was set to coincide with the anniversary of St. Bartholomew's Day. The outcome must have been predictable to the government, and is known in English religious history as the Great Ejection, when between 1,700 and 2,000 clergymen, many of them the cream of the nation's spiritual and intellectual leadership, refused to abjure their consciences and were summarily ejected from their livings. It is estimated that in London alone at least forty graduates of Oxford or Cambridge, including six doctors of divinity, were removed from their pulpits and forced to eke out a living for themselves and their families as best they could, in common with their ejected brethren throughout the land. The sufferings of the ejected clergy have been variously described, but C. E. Whiting's brief account is probably as near the truth as any: 'Some lived on little more than brown bread and water, many had eight or ten pounds a year to maintain a family. . . . One went to plough six days a week and preached on the Lord's day.'[13] Even that was a privilege which was soon to be denied.

Further legislation against Puritan dissent quickly followed. Collectively known as the Clarendon Code, after the Earl of Clarendon, Charles II's Chancellor and chief minister, it included the Corporation Act, which effectually excluded from national or local public office all who refused to conform; the Conventicle Act, which prohibited all private meetings for worship which were attended by more than four persons beyond the immediate family; and the Five Mile Act, which prevented ejected clergy from living within five miles of a corporate town or any town in which they had preached in recent years. The Test Act of 1673 reaffirmed that every Nonconformist, whether dissenter or recusant, should be excluded from all public office, stipulating that those who wished to be considered eligible should receive the sacrament according to the Anglican form at his parish Church. It is quite clear that the years between 1660 and 1690 brought the most severe restrictions upon the Puritan ministry and laity alike. These were the years of real hardship and active persecution, particularly between 1681 and 1687, and notably under the notorious Judge Jeffreys, following the accession of James II in 1635. According to one contemporary record, Jeffreys executed hundreds of Dissenters in Dorset and Somerset and sent hundreds more as convicts to the West Indies.[14] While it is true that these punishments were inflicted for rebellion rather than for religious belief for its own sake, and that not all who were involved in the rebellion were Dissenters, it is also true that many acted from religious motivation, and that the effects of Jeffreys' directives were felt most keenly among dissenting communities. Whole Churches were decimated, some reduced virtually to non-existence. Mercifully, circumstances compelled James to adopt a change in policy, and the Declaration of Indulgence of 1687, and also the Toleration Act of 1689, effectually brought to an end the various repressive measures which had been levelled against Puritan dissent in the preceding thirty years. Thenceforward, freedom of worship was guaranteed to Protestants who found themselves unable to conform to the doctrine, liturgy or constitution of the Anglican Church.

These latter years may be regarded as the time of Puritanism's maturity, and nowhere is this more evident than in the literature of that era. The bulk of Richard Baxter's enormous output belongs to this period. John Bunyan's immortal *Pilgrim's Progress*, and his scarcely less renowned *Grace Abounding to the Chief of Sinners*, both came from these years. John Flavel's works of divinity and devotion, six volumes in all, warm and practical to the end, were the product of Puritanism's later years. And Joseph Alleine's *Alarm to the Unconverted*, which appeared in a modern edition as recently as 1964, was first published in 1672, selling 20,000 copies. So popular did this book prove to be that another edition in 1675 reached 50,000 copies, and numerous further editions continued to appear throughout the following two hundred and fifty years. Many of these writings, and many more besides them, we shall have occasion to sample as our investigation of Puritan beliefs proceeds. Others have argued that together they hold the secrets of our nation's past greatness, the principles of a free society, the motivation for the Church's world mission and, some would add, the key to a revived Protestantism and a completed Reformation.

Some limitations are inevitable in a study of this nature. In this case, the approach has been to concentrate on the specific doctrines which crystallised in Puritanism and radical Dissent and later coalesced in the biblical teachings of the Seventh-day Adventist Church. Since those doctrines were based on Scripture, they can be fully understood only by allowing the Bible to speak with authority as it did in the seventeenth century. The emphasis has therefore been placed on the expository and exegetical reasons for those beliefs which the Bible engendered. This has often been at the expense of their historical and chronological development and of detailed biographical information concerning the men who advocated those beliefs. These omissions are readily acknowledged, and they will no doubt to some degree disappoint the academic purist. The nature of this study suggests, however, that it is more important to understand the doctrines themselves than the men who proclaimed them, and that in order to understand the men it is necessary first to understand the ideas which made them what they were.

Neither is it possible to offer an exhaustive treatment of the doctrines included here. To provide that would almost certainly require a separate volume for each doctrine, and, in any case, some of the areas examined have in fact received more extended treatment elsewhere, as, for example, in G.F. Nuttall's *The Holy Spirit in Puritan Faith and Experience*, E.F. Kevan's *The Grace of Law* and the present author's *A Great Expectation, Eschatological Thought in English Protestantism to 1660*. Some questions, therefore, will remain unanswered, and other questions will doubtless be raised. The purpose of the book is not to examine in exhaustive detail any of the beliefs which have been selected for consideration, but rather to establish their identity within Puritan thought, to assess the fundamental nature of such beliefs vis-à-vis the Bible, and to suggest that in them are to be found the roots of a contemporary Protestant body which, however theologically anachronistic it may appear to some, is nonetheless enjoying considerable popularity on a world-wide basis in the twentieth century.

Some reference to the specific historical links between seventeenth-century English Puritanism and the Adventism which arose in America in the nineteenth century might also be desirable. Again, the purpose of this study precludes anything but the briefest comment. That the essentials of Seventh-day Adventism did appear at various times and in various places in England during the seventeenth century cannot be disputed. Neither can the fact that two centuries passed before those beliefs came together in one body of faith in North America. That many of these doctrines were taken across the Atlantic by the early colonists is also a matter of historical fact. John Cotton, the 'patriarch of New England', had emigrated in 1633, taking with him a firm belief in Christ's second coming and a keen interest in prophetic interpretation. Stephen Mumford arrived in Rhode Island in 1664, and shared with members of the Newport Baptist Church his belief in the perpetuity of the decalogue and the seventh-day Sabbath brought from the Bell Lane Seventh-day Baptist Church in London. Cotton and Mumford are typical of many thousands of seventeenth-century Puritans who arrived as immigrants in the New World, bringing with them beliefs which, in the fullness of time, would give rise to a religious movement encircling the world.

All that remains to be said by way of introduction concerns procedure. The chapter titles are all phrases from the original source material, and it has not been felt necessary to give references for these in the same way that the text itself has been documented. All quotations have been modernised in spelling and punctuation, where that has been necessary, but always in a manner which retains the original meaning. Quotations from the Bible are from the Authorised (King James) Version of 1611, for it is that version which forms the fundamental link between Puritan and Adventist theology. Although the main title of the book specifically mentions England and Puritanism, the careful reader will occasionally note the appearance of characters from the other parts of what is presently the United Kingdom, and from camps not specifically Puritan. He will discover references, for example, to the great Irish Archbishop, James Ussher, and to the seventeenth-century philosopher Thomas Hobbes. It has been argued elsewhere that, from a theological viewpoint, Anglicanism in the seventeenth century differed little from Puritanism in basic doctrine,[15] and those who read Hobbes will find for themselves a fundamental affinity with Puritan theology. Such references, then, are calculated to strengthen the underlying thesis of the book, that in its essentials Seventh-day Adventist belief traces its ancestry through the religious thought which was widespread in the British Isles during the seventeenth century, and which was epitomised in Puritanism. If what follows contributes, in the present ecumenical climate, to a better understanding of that movement, and of the age from which it takes its fundamental character, the arduous tasks of research and writing will have been adequately rewarded.

1. THE SUFFICIENCY OF SCRIPTURE

The Bible points to God as its author; yet it was written by human hands; and in the varied style of its different books it presents the characteristics of the several writers. The truths revealed are all 'given by inspiration of God' (II Timothy iii 16); yet they are expressed in the words of men. The Infinite One by His Holy Spirit has shed light into the minds and hearts of His servants. He has given dreams and visions, symbols and figures; and those to whom the truth was thus revealed, have themselves embodied the thought in human language.

Ellen G. White *The Great Controversy* (1911) pp.v-vi

It were more than brutish madness to doubt of the certain truth and authority of the holy Scriptures which, no less, but much more than any other writings, for their authors are testified and confirmed to be the sacred Word of the ever-living God. Not only testified by the uniform witness of men in all ages, but also confirmed by such reasons taken out of the writings themselves, as do sufficiently argue the Spirit of God to be the Author of them.

James Ussher *A Body of Divinitie* (1647) p.8

It was that renowned theologian of early Puritanism, William Perkins, who, in commenting on II Timothy iii 16-17, spoke of 'the sufficiency of scripture'.[1] A fellow of Christ's College, Cambridge, from 1584 to 1595, and for much of that time preacher at Great St. Andrew's, a Church frequented by the university fraternity, Perkins' influence in perpetuating the Puritan biblical emphasis with succeeding generations of English preachers is beyond question. His fame abroad as a writer was scarcely less than his reputation at home as a preacher and teacher. Many of his works were translated into various European languages, and most of them, particularly those published in English, were read long after his untimely death in 1602. We may be certain that what Perkins had to say concerning Scripture fairly represented the view of mainstream English Protestantism for at least a century to come. Some fifty years later, John Ball, who was deprived of his Staffordshire living and who more than once suffered imprisonment as a consequence of Puritan sympathies, declared plainly, 'the Word of God is the ground of all our faith, whereby we live, be directed, and upheld in all our trials'.[2] The influential Thomas Adams, for over thirty years vicar of Wingrave, Buckinghamshire, and chaplain to Sir Henry Montagu, the Lord Chief Justice and Lord High Treasurer of the realm, described Scripture as 'a perfect and absolute rule'.[3] It would not be difficult to find in the literature of the time a hundred such re-statements of the position that Perkins had earlier defended. Puritanism, as indeed Protestantism as a whole, held that the entire Bible, Old and New Testaments together, was 'sufficient to prescribe the true and perfect way to eternal life'.[4]

Authority
The question underlying the European Reformation in general and the English Puritan movement in particular, as the preceding comments suggest, was that of authority. From what source did the Church and the individual believer receive the faith, and against what standard could that faith, once received, be measured? Who formulated doctrine, and who defined duty? The insistence within Puritanism on Scripture as the answer to these fundamental questions cannot be understood without reference to the centuries of tradition and prescribed religion from which the Church had so lately emerged. John Owen and Richard Baxter, perhaps the greatest of the Puritan theologians of the seventeenth century, both draw attention to that subordination of Scripture to tradition which had characterised mediaeval Catholicism. Owen's defence of the Bible, published in 1659 with the cumbersome title, *Of the Divine Originall, Authority, Self-evidencing Light, and Power of the Scriptures*, confessed that it had been written principally as a corrective to renewed attacks by Roman Catholic scholars on Scripture. Owen was particularly concerned to refute suggestions that the Bible was only a partial revelation of God's will (and hence, by implication, not wholly sufficient), and that Scripture was not valid unless accepted and interpreted by the Church.[5] No self-respecting Protestant theologian of the day could allow such claims to go unchallenged, and the gist of Owen's reply, conveyed in the title of his book, is that the authority of Scripture is above that of the Church, since in Scripture God speaks authoritatively and directly to the individual. Baxter similarly argued that the subjection of Christian belief to the authority of the Church rather than to Scripture was the most injurious of all doctrines emanating from Rome.[6] In making this assertion, Baxter clearly understood how crucial the question of authority was to the whole structure of belief, as well as to the freedom of the individual before God.

Perhaps the case was stated most clearly by the learned James Ussher who, prior to his elevation to the archbishopric of Armagh in 1625, had for fourteen years held the chair of divinity at Dublin. There is no doubt in this thoroughly Protestant mind about the place of Scripture:

The books of holy Scripture are so sufficient for the knowledge of Christian religion, that they do most plentifully contain all doctrine necessary to salvation.... It followeth that we need no unwritten verities, no traditions or inventions of men, no canons of councils, no sentences of Fathers, much less decrees of popes, to supply any supposed defect of the written Word, or to give us a more perfect direction in the worship of God and the way of life, than is already expressed in the canonical Scriptures.[7]

The 'doctrine necessary to salvation' of which Ussher here speaks, points to the dual nature of the authority held by Protestantism to reside in Scripture. It is an authority which extends equally to the formulation of doctrine by the Church and to the regulation of the life of the individual believer. The two cannot be separated. Those who become impatient with the doctrinal controversies which characterised Puritanism fail to understand this relationship and its significance in the eyes of Puritan theologians. Doctrine is important precisely because in the end it is concerned with salvation and with the individual. Sound doctrine is therefore to be pursued and false doctrine is to be avoided, and Scripture is to be the final court of appeal, the objective standard by which the faith of both Church and believer is to be measured. So Ussher adds, 'From them only [the Scriptures] all doctrine concerning our salvation must be drawn and derived.'[8] The Baptist pastor, Henry Denne, concurs: 'Wheresoever the Protestant confessions do go hand in hand with holy Scripture, we do rejoice to follow them.' On the other hand, if the Church, even the Protestant Church, has deviated from this authoritative rule, 'their example must not be our precedent'.[9] Quite clearly, most shades of opinion within the English Church of the seventeenth century agree that the Bible, as opposed to tradition and to creed, is the final source of authority.

It is at this point that Richard Baxter registers a note of disquiet. Baxter, learned, moderate, and devout, and widely regarded as one of the most eminent divines of his age, was a prolific writer and an indefatigable preacher. Later generations have acknowledged his profound influence on the religious life of his own and succeeding generations. His *The Saints' Everlasting Rest* must be regarded as one of the most significant works of Puritanism, if not of Protestantism as a whole. Published first in 1650, and re-issued in numerous editions well into the nineteenth century, this book, written 'by a dying man to dying men', has exerted a lasting influence on countless thousands of readers. The *Saints' Rest* is an admirable example of Puritanism's concern with the salvation of the individual and with practical godliness rather than with institutional and creedal Christianity. Coming as it did a century or more after the beginnings of the English Reformation, it points out the danger, as real to established Protestantism as to established Catholicism, of assigning authority to the establishment rather than to Scripture. Baxter sees clearly the paradox of Protestantism's continuing protest against Rome's subjection of the authority of Scripture to that of the Church, while at the same time being guilty on a similar count. 'The Papists believe Scripture to be the word of God, because their Church saith so', he maintains. Yet Protestants have adopted a similar attitude to Scripture, 'because our Church or our leaders say so'.[10] Baxter's argument, of course, is that it is not sufficient for any Christian to accept the authority of the Bible merely on the basis that this may be the official position of the Church as a whole, or of that section of the Church .to which he may have given his allegiance. There must be a personal conviction, a personal knowledge of the issues involved. George Lawson, a contemporary and often a critic of Baxter, pressed this particular point further. Assent to the authority of Scripture is a fundamental article of faith, yet no Christian should accept that authority blindly 'further than he hath certain reason so to do'.[11] It is a matter, not merely of faith, but also of reason, of understanding. It is necessary for the believer as an individual to know for himself why he should accept the authority of the Bible and why he should regard it as an inspired revelation.

The ground for accepting the authority of Scripture is its own claim to be the Word of God, and it is therefore desirable to understand the 'certain reasons' which led English Protestants of the sixteenth and seventeenth centuries to accept without hesitation the Bible's claim to inspiration, and hence its authority in dogma and in life. Why was Scripture so positively held to be the Word of God rather than a collection of human writings? What precisely did William Perkins have in mind when he stated that the evidences for the divine origin of the Bible were 'not to be found in any other writings in the world'?[12]

Inspiration
We may begin, as Puritanism itself began, with the fact of the Bible's existence. We are to be reminded here that there was nothing fortuitous in the permanence of the Bible. No other book had aroused such universal antipathy. No other book had survived such sustained and rigorous opposition. Yet Richard Baxter enquires if the time ever existed when all the Bibles in the world were destroyed together?[13] If the blood of martyrs was the seed of the Church, so too were the ashes of Scripture. 'They could burn these witnesses by thousands, but yet they could never either hinder their succession or extinguish their testimonies,'[14] so writes Baxter in *The Saints' Everlasting Rest*. It may be difficult for those who live in the twentieth century with the Bible translated into hundreds of languages and dialects and with free access to an almost bewildering variety of versions, to understand the force of this argument to those who lived so much nearer the age of Bible-burning and persecution. John Goodwin, whose *Divine Authority of Scriptures* (1648) proved to be an able defence of the traditional Protestant doctrine of Scripture, saw the position clearly enough. History bore witness to the fact that the best brains, the strongest hands, and the most plausible eloquence had united in sustained attempts to eradicate the Scriptures and to counter their influence:

> And yet we see that they stand, and are as mighty, and as like to stand still in the world, as ever; all their enemies, with all their councils, imaginations, attempts, and machinations against them, from first to last, are fallen, and ready to fall before them; whereas many other books and writings, which had no enemies, no opposition, either from devils or men, nay, which had friends in abundance which loved them and looked after them, are wholly perished and lost.[15]

The continuing existence of the Bible, despite the repeated and determined attempts of its enemies to destroy it, spoke strongly of a providential care.

Not only had the Bible itself been guarded from destruction, but its message similarly had been preserved from corruption. To demonstrate this particular truth was the object of John Owen's *Divine Originall*, the title page of which declared it to be a 'vindication of the purity and integrity of the Hebrew and Greek texts'. Owen's learning well suited him for this task, and it is to his credit that he recognised the importance of textual accuracy to any respectable defence of Scriptural authority. It is of more than passing interest that the reliability of the text was questioned long before the nineteenth century. Owen castigates those who 'with a show of learning have ventured to question almost every word in the Scripture,'[16] and among the reasons which he presents for accepting the received text of Scripture as authentic and reliable are the following:

1. The concern of the original writers to be accurate;
2. The care taken by the Jews, before and after Christ, to preserve authentic copies of the Old Testament;
3. The concern of the Masoretes[17] to preserve the textual accuracy of the Old Testament;
4. Christ's attitude to the Old Testament, thereby giving it the final seal of approval;
5. The determination of the Christian Church to preserve accurate copies of Scripture;
6. The care taken by copyists to ensure accuracy;
7. The concurrence of available manuscripts.[18]

Time has not diminished the combined strength of these arguments, and we can understand what Owen means when he says that in all this the providence of God may be seen in preserving His Word and ensuring its essential accuracy. Of course, variations do appear in the text of differing manuscripts, but these are of no great significance as they do not affect the essential message. In this Baxter agrees with Owen that any errors caused by copyists or printers are 'of no great moment, as long as it is certain that the Scriptures are not *de industria* corrupted, nor any material doctrine, history, or prophecy thereby obscured or depraved'.[19] As Baxter further somewhat dryly remarks, God had not taken it upon Himself to supervise every printer to the end of time; what did matter was that the text had survived without material corruption.

Further testimony to the unique character of the Bible could be found by those who were willing to read it and consider its message. John Owen contended that sufficient internal evidence could be seen within Scripture itself to convince the honest reader of its divine origin. 'The authority of God shining in them, they afford unto us all the Divine evidence of themselves',[20] Owen wrote of the several books of Scripture. William Perkins had put forward a similar argument years earlier. Let any discerning person read the Bible, let him duly note the content, the style, and the purpose of each part and of the whole together, 'and he shall be resolved that Scripture is Scripture, even by the Scripture itself'.[21] The intrinsic character of the Bible is better appreciated in the light of its design, its unity, its 'sweet concord and perfect coherence', as James Ussher described it, which stood out as a more objective testimony to its supernatural origin. Referring to the unity of theme and purpose evident in the various books of the Bible, Ussher pointed out that they had been written by some forty men of different backgrounds, under different circumstances, and at different times. Yet, as Ussher says, 'There is a most holy and heavenly consent and agreement of all parts thereof together, though written in so sundry ages, by so sundry men, in so distant places'.[22] It was difficult to disregard the unique character of the Bible when considering the question of its origin.

One of the most telling arguments in favour of the inspiration of the Bible was fulfilled prophecy. The capacity to foretell the course of future events 'whilst there is yet nothing at all in being ... likely to produce them, or to contribute towards their being'[23] is beyond human ability, and is a mark of divine foreknowledge. Man of himself is unable to predict future events with any degree of detailed accuracy. Yet the Bible contains such predictions, many of them concerning events which were to occur hundreds of years in the future, and which have been accurately fulfilled. Richard Baxter mentions in this respect the Old Testament prophecies concerning Christ. 'There is scarce any passage of the birth, life, sufferings, death, resurrection, ascension, or glory of our Saviour,' he says, 'which are not particularly prophesied of in the Old Testament.'[24] It is the verifiable fulfilment of these and other prophecies that gives confidence in Scripture, and also of course in those prophetic utterances which have yet to be fulfilled. The knowledge of fulfilled prophecy led William Perkins to declare:

Now there is no man able of himself to know or foresee these things to come. Therefore this knowledge must rest in Him alone who is most wise, that perfectly understandeth and beholdeth all things that are not, and to whom all future things are present, and therefore certain.[25]

John Goodwin adds that only He who can 'read the long roll of time from the one end of it unto the other' can truly foretell the future.[26] The conclusion which early Puritanism drew from the fulfilment of prophecy was that God had spoken to man through His Word.

A further consideration which brought strength to the other arguments supporting inspiration was found in the inherent power of the Bible. Here was a living force over the minds and lives of men and women such as no other book or collection of books could provide. 'No writings of man,' says John Ball, however persuasively set forth 'with wit, words, orders, or depth of learning, can so enlighten the mind, move the will, pierce the heart, and stir up the affections, as doth the Word of God'.[27] Although contrary to man's nature and disposition, the Bible, when preached and explained under the power of the Spirit, 'convinceth and condemneth men of sin, it turneth and converteth them to itself, and causeth them to live and die in love and obedience thereof'.[28] This it could never do were it simply of human origin — so argues William Perkins. John Goodwin is even more specific: 'The covetous man it makes liberal, the oppressor it makes merciful, the earthly-minded it makes heavenly, the fearful it encourageth, the proud it humbleth, the unclean it purifieth, the profane it sanctifieth ... it takes away the heart of stone, and gives men an heart of flesh.'[29] Such testimonies to the intrinsic and unique power of Scripture are to be found in abundance on the pages of Puritan doctrine and devotion. They are the testimonies of experience and of observation. We may pause to note one more. John Flavel, cast in the mould of the true spiritual shepherd, and bound with invisible ties of concern for the eternal welfare of his people in Dartmouth, has seen the power of this living Word at work in the lives of his congregation:

Can the power of any creature, the word of a mere man so convince the conscience, so terrify the heart, so discover the very secret thoughts of the soul, put a man into such trembling? No, no, a greater than man must needs be here. None but a God can so open the eyes of the blind, so open the graves of the dead, so quicken and enliven the conscience that was seared, so bind over the soul of the sinner to the judgement to come, so change and alter the frame and temper of a man's spirit, so powerfully raise, refresh, and comfort a drooping, dying soul.[30]

We sense Flavel's conviction, and understand his conclusion. This must be the power of God and if there were no other arguments to bring forth, 'yet this alone were sufficient to make full proof of the divine authority of the Scriptures'.[31]

For such reasons English Protestants believed in the inspiration of the Bible and hence in its authority as the living Word of the living God. This did not lead, as some have suggested, to bibliolatry. That might have been the case if the dominant concept of inspiration had been that which later became known as 'verbal inspiration'. It was widely agreed in Puritan theological circles, however, that this view, which held that each word of Scripture had been given directly to the original writers, was too narrow. 'The true and proper foundation of Christian religion is not ink and paper, not any book or books, not any writing or writings whatsoever, whether translations or originals,' John Goodwin argued. The Christian faith, he continued, was 'that substance of matter ... concerning the salvation of the world by Jesus Christ which [is] represented and declared both in translations and the originals but [which is] essentially and really distinct from both'.[32] Baxter made a distinction between the basic doctrine of Scripture and the words which gave that doctrine expression: 'The one is as the blood, the other as the veins in which it runs.'[33] To Goodwin, again, the concept of Scripture means, 'The matter and substance of things contained and held forth in the books of the Old and New Testament,' but not 'all the letters, syllables, words, phrases, sentences, and periods of speech' found either in manuscript or translation.[34]

A favourite expression with Puritan theologians was that the original writers of the Bible were God's 'penmen'.[35] This conveyed the thought that their role in the formulation of Scripture was not entirely passive, in the sense that they received the words of God in much the same way as a secretary might receive a dictated letter. Rather, the mind of each writer had been subject to the operation of the Holy Spirit, thereby receiving in thought-form the message of God, with the freedom to transmit that message in words and phrases of his own choosing. The message was thus wholly the message of God, transmitted through human personality in human language. The Puritan theologians readily saw that this in no way detracted from the doctrine of inspiration, and John Goodwin representatively declares without hesitation, 'I fully and with all my heart and all my soul believe them to be of divine authority.'[36]

In practice, this meant that no particular version of the Bible could claim to be the Word of God more than another. The Authorised Version of 1611, the Geneva Bible of 1560, Coverdale's version of 1535 and, beyond them, translations in other languages, all contained what Goodwin described as the 'substance' of Christian faith, and were therefore equally to be esteemed as 'the Word of God'. It was the authority of this Word, prized above that of priest or prelate, which gave character and meaning to English Protestantism, and John Flavel spoke intelligibly to both Church and believer when he advised 'keep the Word, and the Word will keep you'.[37]

The Purpose of Scripture
In offering this advice Flavel makes it clear that he is thinking more of the individual believer than of the body corporate: 'As the first receiving of the Word regenerated your hearts, so the keeping of the Word within you will preserve your hearts.'[38] Flavel captures in this sentence the two fundamental purposes of Scripture. The Word of God led a man initially to the experience of salvation, and then enabled him to proceed in that experience. It converted him and kept him. The emphasis in both cases is on that personal religion for which Puritanism strove and which is one of its chief characteristics. The authority of Scripture was only worked through to its logical conclusion as it was demonstrated in the lives of people, and that demonstration was to be seen in both unbelievers and believers. It was to be seen in leading the unbeliever to faith and in leading the believer to greater faith.

To the unbeliever, Baxter addressed one of his best-known and influential works, *A Call to the Unconverted*, in which he explained that the normal method by which God worked to bring a man to a saving knowledge of Himself, was through the Bible. 'If you will be converted and saved, attend upon the Word of God,' he advises, and 'Read the Scripture, or hear it read and other holy writings that do apply it. Constantly attend on the public preaching of the Word.'[39] In this way the purpose of Scripture is to be fulfilled, and men will be 'born again ... by the Word of God, which liveth and abideth for ever'. (Perkins says that the Word 'being preached by the Minister appointed by God, converteth nature, and turns the heart of man unto it,' *Cases of Conscience*, 1651, p.133; John White adds, 'Thy heart is as hard as a stone ... but this word is as a hammer, that breaketh the rock in pieces ... a fire to kindle holy affections in thee ... his furnace to purge out the dross of thy natural corruptions,' *A Way to the Tree of Life*, 1647, p.343.) To those who have already responded to the saving Word of Scripture, Flavel offers similar counsel: 'Let the Word of Christ dwell richly in you; let it dwell, not tarry with you for a night, and let it dwell richly or plentifully; in all that is of it, in its commands, promises, threats; in all that is in you, in your understandings, memories, consciences, affections and then 'twill preserve your hearts.'[40] There can be little doubt that the lives of countless Englishmen and their families were ennobled and enriched by the preaching ministries of Baxter and Flavel who sought to confront saints and sinners alike with the living, saving truths of Scripture.

The desire to convince men of their need of the Bible and its message understandably resulted in certain emphases. Chief among these, if we analyse Puritan theology aright, was that the main design of Scripture is to reveal Christ and to lead men to a personal knowledge of the salvation which God had provided in Him. While the remaining chapters of this present volume will largely seek to examine various aspects of this vast theme, we may note here some of the forms in which it found a basic expression. Flavel declared, 'The knowledge of Jesus Christ is the very marrow and kernel of all the Scriptures,' and went on to show how both Old and New Testaments were 'full of Christ', how 'the blessed lines of both Testaments meet in Him'.[41] Thomas Adams, who on account of his preaching and writing later came to be known as 'the Shakespeare of Puritan theologians', maintained that Christ was 'the sum of the whole Bible; prophecied, typified, prefigured, exhibited, demonstrated; to be found in every leaf, almost in every line'.[42] The great characters of sacred history were types of the Christ who was to come, stars shining in a light borrowed from the sun which was, in the fullness of time, to arise on a darkened world, a concept more fully outlined in chapter two. And William Perkins, whose theology, though expressed with less rhetoric, was good theology nonetheless, succinctly concluded, 'The scope of the whole Bible is Christ with His benefits, and He is revealed, propounded, and offered unto us in ... the Word.'[43]

The relationship between doctrine and salvation in Puritan theology has already been noted. The repeated emphasis on sound doctrine in the Pauline Epistles did not pass unnoticed in the seventeenth century. Those who remembered their Church history were reminded of many who had made shipwreck of the faith and who had wrought havoc in the Church through doctrinal deviation, particularly concerning Christology or those doctrines relating to the person and work of Christ. If it was necessary to believe in Christ for salvation, it was equally necessary to believe correctly. And since the practice of religion depended upon a correct understanding of duty and obedience as set forth in Scripture, it was also necessary that the specific doctrines relating to the Christian life should be clearly understood. Flavel speaks of 'many honest, well-meaning, but weak Christians ... easily beguiled by specious pretence of new light' and 'pliable to many dangerous errors'.[44] The seventeenth century undoubtedly had its share of these — Ranters, Muggletonians, Seekers, Diggers, Levellers, Fifth Monarchy Men, to name a few — whose sincerity could not generally be questioned, but whose interpretations of Scripture were at the best doubtful, and whose Christology was generally distorted. It was to guard the feet of the saints from such slippery paths that moderate religious opinion in the seventeenth century expressed its concern for sound doctrine. Thus, in answer to a question about the purpose of a written revelation such as the Bible, John Ball replied, 'That it might be an infallible standard of true doctrine, and ... that it might be the determiner of all controversies'.[45] It must be conceded that had the Church at all times stood by that axiom there might have been less division and less misunderstanding.

One cannot read far into Puritan theology, or for that matter into Puritan history, without recognising the importance accorded to individual conscience in the outworking of salvation and the application of doctrine. Much has been written about freedom of conscience and the freedom of the individual in matters of faith, and of the contribution made by the seventeenth century to human progress in this respect. Without detracting in any way from what is certainly a basic human freedom, it must be understood that in moderate Puritan eyes the conscience was only truly free as it was captive to the Word of God. Conscience was that inner light given to every man, as part of the general revelation of God in the world, to prompt him to seek and follow ways of truth and goodness, yet insufficient of itself to lead to a saving knowledge of Christ. Conscience can only be completely effective in the context of knowledge, that is to say in spiritual terms, when enlightened with truth. The light within, Joseph Alleine specifically states, is incapable of leading a man to salvation 'without the direction of God's Word'. On the other hand, 'a well informed conscience', Alleine argues, 'instructed in the Scriptures, and well studied in the mind of God ... may be a great help to a Christian'.[46] The Bible therefore finds a further important function as a guide to conscience. A Christian instructed in Scripture will not only know in general terms that he ought to do right, but he will know from the Word what to do. Flavel says, 'If Scripture and conscience tell you such a way is sinful, [you] may not venture upon it.'[47] It is Scripture and conscience together which provide constraint. Alleine, prevented from serving his congregation by the harsh legislation which followed the Restoration of the Monarchy in 1662, therefore declares, 'My brethren, if God deprive you of the preacher in the pulpit, take the more earnest heed to the preacher in your bosom.'[48]

Understanding the Bible

Given the inspiration of the Bible, the most important question of all comes at the level of personal understanding. How shall the Bible be interpreted? How shall its saving truths be appropriated? By what method is the water of life to be drawn from the well of salvation? Thomas Adams, with a characteristic turn of phrase, chides those who are willing to accept the applications of Scripture pressed upon them by the preacher, without understanding the reasons thereof for themselves, 'as if they had only need to have their hearts warmed, and not to have their minds warned, and enlightened with knowledge. But alas, no eyes, no salvation'.[49] One writer complains bitterly of 'the prattling housewife and the old dotard' taking it upon themselves to interpret Scripture, 'readily teaching that they never learned, and abundantly pouring out that which was never infused into them'.[50] He is, of course, making the observation that false conclusions can be reached as a result of incorrect and uninformed methods of interpretation. Hence the need for a ministry trained, among other things, in the principles of biblical interpretation and with a knowledge of the original languages in which the Bible was written. Hence also the need for the preacher to expound Scripture to the people of God, and for the Church to expect such exposition. God speaks to man immediately in the Bible and mediately by those who understand Scripture and who are called to teach and expound it. (George Lawson, for example, says that God speaks 'immediately' to the Prophets, 'mediately' by the Prophets who are inspired and 'mediately' by those appointed to teach Scripture who are not inspired, *An Exposition of the Epistle to the Hebrews*, 1662, p.3.) For all that, however, the Bible was essentially an open book and each individual believer could attain to 'that knowledge of the mind and will of God revealed in the Scripture, which is sufficient to direct him in the life of God, to deliver him from the dangers of ignorance, darkness, and error, and to conduct him into blessedness'.[51] For this reason personal Bible study must complement the preaching of the Word in public.

Two factors, the Holy Spirit and reason,' combine in bringing men to a saving knowledge of Scripture. The great importance of the Holy Spirit in the study of the Bible must never be forgotten. 'The Word alone, though never so excellently preached, conduces no more to the conviction and salvation of a sinner than the waters of Bethesda did, when the angel came not down to trouble them, but when one is under the tutelage of the Spirit,mediating the written word, 'then Christ speaks to the heart'.[52] Thus John Flavel explains the relationship of Word and Spirit. 'The Word and Spirit go together ... the Word is dead without the Spirit,' argues Richard Sibbes, and 'Therefore attend on the Word, and then wait on the Spirit to quicken the Word, that both Word and Spirit may guide us to life everlasting'. [53] The inspiration of Scripture had been directly effected by the influence of the Spirit on the minds of the original writers. Now that same Spirit illuminates the minds of those who read and hear the Word. So the Spirit becomes both author and interpreter, ensuring that the divine message contained in Scripture is both available and intelligible. The illumination of the human mind by the Spirit is therefore crucial in the process of understanding the Bible. Indeed, it is a most pernicious error, and a primary source of confusion, misunderstanding, even heresy, that Scripture can be understood and interpreted 'without the effective aid and assistance of the Spirit of God'.[54]

Yet the Spirit does not supersede reason. Man is a rational creature and God approaches him through his rationality, the Spirit enlightening the mind in a manner that does not dispense with the normal processes of thought. So John Flavel speaks of those 'natural qualifications' necessary to arrive at an understanding of the Word, 'clearness of apprehension, solidity of judgement, and fidelity of retention'.[55] Those who would deny us the use of reason in the understanding of Scripture 'would deal with us,' says John Owen, 'as the Philistines did with Samson, first put out our eyes, and then make us grind in their mill'.[56] Richard Sibbes, one of the great devotional preachers of Puritanism, points out 'There is strong reason in all divine truth ... and it is a part of wisdom to observe how conclusions rise from principles, as branches and buds do from roots.'[57] It is the free access of the Spirit to the mind of man and the full use of reason which together result in the understanding of Scripture.

In practice, however, the tendency to lean to one's own understanding in seeking to arrive at an acceptable interpretation of the Bible is always present. It is easier for a man, even a regenerate man, to think his way through to a conclusion than it is for him consciously to seek the enlightenment of the Spirit. We have noticed Thomas Adams's strictures against those who submissively accept suggested interpretations without taking the trouble to examine for themselves the Scriptural evidence. John Flavel is equally anxious over those who come to the Bible in order to substantiate views already formed. 'They bring their erroneous opinions to the Scriptures ... and force the Scriptures to countenance and legitimate their opinions,'[58] he says. John White offers appropriate counsel:

We must be very careful that we bring with us our minds free, and not prepossessed with any opinion which we have either framed in our own fantasy, or received from others. A mind forestalled by an erroneous conceit is no fit judge of any truth, or of any testimony concerning truth, but as coloured glass transmits the light, and represents it to the eye infected with the same colour with which itself is dyed ... so happens it with a mind prepossessed with any fantasy, it apprehends and judgeth all things according to that opinion which itself hath entertained.[59]

The quest for spiritual truth is impeded by coming to Scripture with prejudice and preconceived opinion. John Owen speaks more strongly yet, contending that most of the heresy which has infected Christian doctrine through the ages has arisen from men 'lighting on some expressions in the Scripture, that singly considered seem to give countenance to some such opinion as they are willing to embrace'.[60] The implication is that coming to the Bible with preconceived opinions results in less than an objective study of the text, and hence in the perpetuation of error. In attempting to understand the Bible, it is essential to approach it with an open mind, seeking the consensus of Scripture as a whole, with a willingness to learn and a readiness to change one's opinion, should that prove necessary.

Puritanism was particularly disturbed by two influences from the past which tended to shape biblical interpretation in a manner likely to restrict the full discovery of truth. The first of these influences was tradition, that immense body of comment and exposition which had been handed on from generation to generation, and which found its fullest expression in the writings of the Church Fathers. It must not be thought that Puritanism wanted to discard these writings altogether. On the contrary, it was generally agreed that much truth and wisdom could be found in patristic literature. But the Fathers also had been human, and on that count liable to error, and their writings must be read with discernment. Humphrey Hody, an outstanding Oxford professor of the late seventeenth century, who was not a Puritan at all, stated the case as clearly as any Puritan writer could have done. 'I desire as much as any man to pay a just deference and regard to the judgements of the ancient Fathers,' he said, 'but it must be confessed that though their authority be great in matters of tradition, yet the reasons and arguments which they produce to confirm their doctrines are not always convincing.'[61] John Owen spoke with equal clarity for Puritanism when he argued that an exaggerated deference to the opinions of the past had been the major weakness in Judaism at the time of Christ and in Catholicism at the time of the Reformation:

> What their forefathers have professed, what themselves have imbibed from their infancy, what all their outward circumstances are involved in, what they have advantage by, what is in reputation with those in whom they are principally concerned, that shall be the truth with them and nothing else. Unto persons whose minds are wholly vitiated with the leaven of this corrupt affection, there is not a line in the Scripture whose sense can be truly and clearly represented. . . . If men will not forego all pre-imbibed opinions, prejudices and conceptions of mind however riveted into them by traditions, custom, veneration of elders, and secular advantages . . . they will never learn the truth, nor attain a full assurance of understanding in the mysteries of God.[62]

Tradition, therefore, must be given its due place, but no more, in the interpretation of Scripture.

The related danger to correct interpretation from which Puritanism withdrew was that of philosophy. It recognised the threat to sound doctrine contained in a system of interpretation which was influenced by the presuppositions and methods of Greek philosophical speculation. There was little doubt in thorough-going Protestantism that influences of this nature had been brought to bear on biblical interpretation in the past, and the significance of Puritanism's desire to be free of all such doubtful influences and to achieve a purer understanding of the Word must not be underestimated. We turn here to Francis Bampfield, yet another learned and godly Puritan divine who, after the Restoration, was frequently imprisoned for preaching without the required authorisation, and who died in Newgate gaol in 1683. Seven years before his death Bampfield had published an unusual treatise on Scripture as the revelation of God's will, applicable to all aspects of human learning and experience, in which he argued that the divisions in the Christian Church were a consequence of human interpretations placed on the Bible, and that ministers and preachers were responsible for perpetuating such error. Concerning the influence of philosophy on the interpretation of the Bible, Bampfield writes:

> What an enemy to the doctrine of salvation by faith in Christ was the Grecian philosophy! What a disfigured face has it put upon religion by its mythologising vanity! ... And what is yet further matter of more lamentation, those who have the name of the scholastic learned among Christians, do still pertinaciously adhere unto many of the philosophic errors ... subjecting theology to philosophy and Christianity to sophistry.[63]

The argument that underlies the whole of Bampfield's interesting treatise is that the principles and presuppositions of pagan philosophy have been allowed to mould the interpretation of the Bible and hence the formulation of Christian doctrine. Possibly nothing characterised Puritanism as a whole so much as its desire to come to grips with the real meaning of Scripture and to submit to its authority, and in order that this might be achieved, the dangers inherent in both traditional interpretations and philosophical principles were to be avoided.

Progressive Revelation

One final factor of immense significance must be mentioned if we are fully to appreciate the quest for truth so characteristic of Puritanism. The possibility, noted earlier, that the Fathers of the Christian Church might have erred in their understanding of the Bible unavoidably implied that later interpreters, Puritan theologians among them, could also reach erroneous conclusions. No man or generation of men could claim to have arrived at a perfect knowledge of Scripture. Truth, or more correctly, the understanding of truth, is progressive. God reveals Himself and His will to men as He sees fit and in accordance with the divine purpose. Man must seek continually for further light, his mind must ever be open to receive more knowledge, deeper insights. Thus the future continually beckons those who desire to progress in the way of truth. 'Well may it be conceived,' wrote John Goodwin, 'not only that some, but many truths, yea and those of main concern and importance, may be yet unborn and not come forth out of their mother's womb (I mean the secrets of the Scriptures).' Goodwin goes on to speak of the 'endless variety of the riches' contained in Scripture, of 'the unknown abyss of truth' to be found in the Bible.[64] All this is but the fuller expression of the conviction voiced by John Robinson to the Pilgrim Fathers on their departure for the New

World in 1620, that God had more truth and light yet to break forth from His Holy Word.

This belief that the future would bring greater understanding of the truths of the Bible was deep rooted in Puritan theology and fundamental to its very existence. It is found in writings representative of all shades of opinion, but few express it as forcefully as Goodwin. At the beginning of time, Goodwin argued, truth made its entry into the world 'like the first dawning of the day'. The light, though perceptible, was barely so, shrouded yet by darkness. Again, it was 'like the corn, [which] when it first sprouts and peers above ground, hath nothing of that shape and body which it comes to afterwards'. In such an undeveloped manner the Gospel had been first proclaimed to man. Then, as time passed, God's message to man became clearer, further editions of the truth appeared, revised and enlarged, as for example in the time of Noah, and in the time of Abraham, and notably in the time of Moses, until eventually God revealed Himself more fully than in any previous age in the person of His own Son 'to be published and preached throughout the world'.[65] Yet even this the ultimate revelation of God confronts men in Himself with undiscovered truth, calling each succeeding generation to a richer and more enlightened faith. 'The knowledge of Christ is profound and large ... a boundless, bottomless ocean,' says John Flavel. In seeking to arrive at this knowledge in its fullness men go through an experience akin to that of discovering and inhabiting a new and unexplored country. At first they colonise the coastal region, gradually penetrating further inland until at length the whole land is traversed and occupied. So with the knowledge of Christ, suggests Flavel. But there is a difference: 'The best of us are yet on the borders of this vast continent.... Though something of Christ be unfolded in one age, and something in another, yet eternity itself cannot fully unfold Him.'[66] So, too, with the knowledge of Scripture in its entirety. The saving truths of the Bible are not comprehended in their fullness at one time, but rather as God chooses to reveal their significance to men. Thus, in the age succeeding Constantine, marked as it was by Christological controversy, the truth to be asserted concerned the deity of Christ. At the Reformation, when the emphasis had for so long been placed on works and merit as the way of salvation, the time had come to emphasise the redemptive work of Christ and justification by faith. In the latter ages the emphasis was to be placed on the hope of the Kingdom of God.[67] Thus at no time in the past or in the present had the Church possessed an absolute knowledge of truth. Only as she remembers her fallible humanity and responds to the promise of the future will she move forward towards a complete understanding and fulfilment of Scripture.

For those who lived in the latter ages of world history, (in the immediate context, this applied to those living in the seventeenth century, who believed that theirs was the last age, and that Christ would soon establish His Kingdom,) the doctrine of progressive revelation and progressive understanding had a special significance. At that time truth was to come to ultimate fruition. 'God's people went into mystical Babylon gradually,' argued Henry Danvers, referring to the mediaeval suppression of the Bible and the ensuing decline in biblical theology. 'So must their coming out be, some at one time, and some at another,' he continued.[68] Goodwin believed that the Bible itself foretold a discovery of truth and sound doctrine before the final consummation. Commenting on Daniel xii 4, which speaks of an increase of knowledge at the end of time, Goodwin explained that the text promised a greater understanding of Daniel's prophecies in particular and a deeper knowledge of the Scriptures as a whole in the last days.[69] 'All spiritual light is increasing light, which shineth more and more unto the perfect day,' said Flavel.[70] Each generation within the Church, therefore, must be open to the future, open to the Word of God, and open to the guidance of the Holy Spirit. Thus led, both the Church as a body, and the believer as an individual, may rightfully anticipate a deeper knowledge of the Word, written and Incarnate, continuing growth towards maturity in Christ, and lasting satisfaction in the pursuit of truth.

2. THIS INCOMPARABLE JESUS

> Christ was treated as we deserve, that we might be treated as He deserves. He was condemned for our sins, in which He had no share, that we might be justified by His righteousness, in which we had no share. He suffered the death which was ours, that we might receive the life which was His.
>
> Ellen G. White *The Desire of Ages* (1898) p.25

> If every leaf, and spire of grass, ... nay, all the stars, sands, and atoms, were in so many souls and seraphims, whose love should double in them every moment to all eternity, yet would it fall infinitely short of what His worth and excellency exacts. Suppose a creature composed of all the choice endowments that ever dwelt in the best of men since the creation of the world, in whom you find a meek Moses, a strong Samson, a faithful Jonathan, a beautiful Absalom, a rich and wise Solomon; nay, and add to this the understanding, strength, agility, splendour, and holiness of all the angels, it would all amount but to a dark shadow of this incomparable Jesus.
>
> John Flavel *Works* (1716) I p.169

Few Puritan preachers understood the redemptive purpose of Scripture more plainly, and few pressed the claims of Christ upon their people more persistently or more persuasively than John Flavel. The son of a Puritan minister who had died in prison for his refusal to conform to the prescribed religion of the day, Flavel knew well the price 'which might be required for pursuing the Puritan ideal of a thoroughly biblical faith. His writings, particularly the *Fountain of Life* and *Method of Grace*, are said to have influenced, among others, Jonathan Edwards, the early American theologian, George Whitefield, the eighteenth-century preacher and theologian, and Archibald Alexander, the first professor at Princeton Theological Seminary. Whitefield ranked Flavel with John Bunyan and Matthew Henry, and Alexander is recorded to have declared, 'To John Flavel I certainly owe more than to any uninspired author.' Flavel was one of the last in a long line of Puritan divines whose chief energies were spent in extolling the merits of Christ, and we shall have occasion, as this chapter unfolds, to observe Flavel's Christology and to examine its implications in some detail.

The Knowledge of Christ
Insistent as Puritanism was on a thorough understanding of Scripture, its

real character can never be seen simply from that standpoint. A century before John Flavel, in those years which saw the beginnings of true Puritan theology, William Perkins had laid a solid foundation for the Christocentric emphasis which was to emerge in Puritanism, and which was perhaps to be its most significant contribution to evangelical Protestantism. To Perkins, a knowledge of Christ was the most important knowledge that a man could obtain. It was a knowledge that emerged from Scripture and to which Scripture pointed as its ultimate objective, a knowledge which was to grow from due consideration and which was to be based on understanding: 'Man must know Christ, not generally and confusedly, but by a lively, powerful, and operative knowledge.'[1] Perkins advocates here what today might be called a rational and experiential knowledge. The Christ of Scripture must become the Christ of theology, who in turn must become the Christ of experience. John Goodwin, whom we met earlier as an eminent seventeenth-century theologian, argued that Christ's work for man must be understood and that it must be understood in its totality. Re-echoing the fundamental issue raised by the great mediaeval thinker Anselm of Canterbury, *Cur Deus Homo* — Why God became Man — Goodwin asks again, Why is Christ both God and man? What does this mean for mankind? There are related questions also, which Goodwin feels should be considered with care: Why was He born of a virgin? Why did He come to live on earth? Why had He died on the cross? And why had He been raised from the dead?[2] These were momentous questions, issues of eternal consequence, demanding intelligent, rational answers. Faith accepts Christ, to be sure, but it is stronger when fortified by understanding. John Bunyan, writing nearly half a century after Goodwin, and a century later than Perkins, maintained the Christological emphasis with equal conviction: ''Tis not . . . enough for us that we exercise our thoughts upon Christ in an indistinct and general way. We must learn to know Him in all His offices, and to know the nature of His offices also.'[3] Blind faith opens the door to heresy and to the devil, says Bunyan. There must be more than a superficial understanding of Christ and His work. The believer must know why Christ is referred to in Scripture as Saviour, and as Priest, Prophet, King, Sacrifice, and Advocate.[4]

It is not difficult to find the reason for this deep-rooted concern with the person and work of Christ. Puritanism's insistence on the Bible as the norm of Christian faith and practice was due to the recognition that Scripture reveals a way to salvation posited on grace rather than on works. In that sense the Bible is a means to an end, since it shows man how he may be saved. 'All that Christ was, and all that He did, and all that He suffered, meet together in that great and common effect, the salvation of them that believe,'[5] explained Goodwin. Christ is God's gift of grace to mankind, the divinely appointed way of salvation, all-sufficient to meet the deepest spiritual needs of sinful men. Are we at enmity with God?, asks Flavel. Christ is our reconciliation. Are we sold to evil and to the devil? He is our redemption. Are we condemned before the divine law? He is our justification. Has sin polluted us? He is the fountain opened for sin and uncleanness. Have we lost our way? Have we wandered from God? He is the way to the Father.[6] It is at this point that Flavel speaks of 'the sensible sinner'. We must not allow the significance of the phrase to escape us. The 'sensible sinner' is the prodigal who, to use the words of Scripture, 'comes to himself'. He is the one who recognises his desperate condition and who as a consequence weighs carefully the claims of Christ. He does not merely believe in Christ, he first thinks about Him. Indeed, his belief is a consequence of his consideration. Hence Flavel concludes that rest is not as welcome to the weary, nor food to the hungry, as 'Christ is to the sensible sinner'. It is impossible to read Puritan devotion at any period of its development without quickly being confronted with the fact that in Christ alone is the way of salvation, and without realising that if men would know the way of life they must understand the way of Christ.

Nor was the way to attain this knowledge beyond the reach of any who might seek it. With the Bible accessible in the vernacular, public exposition of the Word a weekly event in the Puritan pulpit, and the works of popular theologians and preachers available from the booksellers, it was relatively simple for the man or woman who wanted to understand more about Christ to do so. According to Perkins, three steps are necessary in coming to a saving knowledge of Christ, 'consideration', 'application' and 'affection'. 'Consideration' entails a careful appraisal of the historical facts concerning Christ and an honest appraisal of one's own spiritual condition. Was Christ a real person in history? Were men sinful and in need of salvation? These were the questions to be answered, and an objective consideration of the facts concerning Christ as Saviour and men as sinners is the basis of a true knowledge of Christ. 'Application' involves the recognition that the facts concerning Christ and men in general are relevant on a personal level. 'The second part of knowledge,' says Perkins, 'is application, whereby thou must know and believe not only that Christ was crucified, but that He was crucified for thee.' Christ is not only God's gift to the world as a whole, but also to each individual. The cross is more than an historical event in time, it also has a meaning within human experience. 'Affection' is 'application' as a continuous process in which the individual believer, having initially taken the knowledge of Christ to himself, now repeatedly makes that application. It is perhaps more akin to what is conveyed by the modern term 'commitment', in which the believer continually makes a conscious response to the claims of the Gospel. It is experiential knowledge. In Perkins's terminology it was 'transforming knowledge' by which the great truths concerning Christ become a permanent force in the life.[7] Thus, through 'consideration', 'application' and 'affection', a knowledge of Christ, which may begin as little more than superstitious awe, becomes an intelligible, responsible, transforming experience, giving meaning to the present life and assurance of a life to come.

It was the burden of the Puritan preacher to bring his people to such a knowledge. There can be little doubt that the theologians of the time were anxious to define doctrine correctly and to communicate it to their people. But in the last analysis doctrine was only valid if it could be seen to have a bearing on the eternal welfare of those who heard it. 'I could find no one part of Divinity more profitable ... than that which consisteth more in experience and practice, than in theory and speculation,'[8] said John Downame in his *Guide to Godlynesse*. For this reason, if for no other, the doctrines of Christ and salvation were of supreme importance. Perkins advised his readers to begin their study of Scripture with Paul's Epistle to the Romans and then to go on to the Gospel of John. The implication is clear. No two books of Scripture together spoke more specifically of the person and work of Christ. The titles given by prominent writers to works of doctrine and devotion reveal a similar purpose. Thomas Taylor's *Christ Revealed* (1635), Richard Sibbes' *Christs Exaltation* (1639), John Goodwin's *Christ Lifted Up* (1641), Joseph Truman's *The Great Propitiation* (1669) and John Bunyan's *The Work of Jesus Christ* (1688),all indicate a compulsion to make known God's way of salvation in Jesus. In its doctrinal emphasis Puritanism was indebted to the Pauline assertions that in Christ dwelt all the fullness of the Godhead, that in Him were hidden all the treasures of wisdom and knowledge (cf. Colossians ii 3, 9). It was a fullness which time could not diminish, a treasure-house which no man could exhaust. Flavel, then, speaks for generations of Puritan preachers when he declares, 'The blood of Christ doth never dry up. The beauty of this Rose of Sharon is never lost or withered ... every further prospect of Christ entertains the mind with a fresh delight. He is as it were a new Christ every day, and yet the same Christ still.'[9] Charles Wesley was later to confess to being lost in wonder, love and praise. Flavel knew already of the experience which finds words inadequate. 'The longer you know Christ, and the nearer you come to Him,' he declared, 'still the more do you see of His glory.'[10] It was a knowledge without end, an experience beyond description:

> Set ten thousand, thousand new-made worlds of angels and elect men, and double them in number ten thousand, thousand, thousand times. Let their hearts and tongues be ten thousand times more agile and larger than the hearts and tongues of the seraphims that stand with six wings before Him; when they have said all for the glorifying and praising of the Lord Jesus, they have spoken little or nothing.[11]

This experience, available to each believer as certainly if not as rapturously as to Flavel, emerged from Scripture, and was to guide the Christian in his search for spiritual truth.

The Fulfilment of Type and Prophecy
This knowledge of Christ which was to begin with 'consideration' and proceed to 'affection' was derived initially, despite William Perkins' counsel to read first the Epistle to the Romans and the Gospel according to John, not from the New Testament, but from the Old. Its very substance,

said John Owen, 'lies in the bowels of the Old Testament'. It is Owen's argument that recognition of the Messianic nature of the Old Testament is essential if its message is to be grasped. It is the 'bond of union', without which the constituent parts would be 'loose, scattered, and deformed heaps'. 'Him it promiseth, Him it typifieth, Him it teacheth ... Him it calls all men to desire and expect,' says Owen.[12] It is upon the foundation of Old Testament promise that Christ's claim to Messiahship rests. John Flavel claimed that the Old Testament prefigured the redemptive work of Christ as the dawn bears witness to the approaching day. 'It was with Christ the Sun of Righteousness,' he wrote, 'as it is with the natural sun that illuminates the hemisphere before it actually rises or shows its body above the horizon.'[13] The light that is discernible before the rising of the sun signified the knowledge of Christ as foreshown in the Old Testament.

Principally, Christ was typified in the Old Testament by its characters and its events, 'by holy persons, and by holy things,'[14] as Thomas Taylor explained in his *Christ Revealed*. Taylor, one of the earlier Puritan divines of the Cambridge tradition, had become Doctor of Divinity at Oxford shortly before his death in 1633. The title of his book reveals its intent: *Christ Revealed, or the Old Testament explained. A Treatise of the Types and Shadows of our Saviour contained throughout the whole Scripture.* It proved to be one of the most lucid treatments of Old Testament typology which Puritanism produced and illustrates admirably the Puritan understanding of Old Testament characters as types of Christ.[15] His eternal pre-existence had been prefigured in Melchisedec the priest-king whose ancestry was one of the great mysteries of Scripture, 'without father, without mother, without descent, having neither beginning of days, nor end of life,'[16] to use the words of the Authorised Version. His birth had been prefigured in that of Isaac, born, not according to natural law, but according to promise, a child of miraculous conception. His baptism had been typified in the anointing of David as King of Israel, at which time the Spirit of God came upon Him in a special way to enable Him to accomplish the work for which He had been chosen. His life of rejection, temptation, and suffering, and ultimate preferment to a position of influence, had been foreshadowed in the life of Joseph. Moses, who had predicted the coming of a Prophet like himself, typified Christ in His offices as shepherd and deliverer. The final events of Christ's life had been prefigured in the experience of Jonah, willingly accepting death as the consequence of God's wrath that others might live, and rising again from the darkness of the tomb to new life on the third day.[17]

If these were the more obvious representations of the coming Messiah, it is only necessary to read Taylor and others who wrote in similar vein to discover how a careful study of Old Testament characters revealed deeper truths concerning Christ. Andrew Willett, who had obtained his Oxford doctorate of divinity in 1601, and who is chiefly remembered for his *Synopsis Papismi*, a polemical work designed to counter the claims of the Jesuit writer, Robert Bellarmine, had also written a commentary on the book of Leviticus, in which he argued that Christ's life and work had been set forth in detail in the typological forms of the Old Testament. Willett's observations on Joshua will serve as an example. In the first place, the names Joshua and Jesus had the same basic form in Hebrew, and signified Saviour. As Joshua was to deliver his people, bringing them to the reality of God's promises in Canaan, so Christ in a spiritual sense would make possible the reality of a new and better life. As Joshua fought and conquered many enemies in bringing the children of Israel into the promised land, so Christ would overcome the devil and all his hosts in order to bring His people to the heavenly Canaan. In commanding the sun to stand still, Joshua demonstrated that power over nature which Christ was also to demonstrate in His miracles. As Joshua saved Rahab from certain death on account of the scarlet cord hung in the window, so Christ by His blood saves every penitent sinner from eternal death. Joshua had commanded twelve men each to erect a stone in Canaan as a memorial to the crossing of Jordan. So Christ, by taking twelve men and commanding them to preach the Gospel, had erected an everlasting monument to the amazing work of God in the salvation of the human race.[18] It is possible in a similar way to analyse virtually all those characters whose lives are recorded in any detail on the pages of the Old Testament — Adam, Abraham, Noah, Elijah, Elisha, Solomon, Zerubbabel, even Cyrus, if we are to accept the record of Puritan theology — all in some way or in many ways symbolising the life and work of Christ.

The second category of Old Testament typology, according to Taylor, was 'holy things'. By this we may understand both objects and events which figured in the Old Testament narrative and which were widely believed to have deeper significance than the meaning which was literal or obvious. The Ark of the Covenant, in which the Law of God had been kept inviolate, prefigured Christ by whom the Law would be kept inviolate.[19] Jacob's ladder pointed to the one true Way by which men could have access to heaven. The pillars of cloud and fire which led Israel through the wilderness experience represented Him who would lead His people to the Land of Promise. The manna which fed Israel on the way symbolised Christ as the Bread of Life, that divine provision for the spiritual needs of all men.[20] The burning coal from the altar in Isaiah's vision of the throne reminded Andrew Willett of the nature of fire, that which burns and that which is burned 'incorporate together', a symbol of the nature of Christ being God and man intrinsically and inseparably combined.[21] The brazen serpent and its upraising in the sight of the people was both object and event representing Christ on the cross, lifted up for the healing of those who would look to Him in faith.[22] Other Old Testament events were equally significant. The Passover Lamb, offered annually as a reminder of the miraculous deliverance from Egypt was a symbol of Christ, particularly in the application of its blood and the eating of its flesh, which pointed forward to that greater deliverance which Christ would make available through communion with Him.[23] The death of Abel prefigured the death of Christ, as also did the smiting of the rock in the wilderness by Moses,[24] impetuous acts of wrath which were to remind men for all ages to come of the wrath of God levelled against human sin and of the life-giving stream opened for the healing of their wounds. Even the annual ceremony of the scapegoat on the Day of Atonement was generally held to symbolise Christ,[25] as of course did the whole elaborate ritual of the Sanctuary service and the offices of the Levitical priesthood.

From type and symbol we turn to the specific prophecies of Christ with which Puritans understood that the Old Testament abounded. It was the direct fulfilment of Messianic prophecy in the life and ministry of Christ which justified His claim to Messiahship and hence the validity of His person and work. This John White suggests when he concludes, 'Seeing our Saviour so fully answered all that had been foretold of Him by the prophets, it is evidently and fully proved that He was the same Messiah that was promised and spoken of by the prophets.'[26] The argument is simple enough to follow. Since the Old Testament predicted the coming of a Saviour-Redeemer in specific terms hundreds of years in advance, the One in whom such predictions had been realised must therefore be that promised Messiah. The evidence as gathered together and presented by John Flavel is still impressive. Flavel, who lists most of the Old Testament references to Christ, places them in six categories: His person and office, His birth, His life and teachings, His death, His burial, and His resurrection. The first promise of a Redeemer had, of course, been recorded in Genesis iii 15, with the assurance that the seed of the woman would bruise the serpent's head. From that time forward the promise had been reiterated and elaborated. Shiloh would come, Judah's issue, to rule with equity and to gather together His people (Genesis il 10). A prophet comparable to Moses would arise from among Israel's ranks, a teacher and a leader speaking the words of the Most High (Deuteronomy xviii 15). In contrast to the present Levitical priesthood, God would provide an eternal Priest for His people, after the order of Melchisedec (Psalm cx 4). Thus, as the years unfolded, the concept of the promised Redeemer grew steadily more discernible. The time, the place, and the manner of His birth had been predicted in Daniel ix 24, Micah v 2 and Isaiah vii 14. His life of miraculous teaching and healing, to which the Gospels bore abundant witness, had been foretold,to mention but two references, in Isaiah lxi 1, 2 and xxxv 4, 5. His death had been predicted in Daniel ix 26 and Isaiah liii 5. He had Himself referred to the experience of Jonah as a 'sign' of His own burial and resurrection (Matthew xii 39, 40).[27] Commenting on Isaiah ix 6, Joseph Alleine observed that Christ was appropriately called 'Wonderful', since something remarkable and entirely beyond normal human experience, marked His conception, His birth, His life, His death, His resurrection, and His ascension.[28]

These great Messianic promises were seen as gaining added strength when considered in the light of certain key chapters in the Old Testament which spoke almost entirely of the coming Redeemer and His work.

Together they provided an argument for Christ's Messiahship which was difficult, if not impossible, to ignore. We are reminded of Psalms xxii-xxiv and cx, and of Isaiah liii, passages which were seen as containing not only an outline of the main events of Christ's last days on earth, but also as providing many of the details. They foretold, for example, the piercing of His hands and feet, the casting of lots for His garment, His silence in the presence of His accusers, and His burial in the tomb of a rich man. Possibly no chapter in the Old Testament, however, was better known in Puritan circles for its Messianic content than Daniel ix, the prophecy of seventy weeks, representing four hundred and ninety years of literal time. This provided a chronological framework for the Messiah's appearance which could be substantiated by verifiable historical events. Most well-informed Bible students in the latter part of the seventeenth century would have known of the discussion which was said to have taken place in Poland in 1656 between a group of distinguished Jewish Rabbis and some Roman Catholic theologians concerning this very prophecy. It had been said that the Rabbis found the evidence for Christ's Messiahship as argued from this chapter so hard to refute that they had withdrawn from the meeting and pronounced a curse upon any Jew who would thereafter attempt to compute the chronology of Daniel ix.[29] However that may be, it is certain that Bible students in England from the sixteenth century onwards found strong support in this particular chapter to substantiate the fulfilment of many other Messianic prophecies which were contained in the Old Testament as a whole.

Thomas Adams, never at a loss for an appropriate simile or metaphor, declared, 'He was too rich a jewel to be exposed at the first opening of the shop'. He speaks, of course, of the Old Testament foreshadowing of Christ. Therefore, Adams continues, He was prefigured in 'obscure shadows: the tree of life, Noah's Ark, Jacob's ladder'.[30] Those who searched the pages of the Old Testament with care and devotion could find many further allusions. He appeared in the likeness of a man in Ezekiel's vision of the wheels. He was Aijeleth Shahar, the hind of the morning in Psalm xxii, relentlessly pursued to the death (cf. the inscription at the beginning of the Psalm, with verses 12-16). He was Zechariah's smitten Shepherd, Aaron's rod that budded, David's anointed Conqueror from the ivory palaces, Haggai's Desire of all nations. He was the Rose of Sharon, the Lily of the Valley, the Altogether Lovely One, the Apple Tree among the trees of the wood.[31] 'Shadows of Christ to come, shadows of salvation,' says Christopher Love of the Old Testament revelation. 'They had the same Christ as we have,' he continues, 'the same Gospel preached to them as now we have,' calling on I Corinthians x 4.[32] And if the same Gospel, then the same salvation. Christ was, therefore, to quote Thomas Adams again, 'longed for and looked for, more than health to the sick, or life to the dying'.[33]

The Person of Christ

A further Old Testament allusion to Christ, was that of Zechariah's two staves, Beauty and Bands, with which the Lord gathered the flock which had been forsaken by careless and unconcerned shepherds. The text was held by some seventeenth-century interpreters to signify Christ as the good Shepherd in His two natures, human and divine. Whatever the merits of such an interpretation, the importance of a correct Christology is here emphasized. Puritan preachers as a whole were well acquainted with Christian history, and were aware of the dangers which had beset the Church over the centuries in this sensitive area. Hence they recognised the importance of understanding, as far as the limitations of human finiteness would allow, the unique character of Christ, since that very uniqueness was an intrinsic element in the doctrine of redemption.

The position that Puritanism sought to defend was the received doctrine of Scripture which held that Christ was both human and divine, a mysterious and unique being, at the same time Son of God and Son of Man. Schooled in the original languages of Scripture, as the Puritan brotherhood of preachers was, the significance of the Greek words used of Christ in the New Testament could not be overlooked. He was, according to Paul, 'the firstborn (*prototokos*) of every creature' (Colossians i 15), and in the words of one of the best-known New Testament phrases, 'the only begotten (*monogenes*) Son' of the Father (John iii 16). *Prototokos* signifies 'first begotten', in the sense that what God begets is God as opposed to that which God creates, which is not God. Christ is the begotten *prototokos* of the Father, the firstborn of a new humanity, but nevertheless God. Commenting on Colossians i 15, Nicholas Byfield observes, 'He is the Son of God by generation ... born as man and begotten as God.'[34] Thomas Manton says 'God cannot make a creature equal to Himself nor beget a Son unequal to Himself'.[35] *Monogenes*, translated in the New Testament as only-begotten, literally signifies 'the only one of His kind', and refers to Christ's uniqueness. There is no other being like Him, God and man mysteriously and wonderfully blended in one personality. The Scottish preacher George Hutcheson argues that God has many sons by creation and adoption, but only one by 'eternal and incomprehensible generation.... One in essence with the Father, co-existing with Him from eternity,' who 'became true man and did take on our nature with all the essential properties thereof, and all the common infirmities thereof, yet without sin'.[36] Christ is, then, not merely adequately described by these Greek words of the New Testament. He *is* the *prototokos*. He *is* the *monogenes*. There are no others.

The doctrine of Christ's human nature presented little difficulty. He had been born and reared as all men are born and reared, dependent on His parents, but growing onwards to maturity and responsibility as all children mature and become individuals in their own right. He lived the life of an ordinary human being, eating and sleeping, working and resting, a life of toil and reward, of social relationships and communal worship. He was a

man among men, a human being, 'made in the likeness of men', as
Scripture had said (Philippians ii 7). No, the truth which the theologians of
Puritanism sought to establish with a clarity which could not be denied,
was the truth concerning Christ's divine nature. No writer expressed it
with greater theological precision than did David Dickson. As Professor of
Divinity at Glasgow University between 1640 and 1650, and at Edinburgh
from 1650 to 1660, Dickson's theology was of some significance, particularly in view of his reputation as a commentator on Scripture. In his
exposition of the Epistle to the Hebrews, Dickson reminds his readers that
the Son is a separate being in the Godhead, 'having His own proper
subsistence distinct from the Father'.[37] Dickson then describes the Son's
equality with the Father, and the Son's responsibility in the redemptive
purposes of God to reveal to men the character and nature of the Deity.
This He could do only if He were Himself God, and Dickson's conclusion is
that Christ is fully divine:

> The Son resembleth the Father, fully, and perfectly, so that there is no
> perfection in the Father but the same is substantially in the Son. As the
> Father is eternal, omnipotent, omnipresent, infinite in wisdom, good-
> ness, mercy, holiness, and all other perfections, so is the Son omni-
> potent, eternal, and all that the Father is.... Christ is of the same
> nature, and essence, with the Father, consubstantial with Him, because
> begotten of Him, in Himself, without beginning, the Son being eternally
> in the Father, and the Father eternally in the Son, of the self-same nature,
> and Godhead.[38]

Dickson unquestionably speaks for Puritanism as a whole, demonstrating
the latter's essential unity with the theology of the Thirty-Nine Articles of
Religion which on this point state that Christ was 'very God and very Man'
in whom 'two whole and perfect natures, that is to say, the Godhead and
manhood, were joined together in one person'.

What, then, were the grounds from which this reaffirmation of Christ's
divinity proceeded? The most obvious reason, and to many the most
convincing, was that Christ's sinless life testified to His divinity. Even the
most superficial reading of Scripture led to this conclusion. 'No man ever
convicted Him of any sin, either in word or deed,'[39] said Richard Baxter,
claiming that history, which bears witness independently of Scripture to
Christ's existence, says nothing which detracts from the sinlessness of
His character. The writings of the Jews, His greatest enemies, under
whose malicious scrutiny He lived, are silent. They contain no accusations of sin. 'He was so far from pride, worldliness, sensuality, malice,
impatience, or any sin,' continues Baxter, that the world had never seen
such an example of godliness. 'He was the most excellent representative
of the Divine perfection: the omnipotence of God appeared in His
miracles, the wisdom of God in His holy doctrine, and the love of God in
His matchless expressions of love.'[40] It is Baxter's contention, and with
him the contention of Puritan theology as a whole, that all the attributes of
Deity are found in the life and teachings of Christ. No man could live the

life of God without being God.

It was when men studied the Bible in depth, however, that they discerned textual evidence establishing the truth of Christ's divinity. We may note in this respect the doctrine of creation. The biblical explanation of origins was that of fiat creation, as set forth in Genesis and as substantiated in the New Testament doctrine of Christ. 'In the beginning, God created the heaven and the earth' (Genesis i 1), was the premise from which the Old Testament narrative unfolded. Man could only rightly understand his being and his destiny as he remembered his origin. The New Testament, however, threw more light on the process of creation. The Gospel according to John began with a similar unequivocal statement of origins. 'In the beginning was the Word, and the Word was with God, and the Word was God. . . . All things were made by Him, and without Him was not anything made that was made' (John i 1-3). According to John, the divine Word, the *Logos*, had been responsible for the creation of the world and all that it contained. But who was the Word? John explains that the Word was He who was 'made flesh and dwelt among us' (Verse 14). The Word was none other than God incarnate, the One who had been with the Father from the beginning, but who had, in Paul's words, 'made Himself of no reputation' and who had been 'made in the likeness of men' (Philippians ii 7). This living Word, as He had existed in heaven before His incarnation, had been the active agent in creation. Paul himself stated this truth. Writing of Christ in the Epistle to the Colossians, he declared, 'For by Him were all things created, that are in heaven, that are in earth, visible and invisible ... all things were created by Him and for him' (Colossians i 16). These passages, and others like them, were fundamental to the structure of Puritan theology, and, commenting on the text just quoted, George Lawson summed up, 'Christ is not merely man as they affirm, but the Word by which all things were made.'[41] The argument, of course, is that only God can create that which is seen to exist from that which does not previously exist, and since Christ is repeatedly stated to be the Creator of the world and all it contains, He must, *ipso facto*, be divine in the fullest sense of that word. Francis Bampfield reached the same conclusion from certain texts in Hebrews. Putting together the statements in Hebrews i 2, 8-10, iii 4 and iv 10, Bampfield says of Christ, 'He was the LORD in the beginning who laid the foundation of the earth, and the works of whose hands the heavens were.'[42] Bampfield's treatise, *All In One*, in which this statement appeared, had in fact been written largely to explain the implications of the biblical doctrine of creation, and the emphasis on Christ as Creator as well as Redeemer, appears as a recurring theme in that work.

We may follow Bampfield further as he pursues this argument, for in so doing he draws attention to additional textual evidence substantiating the divinity of Christ. Throughout the Old Testament the title Jehovah, or JHWH, in its contracted form, is used exclusively of God. The name appears nearly seven thousand times in the Old Testament and has the meaning of 'the eternal One', or 'the self-existent One'. It is always translated either as LORD or GOD, and always appears in the text of the Authorised Version in a capitalised form. Jehovah or JHWH was the special name of the Creator-God, the living God, the divine, self-existent One, whom Israel worshipped. Bampfield's argument is that this name is taken by the writers of the New Testament, under the inspiration of the Holy Spirit, and applied to Christ. The prophet Isaiah declares, 'Prepare ye the way of the LORD [JHWH], make straight in the desert a highway for our God' (Isaiah xl 3). In the New Testament this prophetic statement is said to be fulfilled in John the Baptist, the one who came to prepare the way for Christ (Matthew iii 3). Through the same prophet Isaiah, JHWH Himself declares that ultimately every knee will bow to Him, every tongue will acknowledge Him (Isaiah xlv 23). Paul twice uses this passage with reference to Christ, in Romans xiv 9-11 and Philippians ii 10-11. Christ is the LORD to whom every knee will bow, and whom every tongue will confess. And in John xii 37-41 two further Old Testament references to JHWH are said to meet their fulfilment in Christ. The JHWH of the Old Testament is to be identified with the Christ of the New Testament, and since JHWH is God in the absolute, the same must also be concluded of Christ. Therefore Bampfield says, 'If there be a due diligent comparing of the Old Testament with the New, it will thereby evidently appear that the same who is Christ in the one is Jehovah in the other.'[43]

Jesus Christ, then, is unique. There is no other being in heaven or on earth comparable to Him. He is the *prototokos* and the *monogenes*, the only one of His kind, human and divine, fully man and fully God. 'Great is the mystery of godliness,' the apostle Paul had declared, and nowhere did the mystery appear more profound than in the incarnation, when God was 'manifest in the flesh'. It would be easy enough to dismiss these concerns of seventeenth-century divines as obscure and irrelevant theologising. Lest we reach that conclusion too hastily, we must listen again to John Flavel. It is precisely because of this uniqueness, Flavel argues, that Christ is able to be man's Saviour. Christ alone, and no other being, can be now or ever become what He is and ever will be by virtue of the union of the human and the divine which has been accomplished in Him. 'Who but He that hath the divine and human nature united in His single person,' asks Flavel, 'can be fit to lay His hand upon both?'[44] He is the link between heaven and earth, the bridge from death to life. Here is the mystery of godliness, the mystery of the Gospel, the mystery beyond human comprehension, that the Creator in the unique person of Christ has descended to the level of the creature thereby to become the mediator between God and man.

The Redeemer

All that the Old Testament foretold of Christ in type and prophecy and all that Scripture in its entirety said of His humanity and divinity was, in the end, for one purpose. Men must come to understand the immense significance of the cross and of Christ's work as Redeemer. They must know why He had come and why He had died and in what way His life and death affected them. This was that knowledge which more than any other it was essential to have. To fail in communicating the meaning of these things would be to fail at the most crucial point of all, and no Puritan preacher worthy of his calling would be found wanting in that.

The death of Christ on the cross had been necessitated by sin. Of that basic truth there could not be the slightest doubt. 'This is that deadly poison, so powerful ... that one drop of it shed upon the root of mankind hath corrupted, spoiled, poisoned, and undone his whole race at once,'[45] said Joseph Alleine. Alleine's *Alarm to the Unconverted*, in which this statement appeared, is a work whose influence on the spiritual life of the age must be ranked with Baxter's *Saints' Everlasting Rest* and Bunyan's *Grace Abounding*. Since the cross could only be understood adequately from the standpoint of sin, it was essential to press home the awfulness of sin and its consequences. Alleine therefore continues, 'This is the traitor that sucked the blood of the Son of God, that sold Him, that mocked Him, that scourged Him, that spit in His face, that pierced His side, that pressed His soul, that mangled His body, that never left till it had bound Him, condemned Him, nailed Him, crucified Him, and put Him to open shame.'[46] But where is this 'traitor', this 'butcher', this 'bloody executioner', to be found? Is sin dead or alive? Is it merely an abstract principle outside human experience, at work at one given time in history to achieve the death of the Son of God? No, says Alleine, sin is inside human experience, it is ever-present in man, it is an inseparable part of human personality, and what it accomplished at the cross it accomplished through human beings and on behalf of all humanity. Therefore, says Alleine, 'Study the nature of sin till thy heart be brought to fear and loath it.'[47] The cross is God's way of dealing with the consequences of sin in human experience. 'If he take them not away by the blood of His cross, they can never be taken away,' John Flavel says of man's sins, and 'They will lie down with you in the dust, they will rise with you and follow you to judgement.'[48] The death of Jesus had been caused by sin and only in that context could it be understood.

How did seventeenth-century preachers understand, and how did they explain, the death of Christ? What did they comprehend by the terms 'redemption' and 'salvation'? Flavel poses a significant question in this respect when he asks, 'Did Christ finish His work for us?' Was all that is requisite for man's salvation accomplished on the cross? Christians of every generation who have thought about their faith have come, sooner or later, to this question. To Flavel, it was rhetorical and the answer follows immediately: 'Then there can be no doubt, but that He will also finish His work in us. As He began the work of our redemption, and finished it, so He that hath begun the good work in you will also finish it in your souls.'[49] The conclusion Flavel reaches concerning the death of Christ is something of a paradox. Christ's work was effective, yet it was incomplete. It was finished in its accomplishment, yet unfinished in its application. The key to the paradox lies in Flavel's word 'redemption', and in the relationship of this redemption to salvation as a process in time and in the individual. Redemption was accomplished and finished on the cross. Salvation was not complete until the work of the cross had been translated into human experience. Flavel explains further: 'When we say Christ finished redemption-work by His death, the meaning is not that His death alone did finish it, for His abode in the grave, resurrection, and ascension, had all of them their joint influence into it.'[50] The argument was put clearly enough by John Durant in the introduction to *The Salvation of the Saints*. Durant, a leading minister among the Congregational Churches of Kent in the middle of the seventeenth century, expressed disappointment that many Christians were satisfied to accept the work accomplished on the cross, without obtaining a fuller knowledge of salvation. Durant's argument was that salvation depended on the total work of Christ and not merely on His death. While it was not to be disputed that His death lay at the heart of the matter, that it was the key to the mystery of salvation, yet it was not the sum total of Christ's work. Salvation had been 'purchased' but not 'completed' at the cross. There remained beyond the death of Christ 'a great deal more to be done ... to apply it unto us'.[51] This meant, in specific terms, Christ's priestly ministry in heaven and His coming again at the end of the age, themes which will be discussed later.

This desire to see the cross in perspective, to understand it in relationship to the rest of Christ's life and work, was not intended to minimise in the slightest the immense significance of His death. Flavel, whose thoughts on this matter are quite clear, and whose alliegance to sound Christology has already been demonstrated, was at pains to put beyond any possible doubt the completeness and centrality of the cross:

> All that was to be done by way of impetration [achievement] and meritorious redemption, is fully done. No hand can come after His. Angels can add nothing to it. That is perfected to which nothing is wanting and to which nothing can be added. Such is the work Christ finished. Whatever the law demanded is perfectly paid. Whatever a sinner needs is perfectly obtained, and purchased. Nothing can be added to what Christ hath done.[52]

The efficacy of Christ's monumental act on the cross is equally conveyed by Joseph Truman in his *Great Propitiation*, intended principally as an exposition of the doctrine of justification by faith, but warm throughout with the desire to make the historical act of the cross relevant to contemporary human need. 'He is able to save to the uttermost them that come to God by Him,' says Truman, quoting Hebrews vii 25, and 'No spot or stain is of so deep a dye that the blood of Christ cannot wash it out, no disease so desperate that He cannot cure it. ... This red sea of Christ's blood is large enough, deep enough, to drown the tall Egyptian host of thy sins.'[53] Redemption is therefore complete, and the blood of Christ powerful to cleanse and to save. Redemption leads onwards to full salvation, however, as Christ becomes a reality for the individual, and Flavel concludes, 'as He presented a perfect sacrifice to God, and finished redemption work, so will He present every man perfect and complete, for whom He here offered up Himself'.[54]

The consequences of Christ's finished work in the believer will be examined more fully in a succeeding chapter. For the present, we must pursue the theme of redemption as it was variously set forth in Puritan theology. This 'foundation' of the faith, as Baxter had described it, had been well laid in the event and was equally well handled in the explanation. Space will permit examination of only two or three of the more salient concepts by which the meaning of Christ's death was explained by Puritan theologians. The first is the word 'ransom'. A ransom was the price to be paid in order that a hostage might be freed. Christ's death was a ranson, for it was in this connection that Christ became, in terms of Old Testament custom, the 'Goel', the one who provided the required price. Man had sold himself and his inheritance into slavery, and was unable to redeem himself from bondage. When such a situation arose in Old Testament times, it was customary for a near kinsman to exercise the right of redemption. This was usually the elder brother on the mother's side, the heir to the family wealth. From his own resources he would provide the necessary ransom, thereby obtaining the release of the one in bondage. Such a benefactor was the 'Goel'. So with Christ. He, the elder Brother, the Heir of all things, had by the gift of His life paid the price required, provided the way of release, and procured the assurance of new and eternal life.

It is equally true that Christ is more than the 'Goel'. He does not simply pay the required price, the ransom — He gives Himself. He does not only set the captive free, He takes the place of the guilty man and vicariously bears his punishment. Christ is man's substitute. Richard Sibbes comes to this point by recalling that Christ was the second Adam, and as such died a substitutionary death on behalf of all those whose right to life had been forfeited by the first Adam. 'Christ died,' he says, 'as a public person, in whom dying all die.'[55] When men die in the ordinary course of events their death holds no meaning or significance beyond that which is common to every man. But with Jesus it is different. 'Christ died alone and singular in this respect,' says Sibbes, 'Because in Him dying, all died that were His.'[56] Christ's voluntary death is the death which is required of all men as a consequence of sin. 'You may sit under Christ's shadow with great delight, shaded from the heat of God's displeasure,' says Joseph Truman, continuing, 'He was scorched with God's wrath that we might be cooled, shaded, comforted, by that shadow that He hath made for wearied souls by being hanged on a tree.'[57] In taking man's place Christ bears vicariously in His body the consequences of sin deserved by sinners themselves.

The ultimate consequence of Christ's death, both in terms of Scripture and in terms of Puritan theology, is reconciliation: 'When we were enemies, we were reconciled to God by the death of His son' (Romans v 10). By sin man had been alienated from God, by the cross that alienation had been terminated. Man had broken the relationship. God had moved to restore it. Those who had been put at enmity by sin, were now, through the cross, placed in a new relationship. This is what is conveyed by the theological terms 'reconciliation' and 'atonement'. Those who were estranged had been brought together, made 'at one'. This is fundamental Christian doctrine and none understood it better or proclaimed it with greater certainty than the Puritan preachers whose writings have been cited in this chapter. Thomas Adams declared:

God sees all our violations of His law, knows every peccant act better than our own conscience, but, withall, He sees the atonement made in the sacrifice of His own Son, a satisfaction able to pay all our debts. Hence no sin shall oblige us to condemnation, no debt shall bear an action against us. The rich creditor sees many items in His books, knows what debts have been owing, but withall, He sees them crossed and cancelled.[58]

The atonement had been made. It is sufficient and satisfactory. The barrier of condemnation has been removed; God and man are brought together. John Flavel, lucid and concerned as ever, explains, 'Reconciliation or atonement is nothing else but the making up of the ancient friendship betwixt God and man which sin had dissolved, and so to reduce these enemies into a state of sweet concord and sweet agreement.'[59] Baxter adds that the sufferings of Christ on the cross were 'to bear what was due to the sinner, and to receive the blow that should have fallen upon him, and so to restore him to the life he lost and the happiness he fell from'.[60] If this introduces the idea of substitution, it also emphasises the idea of restoration and reconciliation, the ultimate objective of Christ's redemptive work.

We return now to John Flavel. He seems not only to grasp the meaning of redemption, but almost to have the facility to feel within himself the dire consequences of sin, and the price of man's redemption. In a moving comment on the phrase 'I come to thee' in the prayer of Jesus recorded in John xvii, Flavel says all that needs to be said by way of conclusion on the redemptive work of Christ:

There is much in these words, 'I come to thee'; I, thy beloved Son, in which thy soul delighteth; I, to whom thou never deniedest anything. 'Tis not a stranger, but a son; not an adopted, but thine only begotten Son. 'Tis I that come. I am now coming to thee apace, my Father. I come to Thee swimming through a bloody ocean. I come treading every step of my way to thee in blood and unspeakable sufferings; and all this for the sake of those dear ones I now pray for.[61]

Jesus and the Individual

At the beginning of this chapter the insistence within Puritanism on a knowledge of Christ was noted. The chapter will conclude on a related heme. In the pursuit of spiritual truth the knowledge that is of ultimate value is that which is experiential. The second of Perkins' three steps to a true knowledge of Christ was, it will be recalled, 'application'. That is to say, knowledge only becomes experiential when it is received and assimilated by the individual. Historians of the period have drawn attention to that peculiarly Puritan practice of keeping a spiritual diary, a detailed daily record of the vicissitudes and victories of the Christian life. Nothing so clearly demonstrates the essentially personal character of faith in Puritan England as do these diaries, specifically recording such matters of daily personal religion as answers to prayer, blessings received, books read with profit, temptations overcome or not overcome, the high points of religious experience such as the time and place of one's conversion, the name of the preacher responsible, and the names of succeeding ministers used by God to guide the believer in his journey to the Kingdom. Bunyan's *Pilgrim's Progress* is not the chance product of an isolated visionary unacquainted with the every-day experiences of his contemporaries. Its significance is that it reflects the spirit of mature Puritanism, the hopes and fears, the temptations, the defeats and the victories, of ordinary men and women whose chief calling in life was to reach the heavenly City. Pilgrim is every man, more or less, and his struggle the measure of an intense, individual involvement. It all speaks of something very real and very personal, a yearning for the essentials of the Christian faith to be worked out in the life of the individual believer.

In nothing is this experiential emphasis more necessary than in the believer's relationship to Christ. 'Thou must know and believe,' Perkins reiterates, 'not only that Christ was crucified, but that He was crucified for thee, for *thee*, I say, in particular.'[62] The figures by which Puritan preachers sought to emphasise the necessity of applying Christ's work to the individual were many. Sin had been portrayed as a wound in Scripture, and Christ as the One who had come to heal. Yet, as Flavel rightly points out, the balm must be brought to the sore for healing to occur. 'Never was any wound healed by a prepared but unapplied plaster,' he says; or, to change the figure, to what purpose is a coat, unless it is worn? So Flavel continues, 'never [was] a body warmed by the most costly garment made but not put on'.[63] George Downham, many years before Flavel, had made the same point: 'For though the obedience of Christ ... be a robe of righteousness and our very wedding garment to cover our nakedness and our sins, yet it will not cover us, unless it be put on'. Again, of what use is food unless taken into the body and assimilated? Downham therefore adds, 'Though His body be meat indeed and His blood be drink indeed to nourish us unto eternal life, yet they will not yield nourishment unto us, unless we eat His body and drink His blood.'[64] All that Christ was, all that He had become, and all that He had accomplished is in vain unless translated into individual experience. Perkins had drawn attention to the frightening possibility of being but a superficial follower of Christ. Herod, he pointed out, had been interested in Christ, but for the wrong reasons.

He had heard of Christ's works and wanted to see Him perform a miracle, but he did not want to hear His word or accept His authority. Similarly, Perkins argued, there were those who would read the Bible to gather facts or learn from its history, but who were not willing to accept and practise its teachings, or to become followers of Christ in a real sense. 'Let us therefore labour,' Perkins advises, 'that with our knowledge we may join obedience, and practise with our learning, as well to be affected with the word of Christ, as with His works'.[65] Men must be confronted with Christ in His saving fullness, persuaded of their need to receive Him, and instructed in the way by which they might do so. This is a recurring emphasis in Puritan literature from the early days of William Perkins in the 1580s to John Flavel more than a century later.

How to receive Christ was, without doubt, the most important question of all, and it is in this context that Flavel uses the word 'assent'. 'Receiving Christ necessarily implies the assent of the understanding,' he says. Flavel is concerned with more than understanding alone. The facts must be heard, they must be understood, but they must also be accepted. A decision is required when the evidence has been presented and explained. The assent, therefore, that Flavel requires is 'the assent of the understanding to the truths of Christ revealed in the Gospel: His person, natures, offices, His incarnation, death and satisfaction'.[66] Although such assent is not in itself faith unto salvation, it is 'the foundation and groundwork of it'. It is the third link in a chain, hearing and understanding being the first two, which leads fallen man to an experiential knowledge of Christ. To enter into this experience, then, it is necessary to understand, to agree and to accept. All are functions of the mind, faith included, and all require individual involvement and personal consideration. Only in this way are the merits and claims of Christ in all His fullness brought home to the needs of the individual. Richard Sibbes summarises all we have endeavoured to portray in this chapter of the Puritan understanding of the person and work of Christ. In Sibbes' words, 'He died for us, He gave Himself for us, He rose for us, He ascended for us, He sits at the right hand of God for us.'[67] It is all 'for us'. Therefore Sibbes urges, 'When we see Him die, think we die with Him; when we see Him buried, think ourselves buried with Him; when we see Him rise, think He is there to prepare a place for me.'[68] It is 'for us', to be sure. But, in the end, as Sibbes says, it is 'for me'. Christ and His cross confront the Church and the world. They also confront the individual. Together they provide the way of salvation for needy men. Sibbes and Perkins, Baxter and Alleine, together with the host of Puritan preachers who were their contemporaries, their brethren in a common calling, would surely have endorsed Flavel's conclusion, 'Before Him was none like Him; and after Him shall none arise comparable to Him.'

3. THE LORD OUR RIGHTEOUSNESS

In justifying the sinner God acquits him, declares him to be righteous, regards him as righteous, and proceeds to treat him as a righteous man. Justification is the act of acquittal and the accompanying declaration that a state of righteousness exists. Charges of wrongdoing are cancelled, and the sinner, now justified, is brought into a right relationship with God that Paul describes as being at 'peace with God' (Romans v 1).

'Justification' *Seventh-day Adventist Bible Dictionary* (1960) p.616

There is no vein in all the body of the gospel, no point whatsoever in Christian Religion more tender, and wherein the least variation from the truth and mind of God may endanger the soul, than this of Justification. An hair's breadth of mistake in this, is more to be feared than a broad error in other points. The truth is, that if a man be of a sound and clear judgement in the doctrine of Justification, and shall so continue, he may find a way into life through the midst of many errors and mistakes in other Articles and arguments of Christian Religion. But if he stumbles ... with the counsel of God about his justification, he is in danger of perishing for ever.

John Goodwin *Treatise of Justification* sig. d3r

Two words appeared in the previous chapter which now require more careful consideration if we are to grasp the thoroughly Protestant nature of Puritan theology. Nowhere was Puritanism more sure of itself than in its understanding of the way of salvation, and in its contention that in Jesus Christ God had provided the complete answer to man's terrible spiritual dilemma. 'Righteousness' and 'justification' are the words in question, and together they suggest the real nature of human need as well as the nature of God's provision. In seeking to discover what righteousness and justification meant to the Puritans we shall see again the crucial declaration of the Reformation that man's salvation is not of himself but of God. Righteousness and justification, in this context, are concepts implying that man, outside of a relationship with Christ, is unrighteous and unjustified. They further indicate that the way of salvation should be understood as the process by which God enables man to be righteous instead of unrighteous, to move from a condition in which he is unjustified to one in which he experiences justification. If this sounds too much like high theology, it must be remembered that these are words used repeatedly by the apostle Paul in explanation of God's way of grace, and it was the strength of Puritanism that it sought to come to grips with the whole message of Scripture. We must begin, however, with another word which also appeared in the preceding chapter. It is the word 'sin', for it is sin which necessitates a response by God to man's lost and hopeless situation, and

it is this divine response which results in his justification and righteousness.

Sin and Unrighteousness
If man looked dispassionately at himself and at humanity in general,
Puritanism contended, he would see clearly enough that the Bible was
unquestionably correct in declaring the human race to be unrighteous.
'There is none righteous, no, not one.... For all have sinned, and come
short of the glory of God,' the apostle Paul had stated (Romans iii 10, 23).
This description of man's natural condition was beyond dispute. It applied
to all men, in all lands, and at all times. No human being could claim
immunity from this generic condition. It was part and parcel of man's
humanity. Sin was 'a desperate disease' which struck at the very heart of
man's being and threatened the continuity of human existence, a malig-
nancy which had contaminated the race, said Joseph Truman.[1] Man's
inherent nature, to use Thomas Gataker's analogy, was 'a general seed-
plot of evil', a garden run wild in which 'the seed and spawn of all sin' had
given rise to 'spiritual weeds of all sorts'. The analogy was a good one, for
it underlined the innate human tendency to be overcome by evil. Man was
'addicted unto' sin, 'wedded unto' it, 'carried away' with it, phrases which
all bring their own particular meaning to bear on the reality of the human
predicament.[2] To recognise this fundamental truth of human nature was
to take the first step towards salvation.

But how had this condition arisen? What were its consequences? And
how could it justly and satisfactorily be resolved? The answers are
derived, to begin with, from Paul's argument in the Epistle to the Romans.
'By one man sin entered into the world,' Paul said, 'by one man's
disobedience many were made sinners' (Romans v 12, 19). The one man
was the first man, Adam, as Paul further emphasises in his first letter to the
Corinthian Church when he declares, 'As in Adam all die, even so in Christ
shall all be made alive' (I Corinthians xv 22). Puritanism understood that
the strength of this promise of new life in Christ lay in the reality of the
present life derived from Adam. Men are made alive in Christ, because
they are dead in Adam. The reality of the life available in Christ is in direct
relationship to the reality of man's death in Adam. Man's sinful condition
with its dire implications, then, is a direct and immediate consequence of
Adam's first sin. 'Adam must be considered not as a private man, but as a
root or head bearing in it all mankind,' says William Perkins, 'a public
person representing all his posterity.'[3] James Ussher uses similar
language. Man's first parents were not merely individuals in their own
right, but were 'the head and root of all mankind', representatives of the
race as a whole. Adam had been promised life for himself and for his
posterity, and had he not sinned, Ussher argues, he would have received
the promise, even as those potentially in him would also have received it.
Since Adam did sin, however, the promise was forfeited and Ussher
speaks instead of 'our participation with Adam's fall'.[4] George Downham
says that Adam's sin was more than a personal act. It was 'the sin of

mankind', since all men are now directly and individually involved in Adam's sin, and since they now receive the consequences of disobedience rather than the consequences of obedience.[5]

To see how this is so it is necessary to understand the nature of Adam's original sin. Downham explains that two things happened to Adam when he sinned. He became guilty, and he became inherently sinful. He stood condemned before the holiness of God's character and before the requirements of His law, and he lost the moral uprightness with which he had been endowed when created in the image of God, and came instead to possess a 'disposition' and a 'proneness' to evil.[6] He is sinful and therefore guilty in a legal sense before God's law because of an act of disobedience, and he is sinful and therefore guilty in an actual sense in himself as a consequence of lost righteousness and a fallen nature which is now disposed to evil. The corresponding sinfulness and guilt in mankind as a whole comes as a result of the natural relationship to Adam. Man's 'participation' in Adam's sin is also to be understood in a legal sense and in an actual sense. Both aspects of man's sinful condition must be grasped if the amazing provision for man's salvation by God in Christ is to have any significance. Since Adam was the representative head of the race, and all men were therefore in him, of him, and one with him, Adam's sin is imputed to them and they become guilty by virtue of Adam's sin, since that sin was the 'sin of mankind' as a whole. Concerning the imputation, or reckoning of Adam's sin to his posterity, John Flavel says explicity that men born after Adam become 'guilty of Adam's sin' by 'natural generation'.[7] Downham explains that by the actual transgression of Adam 'all his offspring were made guilty of sin and subject to death,' not simply because Adam's disobedient nature is inherent in them, but because his sin is 'imputed to them, as if it were their own, because they were in him originally'.[8] Since Adam stood at the head of the race and all men are in him, the effects of Adam's sin are imputed to them even as the righteousness of the second Adam and its effects are imputed to those who are 'in Him', as we shall see shortly. This is the logical conclusion and explanation of the Pauline argument that 'by the offence of one [Adam], judgement came upon all men to condemnation' (Romans v 18). Men share in the consequences of Adam's sin and guilt because they are children of Adam and because Adam was the head of the race. The human race as a whole is both sinful and guilty in Adam and each man shares individually in Adam's guilt because he belongs to the race and is part of it.

By natural generation, however, men also receive the sinful nature which became Adam's by sin, and are therefore born with a tendency to evil. Ussher uses the illustration of a slave. The progeny of a slave, he says, will remain slaves in every generation for ever, unless granted freedom.[9] Flavel points to the 'original rectitude' with which Adam was created, and argues that men were deprived of that moral uprightness of character because Adam could not transmit to his posterity by natural generation that which he had lost.[10] He could only transmit a propensity to evil. Perkins thinks that every child, as a descendant of Adam, inherits Adam's fallen, sinful nature 'and thereby is made a sinner, not only by imputation of Adam's offence, but also by propagation of an aptness and proneness unto every evil, received together with nature from Adam'.[11] Ussher defines two categories of sin, 'imputed or inherent', one the sin of Adam, the first and seminal sin of the race, the other the sin received by natural conception and birth, man's sinful nature and the outworking of that nature in life, so that man 'of himself can do nothing but sin'.[12] Perkins finally sets the seal on man's hopeless condition by adding that the natural inclination to sin is self-perpetuating. Every sin committed leads to further sin and to a deeper bondage to the principle of sin: 'So a sinner, the more he sins, the apter is he to sin, and more desirous to keep still a course in wickedness.' [13] Man is guilty before God, therefore, not only on account of Adam's sin, reckoned to be his by virtue of his identity with the race, but, even more explicitly, on account of his own sinful nature and the effects of that nature in his life and actions. Baxter concludes that Christ had come 'to seek and to save that which was doubly lost,' those who are both 'guilty' and 'unholy'.[14]

The term which frequently and correctly expresses man's guilt and sinfulness is 'unrighteousness'. Sin in human experience, either imputed or inherent, leads to this condition of unrighteousness. Man, who was created in the image of God and therefore righteous, has by sin lost the moral uprightness with which he was endowed in the beginning, and is now by birth and by experience unrighteous. Baxter, again, says that man is the subject of 'a two-fold unrighteousness', by which he means that the guilt of Adam's imputed sin gives him an unrighteous standing before God, and that the sin which is part of his nature and which is now seen in his life and actions gives him an unrighteous character.[15] Man's unrighteousness has a legal aspect and a moral aspect. He is unrighteous when measured against the holiness of God's character and the requirements of His law, and he is unrighteous in himself since he has a fallen nature, a propensity to sin and evil which causes him by nature to think and act sinfully. Righteousness and unrighteousness are key words in Paul's Epistle to the Romans, and his argument is that the Gospel reveals a righteousness provided for man, a righteousness which results both in guiltlessness and in holiness of life. Baxter concludes that since man is doubly unrighteous it is the purpose of God through the Gospel to restore him 'to that two-fold righteousness which he lost,' that is, to freedom from guilt and to holiness of life.[16] Righteousness, then, as far as the word may be applied to human experience, results from God's response both to man's guilt and to his inherent sinfulness. It is guiltlessness and holiness, and only the gospel which proclaims such a righteousness is in truth the Gospel.

The Righteousness of Christ

Whence comes righteousness? This is crucial not only in Puritan theology, but in the application of the Gospel to each individual life. Thomas Gataker is certain that this righteousness cannot be discovered or effected within normal human experience. It is like a rare plant, he says, 'that grew once in Paradise, but upon the fall of our first parents, it left this world and is not now to be found here on earth'.[17] It is not in man or of man, and if man is to experience it, it must be provided for him. But how? John Owen argues that the 'great fundamental promise' contained within the Old Testament as it looked forward to the future, was that the day would come when God would provide man with the righteousness he so desperately needs. This may be seen in passages such as Psalm lxxii 1-7, Psalm lxxxv 9-11, and Isaiah lx 15-21, where the redemptive purposes of God culminate in the specific promises of a righteousness that will one day be revealed.[18] This is not to say that righteousness was not available to those who lived in Old Testament times. It is merely to emphasise that in the revelation and reception of God's own Son these promises of righteousness would become tangible; hence Jeremiah's great Messianic promise declared, 'This is his name whereby he shall be called, THE LORD OUR RIGHTEOUSNESS' (Jeremiah xxiii 6). God's promises of righteousness for man are to be fulfilled in Christ. Man has no righteousness of his own, nor is there any possible source or means in all creation by which he can obtain it. 'Wherefore,' says Owen, 'Jehovah Himself becomes our righteousness.'[19] God Himself provides the righteousness man needs, and He does it in and through the person of Christ. Baxter adds that the righteousness which man may have as the basis of his salvation 'is wholly in Christ, and not one grain in ourselves,' and that nothing can, or need, be added to that righteousness in order to make it sufficient for salvation.[20]

We may pause at this point to note that one of the most lively debates which occurred within Puritanism centred on the question of righteousness and justification. The main concern of this debate was to establish the difference between the Protestant and Roman Catholic doctrines of justification, an issue of sufficient importance in the view of most Puritan theologians to warrant careful and detailed examination. Reference has already been made to one of the best expositions in Puritan theology of this topic, George Downham's *Treatise of Justification*, a work exceeding five hundred pages, written specifically to counter the Jesuit Robert Bellarmine's doctrine of righteousness and justification. The debate as a whole need not detain us, except to illustrate the thoroughness with which Puritanism approached the doctrine of righteousness in Christ. From the basic proposition that it is God's righteousness revealed in Christ which saves man, Downham proceeds to examine the nature of this righteousness. How shall it be understood in its fulness? What is the righteousness of Christ which saves? Downham discerns a 'negative' and a 'positive' righteousness in the life of Christ, the absence of all sin and evil in His nature, and the presence of all virtue and holiness in his life. It is with this second aspect that Downham is most concerned. The 'positive' righteousness of Christ is itself also of a two-fold nature. It consists of perfect obedience to the requirements of God's law, and of a perfect satisfaction in meeting the penalty demanded when that law is broken. The former is seen in Christ's life, the latter in His death. Christ's perfect obedience is in reality holiness, that is, holiness of nature which is seen in holiness of life and which results in actual obedience to all the requirements of God.[21] There is also a passive obedience in Christ's righteousness, which manifests itself most clearly in His willing submission to the sufferings of the cross. It is the sum of both Christ's perfect obedience and His perfect satisfaction, His holiness of life and His sufferings on the cross, which together constitute the righteousness by which man is saved.[22] Ussher describes the righteousness of Christ as 'original' and 'actual', the one the inherent sinlessness of His nature, the other the actual sinlessness of His life. By His death, says Ussher, Christ took away the effect of man's unrighteousness, by His life He provided that righteousness which man needed.[23] It is really unnecessary to pursue any further these definitions of the righteousness of Christ, for whether we follow Downham, or Ussher, or any of the major Puritan spokesmen, we reach the same conclusion: 'Of God, Christ is made unto us righteousness.... Instead of our own, we have His, we have gold for dung.'[24] Christ, in His person and in His accomplishments in life and in death, has become 'the Lord our Righteousness', and that righteousness is totally sufficient for man's salvation.

It should now be possible to discern more clearly the strength of Paul's argument that Christ is the second Adam. The fact that Christ's righteousness may become man's righteousness is due to the similarity of the relationships between Adam and man, and between Christ and man. Christ stood at the head of the human race as Adam had stood at the head of the race. He took Adam's place, which had been forfeited by sin. It is only in this context that Christ's righteousness can be understood as being available for man. 'This righteousness is in Christ, not as in a person severed from us, but as in the head of our common nature,'[25] says Ussher. Since all men were sinners in Adam, because they were 'in his loins, he being the head of our common nature,' all may also become righteous in Christ on similar grounds, particularly since the relationship between a man and Christ is deeper than the relationship between a man and Adam.[26] Baxter explains it as follows:

> As human nature sinned in Adam actually in *specie* and in his individual person, and all our persons were seminally and virtually in Him, and accordingly sinned, or are reputed sinners, as having no nature but what he conveyed who could convey no better than he had ... even so Christ obeyed and suffered in our nature, and in our nature as it was in Him, and human sinful nature in *specie* was universally pardoned by Him and eternal life freely given to all men for His merits.[27]

It is thus the relationship of Christ to the human race which makes it possible for His righteousness to become man's righteousness. He is the second Adam, the One who stands at the head of humanity, taking the place of the first Adam in whom humanity was lost. Otherwise, as James Ussher points out, it would be as irrational to believe that one person's righteousness could be accepted for another, as to think that one person's food or clothing could be of actual benefit to another. There must be a logical basis for believing that Christ's righteousness can be of benefit to all other men, and that basis is His relationship to the human race. Although the truths of the Christian faith cannot be grasped or assimilated entirely by reason, it is not unreasonable, Ussher concludes, 'that a man owing a thousand pounds and not being able of himself to discharge it, his creditor may be satisfied by one of his friends'.[28] Man's deficiency has been supplied by Christ, the second Adam, the spiritual root and head of humanity.

It will be recognised that Puritanism reached its conclusions concerning the righteousness of Christ on the basis of Scripture. Reference has already been made to some of the Old Testament passages in question. The New Testament was even more explicit, and Puritan preachers knew the significance of Romans iii 19-26, Romans v 12-19, I Corinthians i 30, II Corinthians v 19-21, to mention some of the more basic passages. Here were to be found the doctrinal arguments by which Paul had sought to explain the truths of salvation in Christ to the early Christian communities. Jesus Himself had proclaimed the same truth in word and in parable, and Puritanism drew its doctrine of righteousness equally from the teachings of Christ. One illustration must suffice. In the parable of the wedding supper in Matthew xxii, Jesus taught that only those clothed in the appropriate wedding garment could be admitted to the feast. Those who arrived clad in attire of their own choosing could not eat with the other guests, even though they had also received an invitation. The point of the parable was that, in accordance with eastern custom, the king had provided a wedding garment for all those who had been invited to the supper. The robe was held to signify the righteousness of Christ, made available without cost to all who would avail themselves of its benefits. Thomas Adams describes this garment in terms of the person and work of Christ as we have already seen them set forth in Puritan thought. The cloth for this rare and costly robe, made all of silk, Adams explains, was spun in His conception, woven in His birth, purified in His life, dyed scarlet in His blood, cut to requirement and pressed in His death, put together in His resurrection, embroidered in His ascension, and so laid away in the wardrobe of heaven, 'from whence it is spiritually taken and continually worn of the elect, ... a robe large enough to cover us all'.[29] It is this righteousness of Christ, beautiful beyond description and costly beyond calculation, which enables all who will accept it to come to the wedding of the King's Son.

If this also sounds too much like irrelevant theology, who better than John Bunyan to tell us of its reality in experience? In *Grace Abounding To the Chief of Sinners*, Bunyan describes the day when the truth first came home to him that in Christ God had provided the very righteousness he needed. He describes how he had been walking in the country, struggling with a conscience smitten by guilt and fear, when suddenly the words flashed into his mind, 'Thy righteousness is in heaven'. Immediately, Bunyan says, the light dawned: 'Methought I saw with the eyes of my soul Jesus Christ at God's right hand. There ... was my righteousness, so that wherever I was, or whatever I was doing, God could not say of me He wants my righteousness, for it was just before Him ... my righteousness was Jesus Christ Himself, the same yesterday, today, and forever.'[30] Bunyan surely speaks here for countless thousands within the ranks of Puritanism, and perhaps for countless thousands before Puritanism and beyond it, for whom this represents a comparable and tangible experience. Nor will it do to dismiss it merely as a subjective attempt to come to terms with the realities of one's own spiritual condition. It is only necessary to read Bunyan, or to read those who describe in a similar way their personal experiences, to recognise that such conclusions are the outcome of a reasoned approach to reality, made in the light of human experience and the teachings of the Bible. The righteousness of Christ becomes the answer to the human experience of sin. So Bunyan concludes, 'Now did my chains fall off my legs indeed. I was loosed from my afflictions and irons, my temptations also fled away. . . . I went home rejoicing for the grace and love of God.'[31] It is this experience which becomes the basis for one of the most universally popular spiritual allegories in Christian literature. After three hundred years men all over the world continue to read Bunyan's *Pilgrim's Progress*. Would this be so if they did not find in it some reflections of a common experience? And yet the significance of this great allegory is that it is rooted in Bunyan's own experience and his understanding of the way of salvation. When Bunyan discovers that the righteousness that saves and satisfies is in heaven, in Christ, he comes to see that which is central in the Christian doctrine of salvation.

Justification by Faith

It is in the doctrine of justification by faith that the righteousness of Christ is explained and applied to the human predicament. A century or more before Puritanism flowered in its fullness, Luther had described the state of the man who had experienced justification as *simul peccator iustus*, 'at the same time a sinner and righteous'. It is still difficult to find a better summary of the consequence of justification by faith than this famous dictum. George Downham quotes it in his *Treatise of Justification* with the explanation that the man 'who before was guilty of sin and damnation ... remaining a sinner in himself ... worthy of damnation, is in his justification absolved from the guilt of sin, and accepted as righteous in Christ'.[32] He is still a sinner by nature, but he is also justified. Justification is an act of God 'without us', that is an act of God external to the sinner in which the guilt of sin is taken away, but which has no real or actual effect on the nature of the individual concerned. It is a 'judicial act' in which God does not yet work to accomplish 'a real change in the party', says Downham.[33] James Ussher explains that the word 'justify' means to pronounce just, to acquit, to free from guilt and condemnation, and hence that it contains a legal or judicial significance:[34] 'Justification is that sentence of God, whereby He of His grace, for the righteousness of His own Son, by Him imputed unto us, and through faith apprehended by us, doth free us from sin and death, and accept us as righteous unto life'.[35] It is the declaration of the Judge that the demands of the law are satisfied and that the defendant may be discharged. The result, says Ussher, is that man may acquire a better righteousness than ever he had or could have had in Adam. When justification takes place, God reckons man to be righteous and declares him to be guiltless, even though in actual fact he is still unrighteous by nature and therefore sinful.

How can this be? How can God come to a decision of this nature and remain just Himself? The answer is to be found, in part at least, in Romans iv 6 where Paul speaks of 'the blessedness of the man unto whom God imputeth righteousness'. In justification God 'imputes' the righteousness of Christ to the one who believes. Justification is defined by Downham quite simply as 'the imputation of righteousness',[36] which in its effect counteracts the imputation of Adam's sin and the guilt of man's own sin. Thus Flavel says:

If Adam's sin became ours by imputation then so doth Christ's righteousness also become ours by imputation, Romans v 17. If Christ were made a sinner by the imputation of our sins to Him, who had no sin of His own, then we are made righteous by the imputation of Christ's righteousness to us, who have no righteousness of our own.[37]

Downham explains it in terms of the relationship between Christ and the individual sinner:

By imputation, as our sins were made His, so His righteousness was made ours. And as for and by our sins He was condemned, as if He had been a debtor, that is a sinner ... so by and for His satisfaction, which He performed for us, and which the Lord accepteth in our behalf, as if we had performed the same in our own persons, we are justified. And yet through our sins being imputed to Him, He was reputed and as it were made a sinner, and through His righteousness being imputed to us we are made righteous in Him, yet ... He in Himself was just, and we in ourselves sinners.[38]

When it is said that the righteousness of Christ is made man's by imputation, it means that the righteousness of Christ is reckoned to belong to man even though experientially this is not the case. It means that it is counted as man's when in fact it is His, in the same way that man's sins were counted His when in fact they were man's. The requirements of justice are met, for God accepts the righteousness of His Son as the righteousness man must have, and the debt which man could not meet from his own resources is paid in full. By the imputation of Christ's righteousness the guilt of all sin is cancelled for the one who believes.

Mention was made earlier of the desire within Puritanism that the doctrine of justification by faith be seen in its biblical purity as distinct from the Roman Catholic doctrine of justification. This distinction is seen most clearly in the emphasis which Puritanism places on imputation. Downham sets forth altogether seven errors which he finds in the Roman concept of justification,[39] one of which, probably the most basic if we are also to follow other Puritan writers, is that in the Roman doctrine of justification righteousness is infused into the believer and not merely imputed to him.[40] Thus an actual change takes place in the believer, justification is confused with sanctification, and the door is opened for salvation by works. It is to bring an end to this confusion between justification and sanctification which is the concern at the heart of the Puritan emphasis. 'We are justified and saved by the very righteousness of Christ, and no other,' declares Flavel. That righteousness is inherent in Him alone: 'It was actively His, but passively ours. He wrought it, though we wear it. It was wrought in the person of the God-man ... and is imputed (not transfused) to every single believer.'[41] Flavel is quite clear that in justification righteousness is imputed. It is not infused. It is Christ's righteousness, and in no sense does it experientially become that of the believer. 'It is ours relatively, not formally and inherently,'[42] says Flavel again. Downham points out that the Hebrew word meaning justify, together with its Greek equivalent, 'doth never signify to make righteous by infusion, or by inherent righteousness'. [43] There is, of course, a right-eousness which is imparted (described in a later chapter), but this is always to be distinguished from the righteousness that is acquired through justification, and Flavel even describes imparted righteousness as 'holi-ness', reserving the term 'righteousness' for that righteousness which is imputed in justification.[44] Thus the righteousness which is the basis of salvation is the righteousness of Christ imputed, distinct from and ante-cedent to any other form of righteousness in human experience.

Of all that could be said concerning the doctrine of justification, the aspect of greatest importance is that the imputation of Christ's righteous-ness is to those who believe. Justification is by faith. But how is faith to be understood? What role does it play in the imputation of righteousness and the justification of the sinner? The question is important, and it draws our attention to another issue in the Puritan debate over righteousness and justification. A few writers seem to have thought that faith of itself resulted in justification, and that it was not the imputed righteousness of Christ which brought justification, but the exercise of faith in itself toward God. The danger in this, of course, is that faith must have an object, or it becomes little more than an attitude of mind, an exercise of the will, and hence an attempt to achieve salvation by human effort. Flavel implies as much when he emphasises that faith is essentially a gift of God and not a function of the mind or an act of the will.[45] Downham carefully explains that faith is but the instrument by which the righteousness of Christ is received: 'For faith itself is not the righteousness of God which doth justify or save us, but the instrument to receive God's righteousness'.[46] Faith only results in justification as it focusses on Christ and appropriates to itself His righteousness: 'That faith therefore which doth justify, doth specially apprehend and apply Christ, and the proper object of faith, as it justifieth, is Christ.'[47] 'Faith justifieth,' says John Ball, 'not by any virtue or dignity of its own, but as it receiveth and resteth on Christ our Righteousness, our Saviour, our Redeemer from sin and death.'[48] Faith is only effective in justification as it has an object, Jesus Christ, and as it is the instrument of receiving Him.

A consequence of this is that true faith is more than intellectual assent to certain doctrines concerning Christ. In this sense faith is to be distinguished from belief. The latter may be no more than knowledge of Scripture and a 'bare assent' to its teachings. It will recognise the authenticity of the Bible and its authority in matters of faith, but 'without trust or confidence in the mercies of God' and will, therefore, be nothing more than 'dead assent'.[49] This is not the faith which leads to justification. Justifying faith is not only persuaded that Christ is the Saviour of those who believe, but actually embraces Him as its own Saviour. The man who would be justified 'doth rely, cast, and repose his soul upon Christ his Saviour ... cleaving inseparably to the word of truth ... and feeding upon it as the wholesome food of life'.[50] Downham says that although a man may assent to all the articles of the Christian faith and to all the truths revealed in Scripture yet he is not justified by believing any truth but *the* truth, 'neither is the promise of justification and salvation made to any other belief, but only to faith in Christ'.[51] This does not mean that faith discards knowledge and understanding. On the contrary, it proceeds from right knowledge, and especially from a correct understanding of Scripture. Downham himself refers to the illumination of the mind, the right conception of salvation, the inclination of the will, all as pre-requisites to saving faith.[52] Baxter specifically states, 'The faith with which we are justified by, doth as essentially contain our belief of the truth of Christ's person, office, death, resurrection, intercession, etc., as of the promise of imputation.'[53] It is not that faith excludes knowledge, but that it proceeds from it to trust, to commitment. In Flavel's thinking the antecedents to saving faith are illumination, conviction, and self-despair. Only then does the sinner cast himself in faith wholly upon God.[54] The faith, then, which leads to justification, is the faith which hears, understands, and accepts, but which for all that has as its supreme object Christ and His righteousness.

There is a proper relationship between justification and works, even as there is a proper relationship between justification and knowledge. If understanding is to precede justification, so good works are to follow it. Of this relationship there cannot be the slightest doubt. While good works have no part in coming to salvation, they are nonetheless an evidence that salvation has become a reality. 'Although we deny good works to be either causes of justification or merits of salvation,' Downham explains, 'yet we affirm them to be not only good and profitable, but also . . . necessary.'[55] Among the reasons which may be given for holding to the necessity of good works, is that they are an evidence of justifying faith, an evidence of love to God and to one's neighbour, and an evidence of a right relationship to God. Quoting Romans iv 5, 'To him that worketh not, but believeth on him that justifieth the ungodly, his faith is counted for righteousness,' Flavel explains that the phrase 'worketh not' must not be taken to mean 'an idle, lazy believer that takes no care of the duties of obedience'. True faith is not a faith without works but a faith that results in works. 'An idle faith can never be a saving faith,' he says. What, then, is the meaning of the text? The meaning, Flavel continues, is not that the believer works to obtain righteousness in a legalistic sense, 'to cover himself with a robe of righteousness of his own spinning and weaving'.[56] Flavel will have none of that. Rather, it is that while righteousness is imputed on account of faith apart from works, yet the works are a necessary consequence of that faith which has received the promise. George Lawson is equally certain. Justification is by faith alone 'though that faith be not alone'. Faith results in good works, that is in a way of life which bears witness to righteousness, but all the good works which are to be seen in the life of a believer 'presuppose us in Christ and justified by His merits'.[57] The inevitable conclusion is that good works are necessary in the Christian life, but that they are an aftermath of justification by faith. Before we look more closely at this relationship between justification and sanctification it will be helpful to consider the consequences of justification in respect of the one who has truly come to faith.

The Consequences of Justification

What has been said concerning justification by faith should not be taken to imply that the doctrine was understood by Puritanism only in a theoretical sense. Certainly, there is in justification a fundamentally legal and judicial meaning, as the preceding pages have attempted to demonstrate. It is equally certain that this underlying concept must be grasped if the truth of the Gospel, as the Puritans saw it, is to be appreciated in its fullness. Through the righteousness of Christ imputed, the guilt of sin which is man's by imputation and by experience is cancelled, and the one who trusts Christ and accepts His righteousness is acquitted from the condemnation of divine law and freed from the penalty of sin. This is the theory, and it must be understood. Yet few movements within Christian history have inveighed more against a merely theoretical understanding of the Gospel than Puritanism, and we are now to see the practical, experiential consequences which justification, rightly understood, brought to the lives of those who truly believed. These consequences are, of course, the results which justification in its legal and judicial sense brings with it, and John Goodwin is quite right to point out that 'the effect of this act of God is not any natural or moral change' in the believer, 'but a change in his estate and condition'.[58] The one who believes is given, as it were, a new beginning; he has a new standing with God; he sees himself in a new light. But he does not, merely through justification as such, become a new, or better, or different person. While this must also become a reality in his experience, it does not happen by receiving the imputed righteousness of Christ. Justification gives the believer a new understanding of the past and new outlook for the future in a way that has a real and positive effect on his self-understanding and his attitudes. It is the foundation upon which the whole structure of meaningful Christian experience is erected. It is a doctrine that has both Godward and manward aspects, and the latter is part of the believer's new attitudes to God, to himself, and to the future.

In this sense Puritans saw three major consequences of justification. In the first place, justification results in the forgiveness of sin. With forgiveness the individual experientially enters into that divine act of acquittal by which justification frees man from guilt and condemnation. Sin must be dealt with not only in theory but also in fact, and since it is found as a fact in human experience it must be dealt with on the level of the individual. Justification results in the forgiveness of sin and in a knowledge of such forgiveness. Having defined justification and the imputation of righteousness, John Ball goes on to say, 'It is the good pleasure of God revealed in the gospel, to pardon and justify them from all their sins.' The faith which at the same time brings justification and pardon 'leaneth upon Him ... to obtain forgiveness of sins'.[59] It is a living faith, a personal faith, a faith which 'leans' on Christ, and thus results in personal forgiveness. Downham says that 'the righteousness which we have by justification standeth in remission of sin'.[60] That is to say that forgiveness is grounded in justification. The one cannot proceed without the other. Baxter explains that when saving faith is exercised 'immediately all sin is pardoned'. Such pardon is absolute since it 'extendeth to every sin that is then in being, or ever was on that person'.[61] This is in harmony with Paul's statement in Romans iii 25, that in justification the righteousness of Christ is set forth 'for the remission of sins that are past'. That the knowledge of sins thus forgiven is to be part of the experience of the one who believes is quite clear from Downham, who says that the justification that results in forgiveness brings peace to the conscience and joy in the Holy Spirit, and from William Perkins, who lists four 'inward effects of justification' — a peaceful conscience, a sense of the favour of God, joy in the heart, and the love of God manifest in the life.[62] The inward, experiential nature of forgiveness in all this needs little further emphasis. Justification results not only in acquittal from God's standpoint, that is, in a judicial declaration of guiltlessness, but also in the actual experience of forgiveness from the human standpoint, that is, in a sense of peace, freedom and wholeness.

A second, and equally vital, consequence of justification in the life of the individual is that it establishes a new relationship with God. The original relationship between God and man, which had existed at creation and which the Lord had intended should continue as the condition of eternal life, had been severed by sin. If man was to live again in the hope of eternal life the relationship must be re-established, or a new and equally effective relationship substituted in its place. Many of the seventeenth-century writers who expound the doctrine refer to the 'relative' change brought by justification to the relationship between God and man. 'I call this a relative change,' Joseph Alleine explains, 'because it is not a change in a man's nature, but in his condition.'[63] This is a similar emphasis to the one we noted previously from John Goodwin and underlines that justification results in a new standing with God rather than in any moral or spiritual regeneration. Downham believed that in this respect justification was similar to adoption, redemption and reconciliation, in that there was no real change in the individual concerned but that a new relationship was established. Adoption results in a child becoming a son and heir, redemption results in a slave becoming a servant, and reconciliation results in an enemy becoming a friend. In each case a relationship is changed. So in justification, says Downham, there is a changed relationship, but not a change 'in respect of any inward dispositions or qualities'.[64] It is, indeed, the concept of adoption that most accurately expresses this new relationship. 'Adoption is the power and privilege to be the sons of God (John i 12, Ephesians i 5) derived unto us from Christ,' says Ussher, in explaining the effects of justification.[65] By sin man had forfeited the natural right to be a son of God. By adoption that right is restored. 'When a man therefore hath first a son he becometh a father, which he was not before,' adds Downham. This occurs, not by any change in himself, but by the existence of a new relationship. Similarly, 'When a man is adopted, he becometh the son of another man, whose son he was not before,' not on account of a physical change but by the establishment of a new relationship. So, by justification, God receives man 'into His favour ... accepteth of him as righteous, admitteth him to be His son'.[66] By adoption man could become again what it had been intended that he should be by creation, a son of God and the heir of eternal life.

It is in the light of this new relationship that a third outcome of justification may be better discerned. At no point would we misinterpret Puritanism with more serious consequences than if we were to conclude that justification should be equated with salvation in the ultimate, total sense. While justification is always crucial to man's salvation, it is only a part of the whole process, one step in the pathway that leads from death to life. Joseph Truman maintains that it is 'a gross mistake' to assume that God requires only that it is necessary to believe, to accept Christ as Saviour theoretically, without repentance and obedience, in order to experience salvation. Truman speaks of the believer's 'right to heaven' coming through justification, not in the sense that it is a right which cannot again be forfeited, but in the sense that it is a right which he did not have before justification, but which, of itself, does not result, *ipso facto*, in an

irrevocable state of salvation.[67] Again the relationship between justification and sanctification is critical. Downham says, 'By our justification we
are entitled to God's kingdom, that is, saved in hope. By our sanctification
we are fitted and prepared for God's kingdom into which no unclean thing
can enter. Justification therefore is the right of God's children to their
inheritance.'[68] While, as Downham succinctly states, justification is the
believer's title to heaven, sanctification is his fitness for heaven. It is
justification which provides the believer with his right, his title, to eternal
life. By sin that right was lost, by justification it is restored. It is in this
sense that Downham interprets the wedding garment of Matthew xxii 11,
the robe provided for the prodigal son in Luke xv 22, and the white raiment
offered by Christ in Revelation iii 18. All are garments given to those in
need to enable them to participate in the feast which represents eternal life
in the Kingdom of God. All signify the righteousness of Christ imputed in
justification which makes such participation possible. There is an eschatological significance here, a relationship between the present experience
of salvation and the hope of salvation to come at the last day. Only in the
righteousness of Christ, imputed in justification, can a believer be
adequately prepared for the events of the last day, and Richard Sibbes
advises,

> Therefore, above all, let us get the assurance of the grand point of
> justification, of being clothed with the righteousness of Christ. Let us be
> sure to be found in that, and appear in it. . . . If we be clothed with the
> garments of Christ's righteousness, we may go through the wrath of
> God, for that alone is wrath-proof. . . . It is a righteousness of God's own
> providing. . . . Be sure that you understand it well, that you appear not in
> your own, but in His, and then you may think of that day with comfort.[69]

There is much that could be said of this statement, but the essential truth is
that justification, receiving the imputed righteousness of Christ, is the
believer's right to heaven, the assurance that salvation one day may be his
in all its fullness.

Justification and Sanctification
In concluding this chapter, emphasis must be given to the relationship
between justification and sanctification. There cannot be the slightest
doubt that Puritanism as a whole understood that sanctification was as
necessary to a man's salvation as justification. We have already noted
Downham's view that while justification is the believer's title to heaven,
sanctification is his preparation for heaven. Downham further explains
that sanctification is a necessary consequence of our justification. This is
to be understood, not in the sense that full sanctification inevitably follows
in the life of the one who has been justified, but rather in the sense that
sanctification must accompany justification if the experience of salvation
is to be authentic and complete.[70] It is perhaps Baxter who explains the
relationship most clearly. 'Christ's righteousness is ours for the pardon of
our sin,' he says of justification, 'but not to be instead of faith, repentance,

sanctification or sincere obedience.' The imputation of righteousness is not an alternative to righteous living. Baxter continues with some finality, 'He that hath not these, shall never be saved by Christ's righteousness.'[71] In this context, justification of itself is not enough. There must also be sanctification, which Baxter describes as 'sincere obedience'. It is true that faith 'without external acts of obedience' (that is, good works which do not result from faith) is sufficient for justification. But justification without the consequent works that distinguish genuine faith does not result in salvation. From the point of justification there must be a life of 'sincere obedience'. Believers who profess to have been justified, 'must needs have also a personal righteousness, consisting in the holiness of their hearts and lives, which Scripture most frequently mentioneth, and which all divines confess, calling it by the name of inherent righteousness'. [72] Thomas Gataker therefore speaks of 'the righteousness of Justification' and 'the righteousness of Sanctification'. And to return to Downham, we recall a similar emphasis: 'Although we deny good works to be either causes of justification or merits of salvation, yet we affirm them to be not only good and profitable, but also ... necessary.'[73] Imputed righteousness, the righteousness of theology, must be followed by imparted righteousness, the righteousness of experience.

There are two further related points on which Puritan theologians seem to have been in general agreement. The one is that justification is to be a continual experience in the life of the believer, a repeated act of God on behalf of all those whose humanity causes them to continue in sin and therefore stand in need of forgiveness, rather than one single act at the moment of first belief. The other is that justification and sanctification occur simultaneously in the human experience of salvation. While it may be possible to separate them for the purpose of theological discussion, it is not possible to do so in experience. Although justification and sanctification are separate and distinct concepts, each with their own particular meaning, yet in the reality of experience they are not to be separated, for such a false dichotomy will result in a serious misunderstanding of the way of salvation. For the first of these assertions we will remain with George Downham's *Treatise of Justification*, and for the second we will turn to George Lawson's *Body of Divinity*.

Downham's argument is that as long as a man remains a sinner he stands in need of justification. Since man is never totally free from sin in this life, that is, since he never reaches the point of absolute perfection of nature and conduct, he therefore remains in need of the imputation of Christ's righteousness to remedy the lack of righteousness that is inherently his. Further, since he sins daily and falls short of the divine standard both in conduct and nature, he needs daily the imputation of Christ's righteousness through justification. So Downham concludes, 'Notwithstanding those manifold infirmities and corruptions which remain in us as the relics of original sin, we may be continued in the grace and favour of God, by the continued imputation of Christ's righteousness.'

This is not to be understood as suggesting that at any time justification is incomplete or imperfect: 'No sooner doth a man truly believe in Christ, but the righteousness of Christ is imputed to him, and in and by that righteousness he standeth righteous before God as well at the first, as at the last.'[74] It means simply that daily justification is necessitated by man's inherent sinfulness and his continual need of a righteousness which he cannot provide for himself.

Concerning the relationship between justification and sanctification in experience, Lawson says categorically that God 'never did justify any person, and left him unsanctified'.[75] Sanctification is the inward evidence which the believer has that his justification has been accomplished. Justification can only be sought and received as the believer is open to the inward working of the Holy Spirit. The faith that receives justification is itself a consequence of the Spirit's presence. But the Spirit sanctifies the one in whom He is present, and cannot be present without accomplishing such a work of sanctification. Therefore, says Lawson, justification and sanctification go together in the experience of the individual who truly believes, and it is not possible to separate them in actual experience. It is in this sense, Lawson suggests, that it is possible to think of sanctification as including continual justification. This raises the old problem of whether justification is by faith and sanctification by faith plus works. Lawson's answer is clear enough. Both justification and sanctification are by faith alone 'though that faith be not alone'.[76] The faith which results in justification and sanctification, as was indicated earlier, is a faith that demonstrates its presence by works, that is in righteous living. Such works 'presuppose us in Christ', to use Lawson's own phrase. Hence 'all good works of regenerate persons are virtually in faith receiving Christ, and no such faith continuing can be without good works'.[77] Sanctification, then, is the evidence of justification. The two cannot be separated, and we may justifiably borrow Luther's famous dictum and say also *simul peccator sanctus*, 'at the same time a sinner and sanctified'.

The point of significance in this relationship between justification and sanctification as far as the present chapter is concerned — for the righteousness that belongs to sanctification will be more fully examined in chapter four — is that both imputed and imparted righteousness have their origin in Christ. He is the sole author of the righteousness that saves, since it is His righteousness that is both imputed and imparted. Man must depend totally on the righteousness of Christ for salvation. He cannot look in part to the righteousness of Christ and in part to his own righteousness. Justification and sanctification are based on that righteousness which God has provided in His Son. Downham therefore speaks of 'a two-fold righteousness, the one of justification, the other of sanctification'.[78] Samuel Mather explains the distinction between the two. 'There is a righteousness inherent in Christ, and imputed to believers,' he says, and there is also 'a righteousness inherent in believers, but derived from Christ'. The one is 'the righteousness of justification', the other 'the righteousness of sanctification'. Mather fittingly describes them as the outer garment of justification and the inner garment of sanctification. Both are referred to in Psalm xlv 13-14, he says, where the king's daughter is said to be 'all glorious within', and is brought before the king in a garment of needlework. The former is the inner garment of sanctification, the latter the outer garment of justification.[79] Thomas Gataker likewise writes, 'There is a righteousness imputed and there is a righteousness imparted, the one inherent in Christ and imputed to us, the other imparted by Christ and inherent in us.'[80] It is Christ who is the source of all righteousness needed and experienced by man.

We have now returned to the thought which is central to the title of this chapter. 'The Lord our Righteousness' signifies the absolute and infinite power vested in Christ to save sinful man. It prefigures the righteousness which results in justification and the righteousness which is a result of sanctification. Flavel, indeed, suggests that this name, 'The Lord our Righteousness', is the most meaningful of all names by which Christ can possibly be known since it contains within it the way of salvation in its entirety.[81] It thus becomes evident that the fundamental Reformation doctrine of justification by faith, the doctrine that contends that man's needed righteousness is provided by God Himself, is fully explored in English Puritanism. The righteousness that is available in Christ, when understood as the Puritan preachers understood it, stands as a corrective to all deviations from the *via media* in the doctrine of salvation. It is broad and balanced, Scriptural and satisfying. And so the great Matthew Henry, in whose commentary we find the distillation of Puritan theology perpetuated for all succeeding generations, says of Jeremiah xxiii 6, 'All our righteousness has its being from Him, and by Him it subsists, ... and nothing else have we to plead but this.'

4. THE NEW MAN

Regeneration as explained in the New Testament consists in the implanting of the principle of new spiritual life in man. Under the influence of the Holy Spirit a radical change takes place in man's direction, and this change gives birth to a life that moves Godward.

W.R. Beach *Dimensions in Salvation* (1963) p.164

True conversion is the turning of the whole man to God.... 'Tis nothing less than the total change of the inward temper and frame of the heart, and the external course of the life.... Thy heart and will, love and delight, must turn sin out, and take Christ in, or thou art no gospel-convert.... In all true conversion, there is a positive turning unto God, a whole heart-choice of Him, for your supreme and ultimate happiness and portion, ... and of the Lord Jesus Christ, as your Prince and Saviour.... And thus it brings forth the new man, and the whole frame of your heart and life is marvelously changed and altered.

John Flavel *Works* II (1716) p.727

A favourite text with the Puritan ministry, as the above statement from John Flavel might suggest, was that which contained the assertion of the apostle Paul, 'If any man be in Christ, he is a new creature' (II Corinthians v 17). To this theme the brotherhood of Puritan preachers returned again and again. Even the most superficial examination of the relevant sermons and works of exposition and devotion would reveal an insistence on the doctrine of regeneration which can only lead to the conclusion that it occupied a place of utmost importance in Puritan theology. The emphasis which Puritanism gave to Scripture as the norm of life and doctrine, to the person and work of Christ, to the way of salvation through justification and the righteousness of Christ, culminated in the translation of these doctrines into the experience of each believer. The validity of the Gospel was not its strength as a system of intellectual propositions, however attractive that might be, but its power to change the lives of those who would submit unreservedly to its claims and to its influence. To impress that truth upon their people and to lead them to that kind of submission, was the supreme aim of the pastor who stood in the true Puritan tradition.

The Necessity of Regeneration

Joseph Alleine was unquestionably in the true Puritan tradition. His insistence on the need for personal regeneration has ensured the survival of his only work of any consequence. Born in 1636 and therefore a Puritan of the third generation, Alleine was an Oxford man, a scholar and tutor at Corpus Christi, who later ministered at Taunton, a living he lost in the Great Ejection of 1662. Alleine died at the early age of thirty-four, possibly as a result of the treatment he received while in prison for his evangelical preaching, and his premature death accounts for the fact that he is chiefly remembered for one book, *An Alarm to the Unconverted*, posthumously published in 1672, and later republished under the title, *A Sure Guide to Heaven*. No survey of the Puritan emphasis on regeneration would be adequate without reference to Alleine's book, referred to frequently in this chapter. This will show how Alleine, and those who stood with him in preaching what they believed to be Christ's Gospel in its fullness, understood regeneration and, what is perhaps even more important, why Alleine himself, to quote him briefly at this juncture, stipulates that it is 'the one thing necessary ... upon this one point depends thy making, or marring, to all eternity'.[1]

In its attempt to convey what it believed to be the truth regarding regeneration, Puritanism began where it found man. We return here to the natural human condition, for it is only in this context that the doctrine of regeneration has any meaning. By nature man is sinful, corrupt, wicked and therefore spiritually dead. Thomas Adams says simply, 'By nature a man lieth in wickedness.'[2] This means that by birth and heredity he has an antipathy to faith and goodness. He is dead in sin, self-centred, bent on his own advancement, disinterested in the Word of God and all things pertaining to it. Adams uses a biblical metaphor to press home the point: 'Our father was an Hittite, the swarthy king of hell; our mother an Amorite, leprous and loathesome.' Man is therefore born to despair, 'desperately forlorn, cast into the wilderness, ... exposed to the rage of hellish monsters more ravenous than the wolves of evening'.[3] Thomas Gataker makes further comparisons. The natural heart is like a book that is spoiled by mistakes and misprints, like a manuscript that is 'blurred and blotted'. Again, it is like a wasteland 'wherein weeds of all sorts come up of themselves naturally', and which yields nothing good without careful attention.[4] Alleine uses a different analogy again. Of the natural man he declares, 'You may as well expect him that never learned the alphabet to read, or look for goodly music on the lute from one that never set his hand to an instrument.'[5] Such are 'stark dead in sin', strangers to the ways of God, neither knowing them nor desiring to know them. Thomas Taylor makes the additional important observation that sin affects the entire man. It is a corruption of man in his whole being. It is 'a general disorder of the whole man, and of all parts. Neither is bodily leprosy more general and universally spread over all the members, than sin in the soul, which is seated in all the members. So as from the crown of the head to the sole of the foot, there is nothing found but a general ataxy or disorder in want of all goodness in all parts, and proneness to all evil.'[6] Hence sin pollutes 'the mind with blindness, the will with rebellion against the will of God, the conscience with senselessness ... the affections with all manner of disorder'.[7] Quite obviously, if any man was to come to a saving knowledge of God, a change of the most profound nature must occur in his innermost being.

In the foregoing chapters of this book the Puritan doctrines of Christ and justification have been examined. There can be no doubt whatsoever that these doctrines were essential to Puritanism's understanding of the way of salvation. Equally there can be no doubt that, in Puritan eyes, they were of themselves insufficient to provide eternal life. Alleine himself makes this very clear in a comment on the benefits of the atonement: 'But I must tell you, Christ never died to save impenitent and unconverted sinners (so continuing)'. Alleine then adds quite categorically, 'Without the application of the Spirit in regeneration, we can have no saving interest in the benefits of redemption.' 'I tell you from the Lord,' he says, 'Christ himself cannot save you, if you go on in this state.'[8] John Flavel is equally clear regarding the limitations of the atonement. It will be recognised, of course, that mediaeval Catholic theology had placed little emphasis on personal religion, and this Flavel clearly had in mind when saying, 'Time was when men fondly thought nothing was necessary to their salvation but the death of Christ.' The Reformation, however, had brought new theological emphases, new insights into the meaning of Scripture, and Flavel can continue, 'but now the Lord shows them that their union with Christ by faith is as necessary in the place of an applying cause, as the death of Christ is in the place of a meritorious cause'.[9] This could justifiably be interpreted to go well beyond the mere doctrine of regeneration. Flavel's point, however, is that assent to the death of Christ on the cross is not of itself sufficient for salvation. There must also be 'union with the person of Christ ... a work wrought within us when we are believers,'[10] and the beginning of that work lay in regeneration. As Richard Baxter further points out, Christ 'neither believed in Himself, nor repented by a change of mind, in our stead; nor will [He] save us, if we do it not ourselves'.[11]

There was a further aspect of this doctrine which merits some consideration. The ultimate objective of all Puritan theology and preaching was to enable ordinary men and women to find their place at last in the Kingdom of God. Both the writings of Puritanism itself and the many more recent works that have attempted to explain the Puritan movement, lead us to this conclusion. As William Haller observes of the Puritan saga in his masterly survey of the earlier decades of Puritanism, 'The final scene was the ultimate overthrow of Satan by Christ and His saints, and their triumph in heaven.'[12] It was the calling of the Puritan preacher to keep before his people the reality of this final act in the drama of human redemption. Heaven was to be theirs one day, heaven in all its glory and all its perfection, heaven where to all eternity the saints would live together in the presence of God. All this had rather a significant bearing on the question of regeneration, as Joseph Alleine was quick to recognise. The unregenerate man would be completely out of place in heaven, 'quite out of his element, as a swine in the parlour, or a fish out of water'. Heaven's anthems, said Alleine, would neither fit his mouth, nor suit his ear. Such a man would have no more happiness in heaven than an animal at a well-provided table in the company of learned men.[13] There must be a new creature, a new man, a transformation of the natural mind in all its operations, its judgements, its affections, its power of choice. Only thus would man be at home in heaven, fitted to enjoy the company of saints, angels, of God Himself, and so fulfilling in the end the purpose for which he had been created in the beginning.

It would be easy enough to pursue much further the reasons which Puritanism drew from Scripture to establish the needfulness of regeneration. To do that, however, would run the danger of ignoring the doctrine itself, and it is sufficient to note the utter certainty with which the Puritan preacher sought to emphasise the necessity of this experience in the lives of all who would be saved. 'There is no entering into heaven but by the straight passages of the second birth,' 'No conversion ... no salvation,' 'Never did any, nor shall any, enter into heaven by any other way than this,'[14] Alleine stresses in the opening pages of *An Alarm to the Unconverted*. The change of life which comes through regeneration 'is absolutely and indispensably necessary to every man's salvation,' Flavel insists, and 'the door of salvation can never be opened without the key of regeneration'.[15] Indeed, Flavel will go further and make regeneration the ultimate test of a believer's profession of Christianity:

> If any man, be he what he will, high or low, great or small, learned or illiterate, young or old, if he pretend interest in Christ, this is the standard by which he must be tried. If he be in Christ, he is a new creature, and if he be not a new creature, he is not in Christ, let his endowments, gifts, confidence, and reputation be what it will ... a creature renewed by gracious principles newly infused into him from above, which sway him and guide him in another manner, and to another end than ever he acted before.... This is the rule by which our claim to Christ must be determined.[16]

Here is a note which must not be muted if Puritanism is to be understood and Puritanism's contribution to Protestant theology is to be allowed the room which many would argue it deserves.

The Nature of Conversion

How, then, is the nature of so necessary a work to be explained? This is clearly a fundamental question, and certainly the question which those who sat beneath the Puritan pulpit or pondered over the books and pamphlets which poured from the presses of the age would themselves have asked. What was conversion? How did it take place? What effects did it have on the individual concerned? Was the Church as the body of believers in any way affected? And ought one to know if the touch had fallen upon him?

It may be helpful, in seeking the answers to such questions, to begin by clarifying what regeneration, according to the writers whose works we have already drawn upon, was not. John Flavel, for example, wanted it known that regeneration was not to be confused with moral rectitude, or any 'change made by civility upon such as were lewd and profane'. The teachings of heathen philosophers — and Flavel mentions here Plato, Aristides and Seneca — had resulted in moral excellence in the lives of thousands who 'yet were perfect strangers to the new creation'. It was quite possible for a man to be 'very strict and temperate, free from the gross pollutions of the world, and yet a perfect stranger to regeneration'.[17] Alleine agrees with Flavel, saying that regeneration is neither an outward moral goodness, nor the result of education or greater knowledge of spiritual truth. Again, regeneration is not to be regarded as the inevitable consequence of baptism. This is to touch a tender spot, exposed by the internal debates of Puritanism, to which we shall return later. We must observe here Joseph Alleine's pointed affirmation that 'it is not being washed in the laver of regeneration, or putting on the badge of Christ in baptism'. 'How fondly do many mistake here,' he adds, 'deceiving, and being deceived.' Ananias and Sapphira and Simon Magus had been baptised, yet were found wanting when it came to the test. Any view which even approached that of baptismal regeneration savoured too strongly of the popish element, 'of the sacraments working grace,' fostering the illusion 'that effectual grace is necessarily tied to the external administration of baptism'.[18] In Puritan eyes it most certainly was not.

It followed from this that regeneration was not to be equated with Church membership, or even with a place in the ministry. Thomas Adams remembered the parable of the sheep and the goats and applied it, not only to that separation which would take place at the Last Day, but also to the present experience of believers and professors in the Church. If the goats were to be found among the sheep in that day, it was logical to conclude that they might also be found among them now. Too many in the Church display the characteristics of goats, evidences of the unregenerate nature received from Adam. They seek advantage in high places, there are no limits to their deceptive habits, they disturb the peace of the flock, their passions are uncontrolled, they trample underfoot that which is good. 'They smell of impiety, as rank as goats,' Adams adds in characteristic style.[19] Flavel recounts the experience of a minister known to him who had, for many years, faithfully carried out the requirements of his office. A man of 'rare abilities' and 'excellent natural and acquired gifts', he would 'preach of regeneration, faith, and heavenly-mindedness, though he felt nothing of these things in his own experience'. Happily, one day, while in his study at his books, the light dawned, 'the pangs of the new birth seized his soul,' and the Lord from that day forward 'crowned his labours with unusual success'.[20] Here was a concrete example of the truth that regeneration was not to be confused with status or membership in the Church.

The conclusion which derives from all this is that regeneration was an experience which man could not bring about of himself. To be sure on this point was second in importance only to recognising in principle the necessity of regeneration as such. Man was evil at heart, 'bred and born' that way, and as Thomas Gataker quaintly observed, 'that [which] is bred in the bone, will not out of the flesh'. That which is natural cannot be changed simply by nature itself. 'You may tie or muzzle a wolf so that he cannot prey or bite,' Gataker continues, 'or you may beat him so bound till he be not able to stir. But you shall never be able to beat his wolfish nature out of him.'[21] The same was true of the natural man. Through generations of habitual experience sin had acquired 'the force of a second nature', according to Flavel, making 'regeneration and mortification naturally impossible'. Can the Ethiopian change his skin, or the leopard his spots? Flavel asks, quoting Jeremiah xiii 23, 'then may he also do good that is accustomed to do evil'.[22] And Alleine argues, 'Never think thou cánst convert thyself. If ever thou wouldst be savingly converted, thou must despair of doing it in thine own strength.' [23] If we now seem to have arrived finally at the point of despair, this is precisely where the Puritan preacher would have us. It is only as man recognises his desperate, hopeless condition, only as he sees the sheer impossiblity of bringing about the necessary change in his life, that he is in a position to respond to the divine initiative.

It is, indeed, this question of the divine initiative and the divine action which lies at the heart of the doctrine of regeneration. The truth that Puritanism would proclaim with zeal and conviction above all others is that what man cannot do for himself, God can do for him: 'The first motions towards the recovery and salvation of sinners begin not in themselves, but in Christ;' 'Did not Christ move first, there would be no motions after Him in our hearts. We move towards Him because He hath first moved upon our souls;' 'Christ might sit long enough unsought and undesired, did He not make the first motion.'[24] With these words Flavel identifies the first step of man's long journey home. It is a journey initiated by God, a journey that man would not and could not contemplate of himself. Regeneration is a work begun and completed by God within the life of the individual. Commenting on Ezekiel xxxvi 25-26, a text which contains God's promise to put within man a new heart, Flavel says, 'It grows not up out of our natures ... but it is infused or implanted into the soul by the Spirit of God.' On John iv 14, where Christ speaks of a well of water within man springing up into everlasting life, Flavel refers to 'the infusion of a supernatural ... principle into the soul'.[25] The final outcome is 'a new supernatural being, which is therefore called a new creature, the new man, the hidden man of the heart'.[26]

We should pause to note at this point that when Puritanism spoke in these terms of the divine initiative and the work of God in bringing a man to regeneration, it did not necessarily speak in terms of irresistible grace. That some Puritans may have seen it in this light is not disputed. That many did not is equally clear. Professor Haller is right to advise against conceiving of English Calvinism in too narrow or rigid a sense. Calvinistic though Puritanism was in general terms, it was a Calvinism which was accommodated to the English mind and which reflected that experience of religious thought which had grown up in England over a thousand years or more. It did not as a whole teach that men were unable to resist the grace of God.[27] We may follow John Flavel here, as being representative of mature and balanced Puritan thinking. 'Though it be not in your power to open your hearts to Christ,' he says, 'yet it is in your power to forbear the external acts of sin which fasten your hearts the more against Christ.' Evidently some degree of response to the divine initiative was possible, some measure of co-operation with the power of God at work in the soul. No man is so bound by habit or circumstance to the extent that he cannot, especially with divine aid, make certain decisions and take certain courses of action which would be in harmony with a response to the regenerating power of God. 'Who forces thine hands to steal, thy tongue to swear or lie?' Flavel asks. 'Who forces the cup of excess down your throats?'[28] The implication is clear enough. Man has a degree of responsibility. Though he may not initiate the work of grace, he can and must respond to it and co-operate to the best of his understanding. Flavel therefore presses the application further:

So, though you cannot open your hearts under the Word, yet it is in your power to wait and attend upon the external duties and ordinances of the Gospel. Why cannot those feet carry thee to the assemblies of the saints, as well as to an ale house? And though you cannot let the Word effectually into your hearts, yet certainly you can apply your minds with more attention and consideration to it than you do. Who forces thine eyes to wander, or closes them with sleep, when the awful matters of eternal life and death are sounding in thine ears?[29]

Viewed from a practical standpoint, the purpose of regeneration was to counteract the effects of sin in human nature. It was to give man the opportunity of a new beginning, which would lead to a new life, which in turn would lead ultimately to a new existence. The havoc that sin had wrought in the innermost recesses of the mind was to be remedied by the effects of regeneration. Sin had resulted in total corruption, that is, in the debasement of every aspect of man's mind — reason, will, conscience, memory, affections. Regeneration, therefore, brought a renewing and revivifying effect to every aspect of his mind. This Puritanism had always understood, as William Perkins shows in pointing out that when God accomplishes the change of regeneration, He does not do it as a man might renovate an old house, little by little. God's word, says Perkins, 'both for the beginning, continuance, and accomplishment, is in the whole man, and every part at once'.[30] Perkins singles out at this point the mind as the seat of regeneration, and mentions in particular the conscience, the will, and the affections. Richard Baxter observes, on II Corinthians v 17, that the new man has 'a new understanding, a new will and resolution, new sorrows, and desires, and love, and delight; new thoughts, new speeches

... and new conversation'.[31] Flavel likewise holds that 'all the faculties
and affections of his soul are renewed by regeneration' — specifically
reason, thoughts, conscience, will, affections, emotions and actions; and
Alleine states that 'with the true convert, holiness is woven into all his
powers, principles, and practices'.[32] It thus becomes clear that regeneration effects a change in man at the innermost level of his being, a
change that makes him inwardly a different person, with a new power and
new life in the faculties of the mind.

Evidences of Regeneration
The calling of the Christian minister brought the facility to distinguish
between the converted and the unconverted, and the responsibility to
strengthen the former in his determination and to warn the latter of the
dangers which surely awaited him. To the pastor with any measure of
experience in the spiritual cure of souls, it was easy enough to read the
signs which told of the soul's condition. The unregenerate with no
profession of faith, the 'open sinner' whose life tended wholly to the world,
felt no sense of condemnation or judgement to come, had no spiritual
appetite, no desire to pray, and made no move whatsoever towards Christ
and heaven. 'It was my delight,' Bunyan says of his life prior to conversion,
'to be taken captive by the Devil at his will.'[33] Similarly, the marks of the
unregenerate professor, the person in the Church to whom conversion was
an unknown experience, though less obvious, were nonetheless unmistakable. Formality in religious observance, aversion to total commitment,
love of worldly pleasure, a malicious spirit, cherished sin and unmortified
pride are some of the characteristics appearing in one contemporary
survey. If this appears to reflect a harsh, censorious attitude, it must be
remembered that the true Puritan pastor regarded himself primarily as a
physician of the soul, a work that depended to a large extent on correct
diagnosis.

    The evidences of a genuine conversion, on the other hand, were equally
clear: 'The sap of the tree is not visible, yet by the testimony of leaves and
fruit we know it to be in the tree.'[34] In this way Thomas Adams argued that
it was not possible for an individual to have experienced regeneration
without the life bearing witness to it, and both the individual concerned
and those with whom he came into contact would recognise the change
when it had taken place. It was, as explained earlier, a change that
occurred initially in the mind, and the evidences of that change were
likewise seen first in the mind, that is to say in changed attitudes, which
then would be seen to bear fruit in the life and actions. As Joseph Alleine
observed, it was a work which went 'throughout the mind, throughout the
members, throughout the motions of the whole life'.[35]

    Perhaps the change of most significance came with the believer's new
attitude to sin. 'Before conversion, he had light thoughts of sin,' says
Alleine, 'he cherished it, ... he nourished it, ... it grew up together with
him, it did eat as it were of his own meat, and drank of his own cup, and lay

in his bosom.' But what happens as a result of the regenerating experience? The reply is immediate and unequivocal: 'He throws it away with abhorrence, as a man would a loathsome toad which in the dark he had hugged fast to his bosom and thought it had been some pretty and harmless bird.'[36] Through regeneration an antipathy to sin is born, an antipathy that was not present before. If we may follow John Flavel, this new aversion to sin is due, in part at least, to the fact that regeneration brings a deeper understanding of the very nature of sin. Men have but a hazy concept of sin prior to conversion, without a sense of its reality and presence in them as individuals. Regeneration, however, reveals 'that there is abundantly more evil in their sinful natures and actions than ever they discerned or understood before'. In the day of conviction, the Lord shows each sinner the sinfulness of his nature and practice: 'Conviction digs to the root, shows and lays open that original corruption, from whence the innumerable evils of the life do spring.'[37] Indeed, three of the six characteristics which Flavel puts forward as evidence of conversion concern the change in a believer's attitude to sin. He now has a sense of the enormity of sin, he sees sin in its vileness'; he feels a personal conviction of sin, he is 'pricked and wounded'; and he loses that natural love for sin which marked his outlook before.[38]

Regeneration also brought, as might be reasoned from the new attitude to sin, a new attitude to oneself. It is difficult to define in one phrase what Puritanism meant when it spoke of the new attitude to self which resulted from regeneration. Richard Sibbes says of the natural man that 'he seeks himself in all things, even in his religion. So far as it stands with his own lusts, he will be religious and no further. So long as God's will is not contrary to his, he will do God service.'[39] Alleine, again, says that before conversion 'man seeks to cover himself with his own figleaves ... to lick himself whole with his own duties ... to trust in himself'.[40] Thomas Gataker uncompromisingly declares, 'Every David hath his Bathsheba, and every Bathsheba her David.' Sin leads to self-indulgence of one form or another: 'Some are ambitious, some covetous, ... some lascivious.'[41] How is all this to be defined? Is it self-sufficiency? Or self-righteousness? Or self-dependence? Or self-satisfaction? Or self-gratification? Perhaps it is all of these. Whatever it is, Alleine declares that from conversion 'he casts it off, as a man would the verminous tatters of a nasty beggar'.[42] He is brought to poverty of spirit, to see himself as less than whole, to know that life can only be truly rich and meaningful when self is not at the centre.

There is, consequently, a new attitude to spiritual things, a new sense of spiritual values. It might be considered somewhat patronising today to say that the religious experience we are here considering resulted in less worldliness. The term may betray a holier-than-thou attitude which is incompatible with the spirit of genuine Christianity, and which reminds us of the caricatured view of Puritanism that has persisted through the years, giving Puritan religious experience a negative image. Christians, Puritans among them, have always recognised the legitimate claims of the world in which they live, and have realised that a complete detachment from society is neither possible nor desirable. For all that, however, Alleine's meaning when he describes the outlook of the man who is not yet reborn is clear: 'He found more sweetness in his merry company, wicked games, earthly delights, than in Christ.' He 'minded the farm, friends, [and] merchandise,'[43] necessary activities in themselves but perilous when pursued to the exclusion of heaven and eternity. Conversion brought a change here also, a change that would not pass unnoticed, and that would cause former acquaintances to 'stand amazed to see their old companions in sin, whose language once was vain and earthly, . . . profane and filthy, now to be praying, speaking of God, heaven, and things spiritual'.[44] William Perkins believed that a desire to read the Bible was a certain sign of conversion, and George Downham stressed that a willingness to be subject to the moral law of God indicated a change in the natural heart.[45] Francis Bampfield brings together the evidence for conversion in his own characteristic manner:

> The old carnal state, the old corrupt principles, the old crooked rules, the old selfish ends, . . . the old untoward actings, the old erroneous mistakes, the old formality in worship, the old unscriptural traditions, the old sins, the old man's conversation, and such like; these do pass away, and all things contrary to these, are become new, a whole new man.[46]

John Bunyan's notoriety as the most profane and reckless character in the community was later matched by a reputation for sobriety and godliness, perhaps the most convincing example the age provided of that improbable transformation which yet could become a reality in ordinary human experience. Bunyan's story is well known, and there is no need to recount again the details of that remarkable conversion to which the pages of seventeenth-century English religious history still bear eloquent testimony.

Regeneration, Sanctification and the Holy Spirit

If Puritan theology was sure of the change that occurred in a man by regeneration, it was equally sure of what, at first sight, appeared as a contradiction of this experience. Just as certainly as the believer received a new nature, so he retained his old nature. John Flavel is quite explicit: 'The crucifying of the flesh doth not imply the total abolition of sin in believers, or the destruction of its very being and existence in them for the present . . . notwithstanding its crucifixion . . . it may still, in respect of single acts, surprise and captivate them.'[47] Even the most godly saint who sought sincerely to avoid the corruptions of the flesh and the temptations of the world would have agreed in the end that this reflected the sad reality of life. Indeed, perhaps John Ball spoke from experience when he referred to 'sins of forgetfulness, inconsideration, and passion, whereunto there is not advised consent, . . . sins of simple ignorance, and of unavoidable infirmity which, through weakness, the faithful run into every day'.[48] The point of Thomas Adams' analogy of the goats, quoted earlier, was to remind the believer of the possibility that the 'goatish qualities' could in fact manifest themselves after the believer had come into the fellowship of the Church. John White's book, *A Way to the Tree of Life*, claimed on its title page to describe 'the nature of a spiritual man'. Such a person the author compared to a country which had been conquered by an invading army, but not yet entirely subdued. The chief centres of strength had been taken, and a new authority established in the land. Yet pockets of resistance remained, breaking out in unexpected places and at unpredictable times, causing loss and damage, yet unable to reverse the conqueror's new order or drive him from the field.[49] William Perkins had correctly observed, 'There are in man after regeneration two contrary grounds or beginnings of actions.' They were 'natural corruption, or the inclination of the mind, will, and affections to that which is against the law,' and 'a created quality of holiness wrought in the said faculties by the Holy Ghost'.[50] The latter neither fully nor immediately replaced the former, and hence of the terms variously used to describe the beginning of the believer's life, rebirth is perhaps technically more correct than regeneration, or conversion, or renovation, since it implies the beginning of an experience which is to continue in growth and development, but which does so against the tendencies to evil and the impediments to growth in grace which spring from the continuing presence of the old man.

Three deductions were to be drawn from this. To begin with, it led to inner conflict in the life of the one concerned. Perkins continued, 'Between these ["natural corruption" and "created holiness"] there is a continual combat, corruption fighting against grace, and grace fighting against corruption.'[51] On the basis of Galatians v 17, Flavel argues that the existence of such conflict is the sure evidence that a spiritual life has begun. The implication is that the absence of conflict denotes the activity of the old carnal mind only. Perkins uses the term 'concupiscence', by which he seems to mean the natural tendency to sin, and says plainly, 'It is not quite abolished by regeneration, but remains more or less, molesting and tempting a man till death.'[52] A difference is to be noted at this point, however, between the regenerate and the unregenerate, and it is crucial. It may be seen in this quotation from Flavel: 'Where sin is in dominion the soul is in a very sad condition, for it darkens the understanding, depraves the conscience, stiffens the will, hardens the heart, misplaces and disorders all the affections. And thus every faculty is wounded by the power and dominion of sin over the soul.'[53] It is this dominion of sin that marks the difference between the regenerate and the unregenerate man. The strength of sin is its dominion in the mind of the unregenerate. But as Flavel teaches, this power is broken by regeneration, so that the regenerate man, although still subject to the promptings and tendencies of the old nature, is no longer captive to them. Alleine adds, 'Though sin may dwell (God knows a wearisome and unwelcome guest) in him, yet it hath no more dominion over him.'[54]

A further consequence of the continuing presence of the old nature after regeneration, is that absolute perfection is unattainable for the believer in this life. Perfectionism, to be sure, had its appeal in the seventeenth century as much as in other ages of religious intensity, so much so that one observer writing at the middle of the century names 'Perfectists' as a contemporary sect, and lists it with other deviations that indicated that the Devil had run wild in the Church. Reason and good theology, however, both argued against the doctrine of perfection, and John Ball began with the latter. Since the believer cannot attain to perfect faith or perfect knowledge it must follow that any who seek absolute perfection in Christian experience pursue an illusion. Both faith and knowledge are limited in the actual experience of the sincere Christian. Justifying faith, of course, presupposes imperfection, but even faith itself, since it may grow with the passing of time, is therefore imperfect and 'never comes to the highest pitch of perfection'. Indeed, says Ball, 'absolutely the greatest faith is imperfect.' The same is true of knowledge: 'We know nothing as we should of those things which we know, and many things we are ignorant of, which we should know.'[55] It falls to John Flavel, again, to express most trenchantly the delusion of perfectionism: 'This perfect holiness is reserved for the perfect state in the world to come, and none but deluded proud spirits boast of it here.'[56] This is to lay wide open the beating heart of the perfectionist heresy. Flavel then returns to the old analogy of sin as a disease that must be cured. The cure is only begun in this present life, but 'daily advances towards perfection, and at last will be complete'.[57] This comes close to the well-nigh universal Puritan formula of justification — sanctification — glorification, in which it was held that justification provided an imputed righteousness bringing freedom from the guilt of sin, that sanctification provided an imparted righteousness which gave freedom from the dominion of sin, and that glorification, which would occur at the last day, would bring freedom 'from all the relics and remains' of sin in human nature.[58] Flavel explains patiently:

> Tis a wonderful mercy to have the guilt and dominion of sin cured, but we shall never be perfectly sound and well till the existence, or indwelling of sin in our nature be cured too .... And this our great Physician will at last perform for us, and upon us. But as the cure of guilt was by our justification, the cure of the dominion of sin by our sanctification, so the third and last which perfects the whole cure, will be by our glorification, and till then it is not expected. For it is a clear case, that sin like ivy in the old walls, will never be gotten out, till the wall be pulled down, and then it is pulled up by the roots.[59]

Not until glorification had been realised would the roots of sin in human nature be finally destroyed.

Thirdly, since the old nature remained and perfection was unattainable, it followed that a believer stood constantly in need of justification and the imparted righteousness of Christ. At no time could he stand above the basic provision for his salvation and claim, in effect, that he no longer required a Saviour in an objective sense, external to himself and beyond his own experience. As George Lawson said, 'Though the state of justification be begun, ... yet it is not perfected, but by degrees. For all our life, after our first entrance into that estate, should be a continued repentance and faith every day renewed.'[60] The necessity of daily justification was examined in a previous chapter, and is only mentioned here to emphasise that the doctrine of justification did not release the believer from the obligations of right living and all that that entailed. In Puritan eyes justification and sanctification belonged together and occurred simultaneously in actual experience, as Thomas Gataker indicates when he says, 'For justification also and sanctification are never sundered or severed. All that are truly justified are sincerely sanctified, and all that are sincerely sanctified, are truly justified also.'[61] Thus, the believer who is justified by receiving the imputed righteousness of Christ, is at the same time sanctified by receiving the imparted righteousness of Christ. How this can be so, and what the imparted righteousness of Christ consists of, raises the question of the relationship between sanctification and regeneration.

It is John Flavel who stipulates most clearly that 'sanctification is a progressive work'. Like justification, it is to be a daily experience in the believer's life. But what, precisely, is sanctification? How is it to be explained? And how is it related to regeneration? If it is a progressive work, clearly there must be a point at which it begins, and that point is the moment of regeneration. From that point, as we have seen, a profound change takes places in the life, the attitudes, and the actions of the one who truly believes. But to be effective for eternity, this change must be maintained to the end of the believer's life. Sanctification, therefore, may be defined as the effects of regeneration sustained and strengthened. We should observe carefully what John Flavel has to say here. After describing the condition of the natural man he continues, 'By regeneration this disordered soul is set right again, sanctification being the rectifying and due framing, or as the Scripture phrases it, the renovation of the soul after the image of God.'[62] It is Flavel's use of the words regeneration and sanctification which should be noted. They are used virtually synonymously. Both words are applied to one experience. Flavel then goes on to describe that experience

in which self-dependence is removed by faith; self-love by the love of God; self-will, by subjection and obedience to the Will of God; and self-seeking, by self-denial. The darkened understanding is again illuminated, Eph. i 18, the refractory will sweetly subdued, Psalm cx 3, the rebellious appetite, or concupiscence, gradually conquered, Rom. vi 7.[63]

But, is Flavel speaking here of regeneration or sanctification? By comparing this statement with others which describe regeneration, one would almost certainly conclude that it is the former. Certainly all the elements of genuine regeneration are mentioned here. Yet Flavel says that concupiscence is 'gradually conquered'. This shows Flavel means sanctification.

Again, Perkins sees sanctification as the experience 'by which a Christian in his mind, in his will, and in his affections is freed from the bondage and tyranny of sin and Satan, and is by little and little enabled through the Spirit of Christ to desire and approve that which is good, and to walk in it'.[64] It is statements such as these, and they are found frequently in the pages of Puritan theology, which emphasise the essential similarity between regeneration and sanctification. It would appear, moreover, that sanctification differs from regeneration only in degree and not in principle, that it is a sustained change in the life of the believer, a change which begins with regeneration and which is maintained as the believer's life is open to God and remains subject to those influences which initially contributed to his spiritual rebirth. Indeed, William Perkins uses the word 'conversion' in the sense of sanctification, in much the same way as Flavel uses the word 'regeneration':

> The conversion of a sinner, is not wrought all at one instant, but in continuance of time, and that by certain measures and degrees. And a man is then in the first degree of his conversion, when the Holy Ghost by the means of the Word inspires him with some spiritual motions, and begins to regenerate and renew the inward powers of his soul. And he may in this case very fitly be compared to the night, in the first dawning of the day, in which, though the darkness remain, and be more in quantity than the light, yet the sun hath already cast some beams of light into the air, whereupon we term it the breaking of the day.[65]

While it would not be wise to rest the case too strongly on the use made by one or two writers of certain words, it is nonetheless quite clear that sanctification begins with regeneration and that in all essentials it is a similar experience.

This last statement from Perkins contains a key by which the close relationship between regeneration and sanctification may be established. It is through 'the Holy Ghost by means of the Word' that regeneration is effected. The divine power through which regeneration occurs is the Holy Spirit. Elsewhere Perkins refers to a 'created quality of holiness' wrought in the mind 'by the Holy Spirit'. 'We never knock at heaven's door by prayer, till Christ hath first knocked at our doors by His Spirit,'[66] says Flavel. 'The Spirit of life from God enters into the dead carnal heart ... by way of supernatural infusion,'[67] he explains. It is only by virtue of the active presence of the Holy Spirit that regeneration occurs. Yet the same is true of sanctification. Flavel, again, categorically states that 'sanctification is a progressive work of the Spirit'.[68] Perkins maintains that a Christian is 'enabled through the Spirit of Christ' to grow in sanctification.[69] Gataker says that imparted righteousness, that is, the righteousness of sanctification, is the 'first-fruits of God's Spirit'.[70] Flavel further explains that Christ 'makes a perfect cure' of sin 'by His Spirit'. Justification cures the guilt of sin and sanctification the dominion of sin: 'As He cures the guilt of sin by pouring out His blood for us, so He cures the dominion of sin by pouring out His Spirit upon us.'[71] Both regeneration and sanctification, therefore, take place as a direct consequence of the Spirit's operation, regeneration resulting from the Spirit's initial access to the mind, sanctification developing as the Spirit remains in the mind, to control the thoughts and the actions. Thus, John Owen maintains that the great purpose of God is the sanctification of the Church, and that the principal concept of sanctification in the New Testament 'is the effecting of real internal holiness in the persons of them that do believe, by the change of their hearts and lives'.[72] This change begins with regeneration, and is established as the norm of genuine Christian life by the abiding presence of the Holy Spirit.

It will have been observed that Perkins speaks of more than the Spirit. Regeneration, or conversion, or sanctification, is effected by the 'Holy Ghost by means of the Word'. The Holy Spirit does not normally or principally work upon the mind subjectively, apart from reason or understanding. As George Lawson also points out, the 'means of conversion are the Word and the Spirit'. To be sure, the Word of itself is insufficient without the Spirit, yet, at the same time, 'The Spirit without the Word will not ordinarily do anything'. The 'outward revelation' of the Word needs the inward illumination of the Spirit to make it effective. 'The Word must inform, the Spirit reform,'[73] says Lawson. Such illumination of the mind by the Spirit may be the first work in regeneration, Flavel concedes, but it is not His only work. 'His whole work of sanctification is illuminative and instructive to the converted soul,' and Flavel's conclusion here is that a deeper knowledge of the Word is part of the sanctification experience in the believer by the continuing operation of the Holy Spirit: 'Sanctification gives the soul experience of those mysterious things which are contained in the Scripture.'[74] 'The knowledge of Christ' and 'every grace of the Spirit' grow together in the believer as the full light of day grows from the first spring of morning and as the plant grows surely but imperceptibly from the seed. Sanctification proceeds from regeneration, and Word and Spirit together are necessary at every stage.[75]

Appropriately enough, then, John White in his *Way to the Tree of Life*, a book which both gave 'directions for the profitable reading of the Scriptures' and also described 'the nature of a spiritual man', draws attention to a 'principle of spiritual life, planted in a regenerate person'. This new principle of spiritual life 'is the fountain or root of all those habits of spiritual grace' which properly characterise the life of the believer — habits of faith, hope and love, which, springing from that principle of life, result in 'spiritual motions and operations according to those habits'.[76] What is this, if it is not the indivisible power of the Holy Spirit manifest first in regeneration and then maintained in sanctification? It is the new man, no less. And Joseph Alleine, with whom this chapter began, maintains equally that in regeneration the mind must 'be attentive to God's word' and 'allow full access of the Holy Spirit,' and that in sanctification, which is essential to salvation and which must therefore follow regeneration, the believer must study the Word and be subject to Christ's Law and God's Commandments, and watch for those evidences of the soul in a thriving condition, a strong spiritual appetite, greater spiritual perception and a genuine delight in the religious life as a whole.[77] This would only come, as every Puritan preacher knew, as a result of the Spirit's presence, and it could only indicate, as every Puritan preacher also knew, the existence of the new man.

5. BELIEVER'S BAPTISM

If we take the meaning of the word itself and add to it suggestions made in connection with baptisms recorded in the Bible, it is clear that Jesus was baptized by immersion and that John followed that practice regularly in his baptizing. See John iii 23. Philip did the same when he baptized the Ethiopian eunuch. See Acts viii 36-39. The Bible contains no evidence that baptism by pouring or sprinkling was ever practised in the early Church.

T.H. Jemison *Christian Beliefs* (1959) p.245

As to the manner of baptizing, it was by dipping or plunging in the water into the name of the Father, Son and Holy Ghost; ... agreeable not only to the sense of the Word, which signifies immersion in water, but to the allegory of death, burial, and resurrection; to which the Apostle so properly alludes, Rom. vi; Col. ii ... which said custom of dipping the whole body in water, was changed into sprinkling a little water in the face.

Henry Danvers *A Treatise of Baptism* (1674) p.47

The excursions made thus far into Puritan thought have not entailed any consideration of its chronological development. From the earliest affirmations of Puritan faith in the sixteenth century to the well-defined positions of mature Dissent at the end of the seventeenth century and on into the eighteenth century, the doctrines set forth in the foregoing chapters would, with few exceptions, have met with unqualified approval. They were of the marrow of Puritan theology. They expressed those timeless convictions which the open Word of God inevitably brought to the sincere seeker for truth. Hence we have been able in one breath to quote William Perkins, the Cambridge theologian of the 1580s, and John Flavel and Richard Baxter, both of whom died in 1691, and John Owen, the Oxford academic, and John Bunyan, the Bedfordshire tinker. All of these stood ultimately in the same theological tradition, and their writings were destined to exert a continuing influence on theology for a long time to come. These were the truths on which Protestantism as a whole would more or less be united for the best part of three hundred years.

Now the analysis must take on something of a different character, for the question of baptism was an issue that divided Puritanism, often deeply, and that can only be understood adequately in the context of its historical development and in its relationship to the antecedent doctrine of the Church. Indeed, it was as the doctrine of the Church was pressed to its logical conclusions, in the quest for complete reformation in English Protestantism, that baptism as an issue in its own right came to the fore and became, in the minds of some at least, a matter of utmost importance concerning salvation itself. The first known Baptist Church in England dates from 1612, but for political and ecclesiastical reasons it was not until after 1640 that Baptist convictions took firm root in English soil. Thereafter the future of Baptist Churches was assured. Their number increased rapidly, reaching more than 200 soon after the turn of the century, and the principle of believer's baptism by immersion became established and began to reach out to the whole Christian world. The Baptists were a new breed of Puritan and a new brotherhood of preachers.

The Nature of the Church

Puritanism, classically defined, was essentially a movement for reform in Church government and organisation, based on the conviction that the Reformation had not yet been fully accomplished in the English Church. In fact, one of the most serious charges laid by Puritans against the Episcopal system of Church government as it existed in the Anglican Church was that it tolerated, if it did not encourage, a high percentage of incompetent and unspiritual clergy, 'blind guides' that could not see, 'dumb dogs' that could not bark. John Penry, who was hanged in 1592 on the indictment that his publications concerning the condition of the Church and the necessity of reformation incited rebellion, explained what he, and presumably other Puritans also, regarded as urgent. True reformation meant 'the rooting out of our Church of all dumb and unpreaching ministers,' and 'the placing in every congregation within England ... of preaching pastors and doctors, governing elders, and ministering deacons'.[1] It was intolerable to Penry and to those who shared his views 'that the holy ministry of the Word and Sacraments, and the charge of souls, should in our Church be committed unto such men as are no more able to teach us what belongeth to the pure worship of God, than many a child of six years old'.[2] Edward Dering, reputed to be one of the most able and informed preachers of early Puritanism, had already denounced the inefficiency of the clergy in a sermon preached before Queen Elizabeth. 'And yet you,' he said to the Queen, 'you at whose hands God will require it, you sit still and are careless, let men do as they list.' It was bold talk. The majority of parish priests, Dering maintained, were more taken up with internecine wrangling and disputation than with the spiritual care of souls, 'the parson against the vicar, the vicar against the parson, the parish against both, and one against another, and all for the belly'.[3] Puritanism contended that thorough reformation in Church or society could never be realised while the condition of the ministry remained as it was, and as long as the appointment of the clergy lay in the hands of the Crown or the Crown's representatives.

It was precisely this relationship between Church and State which lay at the heart of the matter. Middle-of-the-road Puritanism had gone a step towards recovering the New Testament doctrine of the Church by challenging the mediaeval Catholic view, perpetuated in Anglicanism, that the Kingdom of God and society were essentially one and the same. It was a doctrine which had resulted in the development of a close relationship between Church and State, a relationship that manifested itself in such practical matters as the appointment of the clergy by public servants rather than by those with true spiritual perception. The normal Puritan view was that the 'visible' Church contained the 'invisible' Church, and would continue to do so for all time, the 'visible' Church being the organised body, the 'invisible' Church being the true company of believers in Jesus Christ. In answer to the question 'Who are the true members of the Church militant on earth?', James Ussher replied, 'Those alone who as living members of the mystical body ... are by the spirit and faith secretly and inseparably conjoined unto Christ their head, ... the elect being not to be discerned from the reprobate till the last day.'[4] The true believer was 'secretly' joined to Christ, not outwardly to be distinguished from the mere professor, and the whole company of the saved would not be known until the Day of Judgement. George Lawson similarly argues, 'In the Church of Christ there are some living members, real saints, who have a real communion with their Head ... and those make up that which we call the mystical Church, of which no profane or hypocritical wretch can be a member.'[5] The visible Church contained a number of this latter sort, however, and only some 'real saints'. While most Puritans would have conceded that the true Church of Christ was the invisible 'mystical' Church, this did not preclude the necessity of a visible Church, an organised body for the purpose of worship and witness, which would continue as such on earth until the purposes of God had been realised. What Puritanism as a whole wanted was less control of the Church by the State, greater freedom in the appointment of the clergy, and a structural reorganisation that would ensure that the affairs of the Church would remain in the hands of those who themselves were truly of the body of Christ. These were the aspirations that kept the fires of Puritanism burning until the English Civil Wars and Cromwell's Protectorate effectively ended the dreams of disestablishment and godly rule.

There were those in Puritanism, however, who saw much earlier than 1660 that these things were not going to happen, and who soon came to question the very principle upon which such hopes were built. As men studied the Word of God more closely they felt that mainstream Puritanism stopped short of the true biblical doctrine of the Church and that only those who were truly regenerate could constitute the Church of Christ. John Smyth, a Cambridge graduate and erstwhile a Puritan preacher in Anglican orders, felt that if a man might be a member of the visible Church without being a member of the true Church, a man might also be a member of the true Church without being a member of the visible Church; he argued that the visible Church should therefore be 'a visible company of saints ... all which are to be accounted faithful and elect,' and that such a 'visible communion of saints is a visible Church, and this is the only religious society God hath ordained for men on earth'.[6] We are moving rapidly here to the idea of the gathered Church, the Church which consists wholly of those with a true and living faith, the Church which is composed of those who have personally and responsibly determined to be followers of Jesus Christ. That was in 1607. John Robinson, whose name has become inseparably linked with the departure of the Pilgrim Fathers from Holland in 1620, had, six years before that event, also written of the unmistakable characteristics of those who were truly in Christ: 'The tree, saith Christ, is known by the fruits: so may the good trees truly planted by faith into Christ, and having in them the heavenly sap and juice of His Spirit ... ordinarily be known by the good fruits of faith, and of the Spirit evidently appearing in their persons.'[7] In 1645 Hanserd Knollys wanted to ascertain who were the true people of God and who were not: 'Those people that are ungodly, unsanctified, are not the people of God. Such may boast of their justification, but they deceive themselves, for God hath no justified-unsanctified people'.[8] Knollys was by then a Baptist, and the leader of a Baptist Church in London, but could not have become either without a clear view of the nature of the Church. Thomas Grantham, another influential Baptist leader of the next generation, likewise affirmed, 'The Church or people of God ought to be a people separated from them that live in wickedness.' Grantham saw 'the great impiety and ungodly living' that characterised professing Christians in the established Church, and sensed that this was detrimental to the Church and that it warranted separation.[9] Joseph Stennett, a prominent Seventh-day Baptist whose piety and learning, after the Declaration of Indulgence in 1687, which suspended legislation against all Dissenters, ensured him a regular Sunday pulpit, set out the Separatist or Independent position as clearly as anyone had done before him:

> We hold that a Church of Christ consists of such a number of persons as are capable of meeting together in one place, to celebrate all the ordinances of social worship which Christ has ordained; that men are qualified for this privilege by making a credible profession of their faith in Jesus Christ, and of their obedience to Him, without which they ought not to be admitted into any Christian Church; and that such a Church as this which, for distinction sake, we call congregational, is independent of all other Churches; and having within itself sufficient power, when duly organised with proper officers, for the administration of all ordinances, and the due exercise of discipline, is not under the jurisdiction or authority of any other Church whatsoever.[10]

Like Hanserd Knollys and others before him, Joseph Stennett had come to hold both Separatist and Baptist views, the genesis of which were to be found in the writings of the early Separatists, now almost a century old, and to which we must briefly return.

In 1608, John Smyth had taken a small band of Separatists from England to Holland to avoid persecution for nonconformity in the homeland. Smyth soon became convinced of the invalidity of infant baptism, and in 1609 baptised himself and his followers, so bringing into being the first English-speaking Baptist Church of the Reformation. Shortly thereafter Thomas Helwys and others of the Smyth congregation in Amsterdam felt impelled to return to England, despite the threat of persecution, to bear witness to their new-found faith. Thus, by 1612, a part of Smyth's Amsterdam congregation led by Helwys had arrived in England and had settled in Spittalfields, in East London. In that year Helwys published *A Short Declaration of the Mystery of Iniquity*, which spelt out in no uncertain terms the basis of his Separatist and Baptist convictions, views that were destined to produce ultimately one of the most vigorous branches of English-speaking Protestantism.

Interestingly enough, the *Short Declaration* was argued from the eschatological stand-point, that the abomination of desolation referred to by Christ in Matthew xxiv had reached its peak in the widespread departure from true faith and true religion that was to be observed on every hand. The prophecy of Revelation xiii had been fulfilled in the ecclesiastical institutions of the day, the first beast signifying the Papacy, and the second beast depicting Anglicanism and Episcopacy. The two were of the essence of Antichrist, and together constituted the mystery of iniquity (II Thessalonians ii 7) being essentially of the same nature — religions of the establishment upheld by the body politic. He further lamented that Puritanism itself also partook of the spirit of false religion, since it was inconsistent in not pressing the Reformation to its logical conclusion by insisting on the abolition of Episcopacy and the establishment of Presbyterianism. Even the Separatist brethren did not go far enough, since they retained the baptism of infants as the basis of Church membership, and infant baptism was 'a worldly baptism ... and not the baptism and ordinance of Christ'.[11] To Helwys it was inconsistent to claim to have broken with Rome and at the same time cling to Rome's doctrine of the Church and to her rite of initiation into Church membership. So he points out that false ministers 'teach you still to retain your first or chief badge or mark of Babylon, which is your baptism'.[12] The implications of this were considerable for those who had been brought up on Foxe's *Book of Martyrs*, first published in 1563 and staple diet for early English Protestants. Helwys did not hesitate to point them out: 'You all have brought your baptism from Rome, and so you are all Christians and believers by succession from Rome, and ... though you say you are not of one body with Rome, yet you are all members of one body with Rome.'[13] In short, separation from Episcopacy was the only acceptable form of Church organisation, and the visible Church of true believers the only true Church, and the baptism of believers the only valid entry to the body of Christ.

The Significance of Baptism
The original Christian doctrine of baptism, as the early Baptists came to see it, did not rest solely, or even principally, upon polemical assertions

derived from apocalyptic prophecy, however valid such interpretations might have been. It rested on a much wider appeal to Scripture, on the New Testament record of Christ's own baptism, on the baptismal experiences of the early Church, and on the explanations of the baptismal rite in the Pauline epistles. It was, moreover, at these very points that early Baptists pressed the charge of inconsistency against mainstream Puritanism. If we may take John Ball and James Ussher as representative of Puritan theology in this wider sense, it appears at first sight that the Puritan understanding of baptism differed little from the basic tenets of the Baptist Churches. Ball says, 'Baptism is the true sacrament of repentance for remission of sins, and spiritual renovation. . . . It representeth and confirmeth our engrafting into Christ.'[14] Given that Ball does not speak here of baptismal regeneration in the traditional Roman sense, Baptist believers would have approved of such references to repentance, spiritual renovation and the representation of new life in Christ, as all being of the very essence of the baptismal rite. Likewise Ussher defines baptism as 'representing the powerful washing of the blood and spirit of Christ, . . . sealing our regeneration or new birth, our entrance into the covenant of grace and our ingrafting into Christ, and into the body of Christ'.[15] Again, Baptists would not have quarrelled with the theory of baptism so expressed. Their point of contention was that Puritanism as such did not practise what it preached. It continued with a form of baptism which belied its true significance and which, when weighed in the balance of a biblical measure, was found wanting. Baptists believed that the Reformation principle of *sola scriptura* was to be applied as much in the doctrine of baptism as in any other doctrine of the faith, yet in reading Puritan theology and observing the life of the Church as a whole, they did not see it so applied.

What did Baptists find, then, when they went to the Bible to obtain their doctrine of baptism? They found, to begin with, that the New Testament laid down quite explicitly certain pre-requisites to baptism, certain conditions upon which the rite was to be administered, and without which baptism would lose its essential significance and become little more than an external form. A basic text was that found at Mark xvi 16, 'He that believeth and is baptised, shall be saved.' This, together with other references, such as Acts viii 36-38 and xviii 8, provided the evidence that baptism, after the New Testament manner,was to be administered as a consequence of personal faith. Hence Christopher Blackwood, an Episcopalian clergyman who had espoused the Baptist viewpoint, wrote in a book appropriately entitled *The Storming of Antichrist*, 'The baptism of Christ requires faith as an inseparable condition or qualification to the right receiving of it, without which it ought not to be administered.'[16] Hercules Collins, who ministered to a Baptist congregation at Wapping towards the end of the seventeenth century, wrote in his *Believer's Baptism*, with equal conviction, that 'actual personal faith is to precede this ordinance'. To ensure that the point would not be misunderstood,

Collins specified that the faith to which he referred was 'not the faith of the Church, nor an imputative faith of the parents in covenant, nor the faith of the gossips[17] or sureties', and only 'a profession of their own faith, as Philip required of the eunuch, Acts viii 37' was 'sufficient argument for any minister to baptise'.[18] Blackwood shrewdly suggests that the practice of catechising and confirming those who had been baptized in infancy indicates a confused understanding of the relationship between faith and baptism. If, on biblical authority, baptism is to follow faith, it seems that a loss of faith normally occurs between baptism and confirmation, 'for otherwise why are they put to their catechism and taught the elements of faith again?' This means, in effect, that God gives faith to infants and then withdraws it, or allows it to disappear, before the 'years of capacity'. Blackwood finds this an unacceptable reflection on the character of God, and 'a plain argument they [infants] never received it [faith] in their infancy'.[19]

A second pre-requisite to baptism is indicated by the need for catechising. To baptize before there is evidence of faith, Collins had argued, was to baptize contrary to the 'unerring' Word of Scripture. A parallel text to Mark xvi 16 was found at Matthew xxviii 19, and this clearly showed that 'there is first teaching before baptizing, not first baptized, but taught first'.[20] Instruction, in addition to faith, should precede baptism, if the rule of Scripture is to be followed. Referring again to this same text in Matthew, Collins adds, 'The order in this commission is first to teach, then after taught and disciplised [sic], to baptize them. Therefore to baptize them before taught is quite contrary to the command.'[21] George Hammon, pastor of the General Baptist Church at Biddenden in Kent, and Colonel Henry Danvers, who had been Governor of Stafford in 1650 and Member of Parliament for Leicester in 1653, were two of many other Baptist apologists to stress the importance of pre-baptismal instruction. Danvers' *Treatise of Baptism* quoted Matthew xxviii 19-20 and Mark xvi 16, concluding, 'First, that men should be taught the doctrine of faith. Secondly, being so taught, they should be baptized.'[22] Hammon was even more specific: 'If those that are to be baptized, are first to be taught and made disciples, than a child of seven or eight days old, which is not capable to be taught, ought not to be baptized.'[23] Here, as in the statements cited previously from Collins, the objective of the instruction which is to precede baptism is discipleship, a relationship which must not be overlooked in seeking to understand Baptist theology. To be a disciple in terms of New Testament usage, means to be a follower of Christ as the result of informed choice. It was recorded in Matthew xxviii 19-20 that Jesus had commissioned His first followers to take the Gospel message to all the world, to teach all nations, baptizing them in the name of Father, Son and Holy Ghost, and to teach the observance of everything which He had commanded. It did not escape the notice of the early Baptist theologians that the Greek word translated 'teach' in verse 19 was not the usual New Testament word for instruction as used in verse 20, but the word *matheteuo*, which carried the distinctive meaning 'to make a disciple' or 'to make a Christian'.[24] Instruction, therefore, in the sense in which it was used in relation to baptism was more than the impartation of knowledge. It was a process which led to commitment. It is not difficult to understand Hammon's concern or his emphasis on the instruction which is to lead to an intelligent commitment to Jesus Christ.

There are, of course, other ingredients of discipleship and the life of commitment, as those who have read through the preceding chapter will understand, and Baptists taught that repentance and regeneration were both necessary preconditions of baptism. Hercules Collins states that baptism is 'a lively representation of regeneration, ... a lively badge, symbol, and sign of regeneration, and the new birth,' and emphasises that 'persons are not to be baptized that they may be regenerated' but because they already have been regenerated.[25] Christopher Blackwood uses Romans vi 3-4, saying that baptism is a 'sign or seal of our death, burial, and resurrection with Christ ... having sin dead in us ... and ... rising again to newness of life'. It is also a sign of the believer's true fellowship with Christ and communion in the Holy Spirit, or 'putting on Christ', and having a 'heart sprinkled from an evil conscience' (Hebrews x 22).[26] It is, in short, the witness to that new life which the believer, justified, regenerated and sanctified, lives in Christ. John Smyth had early recognised this underlying concept of true baptism and had remarked in his *Character of the Beast*, 'That infants cannot have repentance is evident, seeing repentance is knowledge of sin by the law, sorrow for sin by the gospel, and mortification of sin and new obedience, all of which are as much in the basin of water as in the infant baptized.'[27]

The conclusions to be drawn from the foregoing arguments, if not already apparent, relate to the purpose of baptism and to the persons to whom the rite should be administered. Baptists believed that the Bible taught that the essential characteristics of Christian life and experience were to precede the external application of water. Baptism was, therefore, the outward testimony to an inward experience. There was no efficacy in the act, no regenerating or cleansing property in the water. Baptism was a symbolic act, 'a sign or seal' as Christopher Blackwood had said, an indication of something which the candidate for baptism had already experienced. Even John Flavel warns his people of their 'dangerous dependence' on the idea of baptismal regeneration. Baptism without faith, he says, will not result in salvation.[28] Thomas Grantham, the Lincolnshire Baptist, explains that 'baptism was not ordained of God to take away original sin, but for the remission of actual sin upon repentance and faith'.[29] Indeed, to retain anything which savoured of baptismal regeneration was a relic of the Roman Antichrist, which limited the effects of Christ's atonement, and which was to be avoided as earnestly as the plague.

The other conclusion, of course, was that baptism could not properly be administered to infants or to children who had not reached the age of understanding or discretion. 'You may as soon extract water out of a flint, as draw a command to baptize infants out of Scripture,'[30] said John Tombes, whose writings on the subject of baptism show as great a knowledge of Scripture, its original languages, and the writings of the Church Fathers, as those of any Puritan theologian, and whose dexterity in applying the principles of logic and exegesis was equally capable. Henry Danvers shows the degree to which a layman might pursue the arguments against infant baptism in the following extract from his *Treatise of Baptism*, a work strengthened by frequent quotations from Scripture and the testimony of Church historians:

> May it not be referred to the judgement and conscience of the considerate, impartial reader, whether any but the believer can possibly reach or attain these spiritual ends mentioned? And how capable poor ignorant babes are to answer any of them? And whether it is not contradictious [sic] to common sense and experience for any to assert it? For what repentance or faith are they capable to profess? What present regeneration can they evidence? What testimony of a good conscience can they give, in striking or keeping covenant with God herein? And how can they embrace, or improve a covenant on God's part for pardon, purging, justification, sanctification, and salvation?[31]

Hercules Collins would point out to anyone who disavowed the need for believer's baptism by claiming that he had been baptized in his infancy, that only baptism by consent was valid. Alluding to marriage as illustrative of the principle of consent, Collins maintained, 'Its not the bed that maketh marriage, for then fornication is marriage, but it is a lawful consent by covenant.' The same principle applied in baptism: 'It is not a little water sprinkled on the face that makes baptism, but also consent and subjection to Christ's command.'[32] In fact, if the reaction of most infants to the administration of baptism was any measure of participation, Collins suggested that it signified dissent rather than assent. Baptism to be valid requires consent, consent necessitates understanding, and understanding presupposes that the age of discretion has been attained.

If any further evidence against the invalidity or the illogicality of infant baptism was required, Baptists found it in the relationship of baptism and the Lord's Supper to faith and Christian experience. John Tombes argued from I Corinthians xi 28 that 'the Lord's Supper is not to be granted to infants because self-examination is pre-required'.[33] The Lord's Supper is clearly intended for those who are already practising believers, that is, to those who are of the body of Christ through faith and baptism. On this Puritanism as a whole would have agreed with Baptists. Yet Puritans in general would not admit to communion those who had been baptized in infancy but not confirmed in the faith. The point which Baptists wanted to make was that it seemed to them illogical to deny the symbolic elements of bread and wine to those who had received the symbolic application of water. Danvers says that it is 'agreeable both to rule, reason, and righteousness ... to admit men upon profession of faith, to both ordinances'. To Danvers it was 'ridiculous' for those who had introduced infant baptism into the Church to have insisted on the correct order of baptism and communion while omitting to observe the spiritual requirements, and 'much worse' for Protestant reformers to admit infants to baptism and Church membership, but not to communion.[34] Blackwood maintains simply that, since Scripture requires the same prerequisites for baptism and the Lord's Supper, 'no man ought to be received into communion in baptism, no more than he ought to be received into communion in the Supper'.[35]

The indisputable conclusion, then, to which Baptists came from their study of the Bible, was that baptism was only to be administered to believers, upon consent and profession of faith. 'When all is said that can be said,' Grantham wrote in 1689, and by that time everything that could be said in the debate over baptism had been said, 'the Church ought to have pious care that none be admitted to baptism, but such as give some competent account of the work of faith with power in their souls.'[36] It is to the credit of the Baptist Church in succeeding centuries, that it has endeavoured to maintain this high standard. Although Baptists have always been wary of creedal statements as such, at least six Baptist confessions of faith appeared in the seventeenth century, together with a revision of the Westminster Confession. While some of these confessions reflected divergent views on the doctrines of grace, election and the atonement, they unanimously upheld the doctrine of believer's baptism. Thus, *The Confession of Faith of Those Churches which are Commonly (though falsely) called Anabaptist*, issued in 1644, stated in its thirty-ninth article that 'Baptism is an ordinance of the New Testament, given by Christ, to be dispensed only upon persons professing faith, or that are disciples, or taught, who upon a profession of faith, ought to be baptized.'[37] Some would argue that had the English Church accepted that principle from the Baptists of the seventeenth century, its corporate witness in the world to the claims of Christ's Gospel, then and since, might have been the more effective, and its influence upon society the more profound and far-reaching.

Baptism by Immersion

For some thirty years or so the Baptist congregations in England, which numbered more than fifty by 1640, baptized their converts by the traditional method of affusion. Baptists, however, did not rest on the assumption that they had discovered the whole truth of Scripture, and further study brought the conviction that immersion was the mode of baptism taught and practised in the New Testament. From 1641 immersion began to replace affusion as the accepted method in English Baptist congregations, and was soon established as the principle which would give the Baptist Church its distinctive characteristic.

To appreciate the full force of the biblical reasons which led Baptists to practise immersion, it is necessary to return to the Pauline statement on baptism in the sixth chapter of Romans. Here Paul taught that believers were baptized into Christ's death, that they were buried with Christ in baptism, and that they rose from that death and burial to live the new life of faith and commitment (Romans vi 3-4). That this was a crucial passage in the development of Baptist views is clearly evident from the writings of the early Baptist apologists. It is related to the basic concept of the Church and Church membership which undergirded Baptist practice, particularly to the belief that regeneration was an essential experience and that it marked the beginning of true life in Christ. As Baptists read the sixth chapter of Romans it became clear to them that the whole concept of death, burial and resurrection in Christian thought could not be restricted to the actual death, burial and resurrection of Christ Himself, central as those events were to Christian faith. Crucifixion and resurrection were to be translated into the reality of the believer's own experience. Henry Jessey speaks of believers' 'union with Christ, and their communion with Him in His death, burial and resurrection'.[38] Through regeneration and the indwelling presence of the Holy Spirit, the believer was to enter into a personal relationship with Christ, a relationship which brought death to the old self and the old way of life, and which resulted in the birth of a new person and a new way of life. The 'old man' was to die and be buried, and the 'new man' was to rise and live henceforth the life of victory over sin. This was the basis of Church membership, the evidence of the reality of the Kingdom of God, the experience which validated the high claim of the Gospel, and baptism, according to Paul, was the symbolic rite by which the meaning of these profound truths was to be expressed.

It was in the light of these things, that those who came to see the significance of believer's baptism could not grasp why the vast majority of their Puritan brethren were unable to comprehend the inadequacy of infant baptism. Collins therefore asks, 'I would fain know, how sprinkling or pouring water upon the face, doth figure out Christ's death, burial, and resurrection?'[39] It was a pertinent question. If baptism, on account of its very nature, was to signify death, burial and resurrection, either with reference to Christ or in the experience of the believer, in what way could sprinkling, or pouring, or the sign of the cross, convey that meaning? Collins therefore concludes, 'There be no manner of similitude and likeness between Christ's death and burial, with sprinkling a little water on the face'.[40] And Henry Jessey says more fully, 'Baptism is an ordinance of the Lord ... wherein persons repenting and believing in Jesus Christ, yielding up themselves to Him ... are solemnly dipped in water, and arise, signifying, representing, and sealing up to them, their union with Christ, and their communion with Him in His death, burial and resurrection.'[41] It is only baptism by immersion which completely and satisfactorily represents death, burial and resurrection, a point which George Lawson, not a Baptist himself, is willing to concede. 'It cannot be denied,' he says, 'that the whole body descending into the water, and plunged wholly, and after that ascending out of the water again, might resemble Christ's death and resurrection more perfectly.'[42] If the 'old man' is dead, it is logical that he be buried that the new man might live, but, as Collins points out, a man is not reckoned as buried who only has earth scattered over him, 'but he who is in the heart of the earth, and covered with the same'.[43] Danvers speaks of that 'figurative death and resurrection in being dipped in water,' typifying the willingness of the believer 'to die and live with Christ by mortification and vivification'.[44] No method of baptism but immersion could adequately symbolise the spiritual significance of burial, and hence of resurrection.

Early Baptists saw no distinction in principle, and certainly none in practice, between the baptism of John and that which had been practised in the wider Christian community. If Jesus had received baptism at the hands of John, there could be little reason to question the baptism of repentance which John proclaimed, or the method of baptism he used. An important statement in this respect was found in John iii 23, where it was recorded that John baptized at a place called Aenon 'because there was much water there'. Christopher Blackwood observes that this 'would have been needless, had sprinkling been the manner of baptising,'[45] and George Hammon adds that the 'muchness of the water was the main reason why John did stay and baptize at Aenon'.[46] The implication arising from this text was clearly that 'the sprinkling of a little water in baptism is not God's way'.[47] The record of the Ethiopian eunuch in Acts viii gave further textual evidence in favour of immersion. Blackwood's comment here is that, 'Philip and the eunuch they went both of them into the water'. Both the one administering the rite and the one receiving baptism descended into the water, Blackwood maintains, which 'shows that there was an application of the person to the water rather than of the water to the person, as it is in sprinkling'.[48] The supreme example in Scripture was unquestionably that of Christ Himself, of which Collins says, referring to the passage at Mark i 9-10, 'He went up out of the water, which in common sense signifies, He first went down, not only to the water, but into the water.'[49] George Hammon pressed the argument here that Christ's example is the pattern for the Christian at all times and in all matters, 'and that we are commanded to follow His steps, as He hath led us an example; and He, dipped or plunged in water, then Christ's disciples ought to be dipped or plunged also'.[50] The supporting argument to these biblical evidences in favour of baptism by immersion was, to quote Henry Danvers, that if infant baptism had divine authority 'there would have been some precept, command, or example in the Scripture to warrant the same'. The Bible, however, was 'wholly silent' on the matter, there being 'not one syllable to be found in all the New Testament about any such practice'. Hence 'where the Scripture hath no tongue, we ought to have no ear'.[51]

These interpretations of the biblical passages relating to baptism were considerably strengthened by appeal to the original languages of Scripture, particularly to the root meaning of the words translated 'baptism' and 'baptize' in the English versions. Danvers explains that the word 'baptism' comes from the Greek *baptisma* which 'in plain English is nothing else but to dip, plunge, or cover all over'.[52] He cites in support of this definition the Greek lexicons of Scapula and Stephens, both 'great defenders of infant baptism'. According to these authorities, the verb *baptizo*, 'to baptise', is a derivative of the verb *bapto* which specifically means 'to dip'. Hence *baptizo* itself signifies 'to dip, plunge, overwhelm, put under, cover over, to dye in colour, which is done by plunging'.[53] Collins takes up this definition and quoting Leigh's *Critica Sacra, or Philological and Theological Observations upon all the Greek Words of the New Testament* — which, first published in 1639, remained a standard work of reference throughout the century — says, 'The native signification of the word is, to dip into, or plunge under water, as the dyer dips his cloth in his vats.'[54] Collins further adds that the New Testament word *baptizo* is equivalent to the Old Testament word *tabal*, which is used of Joseph's coat being 'dipped in blood' (Genesis xxxvii 31), of Asher's foot being 'dipped in oil' (Deuteronomy xxxiii 24), and of Naaman being 'washed or dipped' seven times in Jordan[55] (II Kings v 14). Hanserd Knollys makes the important observation concerning the words used in the New Testament, that 'the Spirit of God hath inspired the apostles to use one Greek word (viz. *baptizo*) for dipping, and another (viz. *rhantizo*) for sprinkling.' Examples of the use of these words could be found respectively in John i 25-26 and Hebrews ix 19 and 21.[56]

It was also to the advantage of those who advocated believer's baptism by immersion, that they could cite church historians to prove that infant baptism, had been a late modification of original Christian doctrine and practice. Blackwood appeals to the continental theologian David Pareus, Professor of Sacred Literature at the University of Heidelberg in the early part of the seventeenth century, who taught that immersion was the method of baptism known in the apostolic Church: 'The persons baptized were dipped all over in a river, with some tarriance under the water, then they rose up again; dipping showed crucifying and death, ... tarrying under the waters, burial, and coming up out of the water, resurrection with Christ.'[57] A candid, though somewhat sketchy account of baptismal practices in the apostolic Church, appeared in the Anglican William Cave's *Primitive Christianity*. Cave, a Cambridge Doctor of Divinity and a recognised ecclesiastical historian, had been appointed Canon of Windsor in 1684. Although not the work of a Baptist anxious to establish the antiquity of his beliefs, *Primitive Christianity* nonetheless testified to the common practice of immersion in the early Church, and drew attention to the departure from apostolic practice in later centuries and to some of the reasons thereof:

> The party to be baptized was wholly immerged, or put under water, which was the almost constant and universal custom of those times, whereby they did more notably and significantly express the three great ends and effects of baptism; for as in immersion there are, in a manner,

three several acts, the putting the person into water, his abiding there for a little time, and his rising up again, so by these were represented Christ's death, burial, and resurrection, and in conformity thereunto, our dying unto sin, the destruction of its power, and our resurrection to a new course of life.

By the person's being put into water was lively represented the putting off the body of the sins of the flesh, and being washed from the filth and pollution of them; by his abode under it, which was a kind of burial into water, his entering into a state of death or mortification, like as Christ remained for some time under the state or power of death: therefore 'as many as are baptized into Christ,' are said 'to be baptized into his death, and to be buried with him by baptism into death, that the old man being crucified with him, the body of sin might be destroyed, that henceforth he might not serve sin, for that he that is dead is freed from sin,' as the apostle clearly explains the meaning of this rite.

And then by his emersion, or rising up out of the water, was signified his entering upon a new course of life, differing from that which he lived before: 'that like as Christ was raised up from the dead by the glory of the Father, even so we also should walk in newness of life'.

But though, by reason of the more eminent significancy of these things, immersion was the common practice in those days, and there-fore they earnestly urged it and pleaded for it, yet did they not hold sprinkling to be unlawful, especially in cases of necessity, as of weakness, danger of death, or where conveniency of immerging could not be had. In these, and such like cases, Cyprian does not only allow, but pleads for it, and that in a discourse on purpose, when the question concerning it was put to him. Upon this account it is that immersion is now generally disused in these parts of the world, and sprinkling succeeded in its room, because the tender bodies of most infants (the only persons now baptized) could not be put under water in these cold northern climates without apparent prejudice to their health, if not their lives.[58]

In returning to immersion, seventeenth-century Baptists believed that they were recovering the letter and the spirit of baptism as it had been practised in the early Church, and contended that both Scripture and history supported that view. Believer's baptism was only really worthy of the name when belief was translated into experience, and when that experience involved death to sin, burial of the past with its failures and mistakes, and resurrection to a new life in the Spirit. That being so, it is easy to see why Baptists could settle for nothing less than total immersion of those who believed.

The Origin and Implications of Infant Baptism
The major criticism of William Cave's account of early Christian baptism is that it passes too quickly over the centuries which followed the apostolic age, leaving the impression that sprinkling was an acceptable alternative

to immersion, even in the days of the apostles. Cyprian, however, whom Cave cites as an authority for the introduction of sprinkling, lived in the third century and did not himself become a Christian until 246. It is more accurate, as early English Baptists, Tombes and Collins among them, recognised, that the age of Cyprian marked the beginning of a deviation from apostolic baptismal practices which would become well-nigh universal in the Church, and this places the departure from immersion and believer's baptism from about the middle of the third century. In 253 a synod of bishops under the chairmanship of Cyprian debated the question of baptism and concluded that children should not be excluded. Henry Danvers mentioned Pope Victor who, at the very end of the second century, was said to have authorised baptising in fonts as well as in rivers.[59] Collins stated that 'infant baptism was hardly heard of till about three hundred years after Christ,' and Tombes added that what Cyprian had begun, Augustine and Jerome, who died respectively in 430 and 420, steadily and consistently pursued.[60] It is important to recognise, however, as Johannes Warnes so thoroughly demonstrates in his *Baptism: Studies in the Original Christian Baptism* (1957), that throughout these centuries in which infant baptism took root in the Church adult baptism remained the rule, and that it was was not until the sixth century and thereafter that infant baptism eventually prevailed.

The men of the seventeenth century who wanted to restore believer's baptism to the English Church were aware of the past, and of those influences, customs and ideas, which to them were wholly unscriptural, unchristian and illogical, which had led to the departure from the biblical doctrine of baptism. Thomas Grantham drew attention to some of those ideas in *Truth and Peace*, a work which he wrote as a reply to a book advocating infant baptism, written by an Anglican. Grantham recounted that with the passing of time in the early centuries, many began to defer their baptism in the mistaken belief that it was extremely difficult, if not impossible, to find forgiveness for sins committed after baptism. In many instances those who had delayed were overtaken by sickness and, 'afraid to die without baptism, requested that it might be administered to them in their sickbeds'. In such cases immersion was impossible, and baptism was administered in some other manner. Grantham attributes to this custom the introduction of sprinkling as an alternative to immersion 'without any warrant from heaven'. At the other extreme there were those who, in the belief that death without baptism meant eternal damnation, were anxious for the rite to be administered as quickly as possible, often 'with preposterous haste, even to baptise infants as soon as they were born, and sometimes before'.[61] Hence arose the practice of infant baptism. Granted that this was something of an over-simplification of what in fact was a lengthy and sometimes obscure development over several centuries, it nevertheless establishes what to Baptists was, after all, the point at issue, namely that the baptism of infants and the sprinkling or pouring of water in the administration of the rite took their origin from sources other than the revealed Word of God. Grantham puts everything he says about sprinkling and infant baptism firmly in the context of II Timothy iv 3-4, the passage which foretold that the time would come when men would 'turn away their ears from the truth, and ... be turned unto fables,' observing that the prophecy 'had too much of its verification in the early times of Christianity'.[62]

It is indeed this association of infant baptism with what Puritans understood to be the apostasy of the Antichrist which emerges as the most weighty and far-reaching implication of the whole baptismal controversy in the seventeenth century. Even a casual survey of some of the titles Baptist writers gave to their books illustrates this relationship. Thomas Helwys had published *The Mystery of Iniquity* in 1612, and this was followed, when restrictions on the printing of books and pamphlets were lifted in 1640, by Christopher Blackwood's *The Storming of Antichrist* (1644), and Henry Denne's *The Man of Sin Discovered* (1645) and *Antichrist Unmasked* (1646). The full title of Henry Danvers' *Treatise of Baptism* (1674) illustrates the point admirably:

> A Treatise of Baptism: wherein, that of believers, and that of infants, is examined by the Scriptures. With the history of both out of antiquity, making it appear, that infants' baptism was not practised for near three hundred years, nor enjoined as necessary, till four hundred years after Christ: with the fabulous traditions, and erroneous grounds upon which it was, by the pope's canons (with gossips, chrism, exorcism, baptising of Churches and bells, and other popish rites) founded. And that the famous Waldensian and old British Churches, Lollards and Wycliffians, and other Christians witnessed against it.[63]

Danvers' basic position, and his purpose in writing a treatise about baptism, must have been clear to anyone who could read, and if they were not immediately discernible, those who read the first few pages of his book would be left in no further doubt. It must be understood here that the universal concept of the Antichrist in seventeenth-century England, was that it applied to papal Rome. This had been the standard view of English Protestantism for more than a hundred years by the time Danvers' book appeared, and was to continue to be so for many years to come. It is not possible to understand Protestantism at any point in its early history, least of all at this time in English religious history, apart from this underlying conviction. The mediaeval Catholic Church which had dominated Europe for over a thousand years had, in so doing, gradually but surely departed from the beliefs of apostolic Christianity, not only in the matter of baptism, but in many other aspects of the faith. Baptists were, as a much later writer was to describe them 'Protestant Protestants', and the connection between infant baptism and Antichrist could not be overlooked. Danvers writes:

> Amongst all those ordinances and institutions of Christ that the man of sin hath so miserably mangled, metamorphosed, and changed, none hath been more horribly abused than that of baptism; which as to matter

and form, subject and circumstance, hath suffered such apparent alteration and subversion, that nothing but the very name of the thing remains.[64]

Danvers then proceeds to explain why infant baptism was essentially of the Antichrist, pointing out, among other things, that it was not finally regarded as essential 'till imposed by Antichristian canons ... and afterwards continued and re-enforced by so many popes and councils'. Moreover, infant baptism had been effectually used to 'propagate, strengthen, and advance the Antichristian church, state and kingdom,' since by it whole towns and cities, even countries, had been received into the faith regardless of any spiritual qualifications.[65] Much more could be quoted in this vein from Danvers alone, to say nothing of the many other Baptist writers who spoke in similar terms. To ignore the Antichristian connection is to take the risk of seriously misunderstanding the impetus in the early Baptist movement.

The implications which derived from the doctrinal relationship to Rome were of the utmost significance. It suggested, for one thing, that to retain infant baptism gave evidence that the Reformation was incomplete in the Protestant Churches. Danvers, again, with reference to infant baptism, says that it is lamentable 'that the Protestant reformers, who detected and cast away so many Antichristian abominations, should yet hold fast such a principal foundation-stone of their building'. This was particularly apposite in view of 'the rottenness of the popish grounds ... for infant-sprinkling'.[66] Another writer charges both Lutheran and Calvinistic Churches with having 'erred' in retaining 'the baptism which they had from the hands of popish priests ... which they [the Reformers] could never retain without acknowledging the Romish Church to be a true church, and their priesthood to be true, and their ministers to be the ministers of Jesus Christ'.[67] They had further 'erred' in receiving 'all sorts of persons to baptism' indiscriminately, on the assumption that fitness for the rite was derived, in some instances at least, from the supposed godliness of parents. This is to come, in effect, to the heart of the Antichristian apostasy, and the argument is that reformation can only be true reformation in the fullest sense of the term if all the accretions and deviations of Antichrist are discarded. Baptists declared that a thorough reformation called for a repudiation of all Catholic concepts of the Church and baptism, and a return to the unadulterated teachings and practices of Scripture. Possibly no Baptist writer put the case with more discernment than John Tombes who called infant baptism 'a mother-corruption' in the Church, 'that hath in her womb most of those abuses in discipline and manners, and some of those errors in doctrine, that do defile the reformed Churches'.[68] Tombes saw the fundamental relationship between Church organisation and government — 'discipline' — and the life of the individual believer — 'manners' — and although doctrinal soundness was important, it was not as important, in the end, as the corporate witness of the Church to the saving power of the Gospel, demonstrated in the godly living of its members. To retain infant baptism meant to tolerate inconsistencies in life and doctrine which impeded the witness of the Church and prevented complete reformation. Heal this sore, Tombes said, and many, if not all, the ills of the Church will also be cured.

Arising from the question of Antichrist came the question of authority. Tombes also clearly discerned this aspect of the matter. One argument used to sustain the doctrine of infant baptism was that of the covenant, which proceeded on the grounds that the children of believers who themselves had entered into the covenant of grace were also entitled to the benefits and blessings of the covenant, baptism succeeding circumcision as the sign of the covenant. The limitations of this argument were readily apparent to Baptist writers, and need not detain us here. Tombes pointed out that, even if there had been a logical covenant basis for infant baptism, it still could not be specifically proved from Scripture, and hence was founded on 'will-worship, without an institution by precept or apostolic example'. Tombes reminded his readers of the principle from which, as good Protestants, they had never deviated, 'that in God's worship we must not meddle a jot further than God hath commanded'.[69] To do that, and to advocate infant baptism on any other grounds but that of Scripture would be to open the way for a deluge of unscriptural traditions, as 'prelacy, holy days, surplice'. Danvers warned that those who accepted 'the Pope's christening ... necessarily oblige themselves by receiving his law, to embrace also his government, and to be ruled in chief by himself'.[70] This, in Baptist eyes, was the logical and inevitable end of accepting infant baptism, and if others could not see it Baptists could, for to them it raised again the question underlying the whole Reformation. This was the question of authority, that of Church or Scripture, and to Baptists the answer to the question was Scripture, particularly when the Church had so flagrantly and persistently deviated from the Word of God.

It would be hard to determine which consequence of infant baptism was, in Baptist eyes, the more dangerous to the welfare of the Church. Certainly, the one that we shall note in concluding this chapter would have been regarded with the greatest concern. Blackwood puts it quite frankly. Infant baptism, he says, 'fills the Church with rotten members and confounds the world and the Church together'.[71] The word 'confound' is used here in the sense of mixing together rather than in the sense of baffle or confuse, and this was indeed the crux of the problem. How could a distinction be made between the Church and the world? But let us listen again to Blackwood, speaking of the effects that infant baptism produces within the Church, the supposed body of Christ:

Such persons in following times growing up prove often wicked, and many of them only civil men, we know not how to get them out of communion; and so the matter of the Churches come to be so corrupted, that they are made uncapable of reformation; for when the matter of Churches is rotten, what hope is there that the Churches will come into a pure state?... Infant baptism especially serves to Christianise the profane world, who if men enlightened would speak what they think, they must needs say they are not Christians, no, not one tenth part in too many congregations.[72]

We have now returned to the doctrine of the Church, with which this chapter began. The hope that the Church would be purified and thoroughly reformed was to the one end that she might bear witness more effectively to the Gospel of Jesus Christ. For this very purpose she had been brought into existence. For this purpose she had been sustained and strengthened, and brought out of great tribulation. It was the belief of those who advocated believer's baptism that the doctrine they proclaimed with such conviction would contribute significantly to the success of that divine mission.

6. A HIGH PRIEST IN HEAVEN

It is not too much to affirm the utmost confidence of those who follow Christ within the heavenly sanctuary. He has opened the way into the very presence of God. That way keeps our eyes and our lives in union with the very life of God. By His intercession Christ mediates eternal life in spite of our decay. Sins that deserve condemnation He pardons. Not a temptation can assail us that He has not power to repel. Our final salvation in Christ is rendered secure, not by self-confidence in one's righteousness but in humble dependence on our divine Advocate with the Father.

E. Heppenstall *Our High Priest* (1972) pp.63-64

When we consider Christ's going into heaven as our Priest and as our attorney, we may from thence collect grounds of both faith and hope.... When Christ went into heaven as our priest, he did accomplish the business of our purchased inheritance. When He appeared as our attorney to plead it, He ensured it in court of law ... and when He entered as our forerunner .... He possessed it actually, and so evidenceth clearly our sureness of it.

John Durant *The Salvation of the Saints* (1653) pp.162-163

What it meant to belong to Christ as Saviour was well understood in Puritan England, as the earlier chapters of this volume have attempted to demonstrate. It was a tangible and meaningful experience in the Christian life, based upon a sound theological truth. The truth was that of a substitutionary atonement, wrought upon the cross, and to those who had entered into the experience resulting from Christ's vicarious sacrifice, it meant assurance of salvation, forgiveness of sin, freedom from guilt, hope for the future, and fellowship with like-minded believers in the body of Christ, the Church. But what did it mean to belong to Christ as High Priest? What significance did that concept have in Christian life and experience? And upon what biblical or theological basis did belief in Christ's high-priestly ministry rest? Charles Wesley was later to write one of his most stirring and theologically significant hymns on this theme. Set to Darwall's 148th, Wesley's words, 'Arise, my soul, arise, shake off thy guilty fears,' reflect a further essential facet of Christian experience, particularly for those who could sing with understanding the line which followed, 'The holy sacrifice in my behalf appears'. Christians of Wesley's day and earlier would have encountered little difficulty with the Old

Testament imagery here, or with those further allusions to the ever-living Christ making intercession in heaven, pleading the benefits of His blood, shed for all mankind and sprinkling 'now the throne of grace'. The hymn testifies to what, in earlier English Protestantism at least, was widely regarded as basic doctrine, and Puritan theologians, had they lived in a later age, would surely have failed to understand what to them would have appeared as culpable neglect of a theme essential to the fullness of Christian life and to the totality of the Christian revelation.

The Priestly Ministry of Christ

When Jesus had completed His work on earth, He returned to heaven and, in the words of Scripture, 'sat down at the right hand of God', (see, for example Hebrews i 3, viii 1, xii 2, Colossians iii 1, I Peter iii 22). The implications of this event are of the greatest import, if the conclusions of Puritan theology are correct. Christopher Love pointedly referred his hearers to Hebrews viii 4, from which he concluded that it had been necessary in the Divine purpose for Christ to return to heaven in order that He might assume the role of Priest, 'to perform and accomplish His sacerdotal office ... to make intercession for all the elect,'[1] which manifestly He would have been unable to do had He remained on earth. John Owen speaks of the priesthood of Christ and its consequences for Christians in terms of 'the principal mysteries of the gospel', and George Lawson says that Christ's 'perpetual intercession ... is far more beneficial to us than His bodily presence on earth'. Owen continues, 'through Him have we boldness, through Him have we ability, through Him have we access unto, and acceptance with God,' and Lawson asks, 'What should we do if we had not Him our righteous Advocate and Propitiator [sic] with His Father? We were redeemed indeed by His death, but we are saved and justified by His life, because He ever liveth to make intercession for us, and will fully and forever save us.'[2] It can only be concluded that Puritanism saw in the doctrine of Christ's priesthood a fundamental article of Christian faith, drawn from Scripture, and necessary to be understood and proclaimed.

If we pursue Puritanism's emphasis on the priestly ministry of Christ, we shall discern that it arises from two major causes, the first of which is clearly of a theological nature and concerns the fullness of Christ's redemptive work. In order for man to be saved, the death of Christ was a necessity. That premise was unquestioned and unquestionable in Puritan theology. But of equal importance to man's full salvation was that work of Christ which lay beyond the resurrection and the ascension, to be more specific, the work which lay between the resurrection and the coming of Christ at the end of the age. The mature confession of John Owen, that prince of Puritan theologians, was that if the work of salvation had been left as it stood when Christ had returned to heaven, it would have remained forever unfinished, and hence, by implication, many would have remained forever unsaved. 'So great and glorious is the work of saving believers,'

Owen declared, 'that it is necessary that the Lord Christ should lead a mediatory life in heaven, for the perfecting and accomplishment of it.' Owen goes on to speak of the 'sure foundations of our eternal salvation' having been laid in Christ's death and resurrection, and to argue 'that believers could not be saved without the life of Christ following it'[3] (the resurrection). Christ was, to use a biblical analogy, the Alpha and the Omega of Christian faith and hope, the beginning and the ending of the transaction which had commenced in distant ages past. But the Omega could not be written with finality on the last page of redemption's story until Christ's heavenly work of intercession had first been accomplished and perfected. Samuel Mather explained it simply and clearly:

> The death and blood of Christ is not enough to the cleansing of our souls, unless the blood be sprinkled, the death of Christ applied to us. There must be a work of application as well as of redemption. All the precious blood that Christ hath shed will not save a sinner, unless this blood be effectually applied and sprinkled on the soul. Application is a great and necessary part of our recovery and salvation, as well as the blood of Christ itself.[4]

It was the 'work of application' which made Christ's priesthood essential in the way of salvation, a point which drew its significance from the Old Testament sanctuary ritual. It was not enough for the sacrificial animal to be slain in the courtyard and its body offered on the altar of burnt offering. The blood itself must be applied to the altar or carried within the sanctuary and sprinkled ceremonially before the Lord. Similarly, John Flavel explained, 'It was not sufficient that Christ shed His own blood on earth, except He carry it before the Lord into heaven, and there perform His intercession work for us.'[5] The tabernacle ritual depicted the future redemptive work which Christ would initiate and ultimately bring to completion, the sacrifice requiring the application of the blood by the priest, and the application of the blood proceeding from the symbolic death of the sacrificial offering, the one insufficient and symbolically inadequate without the other. So Flavel can argue, 'It was not enough for the sacrifice to be slain without, and his blood left there,' and Owen can say that the efficacy of 'the intercession of the Lord Christ depends upon and flows from His oblation and sacrifice'.[6]

The relationship between Christ's priesthood and the work of salvation as a whole was explained at some length by John Durant in *The Salvation of the Saints*, which appeared in 1653. The title itself indicates the drift of the argument, and the author's thesis is that the priesthood of Christ 'now in heaven' and His second coming 'hereafter from heaven' are both necessary to the final outworking of God's redemptive purpose. Durant, who for many years ministered to a Congregational Church in Canterbury, preaching in the Cathedral until ordered by the authorities to discontinue, is a fine example of the Puritan preacher who sought to make doctrine relevant to the daily lives of his people. Durant explains in the introduction to his book that he had discovered in the course of his pastoral experience that many Christians were content to accept the sacrificial death of Christ on the cross without giving any further thought to the way of salvation. In Durant's view, it was a mistake, made by clergy and laity alike, 'to think all was done upon the cross when Christ died'.[7] Those who studied Scripture carefully would readily discover that this was not the case. As a result of Christ's sacrifice upon the cross, salvation was 'purchased, yet it was not completed,' for 'all was not done at Christ's death that concerned our redemption ... all was not done until the blood of Christ was carried into the Holy Places, which was not until Christ went to heaven to appear as our High Priest.'[8] The title of Durant's book also emphasised that the doctrine of Christ's priesthood was of concern to believers rather than to mankind as a whole. Christ's mediatorial ministry was necessary to the salvation of 'saints'. 'What have they to do with the transactions of Christ within the veil, for whom He died not without the camp?',[9] Durant asked. The doctrine of Christ's priestly ministry principally concerned the spiritual welfare of the professing believer. It proceeded from the assumption that the sacrifice had been made and that it had been accepted. For this reason it was more than ever necessary for all those, ministry and laity alike, who were already of the household of faith to understand just what the doctrine meant, and to sense its significance in the plan of salvation as a whole.

The other reason underlying the importance of Christ's priestly ministry in Puritan theology was of an experiential nature, relating to the individual and to the daily lives of those who had become followers of Christ and who, like Bunyan's Pilgrim, had set their faces resolutely towards the heavenly City. Also like Bunyan's Pilgrim, they were to encounter many trials and difficulties along the way, many temptations and discouragements to faith, many obstacles which would make the journey hazardous, and which in the overcoming would require more than ordinary strength and perseverance. Jesus had told His disciples shortly before His ascension that it was 'expedient' for them that He should return to heaven (John xvi 7), and Puritan theology interpreted this not only with reference to the coming of the Holy Spirit, vital as that undoubtedly was, but also with reference to Christ's priestly ministry. It was of practical benefit to them, in the daily round and common task, that Christ should return to heaven and assume the office of priest. It was of greater benefit than if He had remained personally with His Church on earth. 'His presence and His perpetual intercession there is far more beneficial to us than His bodily presence here,'[10] Lawson declared. Christopher Love agreed: 'We have great advantage by Christ's going-into heaven.'[11] And Bunyan, whose Pilgrim we have already mentioned, comes to the point when he explains that Christ 'has undertaken to stand up for his people at God's bar ... to plead by the law and justice of heaven for their deliverance when, for their faults, they are accused, indicted, or impleaded by their adversary'.[12] Flavel says precisely the same thing when he declares that Christ's priestly ministry of intercession provides 'sweet relief against the defects and

wants that are yet in our sanctification,' and that grace 'by reason of
Christ's intercession ... shall live, grow and expatiate itself in thy
heart'.[13] It is quite clear that we have now passed beyond the realm of
theology, important as that is as a foundation for true faith, and that we
have entered the realm of experiential Christian living.

The biblical basis for such convictions is found, in the New Testament,
in the Epistle to the Hebrews, a book which claimed the attention of some
of the best Puritan minds. A basic passage was Hebrews iv 14-16, which
spoke of the believer's great High Priest having passed into heaven, and
which exhorted the believers on account of that fact to come boldly to the
throne of grace to find help in time of need. The vital outcome of Christ's
priestly ministry, in experiential terms, was that it provided practical,
tangible assistance to all who struggled with the limitations and implications of human nature. The New Testament doctrine of regeneration did
not mean that all the tendencies and promptings of the old life were
completely and immediately eradicated. It meant, rather, the provision of
a new spiritual life which, if sustained day by day, would result in a
continual crucifixion of the old life. This resulted, in effect, in the life of the
believer becoming a battleground between good and evil, a point of
conflict between the old earthly, carnal nature, and the new heavenly,
spiritual nature. This inner conflict was, indeed, the supreme evidence
that regeneration had occurred, and a reason why the believer, though yet
in the midst of conflict, could rejoice, looking forward to ultimate victory.
But in the strength of God alone could that victory be won, and this is what
Puritanism saw as the chief benefit of Christ's heavenly priesthood.
Admonished to 'come boldly' to the throne of grace, the believer's plea for
divine assistance, together with the intercession of His High Priest, and
fortified by the grace He made available for daily living, would result in
victory at last. So David Dickson says that Christ in His office of High
Priest would 'inform our minds, and persuade our hearts to believe and obey
... [He] will intercede for the reconciled to keep him still in grace'.[14]
Flavel freely admits to 'defects and wants' in the believer's sanctification,
confessing that more faith, love, heavenly-mindedness, self-abasement
and spiritual understanding are necessary than are found by nature even
in the most earnest believer. But Christ, being the author and finisher of
the believer's faith, will, through His intercessory work, 'save to the
uttermost them that come unto God by Him'.[15] There is never a time in
the believer's life when the practical benefits of Christ's priestly ministry
are not available, and the one who has accepted Christ may look forward
with assurance to a continual dispensation of grace and mercy.

If this sounds too much like spiritual idealism, it was balanced by the
realistic acknowledgement of that inherent sinfulness which is part of
man's real nature. Given all the determination and yearning for holiness of
which the most spiritually minded believer might be capable, he still
remained a child of Adam, a sinner by nature and by experience, guilty of
sins of omission as well as of sins of commission, and constantly in need

of forgiveness. As Bunyan pointed out, with some discernment, 'the best saints are most sensible of their sins'.[16] It is at this point that the doctrine of Christ's priesthood again becomes a necessity, and at this point that every true Puritan preacher desired to make it a reality. Flavel declares that in Christ's priestly office 'is contained the grand relief for a soul distressed by the guilt of sin'. When all other spiritual cures have been tried, "Tis the blood of this great sacrifice, sprinkled by faith upon the trembling conscience, that must cool, refresh, and sweetly compose and settle it'.[17] Love emphasises that Christ's presence in heaven as the believer's High Priest is 'to make intercession to God His father in your behalf, that your sins might be pardoned, that your souls might be saved, that your bodies might be raised and received into heaven with Him in glory'.[18] We can pass over for the moment the eschatological implications here, significant though they are in relating the past to the future through the present work of Christ. Suffice it to say that no believer's body could be raised in the resurrection, and no soul saved at last, if his sins were not pardoned now. It is important to recognise that this did not apply to those sins of which the believer had been guilty before accepting Christ and experiencing justification, but more particularly to the sins which he had since committed, and to the guilt which he had incurred since becoming a believer. Until Christ's priestly ministry should cease to be necessary, forgiveness was to be found in Him, the only mediator between God and man, and every Puritan preacher recognised the fundamental importance of Hebrews vii 25, 'He is able to save them to the uttermost that come unto God by Him, seeing He ever liveth to make intercession for them'.

The Two Sanctuaries

Vital as the Epistle to the Hebrews was in establishing the reality of Christ's priestly ministry, it was not the only place in Scripture where the doctrine was to be found. Indeed, those who sought to understand Hebrews were inevitably driven back to the Old Testament by the very nature of the epistle, by its constant allusion to Old Testament characters and practice and its frequent reference to the Old Testament text. We may conveniently recall at this point Thomas Taylor's book, *Christ Revealed*, which explained the Old Testament from a Christological standpoint. Taylor believed that all Old Testament ceremonial was intended to prefigure Christ and the way of salvation in Him, so that it was God's purpose that wherever His people of old might go 'some shadow or other should meet them, and preach unto them either Christ or some grace by Christ, or some duty unto Christ'.[19] Taylor speaks of rites and ordinances foreshadowing the glory of Christ's Kingdom and stirring up the hearts of the people with a sense of sin and a hunger for mercy and forgiveness. It is in this context that Taylor specifically refers to God's command for 'the erection and sanctification of a stately tabernacle with all the costly vessels and holy persons' garments'.[20] This, of all Old Testament symbolism, pointed forward to Christ most completely and most richly, and it was only against this background that the Epistle to the Hebrews could be adequately understood.

Taylor, of course, is by no means alone among Puritan expositors in his understanding of the significance of the Mosaic sanctuary. Samuel Mather believes that the sanctuary is full of significance, but admits that without correct interpretation Old Testament ceremonial 'looks like a heap of unprofitable burdens,' and the sanctuary ritual 'appears like a shambles or butcher's slaughter-house'. Yet consider them 'in their sense and meaning,' he says, 'and everything is full of light and glory'.[21] It was precisely to bring out the hidden purpose of the sanctuary and its services that occupied much of Thomas Taylor's *Christ Revealed* and Samuel Mather's *Figures of the Old Testament* and, beyond those, which took up endless pages in those detailed expositions of Exodus, Leviticus, or Hebrews, which epitomised the solid biblical theology of English Puritanism. Even Thomas Hobbes, whose *Leviathan* of 1651 has ensured its author a lasting place of importance in the history of philosophical thought, speaks at some length in that historic work of the Levitical priesthood and its significance, declaring quite plainly, 'our Saviour Christ's sufferings seem to be here figured as clearly as in the oblation of Isaac, or in any other type of Him in the Old Testament'.[22]

With this statement of Hobbes we have come to the first of two symbolic meanings inherent in the sanctuary and its ritual. John Owen defines it again when he says, 'The tabernacle and all that it contained were typical of Christ.' Owen includes in this definition the ceremonial ritual of the sanctuary, and means that all was to be understood of Christ's work rather than of His person, as he explains when he says,'They were all representative of Christ in the discharge of His office.'[23] The extent to which this rule of interpretation was to be applied is clear from the following statement, again from Owen:

> In all these things did God instruct the Church, by the tabernacle, especially this most Holy Place, the utensils, furniture, and services of it. And the end of them all was to give them such a representation of the mystery of His grace in Christ Jesus, as was meet for the state of the Church before His actual exhibition in the flesh. Hence He is declared in the gospel to be the body and substance of them all.[24]

Without pausing too long over the details, we should note that the seven-branched candlestick, the table of shewbread and the altar of incense, all of which stood in the holy place, that is to say in the first of the two apartments into which the sanctuary was divided, respectively represented Christ as the Light of the World, Christ as the Bread of Life and the merits of Christ added to the prayers and supplications of His saints, making them acceptable to the Father. Of the ever-burning candlestick, Owen declares that it represents 'the fulness of spiritual light that is in Christ Jesus and which by Him is communicated unto the whole Church'.[25] Of the twelve loaves of shewbread Taylor says, 'Here was a figure of Christ the true Bread of life ... the most sufficient food and refreshing of the Church, to continue it in life, strength, and good estate from Sabbath to Sabbath till that eternal Sabbath come'.[26] Even the garments worn by the priests in the execution of their duties were symbolic of Christ. This was particularly true of the garments peculiar to the high priest, and here Thomas Taylor points out that the ephod, the distinctive long white garment, signified Christ's absolute righteousness which alone was acceptable to God. The ephod was made of linen, and could not be made of any other material such as wool or silk, since only a substance which 'riseth out of the earth' could adequately represent that righteousness wrought out in the life which Christ lived on earth.[27] The high priest's robe was trimmed with pomegranates and bells, which together represented the efficacy of Christ as the divine-human Saviour. The pomegranates signified God's wrath against sin as allayed through Christ as the juice of the pomegranate allays the heat of fire, and the bells symbolised the sound of Christ's Gospel in the willing ears of sinners.[28] It is not possible to follow in any further detail the explanation of the sanctuary symbolism found in Taylor's writing alone, to say nothing of the many other seventeenth-century writers who pursued this theme, and in any case we shall return later to the significance of the ritual itself. Perhaps all that needs to be added here is one cryptic phrase from Christopher Love. 'The ceremonial law is all gospel,' he says.[29] It would be difficult to find a Puritan theologian of any repute who would have disagreed with that.

We must now take note of the other principal meaning contained in the sanctuary and its ritual. Well before the turn of the sixteenth century, we find William Perkins writing of 'Christ our High Priest being now in His sanctuary in heaven'.[30] From that point onwards, the existence of a heavenly sanctuary was standard theology among Puritan divines, as those who care to read the contemporary commentaries on the Epistle to the Hebrews will readily discover. Indeed, as the writer of that epistle declared, the heavenly sanctuary is the real sanctuary, 'the true tabernacle, which the Lord pitched, and not man,' the Mosaic tabernacle having been fashioned according to a specifically revealed pattern. Christopher Love therefore speaks of the earthly sanctuary as 'a type of heaven', John Flavel says it was 'the figure of heaven' containing 'types or patterns of heavenly things', and George Lawson declares that 'Christ must minister in the heavenly tabernacle ... a tabernacle with two sanctuaries'[31] (that is, with two apartments, a holy place and a most holy place). For Lawson the earthly tabernacle was 'a type of the heavenly temple',[32] a 'shadow' of something far greater than that built by Moses, even though Israel's sanctuary was built at the command of God according to a pattern revealed to Moses for that purpose. Lawson therefore writes:

> The pattern did only direct him to prescribe, as an earthly tabernacle, so carnal offerings, and none other. Yet these, though but shadows, yet were shadows, and obscure significations of heavenly things. For the

sanctuary was a shadow of an heavenly sanctuary, the priest of a better Priest, the service of a far better service. Therefore the pattern itself showed in the Mount, must have some agreement with these heavenly and better things.[33]

Referring to Exodus xxv 40, the high Anglican Thomas Lushington explains that the tabernacle shown to Moses was the 'model' upon which the earthly sanctuary was to be constructed, the latter being 'a sample or copy of that model'.[34] On Hebrews viii 2, the same writer comments, 'Christ is a minister of the true sanctuary and of the true tabernacle, which is God's heavenly habitation ... the true, perfect, solid, and heavenly sanctuary.'[35] It is only necessary to open the relevant literature at the appropriate pages to discover that Puritan writers saw no valid reason to depart from a literal interpretation of those passages of Scripture which referred to the existence of a sanctuary in heaven.

Such certainty notwithstanding, it is also worth noting that many seventeenth-century interpreters, if not most, stopped short of requiring a sanctuary in heaven which corresponded in exact substance to the sanctuary that had existed on earth. While the reality of the heavenly sanctuary is not to be doubted, it is not necessary to insist that it is constructed of boards and skins and precious stones, any more than it is necessary to insist that a seven-branched candlestick or a table of shewbread literally existed in the heavenly sanctuary now that the reality has appeared in Christ Himself. This is the intent of the words 'shadow' and 'figure' used frequently in Scripture and in the writings of the Puritan expositors. The Mosaic tabernacle, and the temple that later succeeded it, magnificent as they were in their day, were inferior to the reality in heaven. Thomas Lushington takes up this point in his commentary on Hebrews, where he argues that Scripture states that the heavenly sanctuary is not 'made with hands', that is to say, 'not of this building ... because it is not framed of visible materials or any other stuff subject to the eye, whereof all handiworks wrought by man's art are made'.[36] The heavenly sanctuary, real as it undoubtedly is, according to the clear testimony of Scripture, is of a far more excellent nature than its copy constructed on earth by men. Its 'form and matter is of another kind, far more fair, pure, sublime, and stable than this which we see. And to this building pertains that heavenly tabernacle of Christ our high priest, which is the temple and residence of the Most High God.'[37] If, as the writer to the Hebrews declared, the Lord had pitched the heavenly tabernacle and not man, it could only emphasise 'how much this heavenly sanctuary differs from the earthly and exceeds it,' being without question 'far more excellent than that which was framed to the likeness of it out of gross and earthly materials'.[38] It was to this heavenly sanctuary and to the right hand of God that Christ had ascended after the resurrection, to begin a new phase of His redemptive work by assuming the role of mediator and intercessor between God and man. If a Christian would understand the way of salvation more fully, it was essential to remember that the Mosaic sanctuary in all its facets and ministrations symbolised the work of Christ, and that it symbolised that work as it had been accomplished upon earth and as it was now proceeding in heaven itself.

The Priesthood and Ministrations

It was in the ceremonial ritual, constantly re-enacted in the Mosaic sanctuary, and later in the temple at Jerusalem, that the clearest and most elaborate delineation of salvation in Christ was demonstrated. In order for this symbolic ritual to be performed, a ministering priesthood as well as a sacrificial system was essential. The books of Exodus and Leviticus prescribed in great detail the manifold requirements of the ritual itself and the functions of the Levitical priests who administered it on behalf of the people. From the moment of its inception in the wilderness, this system became the focal point of Hebrew worship and remained so until, at the time of the evening sacrifice on the day of the crucifixion, an unseen hand mysteriously rent the veil which separated the holy place from the most holy place, implying that the sacred Ark of the Covenant had been laid open to the gaze of all and that the Shekinah glory had departed. Puritan theologians were in no doubt as to the significance of this event. As John Flavel says, 'It was a notable miracle, plainly showing that all ceremonies were now accomplished and abolished.'[39] It indicated, in effect, that the whole system of sacrifices and priests had pointed to Christ and His redemptive work, and that when type met antitype such symbolic representations of the ultimate reality were no longer necessary. The desire of many Puritans to come to grips with the significance of the sanctuary services is better appreciated if it is remembered that both sacrifices and priests were held to represent various aspects of the total redemptive work of Christ.

It would require a volume in itself to describe adequately the various sacrifices prescribed under the Levitical system, the detailed instructions given for each ritual oblation, and the symbolic meaning of every act in the cultic procedures. Some of the more representative interpretations should, however, be noted. A requirement for many sacrifices, including the burnt offering and the sin offering, was that the individual bringing the offering should lay his hands on the victim's head, an act which was widely held to signify the transference of sin. Abraham Wright, vicar of Oakham in Rutland from 1660, observed, 'The party bringing the sacrifices did by this sign, of laying on his hand, acknowledge that he himself deserved to die, but by the mercy of God he was spared and his desert laid upon the beast.'[40] Thomas Taylor spoke in this connection of 'the imputation of our sins upon Christ,' since 'the death which they [sinners] deserved was by the death of the Messiah (the High Priest of the New Testament) removed off them, and transferred upon the beast.'[41] Gervase Babington, Bishop of Exeter from 1595 and of Worcester from 1597, discerningly commented on the nature of the animals designated for sacrifice in his *Comfortable Notes Upon the Book of Leviticus* (1604). Noting that only domesticated animals were to be brought for sacrifice, Babington explains, 'Not a wild hart, boar, bear, wolf, for these kind of creatures being fierce, savage, cruel, and by force brought to death ... could not be figures and shadows of a meek, mild, sweet and gracious Saviour, who willingly would lay down his life for us.'[42] Concerning the burning of the carcase of the sin offering without the camp, Babington says this signified that Christ 'should be led out of the city to a place appointed, and there suffer'.[43] Andrew Willett similarly interprets the ceremony of carrying the ashes of the burnt offering beyond the confines of the camp, as symbolising the burial of Christ outside the city of Jerusalem.[44] Thomas Taylor points to the bullock prescribed for the sin offering (Leviticus iv 14-15), and says that its slaughter at the entry to the tabernacle signifies that by Christ's death, 'as by a door, an entry is made for us into the Church'.[45] Taylor also mentions that the burnt offering which accompanied the consecration of priests and which was to be consumed in its entirety, depicted 'the ardent love of Jesus Christ who was all consumed as it were with the fire of love and zeal towards mankind upon the cross,' and 'the bitterness of His passion in His whole man, who was as it were consumed wholly with the fire of His Father's wrath due to the sins of man'.[46]

With all the offerings, it is the blood that is of the greatest significance. This is particularly true of the daily sacrifice, offered each morning and each evening on behalf of the congregation as a whole, regardless of any individual offerings which would also be brought during the course of the day. It was through the blood that forgiveness was possible, even as one day the blood of a greater sacrifice would make possible the actual forgiveness of all men's sins. Since the remission of sin was the ultimate object of Christ's death, Flavel argues that it is the 'typical blood' of earthly sacrifices that must be allowed to demonstrate how the blood of the antitypical sacrifice would be effective in taking away the guilt of sin and providing forgiveness for all who would believe.

> That the remission of the sins of believers was the great thing designed in the pouring out of this precious blood of Christ, appears from all the sacrifices that figured it to the ancient Church. The shedding of that typical blood, spake a design of pardon. And the putting of their hands upon the head of the sacrifice, spake the way and method of believing, by which that blood was then applied to them in that way, and is still applied to us in a more excellent way.[47]

The objective provision of blood must be accompanied by a subjective appropriation of its benefits and blessings, and in the sanctuary this included not simply the symbolic act in which the individual concerned laid his hands on the head of the sin offering, thereby acknowledging responsibility for its symbolic death, but also the application of the blood by the priest according to the designated ritual. The sacrificial act, although complete in itself, must be followed by the application of the blood and priestly mediation on behalf of the sinner. It will readily be seen that the work of the priest within the sanctuary, the work of applying the blood of the sacrificial victim, depended on the prior offering of the sacrifice itself upon the altar in the outer court of the tabernacle. There could be no ministration of blood until that blood had been shed, no priestly intercession without a sacrificial offering, and so in the final analysis of the whole sanctuary economy, everything centres around the altar and the sacrifices offered there day by day for a variety of prescribed reasons. It is easy to understand why John Owen states without reservation that the most significant aspect of the sanctuary ritual were the offerings and sacrifices, 'For these did directly represent ... that which was the foundation of the Church, and all the worship thereof, the sacrifice of the Son of God'.[48] Indeed, it was for this very reason that, at the commencement of His ministry, He had been announced by John the Baptist as the Lamb of God, 'Because He fulfilled and perfectly accomplished what was prefigured by the sacrifices of lambs and other creatures'.[49] Owen therefore maintains that the ministration of the blood by the priest adds nothing to the efficacy of the sacrifice itself. Both the incense and the blood that were administered within the holy place 'receive their efficacy and had respect unto the sacrifice offered without'. Consequently, Owen argued what is, after all, an important theological truth, 'It must be granted that the virtue, efficacy, and prevalency of the intercession of the Lord Christ depends upon and flows from His oblation and sacrifice.'[50]

The application of the blood was solely the responsibility of the priests. Indeed, only the priests could enter the sanctuary, all others being forbidden even to approach it upon pain of death. Day by day, therefore, according to the instructions pertaining to the disposition of each prescribed sacrifice, the priest would apply the blood to the horns of the altar, or sprinkle it around the altar, or carry it into the sanctuary itself or sprinkle it before the veil which separated the holy place from the most holy. Through the medium of the sacrificial victim which the sinner brought as a sacrifice, laying his hands upon its head, and taking its life, sin and its resulting penalty were transferred from sinner to sacrifice, and through the medium of the blood, which the mediating priest symbolically applied, forgiveness and atonement were individually appropriated. The important lesson was that in every case, sacrifice and application were both necessary, and that under no circumstance could the guilty sinner provide for his own salvation. The responsibility for making the application of the blood, as we have said, rested upon the priests, particularly upon the high priest, but it was delegated by him to the priesthood as a whole, and as John Owen points out, 'in process of time was wholly devolved on them'.[51] In theory, the high priest could minister in the holy place, but if he did so it was as a priest only and not as the high priest. His peculiar work was restricted to the most holy place and was limited to the Day of Atonement which fell annually on the tenth day of the seventh month. Owen maintains that the office of high priest was 'the principal glory of all Mosaical worship,' and that the function of the high priest was 'the hinge whereon the whole worship of the Judaical Church depended and turned'.[52] Furthermore, the high priest, both in his person and office, was 'the most illustrious type of the Messiah and His office, and the principal means whereby God instructed His Church of old in the mystery of the reconciliation and salvation of sinners'.[53] It would be difficult to find anywhere a more emphatic declaration than this concerning the significance of the high priestly office. Christ, therefore, is not merely a priest in heaven, He is the great High Priest, answering in this respect to the requirements of the type as He answered in all other respects to the requirements of all those types which prefigured Him, and hence performing in heaven on behalf of all who believe and come to Him the antitypical functions of the Levitical high priest.

What those functions were, are best understood in the context of the Day of Atonement. There can be no doubt, as the previous paragraph has indicated and as George Lawson further categorically affirmed, that in the whole sanctuary ritual, the sacrifices offered on the Day of Atonement were 'most eminent' and 'most excellent ... to typify the death of Christ'.[54] Samuel Mather comes even closer to the point when he states that of the entire Hebrew system of worship, 'The most full and complete shadow of the great work of redemption' was that which transpired on the Day of Atonement, 'the high priest representing in all he did, that which Jesus Christ the true High Priest was to do indeed in the fulness of time'.[55] Thomas Lushington's commentary on the Epistle to the Hebrews stated:

> The ordinary priests went only into the first tabernacle, for none but the high priest went into the second. And into the first they went always, that is every day daily, for herein they are opposed to the high priest, who went into the second tabernacle once every year.... Christ therefore being to enter into the inmost and most holy place of heaven, to sit at the right hand of God's throne, must needs pass through the large and common mansion of heaven, as the legal high priest entered the second tabernacle by passing through the first.[56]

The biblical basis for this conclusion is Hebrews ix 2-9 and 11-12, concerning which Lushington argues that since the earthly sanctuary consisted of two apartments, 'there should be answerable a double place in heaven, one a holy place, and the other the most holy'.[57] Even if it is necessary to interpret this in the light of the author's previously cited remarks concerning the nature of the heavenly sanctuary, it nevertheless seems to reflect a widespread belief in seventeenth-century theology. Christopher Love says that the most holy place in the earthly sanctuary was 'a type of heaven', and Flavel that 'the Holy of Holies' was itself the very 'figure of heaven'.[58] Lawson stipulates that in order to understand Hebrews ix 11-12 and Christ's high priestly ministry, it is essential to remember that in the antitype, as in the type, there are three factors, a high priest, a tabernacle with two apartments and a ministry 'to be performed by the High Priest in the inmost sacrary and holiest of all'. Lawson further points out that Hebrews ix 11-12 must be understood in the context of verse 7 of the same chapter, which specifically refers to the typical Day of Atonement.[59] As on that day the whole Levitical system came to an impressive and solemn climax, so with Christ's high priestly ministry in the heavenly sanctuary, the work of human salvation would come to a solemn and irrevocable conclusion.

If we pursue one line of Puritan thought along this particular path, we shall note two further important observations. In the first place, as John Owen points out, the special ceremonial of the Day of Atonement took place after the daily morning sacrifice had been offered, and after the sin offering which the high priest brought on that day as a symbolic atonement for his own sins.[60] In other words, the Day of Atonement ritual was set against the background of salvation, since both the continual daily sacrifice and the sin offering represented the sacrificial death of Christ. Whatever the Day of Atonement might signify in its deepest sense, it signified only in the context of salvation in Christ. The offerings representing the supreme offering for human sin remained efficacious throughout the special services of that special day. Christ's broken body and shed blood provided the framework for whatever the Day of Atonement might signify in the scheme of human redemption.

The second important conclusion to be derived from the Day of Atonement is that it carried with it a legal, or judicial, significance. John Owen says quite plainly that the work of the high priest on the Day of Atonement was threefold, '1. To offer sacrifices to God for the people. 2. To bless the people in the name of God. 3. To judge them.'[61] In some way the atonement symbolised here was synonymous with judgement, and the Day of Atonement signified a work of judgement. It is in this context that Lushington speaks of 'a legal High Priest in the tabernacle,' that Lawson describes Christ serving as a priest and an advocate in the 'court of heaven', and that John Bunyan distinguishes between Christ's work as priest and advocate, by saying that as advocate He is 'to plead according to law,' and that 'He has undertaken to stand up for His people at God's bar, and before that great court, there to plead by the law and justice of heaven.'[62] Whatever else may be concluded of the Day of Atonement ritual and of Christ's priestly ministry, it is beyond dispute that Puritan theology clearly understood it to have a legal, judicial significance. Christ was not only sacrifice and priest according to the daily ritual of the sanctuary, He was also judge and advocate according to the high priestly ministry of the Day of Atonement. John Durant therefore emphasises the judicial significance of Christ's priestly ministry in a practical sense:

When justice hath pleaded, 'I am thus wronged by this creature, and I claim satisfaction at his hand, and I expect it,' etc., Christ stands up and saith, 'It is true, there was a trespass made and such damage done, but I came into court and I satisfied for it. Look upon the table, there lies my blood as payment. Therefore now let the party have his discharge, let a particular acquittal (or *quietus est*) be granted.'[63]

Having thus clarified the judicial significance of Christ's heavenly priesthood, Durant then turns to the concept of impending judgement as part of life and as part of the redemptive process itself: 'It is appointed by statute law, that thou must come to a trial. We must die and come to judgement ... the day of trial hastens apace ... the judge is at the door.'[64] Those who are familiar with Seventh-day Adventist sanctuary theology will agree that the fundamentals of that theology are represented here in the Puritan understanding of the Day of Atonement and the judicial function of the Levitical high priest.

The Consequences of Christ's Priesthood
Few writers of the age rejoiced more over the practical consequences of Christ's priestly ministry in heaven than Samuel Mather. 'How should faith triumph in this,' Mather exulted as he pondered over the benefits flowing earthwards to the Church from her great High Priest in heaven. 'Is not our High Priest in the sanctuary?', he asked, 'Is He not clothed with garments of salvation and righteousness? And doth he not bear the names of His people upon His shoulders and upon His breast before the Lord?'[65] The questions clearly were rhetorical and Mather himself knew the answers well enough. Concerned, however, lest any of his readers might not grasp the truth in its fullness as they might, Mather presses home this point: 'Thy particular concernments, if thou art a believer, are written upon His heart with the pen of a diamond, in such lasting letters of loving-kindness as shall never be blotted out.'[66] Mather's exuberance, understandable and justifiable though it would undoubtedly have appeared to most Puritans, was tempered somewhat by John Flavel's more practical and realistic observation that even 'the most illuminated believers on earth have but dark and crude apprehensions of Christ's intercession work in heaven, or of the way and manner in which it is there performed by Him'.[67] Assurance in the reality of Christ's heavenly ministry as it had been prefigured in the Mosaic ritual, necessary and helpful as it was to the believer in his spiritual pilgrimage on earth, was ever to be balanced by the recognition that the reality could never be totally communicated by the earthly shadow, however clear and distinct that shadow might be. It was a lesson well learnt, and those who could remember it would avoid the embarrassments of speculative interpretation which, sooner or later, always characterise the theology of those guided more by enthusiasm than by discretion. To be fair to Mather, it must be said that he also concluded that since Christ had assumed His high priestly office, all things 'typical and shadowy' had disappeared in the glory of 'the Sun of Righteousness'.[68]

The effects of Christ's ministry in heaven may be described as being both practical and doctrinal. Which of these appears most prominently in Puritan eyes it would be difficult to determine. Certainly the experiential benefits which directly contributed to the daily lives of individual believers were of the utmost importance, and since these have already been examined it will not be necessary to recount them again in any great detail. Suffice it to say that in terms of the believer's relationship to God, Christ's priestly ministry meant forgiveness of sin and access to the Father. 'By Him all pardons and spiritual blessings are dispensed and disposed of; and all the promises are performed by Him and in His name, and for His merit,'[69] says Lawson. It meant also the assurance of salvation. 'Christ not only beginneth the believer's salvation, but perfecteth it also. He doth not work a part of man's salvation, and leave the rest to his own merits ... but perfecteth it Himself, even to the uttermost,'[70] David Dickson explains. It meant strength in the daily warfare against the flesh and the Devil. 'Let me advise thee to go to Jesus Christ,' Flavel says when considering the trials and temptations cast in the path of believers by the great adversary, 'Entreat Him to rebuke and command him off. Beg Him to consider thy case, and say "Lord, dost not thou remember how thine heart was once grieved, though not defiled by his assaults?" '[71] And it meant, ultimately, the hope of glory: 'This administration shall not be altered, but shall continue till death shall be destroyed. And then Christ shall deliver up this commission, and God shall be all in all.'[72] In the end it is the Scottish theologian, David Dickson, who summarises the experiential blessings of Christ's priesthood most adequately:

> We have Christ for a priest to us, whose lips always preserve knowledge, in whom are hid all the treasures of wisdom and knowledge, who will inform our minds and persuade our hearts to believe and obey, who will reconcile by His once offered sacrifice, the believer; will intercede for the reconciled to keep him still in grace; will bless us with all spiritual blessings; will take our prayers, thanksgiving, and the spiritual sacrifice of all the good works of our hands, and wash the pollutions from them; will offer them in our name, with the incense and perfume of His own merits; and lead ourselves in, where our lamps shall be furnished, and our table filled, till we go into heaven; and there He will welcome us in a mansion prepared for us.[73]

It was the greater tragedy, perhaps, with grace so freely and readily available, that many would still attempt to find the way to life through works and human merit.

It was precisely this danger which emphasised the doctrinal significance of Christ's priestly ministry in heaven. For all true Protestants, and Puritans were nothing if they were not that, Christ had become the sole and all-sufficient priest of the Christian Church. Had not Paul declared that there was but one mediator between heaven and earth, between God and man (I Timothy ii 5)? And did not Scripture further declare that Christ, being eternal, had an unchangeable priesthood which could not be transferred to another (Hebrews vii 24)? To introduce any other mediator or any other system of mediation was to strike at the very heart of Christ's redemptive work. David Dickson perceived this readily, and laid open the real issue: 'If a man join anything meritorious unto Christ's priesthood, or any mediator for intercession, beside Him, or seeketh by his own works to purchase salvation, he denieth Christ to be able to save him to the

uttermost.'[74] It is not only the matter of meritorious works which chall-
enges Christ's ability to save, but also the introduction of an alternative
mediator or mediatrix, be it saints, or angels, or human priesthood, or even
the mother of Jesus herself. The Levitical priesthood passed from person
to person as a result of death, but Christ's priesthood cannot be thus
transferred to any other person. 'Neither death nor any other infirmity can
interrupt His Office,' Dickson declared. 'To make plurality of priests in
Christ's priesthood, vicars, or substitutes, or in any respect, partaker of the
office with Him, is to pre-suppose that Christ is not able to do that office
alone,'[75] he continues. The real problem, particularly for those early
Protestants who remembered the pit from which they had been dug, was
that all this was again of the essence of Antichrist, particularly in the sense
in which Henry Denne defined it. 'I conceive the great Antichrist to be that
mystical body of iniquity which opposeth Jesus Christ,' he says, and
'Whosoever doth seek to destroy that which the Lord Jesus hath built up, or
to build up that which the Lord hath plucked down, the same is against
Christ, and insomuch a member of the great Antichrist.'[76] It was not
difficult in seventeenth-century England to see how this should be
interpreted. Any religious system proposing a form of mediation or
intercession which in any way detracted from the sovereign work of Christ
must, *ipso facto*, be of the spirit of Antichrist. The New Testament plainly
taught that each individual could have direct access to the Father through
the Son, and that the Son's high priestly office had forever disannulled all
forms of human priesthood. What further evidence for the unscriptural and
misleading nature of the Roman system could true Protestants of the day
require?

The Puritan doctrine of Christ's priesthood also demonstrated the
invalidity of another cardinal point of the Roman version of Christianity. If
Christ was bodily present in heaven, as the New Testament said He had
been since the resurrection, how could He at the same time be bodily
present in the sacrifice of the mass? Earlier generations of English
Protestants had been concerned to arrive at biblical truth, even if it had
meant frank discussion and polemical argument. A century or so later,
many were prepared to take a similar stand. The Roman concept of
transubstantiation, or the doctrine of the real presence, held that, with the
elevation of the host in the mass, the bread and wine were miraculously
transformed into the body and blood of the Saviour, and that Christ was as
truly and bodily present in the sacrament as He had been upon the cross.
To Protestants, this belief seemed as illogical as it did blasphemous. 'If
there were no other argument to overthrow this opinion but this,' Christopher Love said of Christ's actual presence in heaven, 'then that opinion of
transubstantiation is hereby confuted. Christ's body cannot be in heaven
and on the earth both at one time.'[77] David Pareus, the continental
theologian whose commentary on the Book of Revelation was read widely
in England, comes to the same conclusion from Revelation i 7. At the Last
Day Christ will descend bodily and visibly from heaven, and since it is the

teaching of Scripture that He remains in heaven until that day, it is not possible that He can be corporeally present at any time on earth prior to His second coming, much less in the sense of the mass which may require His actual presence in several places at a given time. Pareus concludes that this is a 'strong reason to prove that His body is not in the meantime invisibly hid in, under, or about their host, altar, or chalice'.[78]

It will have become evident to those who have followed the arguments of this chapter, that the priestly ministry of Christ, the inherent symbolism of the Mosaic tabernacle, and the significance of a heavenly sanctuary, were not matters that could peremptorily be dismissed from the body of faith by Puritans. They could not even be treated lightly. These were not peripheral aspects of the faith once delivered unto the saints, but were of the very substance of that faith. Together they occupied considerable space in the revealed Word of God. They concerned Christ's work as the all-sufficient and ever-living Saviour of the human race, and the continuing revelation of divine purpose in salvation. They influenced the daily life of a believer and were inextricably bound up with the doctrine and the liturgy of the Church. They represented something fundamental and imperishable in the Protestant interpretation of the Christian Gospel. Little wonder, then, that Isaac Watts, who stood so firmly in the later Puritan theological tradition, could write with such clarity and conviction of the theme we have examined in this chapter:

Jesus, my great High Priest, offered His blood and died;
My guilty conscience seeks no sacrifice beside:
His powerful blood did once atone,
And now it pleads before the throne.

It is self-evident that only a mind which had grasped the theological truth of Christ's high priestly ministry and which knew its significance experientially could write enduring lines at once so simple and so profound.

7. GOSPEL OBEDIENCE

The ten commandments spoken by God from Mount Sinai are set apart from all the other commands of God recorded in the Bible, by their very nature and the manner of their delivery. They themselves are the best evidence of their enduring character. Man's moral nature responds to them with assent, and it is impossible for an enlightened Christian to imagine a condition or circumstance — God still being God, and man still being a moral creature — where they would not be operative.

Seventh-day Adventists Answer Questions on Doctrine (1957)
p.121

It begets faith, it regenerates, it nourisheth, it makes to be growing, it enlightens, it gives heavenly saving wisdom, it restores and strengthens the soul, it exciteth a lively firm consolation, it joyeth and refresheth the heart, it kindleth a love to God in the heart, it furnisheth with armours against temptations and assaults, it doth guard against captious sophistry and treachery, it leadeth to life, and to eternal salvation. Nothing may be added to it, or taken from it. Moses leads to Christ, and Christ sends to Moses.

Francis Bampfield *All in One* (1677) p.145

The title of this chapter is taken from the theologically conservative Richard Baxter and not, as might conceivably be imagined, from a source more inclined to legalistic sectarianism. To put the phrase in its context, Baxter says, 'Faith is the way to Christ, and gospel-obedience, or faith and works, the way for those to walk in that are in Christ.'[1] This is a useful introduction to the theme we are now to examine, and it opens the way to two propositions of doctrinal significance. Acceptance of Christ's Gospel brings with it ethical and practical obligations, certain duties to be performed in one's relationship to God and man. And the nature of those obligations is to be understood as obedience to the divine will which is revealed in precept and command. Obedience is the sequel to faith, law the concomitant of grace.

The function of God's law in the Christian life, and the relationship of that law to grace and to the Gospel as revealed in Christ, are issues which have claimed the attention of the Church from its earliest days. They are present to a considerable extent in the epistles of Paul, often reflecting actual situations in the Christian Church which made those writings necessary. The provisions of grace and the claims of law are treated elsewhere in Scripture, of course, raising fundamental questions to which answers must be provided if the nature of Christian faith is not to be misunderstood. Christians in the Puritan era understood this as clearly as their brethren in other generations, perhaps more clearly than some, if Dr. E.F. Kevan's comprehensive study of this topic in Puritan theology is a reliable guide. That study, particularly as it is reflected in a condensed form, *Keep His Commandments* (1964), is recommended as a sound presentation of the biblical doctrine as understood in Puritan teaching.

What did Scripture mean when it spoke of 'law'? Did it always mean the same thing? Was the Old Testament a dispensation of law and the New Testament a dispensation of grace, and were they thus inherently contradictory? What place did the Ten Commandments have in the life of a believer? Did Jesus, as some had maintained, dispense with law by His death upon the cross, if not by specific assertion? And how was James ii 12 to be interpreted, which said that Christians would one day be judged by the law of the Ten Commandments? These were important questions then as now, and in tracing Puritanism's answers it is possible that we shall discover some emphases which are still relevant to the life and witness of Christ's Church.

The Nature of Divine Law

To begin with, it was widely recognised by the Puritans that when the Bible spoke of 'law' it was not always to be defined in the same way. The concept of divine law so permeated the whole of Scripture and related to so many important biblical teachings that it was always deemed necessary to clarify the use of the term. If one approached Scripture without being aware of the various meanings which law might have, misunderstandings would easily occur. Furthermore, it was not possible to understand law in the New Testament, without understanding it first in the Old Testament.

In a general sense, the basic Hebrew word for law, *torah*, might mean one of several things. John Owen is quite right in saying that the Jews themselves generally understood it to refer to the Pentateuch, 'the whole five books of Moses', or to 'all precepts that they can gather out of them anywhere'.[2] Law, then, might mean the first five books of the Old Testament or it might designate any specific command which was to be found within those books. George Downham makes a wider application however: 'By the Law in many places is understood the whole doctrine of God contained in the Scriptures of the Old Testament.'[3] So law, as a general term, is not restricted to the Pentateuch, but may also be used of the Old Testament in its entirety. It is in this context that Downham adds, 'The evangelical promises made in the Old Testament are contained in the Law,' and 'the promises of remission of sins, though they be in the prophets, do not belong to the law, but to the gospel'.[4] Thus in the Old Testament both law and grace are found together, law containing gospel, and gospel containing law, and all under the general category of law. George Lawson goes even further, declaring that what is 'explained in other parts of the books of Moses, especially in Deuteronomy [and] in the prophets,' is 'most of all' set forth 'in the New Testament, where it is explained by our blessed Saviour, and the duties thereof pressed by Him, and the apostles, upon all Christians'.[5] In its broadest meaning, then, law applies to the whole Bible and in this sense can therefore be understood fundamentally as the revealed will of God. This may be a rather wider meaning than is normally accorded to law, but it is to the credit of Puritan theologians that they arrived at the underlying meaning of an important biblical concept. Hence John Downame speaks of duty and obedience as the 'main scope and end of all our actions ... that we may hallow and glorify God's name, by doing His will'.[6]

In a more obvious sense, however, law refers to the direct commands of God contained in Scripture and set forth initially in the writings of Moses. It is important to recognise in this connection the distinction made by John Owen, Andrew Willett and John White, to mention three of many seventeenth-century theologians whose names could be cited at this point, between the various laws of the Pentateuch. Not all these laws were of the same character, had the same function, or were to be applied to the same extent. It was normal for Puritans to distinguish between moral, ceremonial, and civil or judicial law. Owen divided the whole Mosaic code into these three sections, 'This whole law is generally distributed into three parts: first, the moral; secondly, the ceremonial; thirdly, the judicial part of it.'[7] The moral law as contained in the Ten Commandments concerned man's spiritual relationship to God and his moral relationship to his fellowmen and hence was, as John White said, 'communicable to all men of what nation soever'.[8] The ceremonial law contained the requirements of the sacrificial system with its ritual and its feasts, and hence applied specifically to the Jews. The civil law likewise concerned the Jewish nation, as 'a state, not as a Church,' to use John White's phrase. These were the laws of health and sanitation, or marriage and property, which pertained to the day-to-day life of the Israelites. While the civil law was not binding in a moral sense, particularly on Gentiles, there was much in it of permanent value to mankind as a whole, and White further observes, 'We cannot conceive that He [God] hath taken so much care to preserve them in vain, nor indeed for any other end than that which is the scope of the rest of the Scriptures, that they might be for our learning and instruction.' White's conclusion is that 'they are preserved unto us for some special use'.[9]

Puritan writers generally felt that it was essential to understand the difference between the moral and the ceremonial law. Since the latter pointed specifically to Christ and the way of salvation to be revealed in Him, it obviously had a more restricted function and a more limited duration. Andrew Willett describes how the moral law was given by God Himself, on Sinai, at one specific time, and says that the commandments were engraved on stone 'to show that they were perpetual,'[10] and that they applied to all people in all times. He then points out that the ceremonial law was given by Moses, from the tabernacle, at various times, and that it was written on scrolls 'not to endure always,' and that it concerned only the Jews.[11] Further, while the claims of the moral law had been binding before it had been delivered in written form, the ceremonial law had been of effect only since it had been given. He might also have added that while the ceremonial law was kept at the side of the Ark of the Covenant within the most holy place of the tabernacle, the two tables.of stone containing the Decalogue were deposited within the Ark itself. Theophilus Brabourne, whom we shall meet again shortly, asked some pointed questions in this respect: 'Will you jumble together the morals and ceremonials, as if both were in the Decalogue, and spoken by God to the people on the mount? Do you read of any ceremonial spoken by God on the mount? Or writ in the tables of stone?'[12] It all told of a fundamental difference between moral law and ceremonial law, and John White sums up by saying that 'from the ceremonial law we are wholly freed by the coming of Christ into the world, who is the body of those shadows'.[13] Thomas Adams concisely states, 'The ceremonial was referred to Him, performed of Him, fulfilled in Him, extinguished by Him.'[14] If that was true, the limited function of the ceremonial law terminated with the coming of Christ in the flesh.

The moral law, on the other hand, was deemed to be in an entirely different category, 'a perfect, immutable, and perpetual rule of righteousness ... universally obligatory to all the sons of men'.[15] 'Take a brief view of the Ten Commandments,' John Ball advised, 'are they not plain, pure ... perfect, just, extending to all, binding the conscience, and reaching to the very thoughts?'[16] The reason for this high view of the Decalogue is not difficult to find. Not only did it relate to the inner nature of man himself and to basic moral conduct, but also to the nature of God. To Puritans the moral law was nothing less than a transcript of the character of God, and the Decalogue a verbalisation of the essence of the divine nature. 'To find fault with the Law, were to find fault with God,'[17] says Ralph Venning. 'For such as God is that made the law, such is that law which He made,'[18] John Dod and Richard Cleaver say in their popular *Exposition of the Ten Commandments*, a work which enjoyed numerous editions in its day. The expression of God's character and will in the moral law is so 'consonant to that eternal justice and goodness in Himself,' that any deviation from that law or any annulment of its claims would mean that God was to 'deny His own justice and goodness'.[19] The law defines sin, as is clearly evident from Paul, so that when a man sins, he transgresses moral law. George Lawson points out in this respect that, 'When man swerves from this rule, he forsakes the wisdom and righteousness of God, and follows his own imagination and the suggestion of the devil.'[20] This must mean that law reflects the righteous character of the Lawgiver, and that conduct not in accord with the moral law reflects the unrighteous nature of fallen humanity. The apostle Paul declared that the law was holy and spiritual (Romans vii 12, 14), and this could only be interpreted to mean that it reflected the glory of a holy and spiritual God. Being then a revelation of the divine character, the moral law contained in the Ten Commandments was intrinsically eternal, never to be repealed or disannulled, a point well emphasised by Francis Bampfield: 'There never was, never will be, a repeal of this law, which is so lively an expression of the holy, righteous nature of Elohim Himself.'[21]

Since it is the moral law which will claim our attention for the remainder of the present chapter, it will be well to note two or three further aspects of Puritan discussion of the Decalogue — necessary for an adequate grasp of the whole subject. One of the most basic truths regarding the Ten Commandments was that it was no new law which had been written on stone by the finger of God at Sinai. The moral law had been written in the heart of man from creation, and merely 'renewed and restored by Moses upon mount Sinai'.[22] This law was 'imprinted in the beginning in the hearts of our first parents'.[23] Asked how the law had thus been communicated to Adam, James Ussher replied, 'It was chiefly written in his heart at his creation, and partly also uttered to his ear in Paradise. For unto him was given both to know good and also to be inclined thereunto. . . . There was something likewise outwardly revealed, as his duty to God, in the sanctification of the Sabbath; to his neighbour, in the institution of marriage; and to himself in his daily working about the garden.'[24] Although John White is not so sure of the method of communication, 'perhaps not by word of mouth, but written in his heart,' he is equally certain that 'moral precepts were given unto Adam,' asserting that the moral law is 'most ancient, most general, and most perpetual . . . being given to our first parents in Paradise, that is, to man as soon as he had any being'.[25] It is this law, given originally to Adam, that is sometimes called natural law, and which is described by Thomas Adams as 'knowledge of certain principles tending to live well . . . planted by God in man, and teaching him how to worship his Maker'.[26] Baxter explains that God has the right to govern man by virtue of creation and redemption, and that He so rules 'by a law which is partly natural . . . and that this law is *norma actionum moralium*,' that is, the norm of moral conduct.[27] To a large extent the fall obliterated natural law as it existed in man from creation, and indwelling sin has further dimmed it in Adam's descendants, so that of God's commandments, 'not one of them is found remaining, since the fall, upon the heart of any natural man, complete, full, and fair, but singularly defaced, blotted and blurred like the limbs of an old worn picture'.[28] Hence the promulgation of the law in a verbalised form at Sinai was not the creation of a new law, but the restatement of that law which had originally been written into the very being of man at creation.

It should also be understood that in Puritanism the Decalogue is not thought of as a catalogue of laws, each with its own specific purpose, but rather as the expression of one all-inclusive law. When Adam sinned he transgressed *the* law rather than *a* law, that is law in its wholeness and its entirety. Adam's transgression was a 'breach of the whole law of God,'[29] Ussher holds. In John Ball's view the Ten Commandments are 'an abridgement of the whole law, the full exposition whereof is to be found in the books of the Prophets, and Apostles'.[30] George Downham provides some support for this view by comparing the Ten Commandments to the reasoned stages of an argument. 'If any one be false, though all the rest be true, the whole proposition is false, and to be denied,' [31] he says. It is in this sense that the words of the Apostle James are to be understood, 'For whosoever shall keep the whole law, and yet offend in one point, he is guilty of all' (James ii 10). All this is because the law is a unity, a totality, a transcript of something which itself is indivisible, the character of the Lawgiver Himself.

If the Decalogue was the expression of moral law in its wholeness as it reflected the character of the Lawgiver, it was also the quintessence of that law. One writer speaks of the Ten Commandments as 'the sum of the law', another of the Decalogue as comprising 'the heads of duties to be performed both to God and man'.[32] This is intended to convey a sense of the comprehensive scope of the moral law in its relationship to conduct and behaviour. Indeed, only as the Decalogue is interpreted in this way, can it be wholly relevant to the wide spectrum of human life, and only thus can it be brought to bear on the whole human encounter with sin. Ussher gives three rules for the application of the law in this way:

1. Whatsoever the law commandeth, it forbiddeth the contrary, and whatsoever it forbiddeth it commandeth the contrary. . . .

2. Whatsoever the law commandeth or forbiddeth in one kind, it commandeth or forbiddeth all of the same kind, and all the degrees thereof. . . .

3. Whatsoever the law commandeth or forbiddeth, it commandeth or forbiddeth the causes thereof, and all the means whereby that thing is done or brought to pass. . . .[33]

The application of the moral law in these broad terms is admirably illustrated by William Perkins' exposition of the Ten Commandments, in which he analyses the scope of each commandment, relating it to experience in the broadest terms. Two examples of Perkins' treatment of the Decalogue will illustrate the point. Of the fifth commandment Perkins says:

He breaks this commandment,

That thinks but a thought in his mind tending to the dishonour and contempt of his neighbour.

That mocks or reviles, or beats his superiors, Gen. ix 22.

That disobeys their lawful commandments, Rom. i 30.

That is unthankful to parents, and will not relieve them if needs be, II Tim. iii 2.

That disobeys God, to obey them, Act. iv 19.

That exalts himself above the Magistrate, II Thess. ii 4.

That serves his master with eye-service, Col. iii 22.

That governs his family, and those which are under him, negligently, I Tim. iii 4.

That is slack in punishing faults, I Sam. ii 23.
That is too rigorous in speeches and punishments, Eph. vi 9.
That marrieth without parents consent.
That chooseth his calling without parents consent, Num. xxx.
That thinks better of himself than of others, Rom. xi 10.
That despiseth aged persons, Lev. xix 32.[34]
And of the sixth commandment, Perkins is equally specific:
He breaks this commandment,
That thinks but a thought in his heart tending to the hurt of his neighbours life.
That bears malice to another, I John iii 15.
That is given to hastiness, Matt. v 22.
That useth inward fretting and grudging, Jam. iii 14.
That is froward of nature, hard to please, Rom. i 30.
That is full of rancour and bitterness, Eph. iv 31.
That derides and scorns others, Gen. xxi 9, Gal. iv 29.
That useth bitter words and railings, Prov. xii 18.
That useth contending by words or deeds, Gal. v 20.
That useth chiding and crying out, Eph. iv 31.
That is given to make complaints of his neighbour in all places, Jam. v 9.
That is a fighter, Jam. iv 1.
That hurts or maims his neighbours body, Exod. xxi 24.
That will not forgive an offence, Matt. v 23.
That will forgive, but not forget.
That doth fare well himself, but gives not alms to relieve the poor, Luke xvi 19.
That useth cruelty in punishing malefactors, Deut. xxii 26.
That denies the servants or labourers wages, Jam. v 4.
That holds back the pledge, Ezek. xviii 7.
That sells by divers weights and measures.
That removes the land mark, Prov. xxii 28.
That by his looseness of life is an occasion why others sin.
That moves contention and debate, Rom. i 29.
That being a Minister teacheth erroneously.
That teacheth slackly, Jer. xlviii 10.
That teacheth not at all, I Tim. iii 2.
That hinders mans salvation any way, Matt. xxiii 13.
That seeks private revenge.[35]
It is only necessary to so apply each of the Ten Commandments to life in this way to see why the Puritans believed that the moral law was to be regarded as the standard of righteous living. There were few indeed within the ranks of Puritanism who would have challenged Perkins' basic proposition that the moral law in its essence touched every aspect of human behaviour and human relationship. Baxter expressed an acceptable view when he said, 'The knowledge of the law is the beginning of

wisdom, and no man is wise without the law.'[36]

Christ and the Law
It would be repetitious to argue that Christian belief stands or falls with the person of Jesus Christ. The truth of that statement is so axiomatic that in a work which examines the historico-biblical foundation of a theologically conservative Christian movement it hardly needs restating. Nonetheless, there has been some confusion regarding Christ's attitude to law, and that not only in more recent times but also in the Puritan era, as Christopher Love implied when despairing of the 'abominable errors' which had appeared in England, specifically 'the abolishing of the moral law'.[37] Whether or not the accusation was completely fair cannot concern us here, but Thomas Taylor listed twelve antinomian errors of the day, the first of which was that 'Christ came to abolish the moral law'.[38] Certainly the view that Christ did abrogate the law has persisted through the years in one form or another, and it would be a serious omission if some attempt were not made to establish the position of Puritan orthodoxy on this point. A hint of the answer we may anticipate is contained in William Strong's assertion that 'the gospel requires obedience as well as the law, and there is a law of Christ to be kept'.[39] The question is whether 'the law of Christ' is synonymous with the moral law enshrined in the Ten Commandments.

The distinction between the moral and ceremonial laws, already noted, is given an important new dimension in the works of many Puritan writers. We may take Richard Baxter as typical in this respect. Writing of 'God's laws' in the Old Testament, Baxter refers to the ceremonial law as 'the law given by Moses to the Church and commonwealth of the Jews,' and to the moral law as the 'law of grace by Jesus Christ'.[40] This choice of words is not accidental, for the more thorough Puritans held that the moral law had in fact been delivered at Sinai by Christ, as He had co-existed in equality with the Father from all eternity. It was therefore quite correct to speak of the Ten Commandments as Christ's commandments, and the Decalogue (literally, the 'ten words', from the Greek *deka* and *logos*) as the written word of the Incarnate Word, since both were the embodiment of the character and will of God. Hence, the New Testament was able to apply Psalm xl 6-8 to Christ, who had come to do the will of God and in whose innermost being the divine law had been written. Francis Bampfield had derived much satisfaction over the years from studying the Bible and discerning how God's revelation to man had been made through Christ. 'It was Jehovah Christ Himself, who, by His Spirit from His Father, wrote upon the two tables the words of the covenant, the ten words or precepts',[41] Bampfield explains. Christ's place in Old Testament type and prophecy has already been examined, as have also Bampfield's own well-defined views of Christ as the JHWH-creator of the Old Testament. It is not surprising, then, to discover that Bampfield regards Christ as the mediator between God and man at Sinai. This would be in harmony with biblical Christology as a whole, and consistent with Bampfield's own understanding of the person and work of Christ in relation to the plan of salvation. He therefore adds:

> Jehovah Christ as mediator did Himself at mount Sinai proclaim this law of the ten words.... It is He who is our one and only lawgiver. It is He whose voice then shook the earth at the mount. It is He who was from His father an angel by delegated office, sent for this, as for many other purposes, to be with Moses in the wilderness. It is He who wrote this law of the ten words in the two tables. It is He who brought His people Israel out of Egypt.... It is He who came down upon that Mount attended gloriously with ten thousands of His holy angels, and promulgated this law.[42]

If this were so, it would hardly be likely that Christ, when He came in the flesh, would disannul the law which He Himself had proclaimed on Sinai for the lasting benefit of mankind as a whole.

There is also the more explicit question of what Christ actually taught concerning the law. John Goodwin says that the moral law 'hath received a new authority and establishment from Christ,' and that the conscience of a believer is bound 'under the gospel to the observation thereof'.[43] Baxter is also convinced that 'this law is not abrogated by Christ,' and that He never intended even to give the impression that it should be. On the contrary, Christ came to 'stablish the law ... and satisfy and glorify the justice of the Legislator'.[44] These views are certainly in harmony with the more obvious statements of Jesus as recorded in the New Testament. One thinks in this respect of the Sermon on the Mount, where Christ emphatically declared that He had not come to destroy the law but to fulfil it, and that until the dissolution of heaven and earth the law would remain operative and relevant to the lives of those who would claim to be His followers (Matthew v 17-18). That He was speaking of the Ten Commandments is evident from the verses which follow, in which He gives the commandments the kind of wide application we saw earlier in the writing of William Perkins.

Jesus had further established the law by giving it a broad spiritual dimension in answering the probing question of the Pharisees concerning which of the commandments in the law was the greatest. Jesus replied that the whole law hung on two commandments, the first to love God with all one's heart, the second to love one's neighbour as oneself (Matthew xxii 36-40). It is little short of a travesty of logic and reason to suggest that in making this assertion, Jesus intended to convey the idea that the moral law had been suspended. Baxter could say, 'The Ten Commandments are summed up by Christ into these two.'[45] Jesus is pointing to the fundamental nature of the law in defining the two tables of the Decalogue as the expression of a relationship of love to God and to man. Lawson fully agrees that 'love is the whole law,' but not in the sense that love dispenses with obedience:

> To love God above all, is the first and great commandment of the first table. To love our neighbour as ourselves, is the last commandment of

the second table. These two are purely moral, especially the former, and the rest are such by participation, as before. Therefore, the first is said to be the great commandment, the last to be like it.[46]

Love is the basis of true obedience, and if a man loves God that love will be seen in willing obedience to the first table of the law, and if he loves his neighbour it will be seen in willing obedience to the requirements of the second table. The 'great commandment' does not supersede the Ten Commandments. It summarises them and puts them in the context of grace and love. Daniel King, the Baptist pastor at Coventry and Warwick c. 1656, therefore asks, 'Did not the great commandment ... take in the particular precepts, the first, second, third and fourth commandments of the first table? And did not the second commandment, "Love thy neighbour", etc., take in the fifth ... and the sixth ... etc?'[47] King's argument is that the whole moral law may be summarised in one word, to say nothing of the two commandments expressed in the teaching of Jesus. So King asks again, 'Did Christ mean to cut off the particular precepts, when He said that these were the commandments?'[48] Does the fact that Christ reiterated the underlying principle of the moral law in two succinct statements dispense with the more detailed formulation of the law itself? Does love renounce obedience? King and Baxter and Downham do not think so, nor do the vast majority of their contemporaries. Together they cry out with the apostle Paul, 'Yea, we establish the law' (Romans iii 31).

The idea that Christ was the lawgiver at Sinai has an important sequel in the New Testament. Christ, who was ruler in Israel, is now the ruler of His Church, and the lordship of Christ over His people becomes an important aspect of His Messianic office. As Creator, He brought His people into existence. As Redeemer, He bought them back from the thralldom of sin. As Priest, He mediates on their behalf in heaven. As King, He will rule over them to all eternity. But as Lord, He has the right to rule currently in the lives of all who have submitted to His authority. All rulers dispense laws and require obedience, but the difference with Christ is that 'He is such a lawgiver as writes His own will in the heart. This is what we may expect from this Lordship of Christ,'[49] says Richard Sibbes. He who once wrote the law on tables of stone, is able, yea, anxious to write it again in the heart of each follower. The result is obedience from the heart, the obedience of love, Gospel-obedience in very truth. It is what Baxter means when he says 'We are created to good works in Christ Jesus,' and it is why William Perkins can say with such confidence, 'We are sure that we know Christ ... if we keep His commandments.'[50] This is the practical outworking of the theological truth which Puritans asserted when they said that the Christian 'is *ennomos*, in the law, or within the law to Christ'.[51] The Christian is not 'under the law', or 'without the law', or 'above the law', but 'in the law', if in Christ. Thomas Manton says of the 'law of liberty', 'I am not *anomos*, without the law, but *ennomos*, under the law to Christ.'[52] He is, as the Greek implies, 'in the law'. The Christian's acceptance of Christ as Master implied a willingness to live in harmony with the law that He would write in the heart.

If the law expressed God's will for human conduct in the present, by the same token it had implications for the future. Indeed, it might be said that the whole redemptive purpose of God moves towards the future, and will only be completely fulfilled as the events of the future come to pass. Puritans knew that future events as outlined in the Bible included judgement, and it is true to say that few generations of Christian believers in the English Church were more aware of impending judgement than those who lived in the seventeenth century. The extent of the eschatological expectations which surged through English Protestantism between 1600 and 1700 was quite remarkable. For much of that century the majority of Christian believers expected Christ to come in glory as He had promised to come at the end of the age. John Seagar, a Presbyterian minister in Devon who, in 1650, wrote a book about Christian hope and the future, strongly believed that 'the certainty of this world's dissolution should persuade us to be universal in our obedience'.[53] It was not sufficient, in view of future events, to have a 'bare and naked profession' of the Christian faith. Seagar urges all Christians to 'strive to practise every known duty prescribed in God's word'. The future affected the present life of believers by calling them to holiness and obedience. With regard to the law, the most important future event was judgement, and this explains the reason for Seagar's insistence on obedience to duty and ethical living of a high standard. Men are accountable to God, and will one day be called to judgement. When that day arrives, every man will be required to give an account of his life, and, if we are to follow Baxter, the standard by which men will be judged in that day is the moral law of God: 'And so Christ, at that great assize, . . . as He governed by a law, so will He judge by a law, . . . so that the mouths of all may be stopped, and the equity of His judgement may be manifest to all.'[54] Christ had not abrogated the law, or even modified it. As long as time should last, the moral law would remain, calling men to obedience and duty, and confronting them at the end as they stood before the judgement seat of Christ. That being so, it was in every man's eternal interest to live in harmony with the law, to submit to the lordship of Christ, and to permit Him to write His own eternal law upon the heart.

The Purpose of the Law: (a) for man in general
If Puritans were sure of one thing concerning the moral law, it was that its first function was to lead sinners to salvation. 'The usefulness of the law,' John Flavel said, is 'to bring souls to Jesus Christ'.[55] It was from a consideration of the law, John White similarly contended, that the natural man is 'brought to prize and value Christ above all things in the world'.[56] Paul's statement about the law being a 'schoolmaster to bring us unto Christ' (Galatians iii 24), was applied by George Downham principally to 'natural and unregenerate men . . . discovering unto them their own damnable estate in themselves . . . that so they might be forced to seek for

salvation out of themselves in Christ'.[57] Actually, the phrase Downham uses, 'a schoolmaster unto Christ', merits comment, since it reflects the sense of the Greek text more accurately than the biblical rendering quoted above. The Greek word *eis*, meaning 'unto' or 'with a view to', is qualified in the Authorised Version by the phrase 'to bring us', so that the text reads, as above, 'to bring us unto Christ' rather than 'unto Christ', which would be a more correct translation. Downham omits the qualifying phrase, and says simply 'a schoolmaster unto Christ'. His meaning is that the law prepares the way for Christ, it points to Him and to salvation in Him, but it does not actually 'bring us' to Him. There is no saving merit in the law. It is merely a preparative, but in no sense does it implement the saving merits of Christ Himself. This meaning is more in harmony with the sense of the original text. But how did the law serve in this capacity? In what way did it function 'with a view to' the salvation available in Jesus Christ?

It may be said that there were three steps in this process. In the first place the law revealed sin. It made men aware of sin. It underlined the existence of sin, and defined its very character. It described the nature of the disorder which necessitated such a costly remedy. The law was given, John Owen said, 'that it might discover sin'.[58] Sin already existed, of course, but by the law it would become unmistakably apparent. Flavel uses a helpful analogy. The law is like a mirror 'to show us the face of sin'. Until that has happened, 'till God show you the face of sin in the glass of the law ... till you have had some sick nights and sorrowful days for sin, you will never go up and down seeking an interest in the blood of His sacrifice.'[59] Theophilus Brabourne argues from Romans v 20, 'The law entered that the offence might abound.' The law underlines the extent of sin, it demonstrates 'the exceeding sinfulness of sin', to quote Paul again. 'It exasperates the sinner,' Brabourne says, 'and so makes sin to be exceedingly out of measure sinful.'[60] This is the function of the law in the natural man. Flavel, again, points out that while the law is unable to provide righteousness, 'it can convince us that we are unrighteous. It cannot heal, but it can open and discover the wounds that sin hath given us.'[61] It is in this sense that Paul speaks in Romans vii 9 when he says, 'For I was alive without the law once, but when the commandment came, sin revived, and I died.' Without a knowledge of the law and a realisation of its holy claims, the old life flourished. But with a knowledge of the law sin, which had appeared to be dead (verse 8), suddenly became very much alive. Its character as an active principle within became apparent, thus opening the way for the old sinful life to give way to the principle of life in Christ through the Spirit. The law reveals sin for what it is. It explains the nature of sin, and the extent of sin in human experience.

This brings us conveniently to the second function of law, which is to convict of sin. The law does not merely demonstrate that sin exists or explain what sin is, it also declares that I am a sinner, that sin resides in me, and that I deserve its consequences. 'It cannot relieve or ease us, but it can, and doth, awaken and rouse us,' Flavel declares. Like a fiery serpent, to use another Flavel analogy, it 'smites, stings, and torments the conscience'. The effect of such inward conviction 'drives us to the Lord Jesus lifted up in the gospel, like the brazen serpent in the wilderness, to heal us'.[62] Clear as this may be, it is Bunyan once more who makes the experience take on an air of reality. Of all the sermons which he had heard, one, more than any other, remained in his mind. The minister had preached one day on the question of the Sabbath and true Sabbath-keeping, not omitting to emphasise the sin of Sabbath-breaking and its consequences. Bunyan reminds us that at that time in his life he 'took delight in all manner of vice,' especially on the Lord's day, and recalls how the sermon made a profound impression on Him. It had been as though the preacher was speaking directly and only to him:

> Wherefore I fell in my conscience under his sermon, thinking and believing that he made that sermon on purpose to show me my evil doing. And at that time I felt what guilt was, though never before that I can remember; but then I was for the present greatly loaden therewith, and so went home when the sermon was ended with a great burden on my spirit.[63]

The seventeenth century could provide many a witness who would readily testify to an experience similar to this, as indeed could every other age in Christian history when the inner, spiritual life has been given the emphasis it requires, and when the law has been given its rightful place as a preparative to the Gospel.

The third step in the process by which the law led men towards Christ,is the logical outcome of the two previous steps. With an understanding of the disease and a sense of personal contamination, the man or woman concerned was now ready to go in search of healing. Downham speaks of sinners who have thus come under the convincing and convicting power of the law being 'forced to seek for salvation out of themselves in Christ'.[64] The whole purpose of catechising, a task pursued with great earnestness in Puritan circles, was that those concerned might 'clearly and manifestly see the way unto salvation'. In John Ball's thinking, this specifically meant to understand the relationship between law and Gospel, 'how one thing dependeth upon another, goeth before, or followeth after'.[65] In this case, law preceded Gospel and paved the way for grace to do its work. James Ussher puts the whole argument with a fair measure of clarity:

> It is a glass, to discover our filthiness, and to show us our sins and the punishment thereof, that thereby we may be driven unto Christ to be purged by Him (Galatians iii 24, Romans iii 20, 27). For it layeth open all the parts of our misery, both sinfulness, accursedness, and impotency or unableness to relieve ourselves, so whipping and chasing us to Christ that in Him we may find deliverance.[66]

This is what E.F. Kevan evidently had in mind when he wrote more recently, 'In Puritan thinking, the sharp needle of the law, as it pricks the conscience, was found to be attached to the scarlet thread of the

Gospel.'[67]

(b) for the believer
The importance of the law in the life of the unbeliever as a preparative to the Gospel, was in the end of no greater significance in Puritan eyes than the law in the life of the believer as a demonstration that the Gospel had done its work. The words almost tumble over themselves in the attempt which Puritan writers make to establish this truth in the minds of their readers. There must be no doubt concerning the continuity of the law, no wavering in the conviction that its claims are as binding on those who believe as they are on those who do not. To falter at this point would be to open the door to 'the gross and vile opinions of antinomian libertines who cry up grace and decry obedience'.[68] No less an error this, than that of the legalist whose misunderstanding of law takes him in the opposite direction of attempting to earn salvation by external obedience. And so we find repeated assertions concerning the rightful place of law in the life of one who believes: 'The law is set forth as a rule of life to them that are in Christ,'[69] 'For as the law saveth us not without the gospel, so the gospel saveth us not without the law,'[70] 'In Scripture, to believe in Christ and to keep the commandments mutually infer one another;'[71] 'The law sends us to Christ to be justified, and Christ sends us to the law to be regulated,'[72] 'The doctrine of faith in Christ makes the law void as to justification, but not as to sanctification;'[73] 'A man cannot be or continue in a justified estate without hearty willingness to obey the gospel,'[74] 'Our sonship does not free us from service, but from slavery; not from holiness, but to holiness,'[75] 'They much wrong God and Christ,' Joseph Truman said frankly, 'that think Christ died to procure liberty to sin or to free men from duty, from obedience to the law. He died to free men from the curse of the law, but not from obedience to it, and from the curse, on condition of their sincere obedience.'[76] The case is stated so repeatedly and so clearly that it is impossible to mistake the Puritan view of the rightful place of the moral law in the Christian life.

An argument which led Puritan theologians in this direction is that which concerns the relationship of the law to sin. As we have seen already in tracing the purpose of law in the process of regeneration and initial acceptance of the Gospel, the law defines sin and points to its existence in the life of each individual. To say that this function of the law ceases with regeneration is either to say that with conversion sin as a principle ceases to exist in any meaningful way for that person, or that sin is immediately and totally eradicated from the Christian from the point of regeneration. Since neither conclusion is theologically or experientially acceptable, it follows that the law-sin relationship as it existed prior to regeneration must continue in the believer's life after regeneration has taken place. That this was true, the Puritans were not in the slightest doubt. The law continues to define sin and continues to reveal its indwelling existence even though regeneration is an accomplished and established reality in the life. The believer stands ever in need of further moral guidance and direction. This is what Ussher has in mind when he answers the question, 'What further use hath the law in the regenerate?' He replies, 'As a light it directeth us. For the world being a dark wilderness, and we naturally blind, we are in continual danger of falling, unless our steps be guided by the lamp of the law.'[77] The law continues to define sin, even though the believer has entered into a saving relationship with Jesus Christ.

Richard Baxter perceptively analyses the logical, or perhaps we should say the illogical, consequences of concluding that the moral law has been abrogated. If no such law exists to regulate human conduct, then there can be no transgression, and consequently no guilt, and therefore no forgiveness of sin. Man must therefore be either perfect or unaccountable for his conduct. Moreover, if such be the case there can be no heavenly intercession by Christ, no application of His blood on behalf of confessing and repentant sinners, no efficacy in prayer, and ultimately no point or merit whatsoever in the death of Christ. The sum and substance of the Christian faith disappear as a consequence of accepting the abrogation of the moral law. But since history and experience both testify to the facts of Christ's death and the power of the Gospel in the lives of those who believe, Baxter says that God's claim to authority in the life of believers is increased. Christ redeems men 'not to be lawless, but to be under a better law'. In terms of law and obedience the outcome is clear: 'The writing of the law in our hearts, freeth us not from it, as it is in nature or Scripture, but doubly obligeth us, and enableth us to perform it. . . . It is the same law that is written in Scripture and in us.'[78]

The preceding quotation confronts us with a further argument, perhaps the most powerful of all in Puritan theology, which establishes the continuity of the law in the life of the believer. This is the covenant relationship between God and His people, crucial in the Puritan understanding of the entire plan of salvation, and the omission of which would be a serious flaw in any study of Puritan thought. The ramifications of covenant theology are many, and we must resist the temptation to wander even marginally from the point under consideration. The Bible spoke emphatically of a new covenant which God would make, or had already made, with His people (see Jeremiah xxxi 33, Hebrews x 16). The term 'new covenant' implied the existence of an 'old covenant', although the Bible itself did not specifically use such a phrase. The new covenant was known to Puritans as the covenant of grace, which could further be taken to imply that the old covenant was a covenant of works. Since the basic idea of the covenant was that of an agreement under which God vouchsafed to save His people, the terms were important. A certain misunderstanding had arisen in the minds of some Christians of the time over the whole concept of the covenants, since it was assumed that the new covenant had replaced the old covenant with a better way of salvation. The inference was, of course, that under the old covenant, salvation was obtained by works, and that under the new covenant it was obtained through grace. It was, therefore, a major concern of Puritan theologians to disentangle the threads of these arguments and to clear away the confusion which always tended to surround the question of the covenants. Were there two ways of salvation, one belonging to the old covenant in the Old Testament and one belonging to the new covenant in the New Testament? Was salvation offered to men under one set of terms at one time in history and under a different set of terms at another time? It would hardly seem to be consistent with the character of God if this was so.

John Owen certainly speaks for the majority of Puritans when he says that there is and has ever been one way of salvation, that which is proffered under the new covenant. In fact, the new covenant had existed before the old covenant so-called, and had ever been the basis of salvation. It was a covenant of grace, and as such had existed from the first entrance of sin into the world. Owen says that this covenant was of the same nature from the very beginning, and that 'it passed through the whole dispensation of times before the law and under the law, of the same nature and efficacy, unalterable, everlasting, ordered in all things and sure'. It was called the covenant of grace since 'the promise of grace in and by Jesus Christ, was the only way and means of salvation unto the Church from the first entrance of sin'.[79] Edward Stennett, the prominent Seventh-day Baptist, complains of the 'thick scales' covering the eyes of those who 'make the covenant on Sinai a covenant of works'. The fact of the matter, as a careful study of Scripture revealed, was that Israel was already under the covenant of grace and therefore in theory at least, a saved people, when the requirement to obey the law was proclaimed. 'They had the covenant of grace from Sinai,' Stennett maintains, 'and the word of faith which Paul [later] preached, was in it; and that word on Sinai was the word of Christ, and Christ was in it, and the author of it.'[80] There was one God, one salvation and one covenant, and that was the new covenant founded on grace, which had from the first entrance of sin been the basis of salvation.

The dichotomy between an Old Testament of law and works and a New Testament of faith and grace is therefore fundamentally false. Faith and grace are always the basis of salvation, law and works the evidence that salvation is full and genuine. John Ball discerns this in the writings of Moses. Referring to Deuteronomy viii 11, Ball claims that disobedience to the will of God as revealed in His commandments is clear evidence that true faith does not exist. And referring to Deuteronomy xxvi 17, he speaks specifically of the covenant of faith, concluding with the inseparable consequence 'that if we embrace God by faith, we must and ought to follow His commandments by our deeds. He that doth not this latter, betrayeth that he hath not with a true heart and faith received the former'.[81]

Under the terms of this everlasting covenant of grace the moral law, far from being abrogated or its claims weakened, is on the contrary upheld and perpetuated. 'Subjection and obedience to Christ, is part of the condition of the new covenant,'[82] says Baxter. It is required of those who have received salvation under the new covenant to seek the will of God, and to obey that will when it is revealed. The moral law exists for this very purpose 'as part of this direction'. Thus, 'when the new covenant sayeth "thou shalt obey sincerely," the moral doth perfectly tell us wherein or what, we must endeavour to do'.[83] Baxter uses the analogy of a redeemed galley-slave to illustrate the point. Freedom is promised to the slave on condition that henceforth he will take his redeemer as his master. Such a decision implies a total acceptance of the gift of redemption itself, and a total willingness to serve and obey in the future. So, Baxter argues, salvation at 'the very first point' is through justification by faith alone, 'without either the concomitancy or co-operation of works,' but the evidence that faith and justification are genuine and permanent is willing obedience and service. Faith of itself is not the new covenant in its entirety, 'but faith with repentance and obedience'.[84]

But we have yet to establish the motive for obedience under the terms of the new covenant. Why should believers obey? What constraint is placed upon them to accede to the claims of the moral law? How are they able to direct their conduct in harmony with a law that is fundamentally contrary to the natural mind? The answer, and it is basic, lies in the relationship that the believer has to the moral law in the new covenant experience. At Sinai the law had been written on tables of stone, reminding man of the moral principles which had been written into his being at creation. In the new covenant, the law is re-written in the fleshy tables of the heart. When man submits to grace and experiences regeneration, God writes into his heart the moral law. It becomes part of his new nature, giving him a new awareness of sin and imparting the desire for holiness and victory. The new covenant, far from dispensing with the law, demonstrates that it is essential for its purposes, and establishes it as the rule of conduct for regenerated believers. Edward Stennett systematically expresses the whole concept of the new covenant experience which results in gospel-obedience as the consequence of grace:

God promiseth to take away the stony heart, and to give hearts of flesh, to write His law in tables of flesh, which is the new covenant. The law is the same, but the tables differ; the same law that was writ in Adam's heart, was writ in tables of stone; the same law that was writ in tables of stone, was writ in the heart of Christ, the second Adam; the same law that was writ in the heart of Christ, is writ in the heart of every true believer in Christ. We have the law by nature in our hearts of stone, as we are the seed of the first Adam; but we have the law by grace written in our hearts of flesh, as we are the seed of the second Adam.[85]

George Downham would merely add to this that Christian believers who do not understand this truth or experience its reality are only 'professors . . . like goats in Christ's flock which are to be separated from the sheep, like the chaff in the floor, which is to be winnowed from the wheat'.[86]

Rigorous though their demands stressing the permanence of moral law as a guide to human conduct might sound in the ears of the twentieth century, the Puritans perceived at least one lasting truth from their study of Scripture. Living that was in harmony with the high moral and spiritual standards of the Ten Commandments was as much a benefit to society as a whole as it was an ornament to the external profession of the Gospel. Such living could be maintained only as the Church herself understood the essential nature of her own message, and submitted to the provisions of grace which made the practical experience of that message a dynamic possibility.

8. THE SEVENTH-DAY SABBATH

Sunday ultimately became ecclesiastically regarded as 'the Christian Sabbath', especially among Protestants, and the Sabbath precept of the Decalogue was invoked to give it a semblance of divine sanction. Nevertheless, there has never been, since apostolic times, a century without Christian observers of the seventh-day Sabbath as sacred to Him who declared, 'The Son of man is Lord even of the sabbath day.
Robert L. Odom *Sabbath and Sunday in Early Christianity* (1977)
p.304

Whereas in matters of such weight as is this of establishing a Sabbath, we ought to bring arguments necessarily and demonstratively prooving and not contingencies; and specially since the raising up this new Sabbath, which hath no commandment for it from Christ or his apostles, makes way for the throwing down the old Sabbath, which stands by an express commandment from God. Let us beware therefore of matching probable human reasons with an infallible divine precept. Yea, do we not lean more to our human reasons in this point, then to God's express fourth commandment?
Theophilus Brabourne *A Discourse Upon the Sabbath Day* (1628)
pp.10-11

It was inevitable that, with free access to Scripture, English Christians would sooner or later come to the question of the Sabbath. As the records of the time reveal, the Sabbatarian debate in England stretched well into the eighteenth century, and it is a measure of its significance that it attracted the pens of Richard Baxter, John Bunyan and John Owen, to mention some of the more prominent Puritan divines, in addition to several doctors of divinity, among them Francis White, Bishop of Ely, Peter Heylin, Prebendary of Westminster and chaplain to Charles I, and John Wallis, Savilian Professor of Geometry at Oxford, all of whom wrote on the Sabbath issue during the seventeenth century. It must not be thought, however, that any of these writers were in favour of the seventh-day Sabbath. They were not. To a man, they wrote against the Christian observance of Saturday. That so many eminent men even considered that a necessity is, nevertheless, some indication of the impact made by the seventh-day advocates, and of the strength of the arguments they produced.

It will be helpful to note at the outset of this chapter a distinction made by

Ephraim Pagitt, who catalogued the 'heresies' of his time, regarding those who advocated the observance of the seventh day. Pagitt distinguishes between the Sabbatarians who 'affirm the old Jewish Sabbath to be kept' and the Traskites 'who would have us observe many Jewish ceremonies'.[1] The distinction is important (even though it was not recognised by many of Pagitt's contemporaries) for it points to a fundamental difference between those who, as Christians, advocated seventh-day observance, and those who had fallen into Judaistic legalism. The Traskites were so named after John Traske who, in 1618, was pilloried and imprisoned for his views which, rightly or wrongly, were understood at the time to savour too strongly of anarchy and sedition. Traske undoubtedly advocated the observance of the seventh day, but in a legalistic manner and accompanied by further specifically Jewish ceremonies, and is therefore not representative of the seventh-day movement in general. One of this wider group understandably complained that attempts 'to introduce some of the Mosaical ceremonies ... occasion slanders upon others and discourage further enquiries'.[2] This was one of the problems faced by those who honestly believed that they could produce solid, scriptural evidence for the observance of the seventh day. They knew, even if others did not, that the wholesale identification of all Sabbath-keepers with legalistic sectarians was unjustified. In this spirit Edward Stennett argued that his observance of Saturday should not be regarded as a barrier to Christian fellowship with those who kept Sunday. Indeed Stennett could point to the fact that many Sabbath-keepers, including himself, held communion with Christian believers who were not Sabbath-keepers, and was confident that those of his Sunday-keeping brethren who knew him well would readily acquit him of any charge of Judaistic sectarianism.[3]

It would be quite understandable if, at a distance of some 300 years, the justification for such confidence in the fundamentally biblical and Christian nature of Saturday observance was not readily apparent. For this reason in the present chapter an attempt will be made to assess the beliefs of that wider group in Puritanism which advocated a return to the observance of the seventh day, and particularly of the arguments which they drew from Scripture to support their views. We shall meet, for example, Theophilus Brabourne, the Anglican minister at Norwich, whose *Discourse upon the Sabbath Day* (1628) was the first major work to appear in the seventeenth century advocating the Christian observance of Saturday, Francis Bampfield, Prebendary of Exeter, who was ejected from his living by the Act of Uniformity in 1662, and his brother Thomas, Recorder of Exeter, who in 1658 became Speaker of the House of Commons. These men wrote at great length in support of the seventh-day Sabbath, producing between them at least eighteen separate works on the subject between 1628 and 1693. We shall meet also the Stennett family of Wallingford, Edward the physician and his son Joseph, that 'eminent and pious divine' who ministered to the Seventh-day Baptist Church at Pinners

Hall in London. He was related by marriage to Dr. Daniel Williams, whose scholarship and devotion to Nonconformity have been perpetuated to the present day in the London library which continues to bear his name. Among other major names is Joseph Davis, whose beneficence bought the Mill Yard Seventh-day Baptist Church property and provided for the support of its ministry and that of other clergymen who stood for the seventh day. Each of these, in his own way, added to the Sabbath literature which continued to appear throughout the seventeenth century.

By the mid 1650s, Brabourne tells us, many congregations in England were keeping the seventh day. Precisely how many there were later in the century it is difficult to establish with finality, but it is almost certain that there were more than the ten or eleven suggested by some later historians. While these congregations consisted in the main of artisans and small traders, they also included Peter Chamberlen, the Royal physician, Nathaniel Bailey, the lexicographer whose etymological English dictionary (c. 1730) became a standard work of reference and formed the basis of Dr. Johnson's *Dictionary*, and Christopher Pooley, a Cambridge graduate who, despite flirting with Fifth-Monarchy views for a while, led a seventh-day congregation in Norwich and remained faithful to the seventh-day Sabbath until his death. What occasioned loyalty among believers of such differing backgrounds to a minority viewpoint, frequently misunderstood and sometimes vilified? And wherein lay the strength of seventh-day convictions? These are important questions, now as then, and where better to look for the answers than in the original writings of those early Puritans who are rightly called Sabbatarians because of their advocacy of the observance of Saturday?

The Origins of the Sabbath

The great strength of the Sabbath doctrine was unquestionably its foundation in the moral law, unassailable in the minds of most Puritans, written into the mind of man at Creation, reiterated in the decalogue at Sinai, and established beyond doubt as the norm of Christian conduct by Christ and the apostles in the New Testament. Even those who were unwilling to accede to the claims of the seventh day were virtually unanimous in recognising the perpetuity of the Decalogue, and the moral obligations implicit in the Sabbath commandment were widely recognised in English Puritanism. John White speaks for this broadly based group when he argues in favour of 'the morality and perpetuity of the fourth commandment in the decalogue'.[4] The inescapable logic of White's argument was readily conceded by many:

> All the laws written in the decalogue are moral and immutable in all things. But the fourth commandment concerning the observation of the Sabbath day, is one of the laws of the decalogue. Therefore this law of the Sabbath is perpetual and unchangeable in all things which are concerned therein.[5]

Archbishop Ussher declared that the Sabbath was to be 'constantly and perpetually' observed, since it was enshrined in one of the 'perpetual commandments', since it was 'written by the finger of God ... whereas no part of the ceremonial law was,' and since it was engraved in tables of stone 'to signify the continuance and perpetuity of this commandment, as well as the rest'.[6] Richard Bernard, the Puritan vicar of Batcombe in Somerset, further pointed out that the law which Paul in Romans vii 12-14 described as 'holy, just and good', was itself 'the law of which the precept of the Sabbath is part'.[7] John Owen asked his readers to 'set aside prejudices and preconceived opinions,' and recognise that 'the institution of the Sabbath' was 'plainly expressed ... in the fourth commandment,' and that 'the weekly observation of a day to God for Sabbath ends' was a 'duty natural and moral' which God's children were 'under a perpetual and indispensable obligation' to obey.[8] It should not be forgotten that this was the standard Puritan view of the moral law and the Sabbath as an institution.

The Sabbatarians agreed with all this. Indeed, it was the starting point of their whole argument, arising as it did from the fourth commandment itself, 'The seventh day is the Sabbath of the Lord thy God' (Exodus xx 10). Brabourne says that because the moral law 'is still in force ... the seventh-day Sabbath, which is part of this law, is also in force'.[9] Since the fourth commandment specifically designated the seventh day as the Sabbath, it was difficult for Brabourne or any of those who followed him, to see how the sacredness of that particular day could be abrogated or how it might be transferred to any other day of the week. Brabourne begins his *Discourse upon the Sabbath Day* by calling the attention of his readers to the fact that only the seventh day of the week can be referred to as the Sabbath, since it is the day so designated in Scripture, and by pointing out that even the gospel writers do not call the first day of the week by that name.[10] Francis Bampfield tells us that he had searched the Word with great diligence for many years to discover the truth of this matter. His conclusion is that throughout Scripture, 'where the Holy Spirit doth speak of a weekly Sabbath day, there the name ... of a weekly Sabbath is given only to the seventh, which is the last day of the week, ... and to no other day of the week'.[11] To Bampfield it is 'evident from the Word, that the whole Scripture doth speak in its true, proper, literal significancy for the seventh-day Sabbath, the scope, sense, and meaning of the fourth command being altogether expressly for it'.[12] We might profitably return to Brabourne at this point:

> The seventh day is the Sabbath, not the third day, nor the fourth day, nor the first day of the week, but the seventh day.... It hath pleased God for our certain information to point directly and distinctly to the day that He would have kept, as by the finger, saying 'the seventh day', touching which word of number seventh it is to be noted that it is not a cardinal number, but an ordinal, notifying which for order. The property whereof is to denote, 1. One, and one only. 2. It notes that individual particular one, which for order is the last of that number. For instance, the third; it

is not any of the three, as the second, nor the first, but it is the last of the three; so the fifth, it is not the fourth, nor the second, but it is the last of the five; so the seventh day is the Sabbath, not the sixth day, nor the third day, nor the first day of the week, but the last day of the week, the seventh, is the Sabbath. So again you see the Lord hath culled out the last of the seven for His Sabbath, and hath not left it indefinite and undetermined.[13]

It was with thoughts such as these in mind that Edward Stennett correctly asked, 'How can the fourth command be moral and perpetual, and binding to all, in all ages, if the seventh-day Sabbath be abolished, seeing there is nothing commanded in it, but the seventh-day Sabbath?'[14] Joseph Davis, a contemporary of the Stennetts, pressed the point on his brethren 'of the Presbyterian and Independent persuasion' who, in their writings, had 'so honourably and plainly confirmed the moral law'. Since the seventh day was 'the substance of one of the commandments', Davis asked what reason could be advanced by those who were 'the Lord's ministers and ambassadors' for teaching that the original Sabbath commandment had been abolished or that the day had been changed from the seventh to the first day of the week? This was to come to the very heart of the Sabbatarian debate, and the advocates of the seventh day did not easily forget what a useful question it was.[15]

As a consequence of the foregoing argument, many Puritans found themselves firmly and uncomfortably impaled on the horns of a dilemma. If the moral law was perpetually binding on all men, as their own theologians taught, then Sabbath observance was clearly as much a moral obligation as the command to honour one's parents, or the commands not to steal or not to kill. It was clearly illogical to deny the strength of the moral law in this matter, and yet it was equally intolerable to admit to the claims of the seventh day, particularly as it was often misconstrued to indicate a leaning towards Judaism. Many found a way of escape by arguing that the Sabbath institution was retained as a moral precept, but that the actual day of the commandment had been changed to the first day of the week in honour of the resurrection. Thus the Sabbath was kept every successive seventh day, and the moral requirements of the Decalogue were retained inviolate. Even the learned Ussher flees in this direction, saying, 'By His special appointment under the gospel it may be Sunday, and yet the substance of the commandment nothing altered'.[16] Others saw the weakness of this approach to the problem and admitted that Sunday could not in any way be regarded as the Sabbath, since the Bible unequivocally referred to the seventh day as the Sabbath, and since Sunday was the first day of the week. Francis White, who had been appointed specifically by Charles I to reply to Brabourne's *Discourse upon the Sabbath Day*, a further indication of the seriousness with which the matter was taken, freely admitted that if Christians were to keep the fourth commandment properly, they must keep Saturday as Brabourne had argued.[17] In general terms, the reply of the 'no-Sabbath' group was that the Sabbath commandment was completely or partially ceremonial, applying only to the Jews, and of no further consequence to Christians for whom the observance of Sunday was not grounded at all in the fourth commandment, but upon the authority of the Church.

Those who supported the observance of the seventh day saw the inherent weakness of these arguments, both of which they regarded as attempts to justify a position which could not be justified from Scripture. In reply to the 'Sunday-Sabbath' advocates, who maintained that the essence of the fourth commandment was retained in the observance of Sunday, they pointed out that it was contrary to reason and to the sound interpretation of Scripture to apply the fourth commandment to the first day of the week when that commandment itself specifically spoke of the seventh day. Francis Bampfield argues from the position that Scripture is always to be understood literally unless there is an obvious reason for interpreting the text symbolically or metaphorically, and that since the moral law 'speaks of the seventh day in express letters and words, as the Sabbath,' it would be illogical and contrary both to reason and sound interpretative principle to make it apply to any other day of the week.[18] Brabourne had come to the same conclusion several years previously, and had spoken of 'the error of our times, which will apply this fourth commandment to the eighth day, or the first day, of the week which is the day after the Sabbath'.[19] In his numerous works on the Sabbath question, Brabourne repeatedly returns to this line of thought, which is based on the use of the ordinal number in the text of the fourth commandment. 'The ordinal numbers are these,' he explains, 'First, second, third, fourth, fifth, sixth, seventh, etc. . . . These notify not all, but one of the things numbered.' Thus, 'By the seventh year of the king's reign is not understood one of the seven years indefinitely, but the last year of the seven definitely and precisely.'[20] Similarly, 'A bond to be paid the seventh day of March is not to be paid upon one of the seven days of March indefinitely . . . but definitely upon the seventh day from the first day of March.'[21] So, Brabourne maintains, the use of the ordinal number in the fourth commandment can only mean that 'the seventh and last day of the seven' is the Sabbath, 'which is our Saturday'.[22] Beyond this, the seventh-day men were quite sure that no authority could be found in Scripture for the substitution of the first day for the seventh.

The other argument for dispensing with the claims of the moral law in respect of the fourth commandment was equally illogical, and therefore equally inadmissable. How could it reasonably be claimed that the fourth commandment was entirely of a ceremonial nature or, worse still, that it was only ceremonial in part? Those who had read the great William Perkins, to mention only one of the early Puritan theologians who had wrestled with this problem, could be in no doubt here. Perkins had met this particular argument back in the sixteenth century and had replied that the Sabbath was a moral issue. 'It was ordained before the fall of man,' he explained, 'at which time ceremonies signifying sanctification had no place.' Those who plead for the ceremonial nature of the Sabbath commandment, Perkins says, do so 'falsely'.[23] Without retracing the ground covered in the previous chapter, the conclusion of Henry Soursby, who succeeded to the pastorate of the Mill Yard Seventh-day Baptist Church in 1678, and Mehatabel Smith, who in 1683 jointly published *A Discourse of the Sabbath*, should be noted. The appeal again is to natural law, to the moral law inscribed in the mind of Adam at Creation. The ceremonial law was given later, but the Sabbath had its origin in the beginning. Seeing, then, 'That the seventh day was a paradise-institution ... clears it from the imputation of ceremonial'.[24] Either the whole Decalogue is ceremonial, or none of it is, say Soursby and Smith. Brabourne, as we might expect, is even more explicit. To think of the Decalogue as a combination of moral and ceremonial laws, he says, is to suppose that God would 'plough in His field with an ox and an ass yoked together'.[25] Brabourne cannot follow the logic of those who would so 'jumble things unskilfully together'. He continues:

> O monstrous, what a hotchpotch have we here! What a mingle-mangle, what a confusion and jumbling of things so far distant together, as when morals and ceremonials are supposed to be here mingled together, the one to last but for a time, the other to last for ever; the one belonging only to the nations of the Jews, the other belonging to all nations; and both of these though mingled in one single word, in the word rest. Was the like ever heard of? Can the like instance be shown in all the ten commandments?[26]

It seemed, then, both logical and scriptural to conclude that the moral law as such, the fourth commandment in its entirety, and hence the Sabbath day in particular, contained moral and spiritual implications that could not be lightly or reasonably dismissed.

The fourth commandment also contained within it the underlying reason for its perpetually binding claims: 'Remember the Sabbath day to keep it holy ... for in six days, the Lord made heaven and earth ... and rested on the seventh day' (Exodus xx 8 and 11). The moral constraint of this Sabbath commandment lay in the creatorship of God. The Sabbath commandment referred to Creation because the Sabbath itself was a memorial of God's creative activity in the beginning. On this fundamental truth both the Puritans who advocated a Sunday-Sabbath and those who stood for the seventh day were agreed. The Sabbath had existed before Sinai, before the moral law had been delivered amidst thunder and lightning in the mount. It came from Paradise, from the Garden of Eden, from the hand of the Creator Himself. Soursby and Smith suggest that the Sabbath is 'founded on the order of creation,' by which they mean that Creation was accomplished in six literal twenty-four hour periods, day following night, one succeeding the other, until the seventh period in the cycle was reached, upon which, having completed His creative work with the creation of man, the Creator rested.[27] This was the evident meaning of Genesis ii 1-3, from which it plainly appeared that God had rested upon the seventh day, blessed it, and sanctified it for a holy purpose. Soursby and Smith say that 'Because God rested on it, therefore He commanded it, and men ought to keep it on that ground'.[28] The Creator has the moral right to direct that which He has created, and it is no less a moral right if exercised in love and for the total benefit of the creature.

Perhaps the most detailed account of the Creation-Sabbath relationship is found in the writings of Francis Bampfield, who maintains that the doctrine of the Sabbath cannot be understood without reference to Creation. The 'true doctrine and the genuine meaning' of the Sabbath lies in the fact that man and the Sabbath were created in the same week. 'Whilst weeks do last,' Bampfield maintains, 'they will live and stand together.' The reality of the Sabbath is no less than the reality of man. It is a 'primitive constitution that must stand firm'.[29] Bampfield finds an argument here, as Brabourne does with the fourth commandment, in the ordinal number as used in the Genesis text. The biblical record is a 'diary ... a plain narrative, containing a clear history'[30] of the origins of man and the world, and the sequence of days in creation week is an integral aspect of this narrative. The 'days of this one created week, which did follow in the same week, were ordinal, and successive, and numerable'.[31] Concerning the first day of that week Bampfield carefully explains:

> There was one day which was the beginning of days ... and this and other distinct days in this week of the creation, are properly a distinct enumeration of distinct days, setting out their daily natural measures.
> ... The evening and the morning of every day were a distinct day, and were distinct parts of every day. The one day was before the second, and the third day was after the second, the fourth followed the third, and the fifth was after the fourth, the sixth succeeded the fifth, and the seventh which is the last day of the week, was the holy close of that week. There is but one seventh day in the week. No other day in this, or in any following week, is properly the seventh day of the week, in the weekly revolution.[32]

The Sabbath, then, was the climax of creation week, the day set apart for the communion of man with his Creator, 'to the nourishing of his soul, the satisfaction of his spirit, the strengthening of his heart, and the enlightening of his mind'.[33] It was a day when man was to remember his Creator, worship Him, and come into fellowship with Him. It is easy to understand why Bampfield concludes of the attempted change of the Sabbath, 'That human invention of transferring the weekly Sabbath from the seventh to the first day of the week has wholly inverted this established order.'[34]

It was possible to draw a further truth from the creation origin of the Sabbath. Obvious though that truth might appear, it nonetheless proved very useful in answering an argument that was brought to bear against the observance of the seventh day. The argument was that which designated the Sabbath as a Jewish institution, having no relevance whatsoever for Christians. This argument was partly met, of course, by demonstrating that the Sabbath had nothing in it of a ceremonial nature, since it was the ceremonial law which pertained only to the Jews. It was completely met by showing that the Sabbath had existed from Creation, hundreds of years before the existence of the Jewish people. If the Jews took their origin from Abraham, as was generally agreed to be the case, the creation origin of the Sabbath forever discountenanced any exclusively Jewish interest in the seventh day. Bampfield makes the important point that 'the Sabbath was made for Adam ... as man,' rather than for Adam as an individual, and 'therefore for all men, all men being in Adam'.[35] Referring to the Markan passage at ii 23-27, where Jesus said that the Sabbath had been made for man, Brabourne affirms that 'the Sabbath was made for man, that is for the good of man', and further that God instituted the Sabbath at Creation 'before there was any distinction of Jew and Gentile'.[36] In any event, the argument is less than convincing in Brabourne's mind since Christians observe the other nine commandments which were also ostensibly given to the Jews and since the new covenant, based as it was in the moral law, was also given to the Jews. 'Will you reject the gospel because it was first given to the Jews?' Brabourne asks, 'Why then do you reject the Sabbath, because it was given to the Jews?'[37]

To summarise, the Sabbath was designated as the seventh day of the week at Creation, given to man as the means of a deepening relationship between him and his Creator, written into his heart as part of the moral law of nature, and enshrined in the heart of the Decalogue at Sinai. To say after that, that it was temporary, or inconsequential, or Jewish, was really to betray a somewhat superficial grasp of Scripture and to display the presence of rather serious weaknesses in the principles of biblical interpretation. At the very least, we understand why Brabourne felt justified in concluding, 'If you slight the seventh-day Sabbath, you slight God's Sabbath, call it what you list.'[38]

The Sabbath in the New Testament

In the final analysis the validity of the seventh day for Christians hung on Christ's relationship to the Sabbath in His own life, and in His attitude to Sabbath observance beyond the resurrection. If it could be demonstrated that Christ had observed the Sabbath Himself and that He had expected that it would be observed by His disciples after His resurrection, the case for the Christian observance of Saturday would be very considerably improved. If it could be further shown that neither He nor His followers had substituted the first day of the week for the seventh day as the appointed day of rest and worship the case would be virtually unassailable. The New Testament evidence was of considerable importance.

In previous chapters we have noted the insistence within Puritan Christology on Christ as the Creator and Lawgiver of the Old Testament. New Testament texts, which Puritans in general drew on to support the theologically important assertion that Christ was the Creator, included John i 1-3, Colossians i 15-17, Hebrews i 1-2 and Ephesians iii 9. This was a fundamental concept in the Puritan system of theology and not one likely to meet much opposition, if any at all. But the seventh-day men observed that this teaching of the Bible was not taken to its logical conclusion. If Christ was the Creator, the Word who had been in the beginning with God, and by whom all things had been made, it followed that He had also created the Sabbath. Building on a previous argument, Francis Bampfield explained, 'It was this Christ who created the first seven days and established their order to continue in their successive courses to the world's end. It was He, who when He had perfected His work ... rested on the seventh day. It was He who blessed the seventh day. It was He who sanctified the seventh day, because in it He had rested from all His work.'[39] In Paradise the Sabbath, like man himself, had come from the hand of Christ. He was, therefore, 'the first seventh-day Sabbath observer, and under all the several administrations of grace, He called upon His people to do the same'.[40] Joseph Davis, commenting on Christ's confirm-ation of the moral law in Matthew v 17-18, says that He established 'every jot and tittle of it, and consequently the seventh-day Sabbath'.[41] Had not Jesus referred to Himself as 'Lord of the Sabbath' (Mark ii 28)? What did this mean if it did not mean that the Sabbath was a day of special significance, directly related to the lordship of Christ over the world and over His Church, in the sense in which the New Testament frequently spoke of Christ's lordship? It was a relationship, moreover, to which His role as Creator and Lawgiver gave a whole new depth of meaning. He was Lord of the Sabbath because as Creator He had made it and given it to the creature for his benefit.

The Gospels also recorded that Jesus Himself observed the Sabbath, not occasionally, but 'as His custom was' (Luke iv 16). One writer says, 'His constant course from His childhood at Nazareth, where He had been brought up, was to keep the weekly Sabbath day.'[42] Indeed, we may be sure that had He not done so, the Pharisees would quickly have brought an accusation against Him. As it was, their accusations were not that He disregarded the Sabbath but that He kept it in a manner which was unacceptable to them (cf. Matthew xii 1-13, Luke vi 1-12). It was well known to Francis Bampfield and those who stood with him on the question of the Sabbath, that no biblical evidence could be produced to show that Christ had ever kept holy any day of the week but the seventh day. They had combed the New Testament for every shred of evidence they could find on the subject, and they knew that they were on firm ground. So Bampfield has no hesitation in declaring, 'This Christ, all His life long ... kept the seventh-day Sabbath, and no other day of the week as such.'[43] Thomas Bampfield makes the similar assertion that throughout the time of His incarnation Christ kept the Sabbath, but adds, 'and surely He under-stood His own institution, and was not mistaken in the day'.[44] Surely, too, if Christ kept the Sabbath, He kept it not as a Jew, but as the founder of the Christian Church. Any other conclusion would open the door to a total rejection of the Gospel on the grounds that it, too, was Jewish. Hence

Christ is 'the great exemplary pattern for His disciples to imitate and
follow'.[45] He rested on the seventh day at Creation, kept it during His life
on earth, thus enjoining on His people, 'both by His own example and
command' the perpetual observance of the seventh day. To Christians
whose first duty was to follow Christ, the evidence was difficult to ignore,
and it is perhaps not wholly surprising to learn that in 1671, John Owen,
erstwhile Vice-Chancellor of Oxford University, spoke in terms of the
possibility that many yet might turn to the seventh day.[46]

The argument most frequently brought against the seventh day was that
it had been discontinued in favour of the first day in honour of the
resurrection. Again, those who observed the seventh day believed that
there was no biblical evidence that such a change had taken place and no
biblical authority for it. They contended that Christ would have authorised
such a major change in accepted practice or, at the very least, that He
would have recognised that it was going to take place after His resurrection. The evidence pointed in the opposite direction, however particularly
that found in Matthew xxiv, where Jesus had spoken of certain events
which were to take place between His resurrection and the destruction of
Jerusalem. In looking forward to that time, Jesus had counselled His
followers to watch for the signs of the impending destruction, and to flee
from the city when they saw that its time had come. In verse 20, He had
specifically urged them to pray that their flight would not have to be in the
winter or upon the Sabbath. Why did Christ, looking into the future, speak
of the Sabbath day in this manner, if He knew that after His resurrection
the day was to become invalid in any case? Theophilus Brabourne
supplies the answer: 'Christ allowed of the ancient Sabbath as a Christian
ordinance in the Church all the times of the gospel after His death, and had
it been a dying ceremony, as many fancy, Christ would not have bidden
Christians to pray to God to prevent their profanation of it'.[47] Since
Jerusalem was not destroyed until the armies of Titus razed it to the
ground in 70, it could only mean that Christ anticipated that the Sabbath
would be observed for almost forty years (Brabourne enthusiastically says
'about fifty') beyond Christ's own time. While this may not seem a long
time in terms of Christian history, it was long enough to discountenance
the view that the Sabbath had been abrogated, or changed, immediately
after the resurrection.

It was not a long step from here to the remaining evidence in the New
Testament. The book of Acts contained several references to Paul's
observance of the Sabbath, among them xvi 11-13 and xvii 2-3, and these
passages led Thomas Bampfield to affirm that 'the same certain evidence'
existed with regard to Paul's attitude to the Sabbath as it did with respect
to that of Christ Himself. 'It was Paul's constant use, manner, and custom
to preach Christ upon the seventh-day Sabbath,'[48] Bampfield maintains.
William Saller and John Spittlehouse jointly confessed that Paul, 'the
greatest opposer of ceremonies of all the apostles', consistently observed
the seventh day, citing in addition to the texts quoted above, Acts xiii 14,

42, 44 and xviii 4.[49] James Ockford, whose anonymous work *The Doctrine of the Fourth Commandment* had been condemned by Parliament in 1649 to public burning, made the useful observation that if the Sabbath had been changed there would have been some record in the New Testament and that in all probability the matter would have been discussed at the council in Jerusalem, which had considered matters of a similar nature and their place in the life of the Christian Church (Acts xv).[50] The reason for the silence of the New Testament on the whole question was aptly summarised by Edward Stennett as being 'beyond the apostle Paul, and all the men in the world, to change the Sabbath'. With some appreciation of the situation which prevailed in the New Testament Church, Stennett adds that with the Sabbath 'kept by Jews and Gentiles in every city ... what a stir would there have been if the apostles had gone about to change the Sabbath. It would have been the ready way to mad confusion, and to put a stop unto the publication of the gospel'.[51] The fact of the matter was well stated by Saller and Spittlehouse when they said that none of the apostles 'did ever neglect the observation of the seventh day of the week as enjoined in the fourth commandment'.[52]

While the Sabbatarian debate took its course in the religious literature of the time, it must not be thought that the Sabbath question was merely the arid, intellectual concern of theologians. To understand the issue with the mind was without question extremely important. Otherwise, for one thing, how could the charge of Judaism be refuted? Brabourne is at pains to point out that to keep the Sabbath on the seventh day is, in itself, no more to be condemned as Judaising than to keep Sunday on the first day. It was possible to observe either Saturday or Sunday for the wrong reason, from a legalistic Judaistic standpoint, so the matter did not rest merely with the day but rather with the underlying motive for worship and obedience.[53] The refutation of this charge has largely been dealt with already, but it is interesting to note a comment by the historian William Cave in his *Primitive Christianity*. Referring to the observance of the seventh day in the early centuries, Cave alludes to the account of Athanasius, Bishop of Alexandria, who had recorded that some Christians 'assembled on Saturdays, not that they were infected with Judaism, but only to worship Jesus Christ, the Lord of the Sabbath'.[54] It was an important observation, not only for Christians of the third and fourth centuries, or of the seventeenth century, but for Christians in every age who have felt impelled by Scripture to worship their Lord on a different day from the majority of their brethren. Brabourne says that if the Sabbath is kept from the standpoint of ceremonial law, that is, as a means of salvation, then 'it were properly called Judaism'. 'But where,' he asks, 'is the Christian that keeps it in this sense?'[55] It was a reasonable question, and not one that was easy for the opponents of the seventh day to answer.

The relationship of the Sabbath to Christ and to salvation, more than anything, dispelled any outward appearance of mere intellectual controversy. Those who observed the seventh day stoutly denied that their

Sabbath-keeping contributed in any way to their justification. Stennett saw in the Epistle to the Galatians that some believers had sought justification by works of the law. Yet such an abuse of the law could not negate its legitimate function. 'How greatly do you err ... in applying those scriptures to us which are freely justified by grace,'[56] Stennett said to those opponents who sought to pin the Galatian heresy to the seventh-day keepers. On the other hand, it was just as necessary to defend true Sabbath-keeping as part of the sanctification experience. The Sabbath is 'a sign between Jehovah and His covenant people that they are a sanctified people,'[57] Francis Bampfield says again. But sanctification is in a very real sense bound up with salvation and redemption, and the Sabbath is therefore a token of 'Christ's love, who having been the Creator, is the Redeemer too, and will be sanctification to His covenant people'.[58] Bampfield sees Christ's own Sabbath observance as part of that righteousness of obedience which He wrought out in His earthly life, part of that righteousness which belongs to the believer by faith. So he asks, 'Wither shall we go to get ourselves clothed with Sabbath righteousness, but unto Him, putting on this Lord Jesus, and making this Jehovah to be our righteousness?'[59] To Bampfield, as to many others, the fullness of God's righteousness is in Christ, and the fullness of Christ's righteousness includes His total obedience to the moral law and hence His observance of the original Sabbath of Creation and the Decalogue. It is James Ockford, however, who comes most unambiguously to the point. 'There can be no Sabbath without Christ,' he declares, not in the intellectual sense, but in the inner, spiritual sense. 'Look principally at the inward Sabbath,' he advises, and 'The invisible part of religion is the chiefest and most essential.'[60] True Sabbath observance, after the mind of the Creator Himself, is an inward experience of the soul, transcending all externals of time, place, or day, but nevertheless retaining such externals as that divinely appointed framework within which the spiritual experience can be realised. So Ockford continues:

> Blessed those that are sabbatising in Christ ... they keep a Sabbath that the world knows not of, and cannot keep, for there can be no Sabbath without Christ. ... The Christian Sabbath consists in our dying to all things within us, and without us, besides Christ; in ceasing from our own wisdom ... and in ceasing from man ... in ceasing from sin, (which is the soul's tumult, disorder, disquiet, as well as pollution) and living to the will of God. ... As Christ was crucified the sixth day, and immediately before the Sabbath, so must we be crucified to all comforts and enjoyments before we can come to a Sabbath of rest and delight in Christ.[61]

It was only as the Lord of the Sabbath became also Lord of the life that the fundamentally spiritual intent of the seventh day could be realised, and its inherent blessings appropriated.

The Identical Seventh Day

Sabbatarians appealed to the biblical account of Creation as well as to the moral law to substantiate their views concerning the seventh day. The creation record, however, provided a further line of argument which the Sabbatarians found useful in putting their case. It gave the only known explanation of the origin of the weekly cycle, a fact which could not be overlooked when it came to establishing the identity of the seventh day of the week. Why did the week consist of seven days, 'and not eight, nor nine, or more, or fewer?'[62] Henry Jessey asked. The reason was that in the beginning God had finished His work of Creation in six days and had rested on the seventh, thus establishing the weekly seven-day cycle. 'Since that time there have been weeks, and the week has been of seven days,'[63] Jessey added. The self-evident nature of the weekly cycle was even used by advocates of the Sunday-Sabbath to prove the perpetuity of the Sabbath institution as such. John Owen says it is a 'great testimony' to the 'original institution of the Sabbath'. Furthermore, the week has been so generally recognised throughout history that there must be some valid explanation of its origin and universal acceptance. 'All nations,' says Owen, 'in all ages, have from time immemorial made the revolution of seven days' the basic period in the calculation of time. The computation of day and night, months and years, by the movements of the sun and moon are of 'unavoidable observation to all rational creatures'. But how, or why, the week originated and claimed universal admittance to man's calculation of time 'no man can give account, but with respect to ... a sabbatical rest instituted from the foundation of the world'.[64] Hence, Francis Bampfield speaks of 'the doctrine of weeks' having been handed down through history from Creation:

> There were seven distinct days severally created in order of time, and no more, which being ended another week begins. An whole full complete week doth consist of seven days, not of six or fewer days, not of eight or more days, because Elohim made all in these several distinct days. He made no less, and He added no more.... A week in its successive returns has a natural existence, a created being, which doth unchangeably establish the six foregoing days of every week to be working days, and the seventh, the last, the closing day of every week, to be the weekly Sabbath day, or day of rest.[65]

Bampfield logically claims, 'It is impossible to find out any proper seventh day, but only the last day of the week,' and that this 'doth somewhat confirm the seventh-day Sabbath ... to be of natural obligation'.[66]

On the basis of the perpetual weekly cycle, Sabbatarians were able to argue that the true identity of the seventh day had never been lost. Brabourne, Bampfield and Stennett, each in his own way sees the strength of this argument. Brabourne says that throughout history 'no day was known to be the seventh but one, namely, Saturday,' and that since 'all divines ancient and modern, call our Sunday ... the first day of the week, so consequently Saturday, if you reckon onwards, the seventh day'.[67]

Bampfield asks two pertinent questions, the first of which is directed at Sunday-keepers: 'Can he that proves which is the first day of the week, but be able to tell which is the seventh?' The second question related to the Moslem practice of Friday observance: 'Do not Mohammedans keep the sixth day of the week as their weekly festival? If their day be the sixth, the most immediately following day must be the seventh.'[68] Stennett contends that those who claim that the identity of the seventh has been lost in the past, 'must imagine that at some time or other the whole world fell asleep at once, and by a chance awaked all together and ... forgot what day it was when they did awake'. On a more serious note, Stennett correctly points out, 'The Sabbath was known in Christ's time and after, and it is strange it should be lost without any man's knowing how or when.'[69] Several of the Sabbatarian writers draw attention to legal procedures in England which required that laws enacted on the seventh day or writs issued on that day should be identified *Sabbatum* or *Die Sabbati*. Thomas Bampfield, in his reply to John Wallis' *Defence of the Christian Sabbath* (1692), which advocated the Sunday Sabbath on the grounds that the identity of the seventh day had been lost, comes back to the point which his brother had made: 'If we do not know which is the seventh day, we cannot possibly know which is the first day, and so cannot possibly keep a day which we know not.'[70]

While the Sabbatarians were understandably anxious to clear themselves from any charge of Judaising in the matter of the Sabbath, they were at the same time clear-headed enough to see that in one respect the Jews were helpful to their cause. Every loyal Jew was living proof that the seventh day of the week was the day commonly known as Saturday. From Moses' time, at least, the Jews had observed the seventh day from generation to generation in unbroken succession. Although Christians in the early Church had worshipped on the same day which the Jews had continued to observe throughout the centuries, the feeling still persisted, quite illogically to the Sabbatarians, that the true identity of the day might somehow have been lost in the dim and distant past. So, as an added argument in their favour, the Christian Sabbatarians could point to the Jews and say that as a race scattered throughout the earth, their religious observance established beyond doubt which day of the week was historically the seventh. Soursby and Smith say that, 'The Jews who have been, and now are, dispersed almost into every city and nation ... never laboured under any difficulty'[71] in determining which day of the week was which. Brabourne explains how the ancient Jewish custom of reckoning the days of the week related each day to the preceding Sabbath. Thus Sunday was called 'the first day of the Sabbath; Monday the second of the Sabbath; etc'. Moreover the Jews then living at Amsterdam, Brabourne says, called 'our Saturday the Sabbath day'.[72] Edward Elwall, the Wolverhampton merchant who really belongs to the brotherhood of eighteenth-century Sabbatarians, observed in his day that 'The Jews, who are in almost every trading nation under heaven, do all know the seventh day, and were never at a loss to know it, but continued to keep it ... in every different longitude and latitude where they live upon the face of the earth.'[73] On this basis, Sabbatarians appealed to the great body of opinion in Puritan England which was concerned with the conversion of the Jews, arguing that the Sabbath was a vital instrument to break down the wall of partition and bring them into the fellowship of Christ and His Church.

Francis Bampfield draws our attention to one further aspect of the Sabbath debate, that is, to the etymological significance of the word 'Sabbath'. The Greek words *sabbaton* and *sabbatismos* were derived from the Hebrew *shabbath* and *shabbaton* respectively, 'the sound and the sense going together do enough speak this to every intelligent man's ear'.[74] These root biblical words from which the English word Sabbath is derived are represented in the ancient Chaldean, Syriac and Arabic languages by *shebath*, which is used of the seventh day of the week and which is linguistically related to the Hebrew.[75] A similar relationship could be seen in many current languages. Thus, Bampfield says, in Low Dutch the seventh day of the week is called *rust-dagh*, the day of rest. In High Dutch, or Teutonic German, the last day of the week is designated *samstag*, 'that is the Lord's day, or the day of the Lord'.[76] Similarly, in French, Italian, Spanish, Portuguese, as well as in Latin, Greek and Hebrew, the seventh day of the week is known by a name which denotes that it is the day of rest, the Sabbath, or the Lord's day.[77] Brabourne points out that the Latin name of the day commonly called Saturday in English is '*sabbatum*, the Sabbath day, as is to be seen in all Latin dictionaries,' and which is used in the legal documents referred to previously.[78] With this not inconsiderable extra-biblical evidence in their favour, it is hardly surprising that the Sabbatarians followed the lead given by their first spokesman of any prominence, and categorically affirmed, 'Sunday was never called Sabbath in the Scriptures, but Saturday the seventh day was ever so called, and so hath it ever been ... to this day.'[79]

The Change to the First Day

If the biblical and historical evidence in favour of the seventh day was as strong as the Sabbatarians believed it was, one question remained to be answered. Why did the majority of Christians observe the first day? How had Sunday-keeping come into the Church and then claimed the rank of a divine institution? The question was in principle one of authority, and since the Bible had not supplied that authority, from whence had it come? The seventh-day men spoke with one voice in emphasising and re-emphasising that no divine authority for such a change existed anywhere in Scripture. This was no side issue, but of the very marrow of the whole Sabbath question. God Himself had not changed the day of rest and worship. Christ had not changed it. The Bible contained no authoritative direction that it should be changed at any subsequent time in Christian history. The following extracts from the writings of the seventh-day advocates reveal how firmly they stood on this point:

> Our clergy say, Christ altered and changed the Sabbath from the seventh to the first day. But this is a notorious slander raised against Christ, for search the Scripture and you shall nowhere find that Christ spake one word against the Sabbath, or about altering or changing it.[80]

> The discerning reader may see how express Christ is in this matter. He exerciseth His power according to His Father's will and word, and the Father, as also the Son from the Father, hath not revealed any such thing in the word of truth, as the change of the weekly Sabbath from the last to the first day of the week. There is no appearance of any such institution or command. Christ came not to make a change in any one of the laws of the ten words.[81]

> Christ calls Himself Lord of the Sabbath. . . . He could easily, with a word of His mouth, have abrogated that day and set up another in its room. If He had so intended it should be, doubtless He would have given it in charge to His apostles, either the first day of the week, when He appeared to them, or some time of those forty days after His resurrection when He abode with them, speaking and teaching the things of the kingdom of God. . . . And we may further note by the way, that in those forty days Christ was with them, teaching them the things of the kingdom of God, He never taught them to observe the first day of the week as a holy Sabbath, for if He had, the apostles in some of their writings would have recorded so special a law of His kingdom.[82]

> For any man to tell us the Sabbath is altered or changed, without one word of God or of Christ to prove it, this is trifling with all understanding men, and deceiving the weak and ignorant. Men may follow their human inventions, and plead that the sixth day is the Sabbath, because it was the day of Christ's crucifixion and because on that day it was that He cried 'It is finished', and bowed His head, and gave up the ghost. . . . And others may plead that the first day is the Sabbath, because on it Christ rose from the dead. And others may plead the fifth day is the Sabbath because on it Christ preached to His disciples His last farewell sermon . . . and because this was the day of Christ's ascension, and the day that He blessed His holy apostles, and that the angels appeared and the clouds received Him up into heaven.

> But alas not one word from God, nor precept from Christ, or any of His apostles, to keep any one of these days one more than another. I challenge any man under heaven to show me one Scripture precept or command for it out of all the New Testament.[83]

In an age when vigorous religious debate was acceptable, and when men were expected to be able to defend their beliefs, it would be reasonable to assume that the foregoing statements, made by men who wrote on the Sabbath question over a period of more than a hundred years, were made with due and careful consideration.

No, the observance of Sunday rested on an altogether different foundation from that of the Sabbath, as Edward Fisher readily admits: 'The Lord's
day is a Sabbath under the gospel by the Church's authority, to be weekly
observed on the first day; so that the Sabbath and the Lord's day differ
specifically, that is, are of distinct natures and kinds.'[84] Fisher was a loyal
Anglican, as was Timothy Puller who defended the traditional moderation
of the Church of England on the grounds of her attitude to the Lord's day.
Admitting that no express precept existed in Scripture for the observation
of the first day, and that no such command was necessary, Puller refers to
that day as 'the weekly festival of the Church', and claims that 'the
perpetual and universal practice of the Catholic Church . . . is a sufficient
proof of the divine right of it'[85] (that is, of Sunday). John Prideaux, Regius
Professor of Divinity at Oxford from 1615 to 1641, when he became Bishop
of Worcester, makes a similar admission: 'The Lord's day is founded only
on the authority of the Church, guided therein by the practice of the
apostles, not on the fourth commandment.'[86] This, of course, was
precisely what the Sabbatarians wanted to hear, for it was what they had
suspected all along, and it sustained them in their determination to recover
the true Sabbath and to call the attention of the Church at large to the
departure from the faith once delivered to the saints which, they contended, had occurred in earlier Christian history.

The issue ran deeper than that, however, as every loyal Sabbatarian
knew, and as he believed every loyal Protestant ought to know. Although
Bishop Prideaux had said that Sunday observance had arisen on the
authority of the Church, guided 'by the practice of the apostles', the
Sabbatarians regarded this as rather less than accurate, since Sunday
observance had commenced at a much later date than the apostolic age.
To come to the point as readily as seventeenth-century Sabbatarians did,
the substitution of Sunday for Saturday as the weekly day of worship was
essentially the work of the Roman Church begun in the third century and
continued in the fourth and succeeding centuries, and a legacy therefore
which Protestantism had inherited from post-apostolic and mediaeval
Christendom. Theophilus Brabourne, it will be recalled, had been a
minister in the Anglican Church at the time he had written his *Discourse
Upon the Sabbath Day*, and had been concerned to put forward his views
in as conciliatory a manner as possible. It was not the Church of England
who was principally in error over this matter, for until recent times she had
been as wheat 'covered in the chaff of Popery'. Only with Luther had the
form of what would later be Anglican doctrine begun to emerge, so that the
first-day error was to be 'imputed to the Romish Church' from whom 'by
succession we had the Lord's day' and who even admitted that the
observance thereof was grounded in tradition rather than in Scripture.[87] It
was in the merciful providence of God that since the Reformation 'the
chaff hath been fanned away,' although in succeeding years there had
been 'a continued warfare' against 'Romish doctrine, both by pen and by
preaching,' as a result of which the Church of England scarcely had had

opportunity 'to bethink herself of any further purification'.[88] Brabourne's appeal was that the time had come for a thorough reformation of doctrine in the national Church: 'Let us rather imitate the more pure primitive Churches from whom the Church of Rome is fled in practice of the Sabbath day, than the corrupted Romish Church from whom we sucked this evil milk.'[89] The real issue, as those early English Sabbatarians could not easily forget, was the ultimate question of authority in matters of faith and doctrine. In this case, it was either the authority of Scripture or the authority of Rome.

The Sabbatarians realised that it was not sufficient to make a general statement of this nature concerning the origin of Sunday observance. Only as the facts were widely known and the background clearly understood could they hope to convince others of the correctness of their position. The first thing they wanted known was that the seventh day had been observed in the early Church for several centuries. Brabourne says, 'For three hundred or four hundred years after Christ, this Sabbath was kept, and that by the purest Churches of the primitive times.'[90] Even John Ley, who replied to Brabourne's initial case for the seventh-day Sabbath, admitted that the Sabbath had been kept by many Christian Churches at least until the Council of Laodicea (364), 'as may be proved out of many authors,' and that in Ethiopia it had been observed until the present time.[91] William Cave records that, especially in the eastern Churches, Saturday was held 'in great veneration', and that 'they usually had most parts of divine service performed upon that day, they met together for public prayers, for reading the scriptures, and celebration of the sacraments and such like duties'.[92] The Council of Laodicea seems to have been widely accepted by both Sunday advocates and Sabbatarians in the seventeenth century as the time when Sunday observance began to have official recognition in the Church, although Cave holds that the Council equally upheld the validity of both days, forbidding any Judaising tendencies in Saturday observance. Brabourne fairly concedes that prior to the Council of Laodicea 'both days were in use,'[93] a fact which has not always been recognised, but which does not detract from the established observance of the seventh day for a considerable length of time in early Christian history. The truth of the matter was that Sunday keeping had gradually replaced Saturday observance over a period of some centuries, and that it had finally received the stamp of approval by the canon law of the Church.

In addition to the Council of Laodicea which had placed Sunday observance and Saturday observance together in the context of canon law, Francis White mentions that in the fourth century and after other 'godly laws and canons were framed by Constantine the Great, and by other succeeding emperors, Theodosius, Valentinian, Arcadius, Leo and Antoninus, and by bishops in their synods, for the religious observance of the Lord's day'.[94] It was quite evident, as William Saller points out, that Rome, although she had 'thrown out God's holy day and set up her own in the stead of it,' did not attempt to hide the fact by fathering the change of the day on Scripture.[95]

Perhaps the most obvious piece of evidence which could be produced in support of this submission was that which could be seen for itself in the Roman version of the Ten Commandments. It must be understood that our forefathers in the English Reformation spoke much more plainly about these matters than we are accustomed to do. When they spoke of Antichrist they spoke not of a vague, mystical figure who was to appear at the end of the age, but of a real and identifiable power which had already appeared in history and which had already acted contrary to the will of Christ. Without making too fine a distinction, the standard view in English Protestantism for one hundred and fifty years after the Reformation was that the Roman system, *per se*, was the Antichrist. It is in this context, then, that Francis Bampfield describes the Roman variation of the Decalogue. 'The Anti-christian party have mangled the ten words,'[96] he charged. He meant by this that the ten commandments as they appeared in certain Roman Catholic catechisms differed from the ten commandments as they had been delivered at Sinai and recorded in Scripture. Bampfield then lists the Roman version as 'they publish them in their psalters and catechisms':

1. I am the Lord God; thou shalt have no other God but me.
2. Thou shalt not take the name of God in vain.
3. Remember to sanctify the holy days.
4. Honour thy father and mother.
5. Thou shalt not kill.
6. Thou shalt not commit adultery.
7. Thou shalt not steal.
8. Thou shalt not bear false witness.
9. Thou shalt not desire thy neighbour's wife.
10. Thou shalt not desire thy neighbour's goods.[97]

A careful comparison of this listing will reveal that the second commandment concerning the veneration of images is wholly omitted, that the original fourth commandment, now the third, is made to speak of 'holy days' rather than of the Sabbath, and that the tenth commandment is divided, in order to retain the original number of ten. The Sabbatarians met this somewhat amazing attempt to change the Decalogue and remove the basis of the seventh-day Sabbath, with understandable antagonism. It was 'unwarrantable', 'unlawful', 'the invention of men', 'a heathenish ceremony'. To quote Ockford, 'The Romish Church have adulterated the very letter of the second and fourth commandment most wickedly.'[98] It was strong language, and we must resist the temptation to allow our inbred aversion to such polemics to hide the basic message it sought to communicate. If we can do that, we shall know what Edward Elwall meant when, some two hundred years after the first dawning of the English Reformation, he wrote:

Heave the Pope quite off your shoulders, and all his inventions of red

letter days, Christmas Day, and Candlemas Day, Crucifixion Day, and
Resurrection Day, and Ascension Day, Andrew's Day, and Anthony's
Day, and all the whole catalogue of saints' days, not one of which God
ever commanded. Take all the Popish rubbish of every kind, throw it
upon the Thames, send it to the Tiber, and say from Rome ye came, and
to Rome we send you again.[99]

The Sabbatarians were convinced that Scripture required the Christian
observance of the seventh day, that Sunday had come into the Church by
way of post-apostolic and mediaeval Catholicism, and that allegiance to
Christ meant allegiance to the day which He Himself had created,
commanded, and kept. With this in mind, we give the last word on this
subject to Elwall, who had faith enough to believe that 'all those that will be
followers of God as dear children, and true followers of the Lamb, will not
make void the sacred ten commandments of God for men's traditions, but
be of those that have the true testimony of Jesus, and keep the commandments of God'.[100]

9. THE WHOLE MAN

Contrary to all ancient and modern anthropological dualism, biblical psychology is *monistic*, that is, it presents man as a perfect and indissoluble unity: body, soul, and spirit.... Its importance for the comprehension of the Bible could not be exaggerated: for the understanding of man this notion is essential.

J.R. Zurcher *The Nature and Destiny of Man* (1969) p.150

Anatomize man, take a view of all his lineaments and dimensions, of all his members and faculties, and consider their state severally, and all are transitory, even all that goeth to the subject man is corruptible, and himself but a bundle of corruption.... If all of man that goeth to his manhood be mortal, where, then, or what, is this immortal thing the soul they talk of?

Richard Overton *Man's Mortalitie* (1644) p.13

Few doctrines which re-appeared during the seventeenth century were met with more suspicion and hostility than those of the Mortalists or 'Soul-Sleepers'. Mortalists believed that man did not possess an inherently immortal soul, distinct from the body, but that Christ had brought immortality to light through the Gospel and that man's hope of eternal life was conditional upon his relationship to Christ and upon the resurrection of the body at the Last Day. In 1646 Richard Overton was sent to the Tower for having written a book which explained the Mortalist viewpoint, and in 1658 Thomas Hall listed Mortalism as one of the 'devilish' errors of the time. It had, as a matter of fact, appeared in England more than a hundred years previously in the teachings of William Tyndale, and had been condemned as heretical in the Forty-two Articles of Religion of 1553. The hostility which Mortalism attracted during the sixteenth and seventeenth centuries was due in large part to the fact that the true position of the Mortalists was misunderstood. It was felt that they were striking at the fundamental gospel hope of eternal life by denying that at death the souls of the righteous went to heaven. That they were not in fact attacking the promise of eternal life will become evident as this chapter unfolds.

The Mortalist viewpoint concerned itself with very much more than theological speculations as to what might happen or might not happen at death. It involved, more fundamentally, the nature of man as a created being, his relationship in redemption to Jesus Christ, the resurrection of the body, and the obligations of living the present life to the total glory of God. All this, and more beside, is contained in a phrase which occurred frequently in the writings of the time, and which provides the title of this chapter. 'The whole man' was man in his entirety, body and soul together, or, as the Mortalists would insist, body and spirit together, constituting the soul or the whole man, a psychosomatic unity which in its wholeness was the object of redemption. These were the views which had early appealed to Wycliffe and Tyndale and which also appealed to men in the seventeenth century like the poet, John Milton, and the philosophers, Thomas Hobbes and Henry Layton.

The Nature of Man

In order to see man as the Mortalists saw him, it is necessary to begin at the beginning. The Genesis record not only asserted that God had created man, but also explained how that act of creation had taken place: 'And the Lord God formed man of the dust of the ground, and breathed into his nostrils the breath of life, and man became a living soul' (Genesis ii 7). Into the body which the Creator had fashioned from the dust of the ground, He breathed what Scripture termed the 'breath of life'. This union of body and breath resulted in 'a living soul', in a rational, functioning entity called 'man'. To understand the Mortalist view it is of the utmost importance to recognise that they held that the Bible nowhere taught that at creation God infused into the body a separate entity called the soul, which in some inexplicable way caused the body to function and provided rationality and personality. Man in his wholeness came into being with the union of the body and the 'breath of life'. Richard Overton says of this divine act, 'When God had moulded, formed, and completely proportionated Adam of the dust of the ground, He breathed in his face the breath of lives, and man became a living soul ... that is He gave that lifeless body a communicative rational faculty or property of life, ... and so it became a living creature, or complete *anthropos*'.[1] Henry Layton observes that as a result of the union of body and breath man 'became a living person,' and that although there is a specific reference in Genesis ii 7 to the creation of man's body, 'there is no mention at all of creating a soul for him'. Layton says that the body thus formed was complete and ready to function in every way, needing only the breath to bring it to life and activity. This provided, 'the blood and humours then pullulant and ready for that operation were tinded and kindled into a flame ... which from that time continued and resided in the blood and humours of the body, acting and moving Adam's whole body and every part'. The life thus begun in Adam was perpetuated and sustained in like manner, 'by the gusts of the ambient air drawn through the lungs'.[2] Again on Genesis ii 7 Thomas Hobbes comments, 'God gave unto him vital motion .... He gave him life and breath, that is, made him a living creature.'[3] Overton says more explicitly:

> That lifeless lump became a living soul, and not such a living soul, another creature, a distinct being of itself, was infused into that formed matter, that had its being before that infusion and can be when the body ceaseth, as is vulgarly supposed. That which was breathed, before it was breathed was not a living soul, but that which was breathed upon

became the living soul. No living soul was ascribed to man before that, so that man was formed, and became a living soul.[4]

In the eyes of the writers who challenged the accepted doctrine of the soul's separate existence and inherent immortality, it was essential to grasp the fundamental truth contained in the Genesis account of man's origin.

It may be seen from what has just been said that a correct interpretation of the phrase 'breath of life' was of some importance. Mortalists insisted that it meant what it said and no more, and that there were no grounds whatsoever for any other interpretation. 'The breath of life which God breathed into Adam's nostrils was not an immaterial intelligent substance,'[5] Layton asserts. It 'signifies no more but that God gave him life,'[6] says Hobbes. The Mortalists believed that it was in this sense that the Bible generally used the word 'spirit' when speaking of the breath in man and other living creatures. This could be clearly seen, for example, in Job xxvii 3, 'All the while my breath is in me, and the spirit of God is in my nostrils.' The literal meaning of this text is found in the margin of the Authorised Version, and is given as 'the breath which God gave him'. The spirit here was no more than the breath which enabled life to continue. Similarly the statement in Ezekiel i 20, 'the spirit of life was in the wheels,' was equivalent to 'the wheels were alive'. And Hobbes explained that Ezekiel ii 2, 'the spirit entered into me, and set me on my feet,' meant 'recovered my vital strength' and not that any ghost 'or incorporeal substance entered into and possessed his body'.[7] The poet John Milton says that the creation record and other passages of Scripture teach that the spirit is to be equated with the breath, and 'that when God infused the breath of life into man, what man thereby received was not a portion of God's essence, or a participation of the divine nature'.[8] Even a convinced opponent of Mortalism like George Downham admits that the Greek word for 'spirit' in the New Testament, *pneuma*, 'being derived from *pneuo*, "to breathe", doth properly signify, in which sense it is often used, … the spirit of the nostrils,'[9] that is to say, the breath. Milton, then, is able to say with some conviction, 'Nor has the word spirit any other meaning in the sacred writings, but that breath of life which we inspire'.[10] It is indeed Milton in the *Treatise of Christian Doctrine* (rediscovered in 1824) who sets forth what is so clearly the basis of the Mortalist view:

Man is a living being, intrinsically and properly one and individual, not compound or separable, not, according to the common opinion, made up and framed of two distinct and different natures, as of soul and body,but that the whole man is soul and the soul man, that is to say, a body, or substance individual, animated, sensitive, and rational; and that the breath of life was neither a part of the divine essence, nor the soul itself, but as it were an inspiration of some divine virtue fitted for the exercise of life and reason, and infused into the organic body; for man himself, the whole man, when finally created, is called in express terms a living soul.[11]

The discerning reader will realise that in all this there is much more than abstruse theological hair-splitting. These issues lie at the heart of some of the most fundamental beliefs of the Christian faith, and it was precisely for this reason that the Mortalists of the seventeenth century wanted them thoroughly discussed and thoroughly understood. The real issue was that man was in essence mortal, subject to death, and not possessing inherently the property to live for ever. Adam, of course, had been given a conditional immortality in Paradise, and this the Mortalists recognised. His immortality had been dependent upon his obedience and when he failed to obey he forfeited the right he might have had to live for ever. Hobbes says that, 'God created Adam in an estate of living for ever which was conditional, that is to say, if he disobeyed not His commandment.' And again, 'Adam was created in such a condition of life, as had he not broken the commandment of God, he had enjoyed it in the Paradise of Eden eternally.'[12] However, since Adam did not obey, he forfeited that eternal life which might have been his, with the result that 'mortality entered upon himself, and his posterity, by his first sin'.[13] We are left to conjecture why Hobbes has not enjoyed the same respect as a theological writer as he has as a philosopher, since on this, as on other aspects of Puritan theology, he gives evidence of a grasp of basic issues at least equal to that of the best Puritan theologians and better than many. On Adam's loss of conditional immortality, Hobbes assures us that what Adam had lost, Christ had regained. 'Christ's passion is a discharge of sin to all that believe on him,' he says, 'and by consequence, a restitution of eternal life to all the faithful.'[14] Man, therefore, still has the promise of immortality, conditional now on his acceptance of Christ rather than on his obedience to God's specific command in Eden. The new dependence on Christ for eternal life and immortality again points to the simple fact that man, to borrow the title of one of Richard Overton's books on the subject, was 'wholly mortal'.

But what of mankind in general? Overton is at pains to stress that all men are mortal by natural generation as a consequence of Adam's mortality, and we may profitably pause to follow his reasoning here. Just as the entire tree is potentially in the seed, so the whole man is potentially 'in the seed of mankind'. All Adam's posterity were wholly in him both quantitatively, and qualitatively, 'so that whatsoever in time is actual by procreation, it was at first potentially wholly in its original'.[15] This means that 'mortal Adam must beget mortal children in his own likeness'. It is wholly contrary to logic and experience, to say nothing of revelation in Scripture, to believe that that which is immortal can 'generatively proceed from that which is mortal'. Scripture lays down the principle that 'that which is born of the flesh is flesh' (John iii 6), and therefore Overton says, 'by this mortal flesh cannot be generated an immortal spiritual soul that can subsist by itself dissolved from the flesh'.[16] Overton also sees in Job x 10-12 a synopsis of the whole procreative process by which man is made, 'from the act of generation even to his breathing,' a process which does not permit any deviation from natural law as laid down by the Creator, and which accordingly has no room at any stage for the supernatural infusion of an immortal soul. 'Whence it is clear,' Overton concludes, 'that whole man, flesh and spirit, is a second act [an act of secondary creation], formed in the womb.'[17] John Locke, the philosopher, states the case very neatly: 'But Adam, transgressing the command given him by his heavenly Father, incurred the penalty, forfeited that state of immortality, and became mortal. After this Adam begot children, but they were in his own likeness, after his own image; mortal, like their father.'[18]

A question of some magnitude presents itself at this stage of the enquiry. If, as the Mortalists maintained, the Bible taught that the whole man *was* a living soul as distinct from *possessing* a soul, how was the word 'soul' to be understood? Since it appeared frequently in the Bible, what did it signify? The short answer to this question was that it meant many things, as used in Scripture, depending upon the context and usage, but that it never meant a separate incorporeal entity such as was commonly believed to inhabit the body during life and then ascend to heaven at death. Hobbes quotes several biblical passages to support the position that the word 'soul' in Scripture 'signifieth always either the life, or the living creature, and the body and soul jointly, the body alive'.[19] Referring to Genesis i 20, in which the words 'creeping' and 'soul' appear in the original for 'moving creature', Hobbes points to the Authorised Version which adds 'that hath life'. 'Soul', here, stands for a creature which lives. In the following verse the original Hebrew text speaks of 'great sea monsters and souls', which is translated by 'great whales, and every living creature that moveth'. Following the Flood, God promised, 'Neither will I again smite ... every thing living,' that is, says Hobbes, 'every living creature' (Genesis viii 21). Again, in Deuteronomy xii 23, the text reads literally 'the blood is the soul,' but is translated by 'the blood is the life'. 'From which places,' Hobbes concludes, 'if by soul were meant a substance incorporeal, with an existence separated from the body, it might as well be inferred of any other living creature as of man.'[20] The argument is, of course, that the Hebrew word 'soul' does not refer intrinsically to an immaterial immortal entity. Indeed, it was generally recognised by biblical scholars that the word 'soul', when used in conjunction with man, generally referred to the person, to the whole man as such. Andrew Willett comments in this respect on Leviticus vi 2, 'if a soul sin and commit a trespass against the Lord,' by saying, 'that is, any person', for by this phrase it is 'usual in Scripture to take the soul for the person'.[21] And Richard Overton points out, 'In Scripture it [soul] is variously used upon various occasions,' as, for example, 'for the stomach, Proverbs xxvii 4; for the eyes, Jeremiah xiii 17; for the heart, I Samuel xviii; for God, Proverbs ix 16, Hebrews x 38, Jeremiah xiv 17; for the dead body, Psalm xvi 10; for the whole man, Leviticus vii 19, iv 1, Acts vii 14, Numbers xv 39, Romans xiii 1, Genesis xii 5, Acts ii 41, I Peter iii 20; for breath, Acts xx 10; for life, Isaiah liii 17'.[22]

Similarly the Greek word, *psuche*, translated as 'soul' in the New Testament, has other meanings, such as mind, life and heart, and in classical Greek several further meanings beyond these, such as will, delight, pleasure, affection, breath, mind, wind, anger, memory, thought, etc.[23] Overton's conclusion from the biblical evidence is similar to that which we have previously noted from Hobbes, 'From these places, those parts may as well be proved so many souls, or spirits of immortality, as from those where it is put for breath, or life'.[24] To this substantial array of textual evidence Henry Layton added the argument that the onus of proving the innate immortality of man lay with those who believed that doctrine to be true. If it could be demonstrated that the soul, during the lifetime of a man, acted even in some instances of itself, and apart from the body, then the immortal soul theory would be worthy of serious consideration. But since it is clearly evident that the soul cannot function without the body, as it cannot think, or remember, or understand as an immaterial entity, there is no ground for maintaining its separate existence. On the basis of the biblical evidence, then, it seemed quite incorrect to the Mortalists to say that the soul was a non-material entity, or that man himself was intrinsically immortal. Instead, they said that immortality was provided through the Gospel, and that eternal life 'was effected, revealed, consigned, and insured to man, in and through Christ, and will be accomplished in no other way than that spoken of by Christ and His apostles'.[25]

Death and Resurrection
The real point at issue between the Mortalists and those who opposed their doctrine centred on death and what happened to man beyond the present life. John Milton stood firm in the conviction that the accepted definition of death, 'which supposes it to consist in the separation of soul and body' was 'inadmissable'. If this was a true concept of death, Milton wanted to know whether it was the soul or body that actually died? Those who believed that soul and body were separated at death would not agree that the soul died, for in their view the soul was immortal, yet the body could not be said to die since by their own definition the body had no life of itself, being merely the house of the soul.[26] The logical conclusion from this was that death was not death at all, but continuing life, a point which Richard Overton was quick to recognise. 'If nothing died,' Overton says, 'but his body, then that died and his soul lived.' This meant that the body returned to its pre-animated state in which it was totally divorced of life, and the soul, having life in itself and being the life of the body, continued to exist after the moment of separation. 'And thus it must needs follow,' Overton concludes, 'that this death threatened [to Adam as a consequence of disobedience] was a mere scarecrow, even nothing at all.'[27] Referring to the related doctrine of eternal hell-fire, John Locke comments, 'It seems a strange way of understanding ... the plainest and directest words, that by death should be meant eternal life in misery.'[28]

The argument, then, revolved around the nature of death, and it seemed to the Mortalists a very short step indeed from belief in an immortal soul to an outright attack on the basic premise upon which the Gospel itself was built, for if there was no death, what need was there for a life-giver? To give the Mortalists their due, it was this very concern which lay at the heart of their position, and which in retrospect has earned them the deserved character of 'Christian Mortalists', as in the work of N.T. Burns, *Christian Mortalism from Tyndale to Milton* (1972).

To Milton, death was correctly defined as 'the loss or extinction of life',[29] and it occurred through a direct reversal of the process by which man had been created in the beginning. The union of the body and the breath had resulted in life, now the dissolution of body and breath resulted in death. When the breath, or the spirit, to use the word in the sense in which the Bible writers frequently used it, left the body, death followed. Indeed, since the soul did not exist as a separate entity, the breath was the only thing which could leave the body at the moment of dissolution. Milton turns here to Psalm civ 29-30, where creation and dissolution are set together in relationship to breath and spirit, and observes that 'Every living thing receives animation from one and the same source of life and breath, inasmuch that when God takes back to Himself that spirit or breath of life, they cease to exist.'[30] Here is the reversal of the creation experience. George Hammon, pastor of the General Baptist Church at Biddenden in Kent and a staunch advocate of the Mortalist view, says that when death occurs the body returns to dust and the spirit 'which liveth or dwelleth in it returneth to God'.[31] Overton argues that since there is 'no immortality in fallen man, ... he is wholly dissoluble'. This means that at death every element returns to its original state, 'His earthly part unto the earth, his moisture or watery part unto the water ... his airy part unto the air, and thus the composition man returneth to his simples, and so ceaseth from his being.'[32] Death, then, obvious as it is and unnecessary as it may appear to explain it, is simply the opposite of life. It is the separation of body and breath as opposed to the separation of body and soul, and it results in the non-existence of that living being called man which hitherto had existed as an intelligent functioning creature.

It logically followed that the condition of man immediately after death, or at any time subsequent to the dissolution of body and breath, was one of total rest, total cessation from mental and bodily activity. George Hammon explained that without that spirit which returned to God at death (i.e. the breath), the body 'is not in capacity, or capable of joy,' and that 'there is no remembrance of time or any thing amongst the dead'.[33] Death is a time of waiting, of resting, metaphorically speaking, of non-being, to be more accurate. Milton, as we might expect, comes with a carefully prepared list of biblical references, of which those relating to David served his purpose as well as any: 'For in death there in no remembrance of thee' (Psalm vi 5); 'O spare me, that I may recover strength, before I go hence, and be no more' (Psalm xxxix 13); 'The dead praise not the Lord, neither any that go down into silence' (Psalm cxv 17); 'While I live will I praise the Lord: I will sing praises unto my God while I have any being' (Psalm cxlvi 2). The Hebrew view of life and death as represented here in the experience of David causes Milton to comment, 'Certainly if he had believed that his soul would survive and be received immediately into heaven, he would have abstained from all such remonstrances, as one who was shortly to take his flight where he might praise God unceasingly.'[34] It was a fair comment on an experience which fairly represented the Old Testament view of death as a whole. Layton speaks similarly of the human experience in general. Breath sustains the body for the duration of life, but when the spirit/breath is withdrawn 'we die and are turned to our earth, and all our thoughts perish; our fancies, intellects and memories, our learning and abilities, as well as our love and our hatred, our passions and affections'.[35] Death brings with it a cessation of the normal functions of the mind. During death, Overton adds, 'There is no more present being to man than to a hidden, abortive embryo, ... no more capability than light to unborn infants, no more oppression or torment than when there is none to oppress, which is to say, he absolutely IS NOT.'[36]

The most accepted definition of death in Puritan theology — and this applies equally to the advocates of the natural immortality of man as to the Mortalists — was that death is a sleep. Indeed, to read Thomas Adams on this point one might be excused for concluding that he belonged to the Mortalist camp himself. 'The death of the godly is often called a sleep,' he says. 'It is said of the patriarchs and kings of Judah, "they slept with their fathers." So Paul saith, "they sleep in Christ". The coffin is a couch ... wherein he takes good rest that hath wrought hard in the work of his salvation before he went to bed.' But it is a sleep that will end, and Adams continues, 'So the godly sleep till the sound of a trumpet shall waken them, and then eternal glory shall receive them.'[37] In the light of statements like this, it is difficult to grasp the fact that Adams did not espouse Mortalism but that he clung to the accepted doctrine of the soul's immortality and its continued existence in heaven after death. Adams' views must be regarded as a measure of the confusion concerning the whole subject of death and immortality which persisted among the immortal-soul advocates, in contrast to the logical clarity of the Mortalist viewpoint. Adams' description of death as a sleep, representative as it was of the wider Puritan concept, was in harmony with the Mortalist position and might well have been the point at which mutual understanding began, had that desire been as genuine as it appears to be today. Certainly the comparison of death to sleep was an extremely important element in the Mortalist position, and for a readily understandable reason it found expression in many of the Mortalist writings. Thomas Lushington, recognising that man is a creature of time, relates the human experience of time to the sleep of death:

For when we are dead, and thereby void of all sense of time, the last moment of our life departing, and the first moment of our life returning (for return it shall at the last judgement) will seem one and the same to us at our rising again to life. They who lie in a deep sleep are not sensible of the time that passeth, though the time be very long, and death is a deeper sleep than any sleep of those that sleep alive. And this is the cause why the holy Scriptures do sometimes speak so, as if we should wholly live till the coming of Christ, or were presently after our death translated to the Lord, and so to the joys of heaven. For they have no regard of the time intercurrent between the last end of our life, and the coming of Christ, and the future happiness of the godly.[38]

Henry Layton likewise emphasises that time is of no consequence in death:

We may observe that death in the New Testament is frequently called and compared to a sleep, and that the most sound and profound. And in such a sleep ... whatsoever time passes over the sleeper's head, he hath no perceivance of. If it be two, ten, or twenty hours, the length or shortness of the passing time doth not at all appear to the sleeper, but at his waking he rises as if he had been but newly fallen asleep. Man's death is such a profound sleep, and his resurrection such a waking. If during that sleep there go over the dead man's head, months or years to an hundred or a thousand, this is no way perceivable by the dead person. When he rises, it will be but as if he had newly fallen asleep.[39]

The objection which many raised to the Mortalist teaching was that it robbed the believer of his hope of heaven and eternal life, leaving him with nothing to look for beyond death. Those who read carefully the preceding statements, and the many like them which could be found in the works of other Mortalist writers, would see that such objections were unfounded. In terms of practical experience, death made no difference to the believer's inheritance. As Overton would say, 'Though there be long time to the living till the resurrection, there is none to the dead.'[40]

It would be a serious distortion of Christian Mortalism in the seventeenth century if some emphasis were not placed on the positive nature of the Mortalist hope. The very word 'sleep' implies life rather than death, and those whose lives were hid with Christ in God were assured that at the appointed time there would be an awakening from sleep. The appointed time was the Last Day, the resurrection day when Christ would come again to break the power of the grave, and call forth its captives to everlasting life. It is difficult, perhaps impossible, to over-emphasise the importance of Christ's coming at the Last Day and the resurrection of the body in the scheme of redemption as Mortalists saw it propounded in Scripture. Layton says that 'the whole profession and practice of Christian religion is vain'[41] without the resurrection of the body. In making this assertion the Mortalists are not simply bringing to a convenient theological conclusion the scheme of redemption. They are declaring that the resurrection of the body is the only way to eternal life, for the resurrection of the body is in effect the resurrection of the whole man. Layton says that which dies also rises 'as wheat comes of wheat, and barley of barley,' so that man in his wholeness will come forth from the resurrection, 'the same person, soul and body, that died shall be revived and rise again'. This means the total man, 'his senses ... intellect, and judgements; his affections and passions, his knowlege and memory'.[42] It is the resurrection which is the focal point of Christian hope, the tangible recreation of man in his wholeness, rather than the survival of a partial, immaterial entity beyond death.

Milton defends the certainty of the resurrection from I Thessalonians iv 13-17, where Paul exhorts the Thessalonian believers to 'sorrow not, even as others which have no hope'. 'Why should they sorrow and have no hope,' Milton asks, 'if they believed that their souls would be in a state of salvation and happiness before the resurrection?'[43] It is to the resurrection that Paul directs the hope of believers, rather than to the survival of the individual soul. If we believe in the death and resurrection of Jesus, Milton argues, then we may have total confidence in the future, for it is God's future in Christ and those who sleep in Christ, 'will God bring with Him, that is, to heaven from the grave'.[44] Hence those who are alive at the coming of the Lord will not go to heaven before those who have slept. All will ascend together. Paul assures those who are still living, in hope, that they will not precede the dead to glory. But as Milton says, there would have been no reason to suppose that the survivors might go to heaven before the dead, 'if they who were asleep had long since been received into heaven, in which case the latter would not come to meet the Lord, but would return with Him'.[45] The eternal reward of believers, dead or alive, is rooted in time to the resurrection of the body at the Last Day, and in history to the resurrection of Christ Himself. Christ's resurrection is the surety of the resurrection of all who believe, and both are regarded in Mortalism as crucial to man's redemption. Any version of the Gospel which depreciates either Christ's resurrection or the general resurrection of the Last Day is in truth less than the whole Gospel. Man in his wholeness must in the end inherit that which man in his wholeness had been created to enjoy in the beginning. Thus, true Christian hope looks forward to the resurrection of the body, and few expounded that hope more picturesquely than did William Hodson in his *Credo Resurrectionem Carnis*:

A clock that is grown rusty is taken asunder by the maker's hand, disjoined wheel from wheel, and pin from pin, not to be lost, but to be repolished and put together again that it may go clearly. So death doth pluck the clock of our life asunder, when it hath struck the last stroke of breath, wheel from wheel, limb from limb, member from member, joint from joint, all to dust and pieces. But when the omnipotent Maker takes it into His own hands, and sets it together again at the resurrection, it shall go well in glory for ever.[46]

The resurrection of the body was, in fact, the resurrection of man in his wholeness, nothing less.

The Mortalists, as might be expected, soon discovered that their views were hotly contested by some of the more orthodox Puritan preachers, and it is an indication of their familiarity with the biblical evidence that they were able to refute the arguments brought against them. One example must suffice. Christ's promise to the thief on the cross was widely interpreted to support the popular notion that the righteous would receive their rewards immediately after death. The Authorised Version reads, 'Jesus said unto him, verily I say unto thee, Today shalt thou be with me in paradise' (Luke xxiii 43). George Hammon had thought about this text in relationship to the biblical doctrine as a whole, and had concluded that it did not support the idea that men go immediately to heaven at death. To begin with, Christ had not ascended to heaven on the day of the crucifixion. Even after the resurrection, He had said to His followers, 'Touch me not, for I am not ascended to my Father,' although later, but still prior to the ascension, He had permitted them to touch Him. Furthermore, it could not be presumed that the thief had actually died on the day of the crucifixion. It was more likely that he had died later. Christ's death occurred at the ninth hour when there were only three hours left before the Sabbath. In accordance with Roman custom, the legs of the two thieves who were crucified with Christ were broken while they hung on the cross to prevent the possibility of an escape from what was known to be a lingering death, which sometimes lasted for several days. The thieves were not dead, probably, when Christ was taken from the cross a few hours before the Sabbath began. Hammon's comment here is worthy of note: 'Although Christ said that day to the thief that he should be with Him in paradise, yet it doth not follow that Christ and the thief were that day to be together in paradise, because the thief was not dead, nor Christ ascended that day.'[47] The more likely explanation of this text, and the one that other Mortalists also would use as being more in harmony with the total revelation of Scripture concerning man, death, and eternal life, was 'that Christ gave him a promise of paradise that day,'[48] a promise that would be fulfilled to the thief, as to all who would put their trust in Christ, at the great resurrection day.

The Doctrine of Natural Immortality

Having set forth what they believed to be the biblical teaching of man, death, resurrection and eternal life, the Mortalists felt that it was equally necessary to expose the true character of the natural-immortality doctrine. If it was not a biblical teaching, from whence did it take its origin? Why had it been almost unanimously accepted by orthodox Christendom? And what were its effects on the beliefs and practices of ordinary Christians within the body of Christ? In seeking the answers given in the seventeenth century to these questions, we will turn first to two extremely able men, who, in the 1690s, attempted to come to grips with the whole question of immortality and resurrection, which had by then rumbled on without a definitive answer for more than a hundred and fifty years since the beginning of the Reformation. Henry Layton's book, *A Search for Souls* (1692), was a genuine attempt to solve the problem of the soul's existence, and had been written as a response to the unsatisfactory theories of man's nature and destiny as Layton found them set forth from the Greek philosopher, Pythagoras, to the sixteenth-century French philosopher, Descartes. It was a judicious piece of work, comprehensive, restrained, and well-argued. Humphrey Hody's *A Resurrection of the Body* (1694) was the work of a renowned scholar, the Dean of Wadham College, Oxford, and Regius Professor of Greek at that University. Although falling short of accepting the Mortalist position, it was nevertheless an important statement of the resurrection hope in the Christian thought of the time.

Layton recognised that the idea of a separate, immortal soul was several centuries older than Christianity, and that it had been particularly strong in the pre-Christian Greek philosophy of Pythagoras, Anaxagoras, Socrates, Plato and Aristotle.[49] Broadly speaking, the Greek view of man, as it eventually came to be associated with the Platonic school, was that dualistic concept which held that man consisted of a body and a soul, in which the material body was essentially evil, and the immaterial soul essentially good. The temporal body housed the eternal soul, which at death sought refuge in another body, though not necessarily in a human body. Hody says that this was 'the common and received opinion of the Greeks' in the pre-Christian age.[50] Into this dualistic thought-world the Christian Church was born, with its basically Hebrew emphasis on the wholeness of man and the resurrection of the body as the means by which man might attain to immortality. Layton says that the majority of early Christian thinkers, particularly the Greek and Latin fathers of the Church, rejected this pagan Greek view, and even Hody admits that belief in the resurrection of the body and soul-sleep were 'not looked upon as heretical' in the early Church.[51] Although both statements are unquestionably correct in principle, we must not overlook the immense pressure of Greek thought which inevitably came to bear on the early Christian apologists, nor Hody's equally appropriate comment that the novel Christian concept 'was by all the Greeks in general exploded, not one Christian doctrine so generally and with so much contempt rejected'.[52] Hody even suggests that the passage in I Corinthians xv relating to the resurrection of the body was written by Paul with such emphatic clarity because the Corinthian believers, with their Greek background, found the Christian view of the resurrection 'a strange and incredible thing'.[53] It is a factor too easily forgotten that in its infancy the Church faced both the open hostility of pagan Rome and the much more subtle hostility of pagan Greek philosophy.

The story of the pagan infiltration of Christian thought in the early centuries is well enough known in general and does not need to be recounted again. What is more specifically to our purpose is that eventually, as with so many other original Christian teachings, philosophical pagan influences prevailed over the biblical doctrine of man, and the Church capitulated to the pressure of Platonic dualism. Once again, Origen of Alexandria is singled out as being responsible for the departure from biblical doctrine, although it is only fair to say that many other teachers were involved in what was again a gradual transition from the Judaeo-Christian doctrine of man, which had characterised the New Testament Church, to that which took its place in the third, fourth, and succeeding centuries. Hody says it is quite clear from the writings of Origen 'and other authors' that Christian teachers in the third century 'asserted with the Platonists that the body is no part of man, but the soul alone is the whole man and that the body is the prison of the soul'.[54] That Christian belief could have come so far in such a relatively short time was due in large measure to the allegorical method of interpreting the Bible, usually attributed to Origen. By this method, that which appeared to be literal in Scripture was given a spiritual or allegorical meaning. Hody refers to Origen's explanation of the story of Adam and Eve as they existed in the Garden of Eden before the fall. Until the entrance of sin they existed without a body, according to Origen. But after sin, 'God clothed them with bodies by way of punishment, and this he [Origen] says is meant by that place in Genesis where it is said that unto Adam and to his wife did the Lord God make coats of skins and clothe them. By coats of skins he [Origen] understands bodies.'[55] It is self-evident that virtually any conceivable conclusion could be reached by this method of interpretation. Just how much responsibility Origen alone must bear for introducing the Platonic idea of the soul into the Church is perhaps a matter for conjecture. Certainly his influence in moulding subsequent Christian thought was very considerable. What is beyond question is that by the fourth or fifth century the doctrine of the soul's immortality and separate existence was well established, and that it was thereafter perpetuated in orthodox Christendom in the West by the mediaeval Church. This accords with Layton's statement, made in 1692, that the doctrine had been part of Roman dogma 'for about the space of eleven hundred years, time enough to radicate and fix the belief of a self-subsisting soul in all believers deriving under that Church, or all that have been subjected thereunto'.[56]

This subtle syncretism of Greek philosophic paganism with Christian belief, while challenged to some extent by the Reformation, had not been wholly eradicated by the sixteenth-century Reformers, hence Layton's further statement that Christian theologians had unwittingly perpetuated Greek dualism since the Reformation by upholding the doctrine of the soul's immortality. To the average Christian in Puritan England, who in all likelihood was more concerned with doctrinal correctness than his counterpart in succeeding generations, this meant that Greek paganism had bequeathed error to the Church of Rome and that the Church of Rome had in turn bequeathed error to the Church of England. The burden of Christian Mortalists in the late sixteenth and seventeenth centuries was to communicate the truth that the concept of an immortal soul was not a Christian doctrine at all, but an idea which had originated in pre-Christian paganism. Hody and Layton were by no means the only Christian thinkers in the seventeenth century to recognise the truth of all this, as Milton implies when he castigates those 'who think that truth is to be sought in the schools of philosophy rather than in the sacred writings,'[57] and as Hobbes declares outright when he says that it was 'by contagion of the demonology of the Greeks' that the Church had come to believe 'that the souls of men were substances distinct from their bodies'.[58]

The point at which all this became intensely relevant to Christian believers in Puritan England was in the continuing opposition of Protestantism to the doctrines of Rome. In the ecumenical climate of the twentieth century it is difficult for the average Churchman to sense the strength of feeling with which early Protestantism rejected the corruptions and deviations which at the time were generally believed to have come into Christian thought during the mediaeval supremacy of the Catholic Church. In some contemporary circles it might well be considered injudicious even to raise such matters. No such reluctance existed in the seventeenth century, however, and of all the errors in doctrine and practice from which Protestantism sought to cleanse the Church of Christ, more were attributable to the doctrine of the soul's immortality than to any other single corruption of which Rome might have been guilty. Thomas Hobbes calls it the 'window ... that gives entrance to the dark doctrines' of eternal torment, purgatory, prayers for the dead, and hence of indulgences calculated to lessen the punishment of those not yet in heaven.[59] Henry Layton says that the doctrine of natural immortality is 'the only foundation' for these and kindred teachings 'which can have no common sense in them, if souls do not subsist in a state of separation'.[60] Richard Overton speaks of purgatory, infant limbo, the invocation of saints, and the adoration of Mary, and declares 'a world of such-like fancies are grounded upon the invention of the soul'.[61] Overton adds that most of the heresies and deviations present in Christian thought take their origin from the doctrine of natural immortality, and further, that 'the kingdom of Antichrist depends upon it'.

Antichrist, of course, throughout the seventeenth century is essentially papal Rome, and Overton's main concern is that the doctrine of natural immortality 'undermineth Christ, undervalueth and lesseneth the purchase of His sufferings, and denieth the resurrection'.[62] This, perhaps, is the most serious charge of all, and one which the Christian Mortalists insisted on pressing. If man inherently possesses immortality, what need is there, in the last analysis, of Christ's death and resurrection, and hence of the general resurrection at the Last Day? Paul said that Christ had brought immortality to light through the Gospel. The Mortalists said that this could not be if man possessed immortality within himself. It was in this sense that Overton, and many others with him in the seventeenth century, began to understand the Antichrist, not as one openly and arrogantly opposed to Christ, but as one who took the place of Christ, a usurper who provided an alternative way of salvation and an alternative system of belief to the faith once delivered to the saints. It is, indeed, the biblical doctrine of man as understood and expounded so clearly by the Mortalists that gives all glory to Christ, and which must be defended against the insidious deviations of Antichrist. Hence Overton concludes that, 'Man hath not wherewith at all to boast ... but is provoked wholly out of himself, to cast himself wholly on Jesus Christ with whom in God our lives are hid, that when He who is our life shall appear, we might also with Him appear in glory, to whom be the honour of our immortality for ever.'[63]

The Body Temple

The doctrine of the whole man, central as it was to Christian Mortalism and its hopes, was in reality restricted neither to Mortalists, nor to the future. The concept of the whole man was widespread in Puritan thought as a whole, and it brought an immediate obligation of immense practical implications to the present life of every professing Christian. Greek philosophy had depreciated the body as something intrinsically evil and in opposition to the spirituality of the soul. This idea, when taken into the Christian Church and translated into practice, had resulted in the severe inflictions of mediaeval monasticism — fasting, flagellation, self-mortification, and self-mutilation — which chastened the body in an attempt to purify the soul. The Puritan doctrine of the whole man placed an altogether different emphasis on the body, since it recognised the essential wholeness of the individual and the corresponding inter-relationship of the mental, the physical and the spiritual. Man was not at war against himself in that sense, but was to live in recognition of the essential wholeness of his being.

Francis Bampfield recognises the interaction of mind and body when he speaks of unrestrained emotions weakening 'the whole man' and causing palpitations of the heart, an impaired appetite, a disturbed digestion and loss of strength. These, in turn, affect mental perception, 'the senses are weakened, the mind is darkened, the imagination is clouded and frighted'. All in all there are, Bampfield maintains, 'many sickening effects upon the whole man'.[64] Symon Patrick, the esteemed Bishop of Chichester, and later of Ely, speaks for an innumerable company of godly preachers when he reminds us of Paul's teaching that 'the body of a holy Christian' is 'the temple of the Holy Ghost' (I Corinthians vi 19). The body, which in the Greek view is but a prison, Patrick says in the apostolic view 'is a temple, when it is in Christ'. When the Lord possesses a man and rules in his life, he possesses also the body and 'makes it a place where God dwells, where God is worshipped and glorified, where God appears and manifests Himself'.[65] Another writer explains that it is a Christian duty to glorify God in the whole man, which it is impossible to do if the body is disregarded and dishonoured, as it undoubtedly will be if a man forgets that his body is 'not for drink any more than for fornication ... or any other filthy service'.[66] The body, then, is not to be despised in the Christian life, and there is much wisdom and experience in Thomas White's conclusions that those delights and comforts of the body which God has created for its necessary recreation are not to be denied to a pious life in their due proportion,' and 'a pious and orderly life, truly and really more abounds with corporal delights than the life of the wicked'.[67]

At few points did the Christian's duty to care for his body as the temple of the Holy Spirit find greater expression in the Puritan pursuit of practical godliness than in the matter of diet. It is possible to read many of the great Puritan theologians whose writings have been quoted again and again in the preceding chapters of this book, and find in them the most specific advice concerning diet and its relationship to the spiritual life. William Perkins, Thomas Adams, Thomas Gataker, John Ball, Joseph Alleine and Richard Baxter, all speak of the believer's duty in Christ to look after his body by exercising a responsible control over what he eats and drinks. If, in an affluent society like our own, these men seem severe over this matter, it is only because they understand the relationship of the body and the mind, and the supremacy of the mind in spiritual matters. We may pause to note only a selection of the relevant comments, and in so doing we shall observe two pieces of advice which are to be found repeatedly in the Puritan concern with food and diet. Alleine and Baxter both plead for moderation in eating and drinking. Alleine fears that over-eating is 'a very common sin' among Christians, and advises all believers to set a special watch upon their appetites. In order to retain a healthy body it is better to eat only as much at one meal as will ensure that one is hungry again by the next meal. There are two forms of intemperance which the Christian must guard against in the matter of diet. They concern the quantity of food which is eaten, and the type of food which constitutes the diet. 'We offend in the first,' he says, 'when we eat more than we can digest,' and in the second when we eat that which is not fit to be eaten.[68] Baxter brings both possibilities together in an unusually frank comment about those who 'abuse their bodies and neglect their health':

> Its ill with men when they cram in their bellies as if they were laying provision in a garner, rather than eating for digestion, and when they are so curious and must have their devouring appetites pleased, that the cook is held in more esteem than the husbandman. . . . Those that are prone to excess, or daintiness of diet, they nourish their own diseases, and are led by the great glutton the devil, whom I will not fear to call the belly devil, which indeed is the worst and most pernicious of all devils.[69]

In Alleine's view too few Christians understand the concept of temperance as it relates to eating, and it is a 'great' and 'common evil' for a man to think that he may eat merely to satisfy his appetite.[70] Baxter adds that while animals may live to eat, Christians should eat to live and that to the glory of God. Therefore, he advises, it is a Christian duty to choose one's food with care, bearing in mind that it must be 'plain or simple', since its first function is to sustain life and since life depends on health and strength, 'for both of which nothing is better than a light and easy diet, as being most helpful to digestion and agility of the body'.[71] On the intemperate habit of over-eating, Thomas Adams observes concerning health, 'We seek it in

THE WHOLE MAN   175

ull dishes and, behold, there we lose it.'[72] And regarding the use of
correct food, John Ball advises that 'dainty meats are very dangerous and
deceitful,' an 'evil' which 'faith doth wisely foresee and watch to pre-
ent'.[73]

There is in the foregoing much of what today would pass as plain good
ense, to say nothing of the knowledge more recently available from
nutritional and dietetic studies. Puritanism, however, did not derive its
theological conclusions from commonsense, useful as that undoubtedly
was on occasions. It required the plain word of Scripture, and when the
Puritan preacher turned to the Bible for guidance on the matter of eating
and drinking he found, interestingly enough, not only that Paul commanded
believers to eat and drink to the glory of God (I Corinthians x 31), but also
that man's diet had been prescribed in the beginning by the Creator
Himself. As they studied the biblical record of human origins, Puritan
theologians discovered that man had been created to subsist on what
would later come to be called a vegetarian diet, and that the use of flesh as
food had been permitted only after the Flood. Richard Overton explains,
Beasts were not given man to eat in the Innocency, but to all flesh wherein
was the breath of life, was given the green herb for meat.'[74] Andrew
Willett and Samuel Mather are a little more explicit. Willett says that in the
beginning animals were 'not yet necessary for food, for the herbs and fruits
were sufficient for man's food,' and Mather, commenting on Genesis ix 3,
which he takes as permission to eat flesh following the Flood, says, 'He
enlargeth their provision of food by giving them a commission to eat the
flesh of brute creatures,' although 'at first there is no mention of any other
provision, but the fruits of the earth'.[75] The high priest of Puritan theology,
William Perkins, makes a similar comment on the same passage: 'After the
Flood flesh was permitted, but blood forbidden, Genesis ix 3-4. From that
time there was commanded a distinction of meats, whereof some were
clean, some unclean.'[76] A perceptive comment on man's original diet
comes from Thomas Tryon, who argues that if man had continued in
obedience he would never have eaten flesh, since all death, including the
death of animals, is the result of sin, with the inevitable implication that
flesh was never intended to be part of man's diet at all. Man, therefore,
was put into a garden amongst innocent herbs, fruits, and grains, which
were intended and ordained for his food'.[77]

With Thomas Tryon we come to one of the most interesting characters
whose writings appeared during the latter part of the seventeenth century.
Tryon is chiefly remembered for a book entitled *Healths Grand Preserv-
tive*, first published in 1682, and soon reprinted with a new title, *The Way
to Health*. The work was remarkable, not only since it advocated a
vegetarian diet in general, but also on account of its apparent foreknow-
edge of medical and nutritional principles which at the time were little
known, if they were known at all. Tryon's views were based on the Pauline
teaching of the body temple and also on the example of the prophet Daniel
and his companions in the court of the Babylonian king, Nebuchadnezzar

(Daniel i 8-16). When confronted with the order to partake of the food and drink provided for the king, Tryon says that 'Daniel entreated leave to continue that clean, simple food they had accustomed themselves unto, viz, herbs, grains, and fruits, and pure water to drink'.[78] Tryon's argument is that if a vegetarian diet has proved beneficial to man in the past, it can have the same effect on men in the present. 'Our forefathers,' he says, 'did not make their stomachs the burial places of dead bodies,' yet they lived 'to wonderful ages in perfect health' on a diet consisting chiefly of 'herbs, fruits, and grains'.[79] Tryon rejects flesh as food on the grounds that it quickly putrifies both before and after consumption, and that it endangers general health and well-being since animals are widely subject to disease. The natural uncleanness of many animals argues against the use of their flesh as food, and the treatment they receive in the abattoir 'renders their flesh still more unwholesome,'[80] Tryon says. His alternative is what is known today as a lacto-vegetarian diet consisting of legumes, grains, fruits, wholewheat bread, cheese and milk, with the observation that their origin is 'more clean' and that they 'afford a more excellent nourishment'. Tryon adds that by overeating with this kind of diet 'the health will not thereby be brought into such danger as by the superfluous eating of flesh'.[81] The general tenor of Tryon's interesting book is summarised in the following quotation:

> Now the sorts of food and drinks that breed the best blood and finest spirits are herbs, fruits, and various kinds of grains, also bread, and sundry sorts of excellent food made by different preparations of milk, and all dry food, out of which the sun hath exhaled the gross humidity, by which all sorts of pulses and grains become of a firmer substance. So likewise oil is an excellent thing, in nature more sublime and pure than butter. And if you do eat fat flesh, let it be sparingly, and not without a good store of bread and herbs.[82]

There may be a reference here to the advantages of what have only recently become known as polyunsaturated fats over the so-called saturated animal fats, although we cannot be sure precisely what kind of 'oil' Tryon refers to. Be that as it may, Tryon would surely have been immensely gratified had he been able to witness the revived interest which many of his dietary suggestions have attracted in more recent years, particularly as much of that interest accords with his own conviction that the body is 'the temple of God, wherein His blessed Spirit delights to dwell, and communicate its gifts and graces'.[83]

The interest which Tryon's views on diet and vegetarianism still arouse after almost three centuries is matched, if not surpassed, by his observations regarding tobacco and the habit of smoking. Tobacco had been introduced into England late in the sixteenth century by Sir Walter Raleigh, and attempts had been made to prohibit it on various grounds both at home and in New England during the seventeenth century. James I disliked its smell; some thought that smoking was contrary to nature; others believed it encouraged farmers to neglect the production of necessary food crops. Tryon, however, opposed the use of tobacco on medical grounds, and in some of his conclusions must be judged to have been far ahead of his time. He describes tobacco as a 'herb endued with extreme qualities' and 'high poisons', useful perhaps as an ointment, and hence 'much safer being applied outwardly, than inwardly taken'.[84] Tobacco is 'one of nature's extremes', he explains, having 'a strong, fulsome, poisonous nature'. It is inherently and irreversibly contrary to man's well-being, since 'there is no way known, or preparation found out, that can destroy its poisonous qualities, or reconcile and make it friendly to man's nature'.[85] Tryon is also aware of the addictive nature of tobacco, classifying it with 'the continual use of such things [which] ... requires their continuation,' and which 'if a man does leave them, at the first nature seems to want them,'[86] and he is concerned to underline the habit-forming pattern of tobacco:

> The first taking of it in pipes is both difficult and troublesome to nature, and there is no preparation known that will make this herb friendly or familiar to nature, but only the continual custom of taking it, which awaken and strengthen its own quality in the stomach, which in the beginning was weak, but by custom is become strong, so great is the power of everything in increasing its likeness, and it becomes as though it were natural. And there is as much difficulty to leave the use of such things (if not more) as there was at first to make them familiar.[87]

The addictive property of tobacco is similar to that 'in brandy' and other drinks with a high alcohol content, 'the more unnatural and greater the extreme is, the more troublesome it is to leave it'.[88] We can only conclude that Tryon would have said of smoking what a contemporary said of drinking:

> It is a high offence to our glorious Creator. It perverts the end of our redemption. It unmans the man, and is a contempt of death, the grave, and hell itself. If men had any reverence for their God, Creator, Saviour, Sanctifier, if any honour to their own nature, if any sense of mortality and of the reference this mortal life hath to eternal life, they would never live it thus, throw away their time thus.[89]

In fact, he did make a similar comment, and with it we may appropriately conclude our survey of the Puritan understanding of the wholeness of man. With due deference to the 'temple of God', Tryon addresses all who are concerned with the continuing health of body and mind. Their obligation before God is to 'make the body, pleasant, healthful, and fit to discharge all its functions ... which must be done by sobriety, gentleness and temperance in meats, drinks, and exercises'.[90]

To live one's present life to the glory of God in Christ, in the whole man, is the believer's anticipation of resurrection and eternal life, in the whole man, by Christ, at the end. There were many in the seventeenth century whose concept of man in life and death was nearer to that which attracts the attention of some Christian thinkers now, than to what characterised most of their predecessors.

10. THE RETURN OF CHRIST

Implicit and explicit throughout the teachings of our Saviour is the necessity of a second advent to complete the work of salvation begun at His first advent. The first advent witnessed the formal establishment of the kingdom of divine grace, announced first by John the Baptist (Matthew iii 2) and later by the Lord (Mark i 14-15) and His disciples (Matthew x 7). ... The second coming of Christ is the great climactic event that brings this age of earth's history to a close and that marks the transition to the ceaseless ages of eternity. The glorious appearing of Jesus Christ is the 'blessed hope' toward which the Christian looks forward in this life (Titus ii 13) as a time when he will be united forever with his Lord (John xiv 2-3; I Thessalonians iv 17).

Seventh-day Adventist Bible Dictionary (1960) p.976

Scripture is express unto a double appearing or coming of Christ. The first was his coming in the flesh, coming into the world, coming unto his own, ... to discharge the work of his mediation, especially to make atonement for sin in the sacrifice of himself, unto the accomplishment of all promises made concerning it and all types instituted for its representation. The second is in glory, unto the judgement of all, when he shall finish and complete the eternal salvation of the Church. ... His first appearance is past and appear the second time he will, ... and the salvation of the Church shall be completed.

John Owen *A Continuation of the Exposition of ... Hebrews* (1680) p.469

The Doctrine of the Second Advent

The passing of the English crown from the Tudors to the Stuarts was to prove a significant milestone in the development of Puritan thought. William Haller remarks that from this point Puritan preachers 'increased in number and influence faster than before, finding a growing audience ever more willing to listen'.[1] As time went on and the full content of the biblical revelation became more apparent, clergy and laity alike became increasingly aware of the eschatological character of Scripture. A renewed emphasis on Christ's second coming, with its associated doctrines, now appears as one of the major contributions which Puritanism made to the recovery of the total biblical message. Probably at no other time in English history has the doctrine of the second advent been so widely proclaimed

or so readily accepted as in the heyday of Puritanism. Furthermore, it is
clear that many of the most eloquent advocates of the second advent in
the seventeenth century were prominent theologians loyal to the norms of
accepted doctrinal orthodoxy.

The certainty with which preachers in Puritan England eagerly anticipated the coming of Christ is matched only by the clarity with which they
understood the doctrine and its related issues. Samuel Smith, one of the
many Puritan divines ejected at the Restoration had, in 1618, written *The
Great Assize, or, Day of Jubilee*, a work which proved to be so popular that
by the turn of the century it had been through no less than thirty-nine
editions. This one book alone must have given an understanding of the
second advent hope to many thousands throughout the land. Joseph
Alleine would rather point his people to Christ's return than to His
resurrection. This was the sure hope of the Church,'built upon the
foundation of that sure word … not … upon the sand of mortality'.
Alleine knows 'how fully doth this word assure us that this same Jesus …
shall appear the second time unto salvation to them that look for him'.[2]
Christopher Love, who also wrote at great length on the theme of the
second advent, argued that the certainty of Christ's coming rested on a
three-fold biblical foundation — 'The immutability of God's decree … the
infallibility of Christ's promise … the impartiality of his justice'. It was a
'promise made by Christ Himself,' and hence 'the great pillar of our
hopes'.[3] John Seagar cited the following texts to support his belief that
Christ would come again: Jude xiv, Psalm ￼ v 3, Matthew xxiv 30,
Matthew xxv 31, Matthew xxvi 34, Luke xxi 37, John xiv 3, Acts i 11, I
Thessalonians iv 15-16 and James v 7-8. He then concluded, 'If the
second coming of Christ in the flesh be confirmed unto us by so many
plain testimonies of Scripture, we should not doubt … but should look
upon it as that which shall be most sure and certain.'[4] When the Bible
consistently declared that Christ would return literally, bodily and personally at the Last Day, Puritan theologians could see no reason to take an
alternative position.

Both Seagar and Love warn against a spiritualised interpretation of this
doctrine, as being contrary to the plain meaning of Scripture. Love points
out that the concept of a spiritualised second advent was a third-century
deviation from Christian orthodoxy introduced by Origen, and that it should
not be regarded as the biblical view. On this point Love explains:

It was the great mistake of Origen, though he holds for the coming of
Christ again, that he pleads for the coming of Christ in spirit. Therefore
the text where it is said, 'You shall see the Son of Man coming in the
clouds of heaven,' Origen understands by the clouds, to be the saints,
because it is mentioned in Scripture that the believers are a cloud of
witnesses. Now this is to pervert the whole letter of the Bible, and turn
all the Scripture into an allegory and metaphorical sense.… I only
mention this to confute those that follow the conceit of Origen, merely to
make Christ's coming to be but a spiritual coming, a coming in the

hearts of saints.[5]

To be strictly accurate, many biblical scholars of the time, Love among them, recognised that the Bible appeared to refer to the coming of Christ in several ways. Love himself drew attention to three apparent comings of Christ mentioned in Scripture, the first in the flesh at the incarnation, another 'spiritual' coming through the Gospel, and the third, His final appearance to judgement at the Last Day. Love stressed that it was Christ's coming to judgement at the end which was referred to, for example, in Colossians iii 4 and John xiv 3, the texts on which his own books, *Heaven's Glory* and *The Penitent Pardoned*, had been based. Therefore, Love says, 'By Christ's appearing here, is meant that glorious manifestation of Jesus Christ upon earth at the time when He shall come at the last day,'[6] and 'The same Jesus that you saw ascend, shall descend, so that it cannot be Christ in His spirit, but in His person.'[7] Christ was to come at the end no less visibly or personally than He had come originally through the incarnation.

Beyond the certainty with which Christ's second coming was anticipated, there is possibly no point of wider agreement among Puritan theologians than on what Love describes above as 'a glorious manifestation'. Ussher's description of Christ coming at the end 'environed with a flame of fire, attended with all the host of the elect angels,'[8] is matched by Robert Bolton's scripturally toned phrase 'coming in the clouds of heaven with power and great glory'.[9] John Owen's exposition of the Epistle to the Hebrews, first begun in 1668, refers to an 'illustrious appearance filling the whole world with the beams of it,'[10] a somewhat later echo, this, of Thomas Taylor's earlier description of the second advent which had appeared in his commentary on Titus, published in Cambridge in 1619. To Taylor, Christ would come 'in such glory as neither the tongue can utter, nor the mind of man conceive'.[11] Baxter adds, 'Methinks I see Him coming in the clouds, with the attendants of His angels in majesty, and in glory.'[12] There are indeed few exponents of the second advent doctrine in the seventeenth century who sense the glory of the Last Day more than does Baxter:

> If there be such cutting down of boughs and spreading of garments, and crying hosanna, to one that comes into Jerusalem riding on an ass; what will there be when He comes with His angels in His glory? If they that heard Him preach the gospel of the kingdom, have their hearts turned within them, that they return and say, 'Never man spake like this man,' then sure they that behold His majesty and His kingdom, will say 'There was never glory like this glory.'[13]

In attempting to explain the manner in which they believed Christ would come, Puritan theologians often compared His second coming at the end of time with His first coming at the incarnation. 'When our Saviour Jesus Christ lived on earth, He came in misery, very base and lowly,' said Samuel Smith, 'but now, He shall come as a king, full of majesty and glory.'[14] Christopher Love, again, is quite explicit. When Christ came the first time,

He came as a servant and in a manner befitting a servant, but 'at His second appearing He shall appear in majesty as a king. In His first appearing He appeared in contempt in a manger, in His second He shall shine in glory in the clouds. In His first appearing, He had only beasts to be His companions, in His second appearing He shall have saints and angels to be His attendants.'[15] Whatever merits, or demerits, there were to be in later interpretations of the second advent doctrine, it is beyond doubt that in the seventeenth century men widely concurred in expecting a glorious visible advent and a personal and literal appearance of Christ at the end of the age, and that in doing so they believed that they were correctly representing New Testament teaching.

But when would Christ's second advent occur? In attempting to provide an answer to this tantalising question, Puritan theologians and preachers were aware that they were wrestling with a problem that went back to the earliest days of the Christian Church. Since Puritan theologians built upon the foundation laid by the great Reformers of the sixteenth century, and since Reformation theology was itself contained within the framework of the New Testament, there was but one answer that could be given to this question: Christ would come soon. Thomas Hall is thoroughly represent- ative of his age in re-echoing the New Testament note of imminence when he says, 'The days we live in are the last days. Our times are the last times, . . . this is the last hour, . . . and upon us the ends of the world are come.'[16] The end of the present order was imminent. As Hall logically points out, 'If the apostle thought the day of the Lord was at hand sixteen hundred years ago, we may well conclude that it is near now.'[17] The Puritan preachers did not seek to dissociate themselves from the New Testament emphasis on the imminence of the advent or from the reiterat- ion of that emphasis given by later generations, and Thomas Adams conveys the accepted view of world history when he says, 'The morning was in the days of the Patriarchs, Christ bore the heat and noon of the day, and we are those upon whom the latter ends of the world are come.' Adams goes on to describe the symptoms of the world's sickness unto death, 'the declination of goodness, the fainting of religion,' by which 'one could see the sun of this world ready to set, and the night drawing on,' the world itself lying 'bed-rid, . . . fetching a thick, sick, and short breath'.[18]

Henry Symons, the rector of Southfleet in Kent, had evidently read several books on prophecy and last-day events. Although he could not agree with Johannes Alsted, professor of philosophy at Herborn, that the end would come in 1657, or with John Napier, the Scottish mathematician, that it would occur in 1688, he could nonetheless agree with many of the illustrious Church fathers of the past, Tertullian, Augustine and Cyprian among them, that Christ's coming was near, and indeed that it was always near in the thinking of a committed believer. 'He is on the wing, He comes post, He will be here before most are aware,'[19] Symons declared. It was in this sense that Hanserd Knollys, who produced several works in the later Puritan period on prophecy and the last days, held that the signs of Christ's

coming were 'to strengthen the faith of His people, that they might upon
Scripture ground believe that this world shall have an end, and that the
Lord Jesus will come again from heaven in power and great glory'.[20] To
believe that Christ's coming was near was only to believe as the apostles
themselves had believed.

The conviction that Christ's coming was at hand was widespread in
England during the seventeenth century, but, as Henry Symons and many
others plainly demonstrate, it was a conviction which could be held
without becoming involved in capricious date-setting or the subjective
and irresponsible interpretation of prophecy. When these men and their
contemporaries studied the Bible they discovered a fundamental and
recurring emphasis on the future and on the events of the last days. They
discovered that Christ himself had spoken repeatedly of His second coming
and the consummation of world history, and that the early church had gone
forth on its world mission seemingly sustained in the hope of an early
fulfilment of Christ's promises. As the Puritan apologist strove to recapture what he saw as the wholeness of New Testament eschatology, he
inevitably identified with these hopes of the early church. Thus to Richard
Baxter the eventful day is 'approaching', 'not far off', and 'comes apace',
and Thomas Adams, whose prodigious exposition of II Peter went to more
than sixteen hundred folio pages, explains:

> The time from Christ's ascension to the world's end, is called *Dies
> extrema*, the last day, because it immediately (without any general
> alteration) goes before it. The end in the apostles' time was not far off,
> now it must be very near: if that were ultima dies, this is ultima hora: or if
> that were ultima hora, the last hour, this is ultimum horae, the last
> minute.[21]

Adams is one of many in the seventeenth century who see the entire post-
New Testament age in an eschatological sense. The last days began in
the time of the apostles and reach down to the Last Day, and it behoves
good Christians to live always in the expectation of a final fulfilment.
Although we are not able to comment on it in detail here, the following
explanation deserves some thought:

> There is a great difference betwixt the last days, and the latter days. For
> the (last days) Hebrew i 2, and the (last times) I Peter i 20 do
> comprehend the whole time under the Gospel; the time, I say, from
> Christ's first coming to His second: but the (latter times) I Timothy iv 1
> do signify only the latter part of the last times. And as the last times, or
> days, have their latter times; so again the (latter times) have their (last
> days) as we may see in the II Timothy iii 1 and in the II Peter iii 3 and of
> the end of these (last days) of the (latter times) are the (latter days) in
> this Prophecy to be understood. . . . [22]

Whatever that might mean in the final analysis, it meant that the last age of
the world had commenced with Christ and that men had been living under
the promise of His return ever since. In professing the hope of an
imminent advent, the preachers of Puritanism felt an affinity with the first

apostles of Christ, and Baxter speaks for many when he exclaims, 'How near is that most blessed joyful day! It comes apace, even He that comes will come, and will not tarry.'[23]

The Second Advent in the Scheme of Salvation

The basis of second advent expectation in the seventeenth century was the unqualified acceptance of Scripture as the sole source of faith and doctrine. To the sincere Puritan the Bible was authoritative, not only in its record of the past and in its guidance for the present life and doctrine of the believer, but also in its delineation of future events and in its promises and prophecies which spoke of things to come. John White, who was a member of the Westminster Assembly, ably argued the intrinsic relationship in Scripture between the past, the present and the future:

> Whatsoever things were written aforehand, were written for our learning; ... the laws for our direction; the prophecies for observation of their accomplishment in answerable events; the promises for our comfort and consolation; the examples of evil for caution, of good for imitation; and lastly the events, ordered by the wisdom and providence of God, for precedents and patterns, representing our state and condition, either what it is at present, and why so, or what we are to expect it may be hereafter.[24]

It is not enough to look to the past and live in the present. Christians should keep an eye open for those events which reveal the outworking of the divine purpose and which fulfil the prophecies of Scripture. Hence they should also look to the future. Indeed, the validity of the past and the present is in their ultimate fulfilment in the future. It is against the background of this fundamental relationship between the past, present and future in the redemptive purposes of God for man, that we can most clearly see the intrinsic rightness of the Puritan emphasis on Christ's second coming.

In *The Penitent Pardoned* Christopher Love sets forth the doctrine of the second advent as an integral element in the historic Christian faith. On John xiv 3 Love comments, 'This text contains in it the most material and fundamental point of all the doctrine of Christianity,' notably 'the great doctrine of Christ's second coming'.[25] John Owen, to whom we have turned frequently in preceding chapters, similarly argued that 'Christ's appearance the second time, His return from heaven to complete the salvation of the Church, is the great fundamental principle of our faith and hope.'[26] Richard Sibbes, whose collected writings must still be regarded as belonging to the classics of Puritan devotional literature, suggested that since the coming of Christ was fundamental to Christian doctrine, it should be desired as such by the Church:

> Such is the disposition of the Church that, before Christ was come, good people were known by the desire of his coming. And therefore it was the description of holy men that they waited for the consolation of Israel. O Lord come quickly, come in the flesh. But now the first coming is past

they desire as much his second coming, and therefore they are described in the epistle of St. Paul, to be such as love and long for the appearing of Christ.[27]
An expectant attitude to the future was, moreover, a characteristic of the true Church, the espoused bride of the heavenly bridegroom, and Sibbes adds, 'as in civil marriage there is a contract, so here, in the spiritual; and seeing there is a contract, there is also an assent to the second coming of Christ; the contracted spouse must needs say "Amen" to the marriage day'.[28] The second advent hope in Puritan theology was related to the revealed purpose of God for His people, and William Jenkyn logically enquired, 'If the other predictions in Scripture, particularly those concerning the first coming of Christ, have truly come to pass, why should we doubt of the truth of Christ's second appearance?'[29] Jenkyn's question, rhetorical though it was, had already been answered by Richard Baxter, 'As Christ failed not to come in the fulness of time, even when Daniel and others had foretold his coming, so in the fulness and fitness of time will His second coming be.'[30]

The foregoing statements suggest that a relationship was recognised in the Puritan understanding of the work of Christ between the incarnation and Christ's coming at the end. This relationship, in fact, saw the second advent as a necessary and inevitable sequel to the first advent. 'The first and second coming of Christ are of so near connection,' Sibbes argued, 'that oftentimes they are comprised together, as the regeneration of our souls and the regeneration of our bodies, the adoption of our souls and the adoption of our bodies, the redemption of our souls and the redemption of our bodies.'[31] Christ must come again to complete the work of salvation which He had begun at His first coming. Indeed, many would argue that that work could not be complete or efficacious until Christ had returned. John Durant says of Hebrews ix 28, 'We have two fundamental points of our Christian religion held forth and confirmed. The first concerns the passion of Christ, the second His coming again. The not right and full believing of these endangers the very foundation of our faith.'[32] Evidently it was not enough to believe in Christ's accomplished work, without believing also in His future work. The second advent was not an appendage to the body of Christian doctrine, merely a convenient way of bringing to a satisfactory conclusion the logical sequence of Christian theology. It was, *per se*, a doctrine of the utmost significance, the climax and crowning glory of the whole redemptive process. So Durant says, 'Christ keeps the crown till the day of His appearance and kingdom, and in that day He will give it to you.'[33] Sibbes had said that at His second coming Christ 'shall perfect our salvation,' and Love that 'you shall then be saved to the uttermost'.[34] Whether it was to effect or complete a believer's salvation, or to make it a reality, or to receive the saint to Himself, it was clear to believers in Puritan England that the final chapter in the saga of human redemption could not be written until Christ had returned to earth, as He had promised He would do at the end of days.

The steps by which it was believed in the seventeenth century that a man might eventually attain to salvation were patiently explained by the Puritan preachers to their people. Assuming, as most Puritans did under the Calvinistic doctrine of predestination, that in the predeterminate counsels of God some men had been elected to salvation, the first step involved his calling to faith and to Christ by the Holy Spirit. When a man became aware of God's call and responded to it by exercising faith in Christ as his personal Saviour, he then experienced justification. This was to be followed by sanctification, the daily commitment of his life to Christ and the inward working of the Holy Spirit bringing victory over indwelling sin and increasing holiness. This was to continue for the remainder of his earthly sojourn, until in fact sanctification was crowned with glorification at the Last Day. Haller rightly points out, 'Election — vocation — justification — sanctification — glorification was more than an abstract formula. It became the pattern of the most profound experience of men through many generations.'[35] In the understanding of most Puritans, glorification at Christ's coming would set the seal upon his experience in this life and effectively translate him to the life to come.

John Milton, the great Puritan poet, drew an argument for the necessity of the second advent from what he called the doctrine of 'complete glorification'. In his *Treatise on Christian Doctrine* Milton contrasts the 'incomplete' glorification to which believers attain in this life with the 'complete glorification which must eventually be achieved in eternity'. Of the latter he states, 'Its fulfilment and consummation will begin with Christ's second coming to judge the world, and with the resurrection of the dead.'[36] To Milton, a believer's glorification is an essential experience in the outworking of the Gospel in the life. It is a process which begins in this life but which is not fully realised until the second advent. Other Puritan theologians shared similar views on the doctrine of glorification. To Christopher Love, glorification was essentially the future, eternal state of the believer 'that we shall enjoy with Christ, when the world is ended,' and which will become a reality when Christ 'shall appear to judge the world'.[37] Thomas Brooks, writing in *The Glorious Day of the Saints Appearance*, states succinctly, 'When He shall appear the second time ... He shall appear glorious, and so shall all His saints.'[38] To Milton, Love and Brooks alike, the believer's glorification is no less than the ultimate purpose of the Gospel, but it is contingent upon the Second Advent.

Puritans in general saw yet another aspect to the completion of Christ's redemptive work. Not only was it essential that Christ should finish His work for the sake of mankind, it was equally essential as far as He was concerned Himself. He had begun a work and it was unthinkable that He should leave it unfinished. Having undertaken the restoration of man to the fullness of fellowship with God and having, at His first coming through the atoning act on the cross, achieved reconciliation between God and man, it was incumbent on Him now to bring everything to a just and satisfactory conclusion. This He would do, and could only do, at His second coming. Richard Sibbes had been persuaded by this argument, suggesting that the Second Advent would bring to perfection not only the Church and the individual believer, but even Christ Himself. 'Christ is in some sort imperfect till the latter day, till His second coming,' Sibbes states. He then goes on to explain:

> The mystical body of Christ is His fulness. Christ is our fulness, and we are His fulness; now Christ's fulness is made up, when all the members of His mystical body are gathered and united together; the head and the members make but one natural body.... Christ in this sense is not fully glorious therefore till that time.[39]

There is much in the writings of Richard Sibbes concerning the vital place of the Second Advent in biblical theology which could profitably detain us. One further illustration will be helpful:

> We have not the perfect consummation and accomplishment of that which Christ wrought in his first coming, till his second coming. Then there shall be a total redemption of our souls and bodies.... There is a double redemption, as there is a double coming of Christ, the first and the second, the one to redeem our souls from sin and Satan and to give us title to heaven; the other to redeem our bodies from corruption, when Christ shall come to be glorious in his saints.[40]

The emphasis in all this is almost that of a divine obligation, self-imposed by the very nature of deity, to bring all to a satisfactory completion. Hence Sibbes writes on another occasion that Christ must come the second time 'to make an end of what he hath begun'.[41]

A further aspect of this line of thought comes from what may be termed the continuity of Christ's work for man. Christopher Love saw the Second Advent, not as an event at the end of time isolated from what had gone before, but as part of an unceasing process which moved towards the complete and harmonious restoration of fellowship between man and God. This process, having begun at the birth of Christ, had continued ever since and included, in succession, Christ's sinless life, His death upon the cross, His ascension, His priestly ministry in heaven, His second advent, the resurrection of the dead, and 'the great doctrine of that everlasting communion that the saints shall have with Christ in heaven'.[42] The writings of both Christopher Love and John Durant argue that if Christ's ascension and priestly ministry could be shown as necessary parts of this continuous work, then it would naturally follow that the Second Advent, with its outcomes of restoration and restored fellowship, would be seen in a similar light. Therefore Love, before he discusses the Second Advent, emphasises the importance in the overall work of Christ of His mediatorial ministry in heaven. Christ had 'entered into the very heavens, that He might appear before God for us'.[43] Love goes on to say that the intercessory ministry of Christ in heaven is to be regarded as even more essential than His personal presence on earth. Only as Christ fulfils the office of high priest in heaven can He adequately make intercession for all men. This He could not do by being bodily present on earth, Love argues, 'therefore we have great advantage by Christ's going into heaven'.[44] John Durant made the same point by referring to the sanctuary services of the Old Testament. In the sanctuary ritual it was not sufficient, Durant stated, merely for the sacrifice to be offered. It was also necessary for the blood of the sacrifice to be taken into the tabernacle itself. The significance of the sacrificial system was incomplete until the blood had been ministered in that way. Durant then continues:

> When Christ died, the sacrifice was slain, the blood was shed, there was no more sacrifice to succeed, all was finished in that respect; but yet all was not done till the blood of Christ was carried into the holy places, which was not till Christ went to heaven, to appear as our high priest.[45]

Only after they have established the necessity of Christ's high-priestly ministry do Love and Durant proceed to discuss the doctrine of the Second Advent in its logical sequence as the consummation of Christ's work for man. Christ had voluntarily undertaken man's salvation in response to human need, and the moral constraint to complete that work was indisputable.

A further important dimension was given to the doctrine of Christ's second coming by Richard Baxter: 'Fellow christians, what a day will that be, when we who have been kept prisoners by sin, by sinners, by the grave, shall be fetched out by the Lord Himself?'[46] Baxter speaks here of a future hope which is related to a definitive event in time. It is 'by the grave', as well as by sin, that men have been bound and prevented from enjoying the fullness of fellowship with God for which they were created. Thus only as the grave is conquered and its captive released can the believer enter into eternal life in the widest sense. The limitations of mortality must be overcome, and when Baxter speaks of an everlasting rest for the saints he speaks of more than the liberation of the soul from the body at death. To be sure, in Baxter's view, as in the view of most Puritans, the saint's rest begins at death when the soul is liberated from the body,[47] but this is only a partial rest. The fullness of the saint's rest is not achieved until after the resurrection when soul and body are united again, and Baxter looks forward confidently to the day when 'perfect soul and body together' come into the presence of God.[48] This essential reunification of body and soul will take place at 'that most blessed joyful day', that is, at the second coming of Christ. In this assurance Baxter can trustingly commit his whole being to the grave:

> O hasten that great resurrection day! When thy command shall go forth, and none shall disobey; when the sea and earth shall yield up their hostages, and all that slept in the graves shall awake, and the dead in Christ shall first arise; ... therefore dare I lay down my carcase in the dust, entrusting it, not to a grave, but to thee: and therefore my flesh shall rest in hope, till thou raise it to the possession of the everlasting rest.[49]

In short, the fullness and blessedness of eternal life can only be realised through the resurrection of the body, at the Last Day, at the coming of

Christ.

This again is Christopher Love's message when he argues that the 'main end of Christ's coming again' is the resurrection of the body.[50] It is what John Durant means when he declares, 'salvation is only yours, at the last day'.[51] The whole doctrine of the resurrection of the body is thus very much a question of a believer's personal salvation. 'You are already redeemed in your souls,' says Durant, 'but your bodies are not yet redeemed . . . in that day you shall have not only soul-salvation, but body-salvation.'[52] The consensus of opinion in Puritan England was that Christian hope lay less in the survival of the soul after death, prevalent as that doctrine undoubtedly was at the time, than in the new creation of the whole man. When David Dickson spoke of 'the full accomplishment of the salvation of the believers' he spoke in terms of Christ's coming and of the resurrection of the body.[53] He who had in the first place fashioned man from the dust of the ground and pronounced him perfect, would yet bring forth from the grave a multitude of men with bodies not subject to 'diseases and distempers, infirmities and deformities, maimedness and monstrous shapes'.[54] The hope of the saints in seventeenth-century England was the hope of a personal and perfected salvation.

The Effects of the Advent Hope

The Puritan belief in Christ's second coming demonstrated that hope was an essential element in the Christian faith. Men learned from their Bibles of a hope set before them (Hebrews vi 18), of a hope laid up in heaven (Colossians i 5), of a hope that the body would be resurrected at the Last Day (I Thessalonians iv 13). They read that the Christian believer was begotten unto a lively hope (I Peter i 3), that he was an heir of the hope of eternal life (Titus iii 7), and that he was to look for the blessed hope, the glorious appearing of Christ (Titus ii 13). It was precisely such hope that encouraged the believer along the path of sanctification to ultimate glorification. The goal to be reached by travelling this path was true godliness, the evidence of fitness for that eternity which was to be spent in the presence of a holy God and holy angels: 'If a man hope for this coming of Christ, he will purify himself for it, even as He is pure. He will not appear in his foul clothes, but . . . will fit himself as the bride for the coming of the bridegroom.'[55] Even as the earthly bride did not spend the time of her betrothal dreaming idly of bliss to come, but in acquiring apparel suitable for the wedding, and in the exacting task of preparing for a new life, even so the Church and the individual believer were to spend the remaining time in preparation for Christ's coming and eternity to follow. One writer declared that belief in Christ's second coming was 'a special means to make Christians thrive in grace and holiness'.[56] Richard Sibbes emphasised that the converse was also true. If the hope of Christ's coming is not seen to work efficaciously in the present life of the believer, 'it is but a false conceit and lying fancy'.[57] Sibbes also notes the positive effects of Christian hope:

If we say this truly, come Lord Jesus, undoubtedly it will have an influence into our lives. It will stir up all graces in the soul; as faith, to lay hold upon it; hope, to expect it; love, to embrace; patience, to endure anything for it; heavenly-mindedness, to fit and prepare for it.[58]

True Christians, therefore, 'always live in expectation of the Lord Jesus in the clouds' with oil in their lamps and 'prepared for His coming'.[59]

All this recaptures both the letter and the spirit of New Testament eschatological hope. Thomas Goodwin is one of many seventeenth-century writers who recognised that the Church in New Testament times lived constantly in the expectation of an early fulfilment of Christ's promise to return. The early Church 'had that day in their eye,' they 'walked in view of it,' consequently they were 'set forth as a pattern' to succeeding generations in the Church.[60] Thus, in Goodwin's view, the whole gamut of eschatological doctrine, belief in Christ's coming, the interpretation of apocalyptic prophecy, the computation of biblical chronology, understanding the signs of the times, the future of the Antichrist, the Millennium and the Kingdom, all, in the last analysis, were to be measured by one criterion. 'The only use of knowing them,' declared Goodwin, was 'to prepare for them. . . . The day and year of the accomplishment of the great matters are hid from us, so that each day and year we may be found ready, whenever they shall come.'[61] It was this emphasis in the New Testament and in the outlook of the early Church which constrained Durant's exhortation, 'It is your work and wisdom, to cleanse yourselves from all filth, and to perfect holiness in a filial fear of God.'[62] The conservative Bishop Joseph Hall of Norwich recognised the inevitable consequence of biblical hope when he said that a true Christian was always ready for the coming of the Lord.[63]

While the Puritan believer looked forward to a definitive event in the future for the ultimate realisation of his hopes, he also understood that, to some extent at least, the future depended upon the present. The Christian's future hope did not rest solely on an isolated event, or a series of events, at the end of time, but rather in the culmination of the divine, agelong process. For the world, this process had been in operation from the beginning of history, for the individual it had begun with the outworking of divine grace at regeneration. There was no future, no hope, for the man who in the present lived only for the present, or for the man who pinned his all on the future, ignoring the legitimate demands of the present. The true hope associated with the last events led both Church and individual towards a future final event only along the path of present and total commitment. Christopher Love preached ten sermons on the coming of Christ and the glory of the future life from Colossians iii 4, all of them based on the three propositions that Christ is the life of the believer now, that Christ will appear in glory at the end of time, and that when He does appear the saints will appear in glory with Him. Love argued that there were three appearings, or comings, of Christ set forth in Scripture, His first appearing in the flesh, when He lived a holy life on earth, secondly His appearing in and through the lives of the believers by the Gospel, and finally His appearing in glory at the Last Day. Love's argument is that the saints will appear with Christ in glory at the end only as His holy life is manifested in them now, in the present.[64] Richard Sibbes also understands this relationship between the believer's present life and the future, returning to the analogy of the marriage of the bride with the heavenly bridegroom at the end of time. Before this marriage can be fully consummated there is to be a threefold union between Christ and His Church — a union of nature, a union of grace, and a union of glory. To Sibbes, the union of nature came through the incarnation, when Christ took upon Himself human nature. The union of grace comes through the effective outworking of the Gospel in human experience, when man partakes of the divine nature. The union of glory will be at the end when the Church, duly prepared and perfected, will be in heaven, in the presence of Christ.[65] The marriage cannot be consummated until this union of glory becomes a reality, but that union itself is not possible without either those of nature or grace. The future, either of Church or of individual believer, cannot be isolated from the present. It is part of the present, the culmination in time of a process in history and in experience.

The reality of this hope in the personal experience of the individual believer finds expression in many ways in the writings of the Puritan Adventists. Richard Sibbes, for instance, sees it as an effective antidote to sin: 'The soul is never in such a tune as when the thoughts of those glorious times have raised the affections to the highest pitch ... so long as it is so affected, it cannot sin ... so long then, as we keep our hearts in a blessed frame of faith, and in a love of the appearing of Christ, they are impregnable.'[66] To Thomas Goodwin, hope guards against the machinations and deceptions of Satan: 'The devil, the shorter his time is, the more he rages and ... seeing these are the last days ... the more should we endeavour to do God service.'[67] To Thomas Brooks, it is a challenge to prepare the whole man for eternity: 'Those that have hopes to reign with Christ in glory, that have set their hearts on that pure and blissful state, ... they will purify both their insides and their outsides, both body and soul.'[68] The total effect of hope on the present life of the believer is wide indeed. It is an incentive to duty and obedience.[69] It is the spring of brotherly love.[70] It is a stimulus to work and to pray for others.[71] It is the root of happiness and contentment in the present life.[72] There is, in short, no aspect of Christian life and doctrine that is not quickened and ennobled by the influence of a positive, biblical hope in the future. This theology of hope is an effective agent which breaks down the barrier between present and future by bringing the future into the present in a form which is accessible to every aspiring believer. In the language of the time, it is eloquently summarised by Thomas Brooks in the introduction to his *Heaven on Earth:*

Holiness is the very marrow and quintessence of all religion. Holiness is God stamped and printed upon the soul; it is Christ formed in the heart; it is our light, our life, our beauty, our glory, our joy, our crown, our heaven, our all. The holy soul is happy in life, and blessed in death, and shall be transcendently glorious in the morning of the resurrection, when Christ shall say, 'Lo, here am I, and my holy ones, who are my joy; lo, here am I, and my holy ones, who are my crown; and therefore, upon the heads of these holy ones, will I set an immortal crown.' Even so, Amen, Lord Jesus.[73]

To Brooks, to Sibbes, to Goodwin, as to the host of Puritan preachers professing faith in the Second Advent, fellowship with Christ in glory was measurably dependent on fellowship with Christ in grace. It is difficult to avoid the conclusion that the second advent hope was an indispensable factor, perhaps even the chief factor, in the spirituality that characterised both Church and individual believer in Puritan England.

Vital as the second advent hope unquestionably was to the spiritual life of each believer, it was of equal significance to the Church as a whole. The entire Church was to draw a blessing from the second advent hope, a blessing which was related to the fellowship of believers with believers in the body of Christ, and it was at this precise point that Sibbes found serious cause for concern. In the preface to his *Glorious Feast of the Gospel* he regrets that many had apparently lost this necessary relationship: 'Alas, Christians have lost much of their communion with Christ and his saints.'[74] The very experience upon which the future glory of both Church and believer rested was being eroded, and the reason was clear: 'They have woefully disputed away, and dispirited the life of religion and the power of godliness into dry and sapless controversies about government of Church and state.'[75] Matters of secondary consequence had come to claim the attention of many influential teachers in the Church, and Sibbes's point of concern is apparent. Let the message of the Church take precedence over its machinery. Let believers recapture that essential unity with Christ and with each other through a re-emphasis of the gospel message in its wholeness. From this premise Sibbes goes on to set forth the doctrine of the Second Advent as an integral part of the total message of the New Testament.

Other influential preachers in the seventeenth century voiced similar sentiments. Edmund Calamy and Stephen Marshall, both moderate and esteemed, deplored the divisions that had appeared in Church and kingdom alike, and Marshall described the multiplicity of sects into which the Church had been divided as an 'epidemical disease ... pleasing to Satan'.[76] The divisions within the Church were clearly an obstacle to the realisation of the divine purpose, and while some undoubtedly expected the desired unity to be realised through Acts of Parliament and the reformation of the established Church, there were many whose discernment was more far-reaching. William Strong's eschatological hope of 'perfect and sweet communion one with another' is contingent upon the communion of each individual believer with God, in Christ.[77] The cure for division within the Church, according to the Moderator of the Westminster

Assembly, lay in the universal acceptance and the individual application of the essentials of the Christian faith. At a time of renewed emphasis on the unity of the Church, it may be that the words of Jeremiah Whitaker are as appropriate now as they were in his own day:

> The way to cure the bleeding distempers of Christendom is for all men to endeavour to get inward persuasions answerable to their outward professions, for as these main principles are more or less believed, so is the heart and life of men better or worse ordered. When the soul is once fully persuaded that Christ is God, that He is the true Messiah, that there is another life besides this, that the Lord Christ is ready to come to judgement, and His reward is with Him, then the soul begins to seek and beg an interest in Christ, to flee from wrath to come, to assure the hopes of heaven, whilst we are on earth. And this hope, when once truly attained, carries the soul far above the comforts of life, and beyond the fears of death.[78]

There is more here than a mere concern with ecclesiastical politics or Church government, more than the unrealistic yearnings of a radical sectarian minority. Hope, the future, Christ's coming, eternal life, all these, in the context of a complete Christocentric Gospel and in the experience of each individual believer, are the basis of a valid ecumenism and the assurance of ultimate triumph. Many in the seventeenth century died in that hope, and counted it a privilege to do so. They had not received the promises, but with the eye of faith had seen them afar off, and the Church in Puritan England was stronger for the advent hope it cherished and for its effect on the lives of those who embraced it.

11. THAT GREAT ALMANACK OF PROPHECY

> Only the God who created the world and who still controls the destinies of men and nations can give any accurate prediction about the future. Hence, when we see various long lines of prophecies like those of Daniel which have been minutely and accurately accomplished by the history of the past two thousand years, only one who has the most obdurate will to disbelieve can deny that the great Jehovah has spoken.
>
> ... the visions of the book of Revelation have picked up these prophecies of Daniel and have enlarged their final portions, giving a profusion of detailed instructions for the guidance of the people of God in the last deadly conflict with the Dragon, the Antichrist, and the false prophet, that awful trinity of Hell, in the closing hours of human probation, just preceding the second coming of Christ.
>
> G.M. Price *The Greatest of the Prophets* (1955) pp.47-48

> I may say, without prejudice to those that went before, that Bullinger in his time, Brightman in his time, Grasserus in his time, Mede in his time, each of these have made their several and respective additions to the clearing of the prophecy. If we endeavour to carry on the work where they left it, at least with the same industry and fidelity, we may, (by the blessing of God) be the instruments of bringing those mysteries to light that were not discerned in former ages. And for my part, I do firmly believe that God will not cease to raise up such, in the times following, as shall clear the things that have lain dark in the prophecies, and do yet remain hid to us.
>
> Nathaniel Stephens *A Plain and Easy Calculation of the Name, Mark, and Number of the Name of the Beast* (1656) p.13

A seventeenth-century lexicon defines almanac simply as 'a calendar',as well as a help to astrological 'prognostication'. It is in this former sense, as a means of reckoning time, that the Anglican scholar, Joseph Mede, uses the word when speaking of biblical prophecy. In context, the phrase borrowed from Mede for the title of this chapter urges Christians to recognise the importance placed on time in Scripture, and refers them to the 'sacred calendar and great almanack of prophecy, the four kingdoms of Daniel, which are a prophetical chronology of times ...'.[1] Daniel's four kingdoms will certainly claim our attention again before this chapter can be concluded, as will other elements of symbolic prophecy. To begin with, however, it will be helpful to hear what the seventeenth century said about prophecy in general, for only when set against that wider background can

Puritanism's interest in apocalytic prophecy and prophetic chronology have a meaning which fairly detaches it from the realm of speculative fantasy. There has been more than enough of the latter at various periods in Christian history to discredit the serious study of prophecy altogether, and it must be said here that while undoubtedly there were extremist tendencies in seventeenth-century England, the majority of prophetic expositors of the time, and there were many, cannot justifiably be placed in that category. We shall have opportunity to examine the views of John Napier, mathematician and inventor of logarithms; Thomas Brightman, whose works on prophecy were seminal to Protestant exposition for three centuries to come; Joseph Mede, one of the most learned and renowned academics of the age; and many others of equal calibre, the long line of whom culminated in Sir Isaac Newton, whose interest in prophecy has been eclipsed by his achievements in science and philosophy. None of these men, and relatively few of their contemporaries, can fairly be regarded as extremist or fanatical. To what can their serious concern with biblical prophecy be attributed?

The Importance of Prophecy

The answer to the foregoing question must inevitably lie in that fundamental view of prophecy which they shared with most biblical scholars of the time. It is quite evident to the Bible student, even today, that a significant proportion of Scripture is of a prophetic character. To those books of the Bible that are obviously prophetic in content, must be added whole chapters and passages of a similar nature in other books. Given the Puritan insistence upon Scripture as the revealed Word of God, it is not difficult to understand why the study of prophecy should be considered necessary. It is not an optional part of the biblical message, or a matter of secondary importance, and to neglect prophecy is to neglect divine revelation. Therefore, as Thomas Hall said, 'It is our duty to take notice of the prophecies delivered to us in the Word of God.'[2] His brother Edmund spoke even more forcefully: 'It is a sin to be wilfully negligent in searching into those prophecies which give light to the times we live in.'[3] The Hall brothers, both incumbents of benefices in the Midlands, Thomas as perpetual curate of King's Norton in Worcestershire until his ejection in 1662, and Edmund as rector of Chipping Norton in Oxfordshire, each published at least two works on prophecy. Thomas argued that prophecy would not have been included in Scripture by revelation only to be sealed from human understanding, and concluded that men should not neglect prophecy on the grounds that it could not be understood.[4] That would be tantamount to saying that a large part of the Bible was of no practical value. Edmund contended that Israel's failure to understand the prophetic texts of the Old Testament was a major factor in the ultimate rejection of her Messiah and the crucifixion of Christ.[5] The implications of that were clear enough for those who cared to think about them.

The positive value of prophecy is clearest, perhaps, when seen in relationship to hope, that large and indispensable element of the Christian faith. The New Testament, as its readers well know, speaks much of hope. Paul desires that believers 'may abound in hope' (Romans xv 13), even asserting that they are 'saved by hope' (Romans viii 24), and the apostle John suggests that hope in the reality of the future life is an important factor tending to godly Christian living in the present (I John iii 3). Nathaniel Homes representatively comments, then, 'True hope keeps up the heart from sinking and desponding.... As the cork bears up the net that it may catch the prey, so doth hope bear up the soul till it catch salvation.'[6] Salvation, again, is something which is not fully accomplished until the last events have run their course and the Last Day has arrived. Then hope will turn to fruition, faith to reality. Faith and hope together lead the believer hand in hand along the pathway to the Kingdom. But it is prophecy as much as any other single factor in the Bible which sustains such hope. Few passages were better known or more frequently quoted by Puritan preachers in this respect than II Peter i 19-21, which assures Christians of every age that they have received in Scripture 'a more sure Word of prophecy'. No writer or preacher whose task it was to set forth the marrow of biblical truth could ignore a fundamental passage such as this or the doctrine which emerged from it. Prophecy came by the operation of the Holy Spirit, and was to lead all who were born in darkness to the light and life of a new day. Therefore, asks William Hicks, 'Is it not a great privilege and blessing to the people of God ... to have a sure Word of prophecy?' and 'Is not this able to bear up their spirits in all their fiery trials, to see that their deliverance draweth nigh?'[7] Here is prophecy as the unfailing well-spring of hope. And commenting on the same text, Thomas Adams stresses that prophecy will retain this function as long as the Church exists on earth: 'There is no end to the use of this saying, till there be an end of the world's being'.[8]

It is Thomas Adams who also explains the purpose of prophecy. Christ had said of certain predictive statements He made concerning His own future, 'I have told you before it come to pass, that, when it is come to pass, ye might believe' (John xiv 29). The fulfilment of predictive prophecy is crucial to its interpretation. Prophecy is not given as a basis for speculation concerning the course of future events. It is not the crystal ball of the Christian seer. It is given to substantiate faith by the verification of its fulfilment in events which can be demonstrated to have taken place. Hence Adams maintains that fulfilment is the most important single factor in the exposition of prophecy, declaring, 'It is the property of a prophecy ... to be fulfilled before it be understood.'[9] Richard Bernard likewise argues that the full meaning of prophecy can only be known in the light of history. Before their fulfilment, prophecies have the ambiguous character of riddles, he says, 'But when the time is come that that which is prophesied be come to pass, then have the prophecies a clear and certain exposition.'[10] Had all would-be interpreters of prophecy in the seventeenth century, and later, heeded this principle, Christ's Church might

have been spared much embarrassment in the realm of prophetic interpretation, and, what is fundamentally more important, might not in later
times have turned away so consistently from the legitimate and necessary
study of biblical prophecy.

It was, indeed, the fulfilment of Old Testament predictions concerning
Christ that authenticated His claim to Messiahship, and that gave credibility to the many prophecies concerning His second coming and the last
events made both by Himself and other biblical writers. George Hammon
points to those Old Testament predictions that Christ would be born at
Bethlehem of a virgin, that He would ride into Jerusalem upon an ass, that
He would be smitten on the face by His accusers, that He would be offered
vinegar to drink, that He would be betrayed for thirty pieces of silver, that
lots would be cast for His coat — all of which predictions, besides many
others, were known to have been fulfilled accurately. The logical sequel to
the fulfilment of prophecy in the course of Christ's life and in the events
surrounding His death is that those prophecies which speak of His second
coming and latter-day events will also come to pass with equal certainty
and accuracy. 'So shall all those Scriptures that speak of His glory and
reign ... be fulfilled in their time,'[11] Hammon says. 'Why should we
doubt of the truth of Christ's second appearance,' asks William Jenkyn,
when the other predictions in Scripture, 'particularly those concerning the
first coming of Christ, have truly come to pass?'[12]

Perhaps in no aspect of the biblical revelation as a whole was the
principle of progressive understanding more relevant than in the study of
prophecy. If the prophetic word reached down to the Last Day and spoke
of future events and the culmination of the present world order, and if
fulfilment of that which was predicted was essential to correct interpretation, then it was axiomatic that with the passing of time the Church would
come to a deeper and clearer understanding of the prophetic message.
Indeed, was this not the most powerful argument to beckon believers of
every age to a serious and sustained study of all prophecy? Once the
purpose of prophecy was grasped and its significance recognised by the
Church, the process of time would result in more faith, not less, since that
very process would bring more prophecy to fulfilment. It is this principle
which leads Thomas Parker to defend the study of Daniel against the
objection that it is not God's will for men to seek into the hidden meaning
of prophecy: 'It was not for Daniel to search and understand the time, two
times, and a half, at the end whereof the kingdom must begin to be set up.
Howbeit, these times are to be unsealed to the last age.'[13] In similar vein,
William Hicks explains that those who lived in the latter half of the
seventeenth century had a clearer understanding of the book of Revelation
than those who had lived in earlier times: 'It is not at all strange if those that
are in this age ... coming nearer unto the accomplishment of the events
and the end of all, should see a little further in the truth of those mysterious
prophecies than they that went before.'[14] Nathaniel Stephens, writing in
1656, noted that Henry Bullinger in 1557, Thomas Brightman in 1609 and

Joseph Mede in 1627 had published contributions (originally in Latin) to the understanding of prophecy, and concluded, 'If we endeavour to carry on the work where they left it, at least with the same industry and fidelity, we may (by the blessing of God) be the instruments of bringing those mysteries to light that were not discerned in former ages.'[15]

Daniel and the Revelation
It was against this background of biblical prophecy as a whole that expositors in seventeenth-century England turned to the study of Daniel and the Revelation. Few generations in the long history of the Christian Church in England have attempted to come to grips with the apocalyptic symbolism of these two books more earnestly than those whose years of influence approximately coincided with the reign of the Stuarts. It would be a daunting task in itself to draw up an exhaustive bibliography of works dealing with Daniel and the Revelation, expositions in part or in whole, which appeared between 1600 and 1700. It was without question the era *par excellence* of prophetic enquiry in English theology, when men of every shade of ecclesiastical leaning — Episcopalian, Presbyterian, Independent and Baptist, to say nothing of the followers of more extreme factions — untiringly bent their best efforts to interpret and communicate the message of prophecy. We must not allow the indiscretions of a relatively few extremists to hide the immense contribution which English Protestantism as a whole has made to the development of prophetic interpretation.

Already in the latter half of the preceding century, following the establishment of Reformation theology in the English Church, a number of influential works on prophecy had appeared. In 1548, John Bale, Bishop of Ossory, published his *Image of Both Churches*, an exposition of Revelation which showed a knowledge of prophetic interpreters from the Church fathers and from mediaeval and Reformation sources. An English translation of the work by the Swiss Reformer, Henry Bullinger, on the book of Revelation had appeared in 1561 with the title, *A Hundred Sermons on the Apocalypse of Jesus Christ*. Another work on the Apocalypse by the martyrologist, John Foxe, was published in Latin in 1587, although it was never translated into English. A year later James VI of Scotland, soon to be James I of England, wrote a brief exposition of part of Revelation xx, a harbinger, perhaps, of that interest in the Millennium which was shortly to appear and which was to have such far-reaching effects on the course of English history. James also wrote a seventy page paraphrase on Revelation. But by far the most significant work of prophetic exposition in the sixteenth century was John Napier's *A Plain Discovery of the Whole Revelation of St. John*, published first in 1593, and reprinted in 1594, 1611, 1641 and 1645, and translated twice into Dutch and four times into French within fourteen years of its first appearance. The interest shown in Napier's work amply demonstrates that as the sixteenth century ended and the seventeenth century commenced, the tide of prophetic enquiry was well on its way in.

Napier, a Scottish laird and a brilliant mathematician, was followed, in England, by Arthur Dent, the Puritan rector of South Shoebury in Essex, who in 1603 wrote a massive treatise on the book of Revelation, entitled *The Ruin of Rome*. The title must be seen in the theological context of early Protestantism, and not merely as an astute attempt to gain readers, although it might well have been that also, for the work went through at least eleven editions in half a century. Thomas Brightman wrote on both Daniel and the Revelation, as did Joseph Mede, the brilliant and unassuming Cambridge scholar. Brightman's exposition of Daniel was printed at least three times, and his exposition of the Revelation, *A Revelation of the Revelation*, was published several times in English, as well as in Latin. It would be too tedious to catalogue the many editions of Mede's various works on prophecy which appeared throughout the seventeenth century, beginning with his famous *Clavis Apocalyptica, The Key of the Revelation*, first published in 1627. Suffice it to say that this book, which enjoyed the almost universal praise of contemporaries at home and abroad, remains his chief work, despite the breadth of his learning and the contributions he made in the fields of philology, botany, anatomy, history and mathematics. These men whose works appeared early in the seventeenth century, together with those of like calibre who followed them for the next hundred years or so, place prophetic enquiry fairly beyond the ranks of sectarian extremism and firmly within the realm of Protestant orthodoxy.

It must also be said that the widespread interest in Daniel and the Revelation which arose in English Puritanism was neither at the expense of Scripture as a whole nor at the expense of other aspects of Christian doctrine. Puritanism in general was interested in the entire Bible and in the totality of the Christian message. When Edmund Hall says of the book of Revelation, 'It is as lawful and as necessary for us to study that, as any other part of the Bible,'[16] he clearly does not mean that the book of Revelation is to be placed above the rest of Scripture in importance, but rather that a study of the Bible which does not include the Revelation (and, by implication, the book of Daniel) is less than whole. A similar emphasis is evident in Napier's question, 'To what effect were the prophecies of Daniel and of the Revelation given to the Church ... if God had appointed the same to be never known or understood?'[17] The objection that the Revelation was a sealed book too difficult to understand, was of no real consequence, as we have already seen. Richard Bernard pointed out that the very title of the book implied 'to make plain secret and hidden things,' and reminded his readers of the purpose and promise expressed in the opening verses of the first chapter. It was quite inconceivable to think that a blessing is specifically promised to those who read the book of Revelation and accept its message, if that very message is incapable of being understood. These opening verses give the Revelation the quality of speaking to the Church universal, and Bernard concludes, 'It as much belongeth unto us now living, as it did unto others in time past, and as it shall unto those which are to come after us.'[18]

To speak in such terms is in effect to raise the question of authenticity. Are the books of Daniel and the Revelation to be regarded as part of the inspired revelation of Scripture, or are they not? William Hicks, for one, is in no doubt about the answer, certainly as far as the book of Revelation is concerned. Its inclusion in the original canon of the New Testament, its ratification by the fathers, Church Councils, and more latterly by the Westminster Assembly, its orthodoxy on such basic issues as the divinity of Christ and the atonement, and the fulfilment of its prophecies, are all evidence of inspiration and authenticity. Similarly, since the prophecies of Daniel are concerned with the ultimate triumph of Christ, they constitute an important part of God's message in Scripture. Joseph Mede speaks of 'the gospel out of Daniel'.[19] Nathaniel Stephens suggests that Daniel, who spoke from 'afar off', spoke nevertheless of 'the coming of the Son of Man in the clouds of heaven'.[20] Thomas Adams, who cannot by the widest stretch of the imagination be regarded as extreme, quotes Bullinger's view that the Revelation is 'the most gospel-like book' which presents 'the Lamb of God guarding and regarding His saints, and giving them triumphant victory over all His and their enemies'.[21] Adams himself says that the writings of John in Scripture are of three kinds: 'He teacheth in his gospel especially faith; in his epistles love; in his Revelation hope.' 'There are other books of the gospel,' he adds, but the latter is 'a book of most happy consolation, which shall successively and successfully accompany the Church unto the end of the world'.[22]

A word more must be said of the allusions to extremism in prophetic interpretation which have been made in this chapter. Those who are familiar with the seventeenth-century scene will not need to be reminded of its propensity to spawn all manner of strange religious sects. It is beyond question that many of these eccentric groups built their hopes on wild interpretations of prophecy. So it was that Charles I and Oliver Cromwell were both at various times depicted as the 'little horn' of Daniel vii, and that the end of the world was repeatedly calculated to occur variously between 1655 and 1700. Historians have for many years regarded such ingenuous interpretations as constituting the substance of all seventeenth-century prophetic exegesis, while overlooking the more restrained and scholarly expository work like that of Napier, Brightman and Mede, for example, which far out-weighed all ill-advised attempts at computing the date of the Last Day or defining the course of future events.

It was, indeed, as a corrective to some of the more extreme views which had appeared that many of the later works on prophecy were written. William Hicks, for one, in the preface to his *Revelation Revealed* decries 'strange and wild applications' of prophecy, made apparently 'as if the actions and revolutions of every petty city ... and every person that divine providence exalts in power and authority somewhat beyond the common boundaries of the ordinary lords and rulers of the nations,were comprised, predicted, foretold, and prophesied of in this book of

Revelations'.[23] Hicks appended to his book an appeal for moderation to the Fifth Monarchy Men, one of the fanatical sects in question. This was in 1659. Half a century before that, Arthur Dent had urged restraint in the computation of prophetic chronology: 'If we knew the day or year when Rome shall fall finally, it would give us too much light into the knowledge of the last day, which God in great wisdom hath of purpose hid from the knowledge of all men.'[24] Edmund Calamy, one of the most respected leaders of moderate Puritanism, pointed out that time had already proved many predictions rash and incorrect. One writer had foretold that the conversion of the Jews would occur in 1650, another that it would take place in 1655, and yet another in 1656. 'Such peremptory assertions and conclusions argue great confidence,' Calamy declared, 'but are built upon such weak foundations that in the issue it will appear that they have deceived both themselves and others.'[25] It is to the credit of the more moderate expositors of the day and the majority of those who have succeeded them in later Protestantism, that they learned from the mistakes of those who took prophetic interpretation a step too far.

Principles of Interpretation
We may now return to the main theme of this chapter, and the quest to grasp the message which emerged from moderate Puritanism's study of prophecy. That quest can only be successful as the underlying principles of prophetic interpretation are first understood. In a sentence, the fundamental rule was that the interpretation of prophecy must be allowed to proceed from the study of Scripture itself. The Bible as it had been received was the key to its own interpretation. Prophecy, as all other aspects of Scripture, must be explained by an objective study of the text, rather than by the application of external ideas which might reflect subjective imagination, prejudice, or the impetus to substantiate preconceived views. 'The Scriptures are interpreters of the Scriptures,and the meaning of the Spirit is to be found out by his own words,'[26] wrote Bernard. The title of Bernard's book reflects his own concern that the study of prophecy should proceed logically and methodically: *A Key of Knowledge for the Opening of the Secret Mysteries of St. John's Mystical Revelation.* The burden of the book is to explain the principles necessary for the correct understanding of prophecy, and Bernard sets out the steps which must be taken in approaching the text itself. Firstly, the whole book must be analysed so that the 'main parts may be easily seen, and so that the chiefest matters and scope may be understood'.[27] Then the contents of every chapter and the relationship of each chapter to the next must be considered, to see 'the orderly laying-down of things successively therein'.[28] This will be followed by careful exegesis of each chapter, 'following the guiding of the Spirit in His own order, word for word'.[29] Bernard's argument is that the text must be allowed to speak for itself. Similar guidelines were laid down by other expositors. Napier's book listed thirty-six propositions pertaining to prophetic interpretation, before proceeding

with the exposition itself, and Mede's *Key of the Revelation* was based on his famous 'synchronisms', seven rules for interpretation which emerged from his study of the various prophecies as they stood in the book of Revelation. One of Mede's lasting contributions to prophetic interpretation was his insistence that a true understanding depended on the relationship of the various prophecies to each other. Such an understanding could only emerge from a careful study of the text itself.

A second principle of interpretation, basic to the communication of the prophetic message, recognised the complementary nature of Daniel and the Revelation. It was impossible to grasp the full scope of prophecy without taking into the account the relationship between these two books. Hugh Broughton, rabbinical scholar and Reader in Divinity at Durham, who wrote on both Daniel and the Revelation, said of the latter in 1610, 'I must advise the reader to learn Daniel before he learn this book.'[30] Referring to the first two prophetic visions of Daniel, the metal image of chapter ii and the four beasts of chapter vii, Mede declared that together they constituted 'the ABC of prophecy'. Professor V. N. Olsen, in a comment on the influence of John Foxe on later prophetic interpretation, says of these chapters, 'From the time of the Ante-Nicene Fathers, these two chapters describe prophetically and historically the linear concept of time and the one-directed movement of history towards the kingdom of God.'[31] It is quite clear that virtually all prohetic exegesis of the sixteenth and seventeenth centuries, both on the Continent and in England, recognised the fundamental significance of Daniel to the interpretation of the Revelation. The concept of time in which everything moves forward to the ultimate realisation of the divine purpose is apparent in both books, and is crucial to an understanding of biblical prophecy. Hence, Mede himself adds, 'I conceive Daniel to be the *Apocalypsis contracta* and the Apocalypse *Daniel explicate* in that ... both treat about the same subject.'[32] Mede explains that what was shown to Daniel in brief, was often later revealed to John in greater detail, but that both prophets speak principally of the same events over one period of time.

In practice, however, those who studied Daniel and the Revelation realised that much apocalyptic prophecy was couched in symbolic language. It soon became evident to these early Protestant expositors that a correct identification of the symbols was crucial to a sound interpretation. Richard Bernard, again, had recognised this, and had made it a major pre-requisite to the interpretation of the book of Revelation:

The words are figurative, the whole prophecy full of metaphors, and almost altogether allegorical. So we must take heed that we look further than into the letter and naked relation of things as they are set down, otherwise the book should be full of absurdities, impossibilities, falsities, and flat contradictions unto other truths of Scripture.... For who can believe a lamb to have seven eyes, a mountain burning to be cast into the sea, and this thereby in a third part to become blood, a star to fall from heaven, locusts to be of so monstrous a shape as is set down in chapter ix, and horses with lions' heads, fire, smoke, and brimstone coming out of their mouths, and a hundred such things? Therefore we must not stick in the letter, but search out an historical sense, which is the truth intended, and so take the words typically and not literally.[33]

Bernard's logic here cannot be faulted. No writer could hope to arrive at a satisfactory interpretation who was unable to explain the significance of beasts, horns, angels, women and other recurring symbols which featured prominently in the prophetic text. A careful study of the available works of the main Puritan expositors reveals a remarkable consensus regarding the fundamental symbols of prophetic imagery.

The question of time in relationship to the fulfilment of prophecy was of the utmost importance. Indeed, it is so large a factor in the text and in the interpretation thereof, that it will merit more extended examination at a later stage. For the present, however, we must note that a day in symbolic prophecy represents a year of literal time. This principle is based on the explicit statements of Ezekiel iv 6 and Numbers xiv 34, and on the verifiable fulfilment of such prophetic time periods as the seventy weeks of Daniel ix. Virtually every Protestant expositor for two centuries after the Reformation adhered to this rule of Scripture. Its precise implications for the interpretation of symbolic prophecy were spelled out by John Napier: 'So then, a prophetical day is a year, the week seven years, the month thirty years (because the Hebrew and Grecian month hath thirty days), and consequently the prophetical year is three hundred and sixty years.'[34] We shall have occasion to return to the day-year principle when we examine in greater detail the prophetic time periods of Daniel and the Revelation.

If days in symbolic prophecy represented years, it was equally important to understand that beasts represented kingdoms, that is, ruling powers, either civil or ecclesiastical, as Thomas Brightman explained.[35] This also meant that the heads and horns which were variously associated with the prophetic beasts likewise indicated successive or derived powers ruling on the earth, 'kinds of governments', to use James Durham's phrase, again either of a secular or a religious nature. Durham, royal chaplain and Professor of Divinity at Glasgow, was one of many moderate expositors who explained that the identification of beasts and their heads and horns as earthly kingdom-powers was a basic principle of interpretation. It followed that seas or waters, out of which nearly all prophetic beasts were seen to emerge, symbolised peoples or nations.[36] Thus an expositor seeking to explain the significance of a beast emerging from the sea (as in Daniel vii 1-7, or Revelation xiii 1-3) could know that it represented a governing power which had arisen from the peoples of the earth.

There were other symbols which also required explanation. What meaning, for example, was to be given to a woman in prophetic symbolism? Scripture itself supplied the answer. 'I have likened the daughter of Zion to a comely and delicate woman,' God had said through the prophet Jeremiah (Jeremiah vi 2). This text is not merely an isolated reference to some obscure incident in the history of Judah in the eighth century B.C. It is also a principle of prophetic language and symbolism. A woman represents God's people. Hence the woman clothed with the sun and cast into the wilderness in Revelation xii depicts God's true Church on earth, while the scarlet-clad woman of chapter xvii, drunken with the blood of the martyrs and in league with the beast with seven heads and ten horns, symbolises the Church that has apostatised. It is in this context that Mede comments on the attempts of the Dragon, identified by the Bible itself as the great arch-enemy of God (Revelation xii 9), to destroy the Church of Christ by error and deception, where he had previously failed to do so by persecution:

> For now the dragon did not behave himself like a dragon as before, that is he professed not himself to be what he was, the sworn enemy of the Christian profession. For if he had done this, the seed of the woman would presently have known him.... Not till it was too late, the Church did know herself to be deceived by the old enemy, and to worship the dragon under this mask.... Who would have judged that under an empire pretending the worship of the Christian religion (and) demolishing idols, horrible idolatry and lately abolished heathenism should be mainly set up, and promoted by laws and edicts?[37]

It was the history of the Christian Church, as it had developed over the centuries, which helped to emphasise why it was necessary to understand the fortunes of the two women of Revelation.

But how could such things be comprehended? How was prophecy to be understood and its message communicated? How was the Church to be preserved from error, protected from the deceptions of the Devil, and presented at last, as the book of Revelation itself predicted, as the bride of Christ, arrayed in a white robe and prepared for the marriage of the Lamb? The answers to these questions are bound up to a large degree with yet another prophetic symbol which appeared frequently in the Revelation. Angels, particularly when depicted as bringing a message from heaven to earth, represented the human instruments chosen by God to carry His truth to men, 'preachers of the gospel', 'God's messengers whether magistrates or ministers', 'men joined together in a body to effect this work'.[38] David Pareus, Professor of Sacred Literature at Heidelberg University, whose commentary on Revelation had been translated into English in 1644, said of the three angels of Revelation xiv, 'These angels represent the preachers of the Gospel in the time of Antichrist.' The first angel represented Wycliffe, the second Luther, and the third 'all evangelical teachers' of the truth, who had proclaimed the Gospel since Luther's time and who would proclaim it until the end of the world.[39] The message of the third angel was of great importance in view of impending judgement, which was pre-figured in the last part of the same chapter and which, therefore, was inevitably linked to the proclamation of the Gospel as symbolised by the angels in the preceding verses.

Important as these principles unquestionably were to prophetic interpretation, the most important single factor was the relationship of Daniel and the Revelation to world history. To have any real interpretative significance, the meaning of the symbols had to be applied within a framework of thought that related all the prophetic visions of Daniel and the Revelation to a continuous process of history, beginning with Daniel in 600 B.C. and stretching down to the final fulfilment of prophecy and the consummation of history. Mede said of Daniel's prophecies that they covered the time 'from the beginning of the captivity of Israel, until the mystery of God should be finished ... therefore Daniel's prophecy is not terminated with the first, but reacheth to the second coming of Christ'.[40] The same principle applied to the book of Revelation, of which Bernard stated, 'It concerneth the whole church to the world's end ... till all be fulfilled.'[41] Brightman, commenting on Revelation i 1, explained, 'The matters should be begun by and by, and should flow from thence with a perpetual course without interruption, although the final consummation should be afterward for many ages.'[42] William Hicks explained more easily, 'This book of the Revelation is a book of prophecies wherein is a discovery of all such notable events and alterations as should happen to the Church of Christ, and her enemies, from her first rise unto the end of all.'[43] This historicist approach to the prophecies of Daniel and the Revelation arises from an understanding of history. Indeed, it may be said, as it was said for three centuries following the Reformation, that history is the key to prophetic interpretation, since history bears witness to the events which fulfil the predictions of prophecy. The value of Dr. L.E. Froom's four-volume *Prophetic Faith of our Fathers* is that it establishes the historicist approach as the norm of prophetic interpretation through Christian history. It has also been said that historicism is *the* Protestant interpretation, and it is doubtful whether Protestantism would have survived to perpetuate Reformation theology without it. It is only, then, as prophecy is studied in the light of history that its meaning becomes clear, and since the events of history can be verified, they effectively exclude any attempt to interpret prophecy from an alternative standpoint.

This is not to say that there have not been attempts to provide other frameworks for the interpretation of prophecy, either in the seventeenth century or since. There have been such attempts, but the fact that they originated at the time when Reformation thought and historicism were making their greatest impact must not be overlooked. The two principal alternatives to the historicist interpretation are preterism and futurism. Historicism, as we have seen, is the approach that sets Daniel and the Revelation within the context of history, and sees the progressive fulfilment of prophecy against that background and in relationship to the onward course of world history. Preterism, on the other hand, says that the prophecies of Daniel and the Revelation were fulfilled in the early centuries of Christian history, while futurism, as its name implies, contends that most prophecies, particularly those in the book of Revelation, remain yet to be fulfilled and will only come to pass at the very end of world history. It is evident that with either preterism or futurism the contents of

Daniel and the Revelation become largely irrelevant to the whole Christian Church throughout history, and that both systems will encourage a selective approach to the study of the Bible, which will tend to avoid or depreciate prophecy as part of the overall revelation of God to man.

The preterist system, which sought to apply the book of Revelation (with the exception of chapters xx-xxii) to the triumph of Catholic Christianity over Judaism and paganism in the early centuries, originated with Luis de Alcasar, a Spanish Jesuit who, in 1569, had devoted himself to the study of philosophy and Scripture in order to stem the flowing tide of Protestantism. Forty years of study resulted in the posthumous publication in 1614, of a 900-page commentary on the book of Revelation, dedicated to the Roman Church, and based on the preterist concept. Some fourteen years prior to this, another Jesuit priest, Francisco Ribera, who had specialised in biblical languages and who was Professor of Theology at the University of Salamanca, had also published a commentary on the book of Revelation which, with the exception of the early chapters, he applied to the last three and a half years of Christian history, at which time, he said, the dreaded Antichrist would arise, deny Christ, abolish the Christian faith, persecute the saints and assume world leadership. Futurism was most ably propounded by yet another Jesuit, Cardinal Roberto Bellarmine. The heart of the argument, again, was the projection of the Antichrist to the future, as a Jew who would arise at the end of time, and in whom would dwell all the powers of the Devil. It was under these circumstances that this futurist concept of the Antichrist first appeared in Christian thought.

Thomas Brightman was one of the first English writers to expose the origin, and the purpose, of futurism as a method of prophetic interpretation. Brightman contended that since futurism projected the prophecies of Revelation into the final three and a half years of history, it thereby denied the historicist emphasis contained within the book of Revelation itself, negated the blessing promised in the opening verses of the book to all who would seek to read and understand, and ignored the course of two millennia of history, the very events of which vindicated the historicist approach.[44] The more relevant point, perhaps, was that futurism had been devised by Jesuit scholars specifically to counter the Protestant understanding of history and of the papal Antichrist, a view that seemed fundamental to many Protestants in the sixteenth and seventeenth centuries. James Durham described futurism as:

> that conceit or dream of the papists, expounding all so literally of an Antichrist who shall come of the tribe Dan, and that shall reign just three years and a half, sitting in Jerusalem.... This dream [was] invented by them to keep their pope from being apprehended as the true Antichrist.[45]

Most Protestant commentators felt that it was necessary to point out, as Durham had done, that the true meaning of the Revelation had been deliberately concealed, even distorted, by the Church of Rome, and

Jeremiah Burroughes spoke for many when he said that due to papal influence there had been virtually no knowledge of the book during the Middle Ages.[46] While it is not possible to understand Puritan interpretation completely without this emphasis, the wider appeal of the historicist approach lay in the inherent strength of its argument. Subject to the irrefutable witness of history, historicism was to the objective mind the only valid basis for prophetic interpretation.

The Conclusions of Historicism

It is with Daniel's four kingdoms, which Mede had described as the 'ABC of prophecy', that any attempt to understand the historicist interpretation must begin. The four kingdoms were outlined in Daniel's second chapter under the symbolism of a great metal image, the meaning of which was explained to the Babylonian king, Nebuchadnezzar, by the prophet himself. The whole prophecy is specifically stated in the text as being a revelation from God concerning the future. The image consisted of four main sections, each composed of a different metal. The head was made of gold, the chest and arms of silver, the lower abdomen and thighs of brass, and the legs of iron. The feet consisted partly of iron and partly of clay. The image stood until it was destroyed by a stone of supernatural origin which struck it on the feet, the fragments ultimately being dispersed by the wind. The stone itself then became a great mountain, filling the whole earth (Daniel ii 31-35). The Bible explained that the golden head represented the Babylonian empire of Nebuchadnezzar, and that the other three parts of the image symbolised three further kingdoms which would successively arise thereafter. The fourth kingdom, represented by the legs of iron, would ultimately be divided into ten, depicted by the ten toes, and the resultant nations would remain disunited until the coming of the stone, which would terminate all earthly kingdoms since it represented the Kingdom of God (Daniel ii 37-44). The stone had been depicted as striking the image in the time represented by the feet, signifying that God would bring to an end the course of human history during the era of those divided nations that followed the iron kingdom. 'These times once finished, all the kingdoms of this world should become the kingdoms of our Lord and His Christ,'[47] Mede said. Of this prophecy, so fundamental to the understanding of all other prohecies in the books of Daniel and the Revelation, Scripture itself declared, 'The great God hath made known ... what shall come to pass hereafter: and the dream is certain, and the interpretation thereof sure' (Daniel ii 45).

These four kingdoms were again the basis of Daniel's second vision, recorded in the seventh chapter. Now the symbols were beasts: a lion with eagle's wings, a bear with three ribs between its teeth, a leopard with four heads and four wings, and a fourth beast, unlike any known animal, but 'dreadful and terrible, and strong exceedingly' (Daniel vii 7). In accordance with the text itself, from which the rule of interpretation was derived, the beasts were understood as symbols of kingdoms (verse 17), the same our kingdoms that had been represented in the earlier vision. Even as the legs of the image had ten toes, so the fourth beast had ten horns, designating the divisions of the fourth kingdom. Again, the vision concluded with a picture of the last events — the judgement, the coming of Christ at the Last Day, and the everlasting Kingdom of God. These were the prophetic revelations which together Mede described as the 'sacred calendar', and which he contended were the yardstick of all prophetic chronology in the Bible.

The reckoning of time according to this 'sacred calendar' was relatively simple. The Bible explicitly stated that the Babylonian empire was the first of the four kingdoms which would successively bear rule in the earth (Daniel ii 38). History provided the identity of the other three. They were the empires of Medo-Persia, Greece and Rome, which succeeded Babylon, and each other, in that order. The Babylonian empire gave way to that of Medo-Persia in 539 B.C., Medo-Persia was finally superseded by Greece at the battle of Arbela in 331 B.C., and Greece in turn was conquered by Rome in 168 B.C. at the battle of Pydna. Thus began that long domination of Western Europe by the mighty Roman empire, a rule which was to last for some six centuries and which was to include within its compass the birth and death of Christ and the birth and growth of the Christian church.

Both of Daniel's prophecies had indicated that the fourth empire would be divided rather than conquered by another world power as the preceding empires had in turn been conquered. It was well known in the seventeenth century that the Roman empire was overrun by invading barbarian tribes from the north, ten of which ultimately settled and survived in those territories of Western Europe which had belonged to Rome. The final blow was struck in A.D. 476, when the last emperor or Rome was deposed and the city of Rome conquered by the Goths. Thomas Parker wrote, 'For about four hundred years the Roman emperors continued in their majesty .. and then began effectually to be broken down, and to be dissolved into ten kingdoms.'[48] Thus the fourth empire of prophecy came to its appointed end and the era of divided Rome's successors began, an era that prophecy indicated would continue until the end of the present world order.

It was in relationship to these two prophecies of Daniel, covering as they did the whole gamut of the future, that the remaining prophecies of Daniel and the prophecies of the Revelation were to be considered. They foretold events of major religious significance which would take place between Daniel's time and the coming of Christ's kingdom at the end. This was particularly true of the Revelation, whose prophecies concentrated on the fortunes of the Christian church as they ebbed and flowed through history, and on the intense battle between good and evil, truth and error, as it would be waged on earth prior to the ultimate triumph of righteousness and peace. Thomas Goodwin, President of Magdalen College, Oxford, taught that the Revelation covered the time from Christ's ascension to the final reign of God, dealing principally with those earthly kingdoms whose fortunes were directly related to those of the church, of which the Roman empire and its successors played the most significant role.[49] Hence William Hicks would write:

> The Revelation is no longer a mystery, but a book of history of memorable acts and passages, wherein is foretold the several changes that shall befall the secular state or Roman Empire, and to the Church of Christ under the dominion of that Empire, until it shall, as the stone prophecied of in Daniel ii, smite the image on his feet and become itself a great mountain, set up upon the top of all mountains.[50]

It would require a book in itself to explain with the necessary detail the meaning of the many lines of prophecy in Daniel and the Revelation. Suffice it to say that Hicks and his contemporaries were able to say of much of the Revelation as of Daniel, 'The things represented in this book are no more mysteries and hidden things, but are clear and accomplished acts.'[51]

Reference was made earlier to the significance of time in prophetic interpretation, and we must now comment, if only briefly, on chronological prophecy. Even the most casual reading of Daniel and the Revelation reveals that several time periods feature in the text, and it is clear that these periods must be calculated correctly if the prophetic message as a whole is to be understood. Puritan expositors recognised that the biblical revelation was set in time and that the historical process was related to the fulfilment of the divine purpose. More than one writer defended the importance of prophetic time periods on the grounds that in the Old Testament God had specified certain periods of time for the accomplishment of His purpose. One hundred and twenty years had been allotted to the men of Noah's age, and seventy years had been determined as the period of Israel's captivity in Babylon. There was, therefore, nothing out of the ordinary in the fact that the same God, when speaking of the future, should also speak in terms of time. One of the most important contributions of prophetic exposition in this respect was the settlement in English religious thought of the conclusion reached by continental theologians, that the time, times, and half a time of Daniel were synonymous with the twelve hundred and sixty days, and the forty-two months of Revelation, and that they all represented twelve hundred and sixty years of literal time. It was during this period that Revelation's woman in white hid in the wilderness and the mysterious 'little horn' of Daniel held sway in the earth. In accord with the historicist view, English Protestantism in the seventeenth century widely regarded this period of time to be largely in the past.

In much the same way as the prophecies of Daniel ii and vii were crucial to the interpretation of all apocalyptic prophecy, so the prophecy of Daniel ix was crucial to the computation of chronological prophecy, for it established beyond doubt the validity of the day/year principle. The prophecy spoke of a period of seventy weeks, that is, weeks of prophetic days, or four hundred and ninety years, foretelling the coming and death of the Messiah within that period of time. John Owen addressed himself to the explanation of this prophecy in his commentary on Hebrews, which must rank as one of the most scholarly expositions of any portion of Scripture to emerge from English Puritanism. Owen noted that the whole period was divided into three sections in the text of Daniel, an initial period of seven weeks or forty-nine years, a second, longer period of sixty-two weeks or four hundred and thirty-four years, and a final week of seven years, together making seventy weeks or four hundred and ninety years in all. A commandment to rebuild Jerusalem was stated by Daniel as marking the beginning of the seventy weeks' period, and Owen said that this command was given by Artaxerxes Longimanus who, in the seventh year of his reign, decreed that the exiled Jews should return to their fatherland and rebuild the holy city. The main issues in the prophecy, Owen contended, concerned the 'anointing' of the Messiah and His 'cutting off'. The Messiah's 'anointing' corresponded to His baptism, which took place at the end of sixty-nine weeks, and the 'cutting off' referred to His death in the midst of the final week of the prophecy. Owen, in fact, says that the seventy weeks as a whole extended from Artaxerxes' decree to the death of the Messiah or a very few years thereafter.[52] If the whole period began with the decree issued by Artaxerxes, which in modern reckoning was in 457 B.C., it therefore ended in A.D. 34, exactly 490 years later. Clearly, the accurate computation of the prophecy depends on a correct starting date, and other expositors besides Owen — among them Henry Bullinger and Sir Isaac Newton — arrived independently at the seventh year of Artaxerxes as the point at which computation should begin.

By far the most significant and far-reaching conclusion to emerge from Puritanism's study of prophecy was its identification of the Antichrist. To be more correct, it was a conclusion derived from earlier Protestantism but clarified and perpetuated in Puritan exposition. Daniel's second prophecy had foretold the rise of another power, set in time after the fall of the Roman Empire and the emergence of the ten kingdoms, and designated in the Bible as the 'little horn' (Daniel vii 8). This horn, in fact, arose from among the ten horns, destroyed three of them in the process, uttered blasphemous words against the Most High, persecuted the saints, attempted to change times and laws, and prevailed for a period of twelve hundred and sixty years (Daniel vii 24-25). Revelation had also foreshadowed the emergence of this power under two further types. Chapter xiii described a beast with seven heads and ten horns, which careful students could identify as the successor of the Roman Empire, having all the characteristics of Daniel's little horn, with the added qualification that after its rule of forty-two prophetic months or twelve hundred and sixty years, it would suffer a mortal wound, and then rise to world prominence regaining its lost influence once again, before the final triumph of the Gospel. Chapter xvii depicted the scarlet whore, 'Babylon, the mother of harlots', riding on the beast, whose seven heads represented seven mountains. As though to emphasise the importance of this power and to impress upon the Church the danger of underestimating its influence, the Apostle Paul had also spoken of it as 'the man of sin' and 'the mystery of iniquity' in his second Epistle to the Thessalonians, and again as the apostasy of the latter times in his first Epistle to Timothy. It was this power, so often and so strongly spoken of in Scripture, that had come to be known in the Church as the Antichrist.

The historico-chronological setting for the emergence of this power, and a careful analysis of all its characteristics so clearly and repeatedly given in Scripture, enabled an identification that shook the mediaeval Catholic Church to its foundations. Edward Haughton, whose book *The Rise, Growth and Fall of Antichrist* (1652) drew on the prophetic statements of Daniel, Paul and John, explained, 'In all they have said of the great Antichrist, they have pointed the finger at the Popes of Rome.'[53] The use of the plural was intentional. The Antichrist was a system, a succession, rather than an individual. David Pareus agreed with this, since the papal system fulfilled all the prophetic characteristics: 'Him therefore we cannot but confidently judge to be Antichrist, for as much as in him all the marks of Antichrist do evidently concur and agree together.'[54] Lest the impression be given that we seem now to be descending into the realm of speculation, we should repeat that this identification was virtually unanimous in all Protestant exegesis in England and on the Continent for at least two hundred years following the Reformation, and that it was based on recognised principles of interpretation within the historicist framework.

Of all that might be said concerning Antichrist, and that would be a considerable exercise in itself, we must restrict ourselves to the Puritan definition of the term. This will, at the same time, explain something of the origin and nature of the Antichrist, as well as underline its importance to the Puritan concept of truth and the purity of the Gospel. We will allow those who wrote with such conviction on these matters in English Puritanism to speak for themselves. David Pareus and James Durham both described the gradual growth of the Antichristian power in the Church in the centuries which followed the apostolic age:

> By degrees ... the apostolic sincerity of faith and order did wear out, and the corruptions, superstitions, and heathenish abominations and idols were brought in, ... for Antichrist's apostasy was not at the highest all of a sudden, but increased by slow paces, till the pride and tyranny of the Roman bishops was lifted up and established.... The beast therefore rose out of the sea, not suddenly, nor in one day, month or year, but by certain steps, continuing almost three hundred years, viz. from Constantine until Phocas, or from Julius I until Boniface III. In this tract of time Antichrist was formed in the bosom of the Church, as it were in the womb of a mother.[55]

Durham writes of the decree of Phocas, in A.D. 606:

> Immediately after this, the light of the Word wonderfully decayed, traditions were obtruded, all public worship was to be performed in Latin, the Scriptures were keeped up from lay people ... litanies, liturgies, and masses were brought instead of the Word and preaching ... plurality of

mediators, and worshipping of saints and angels were brought in ...
heathenish superstitions were brought again into the Church ... images
were set up in the Church, and appointed to be worshipped.[56]
Pareus concludes that from the conglomeration of heresies, errors, traditions and superstitions that crept into the Church in the early centuries, the
'purity of Christian religion was corrupted and depraved, the Church forced
to flee into the wilderness, Christ thrust out of His possession, and
Antichrist set up in His stead'.[57]

It is the combined effect of tradition, superstition and heathenism on the
person and office of Christ, which constitutes the very essence of Antichrist. Edward Haughton puts the case as plainly as it could be put:

> The great Antichrist is one that is pretendedly for Christ, but is really
> against Christ.... The Pope pretends to be more for Christ than any
> man in the world, Christ's vicar, Christ's viceregent, the visible head of
> Christ's Church, Saint Peter's successor to feed the flock of Christ.... I
> tell you, he pretends to be more for Christ than any man alive, but let me
> tell you withall that there is no man alive so much against Christ as he is,
> and therefore most properly called Antichrist.[58]

It is Haughton's argument that the fundamental doctrines of the Gospel and
the redemptive offices of Christ have been supplanted by the doctrines of
Catholicism. Haughton specifies the doctrines in question. The atonement has been superseded by the satisfaction of the mass and other works
of merit. The mediatorial office of Christ has been replaced by the
priesthood. Christ's intercession has given away to the intercession of
Mary, saints and angels. The sole authority of Scripture has been
subordinated to the authority of the Church. The worship of God has
become the worship of images, and salvation by faith alone in the finished
work of Christ has been replaced by salvation by works in the unceasing
observance of saints' days and acts of penance.[59] It is in this sense that
the Papacy is Antichrist, not in the sense of one who is opposed to Christ,
but in the more subtle and dangerous sense of one who provides an
alternative for Christ. Joseph Mede says that the apostasy of the latter
times is a revival of pagan worship-forms which deny the worship due
alone to Christ, and hence that Antichrist is 'a counter-Christ'.[60]

The finality with which early Protestantism and Puritanism identified the
Antichrist might have been tempered by the somewhat more cautious
stand taken by Henry Denne, had that stand been adopted by others. In
retrospect, however, it must be concluded that Denne was ahead of his age
in advocating a view that would only be understood more clearly with the
passing of time. It was Denne's opinion that to limit Antichrist to any
specified man or succession of men was to place too narrow an interpretation on prophecy. 'I conceive the great Antichrist to be that mystical body
of iniquity which opposeth Jesus Christ,' he declared. Denne agreed that
this did refer to the papacy, but argued that it also included whoever sought
to destroy what Christ had erected or to build where Christ had pulled
down. The papacy and the Antichrist differed as did the head and the body,

and whatever might be opposed to Christ in principle, or in effect, was of the essence of Antichrist.[61] Was Denne speaking of any version of Christianity, individual or collective, Catholic or Protestant, then or at any time in the future, which substituted a religion of its own devising for the purity and fullness of the Gospel revealed in Christ? The passage as a whole suggests that he might have been. With that possibility in mind, it only remains to cite a final statement from Thomas Goodwin concerning the latter-day revival of papal influence foretold in Revelation xiii:

There is a generation of men set forth as the beast's last champions, that yet receive the number of his name. And these are reckoned his as truly as the others, as being they who should interdict buying and selling to the beast's opposites, in order untt his advancement. . . . But I fear that they shall proceed yet further, even to an open acknowledgement and professing of the Pope's power, (though perhaps not as infallible head of the Church, yet as universal patriarch of the West) and so endeavouring to effect a union and reconciliation with him.[62]

12. THE WORLD TO COME

The earth originally given to man as his kingdom, betrayed by him into the hands of Satan, and so long held by the mighty foe, has been brought back by the great plan of redemption. All that was lost by sin has been restored. 'Thus saith the Lord ... that formed the earth and made it; He hath established it, He created it not in vain, He formed it to be inhabited' (Isaiah xlv 18). God's original purpose in the creation of the earth is fulfilled as it is made the eternal abode of the redeemed.

Ellen G. White *The Great Controversy* (1950) p.674

This present world shall one day be dissolved, and these visible heavens and earth which now are shall be burnt up and brought to dust. Yet we who are believers, according to the promise under the Old Testament, do look for a new world instead of this, that is, for new created heavens and a new created earth instead of these. ... All the godly meek shall inherit the new created earth, and therein delight themselves in abundance of peace ... all that are truly righteous shall not only inherit, but also shall dwell therein for ever.

John Seagar *A Discoverie of the World to Come* (1650) pp. 60, 63, 64

A Calvin scholar, Dr. Heinrich Quistorp, describes hope as 'the fundamental attitude determinative of the Christian life'.[1] It may seem superfluous to emphasise again how basic this view is to the wholeness of the Christian message, particularly since Paul himself argues in his defence of the resurrection that 'if in this life only we have hope in Christ, we are of all men most miserable' (I Corinthians xv 19). Judged by its own original claims, and by the consistent interpretation of succeeding ages, the Christian faith is strongly and inherently directed towards the future, and unless that orientation is evident in the presentation of the Gospel, the very message itself must inevitably be open to question. We may be quite certain, moreover, that if our Puritan forefathers were by some act of providence to be thrust into the contemporary theological scene, they would view it with profound consternation, concluding that the source of much current Christian doctrine must be quite different from that from which they had drawn their own faith. This is not to suggest that the present is unimportant, or that the Church should not be concerned with the realities of life or the betterment of society, but rather to emphasise once more that to the Christian the present must always be lived in view of that future life which Christ made possible by His death and resurrection, and which, in the final analysis, must be of the greater consequence. That our Puritan forefathers understood all this cannot be questioned, and when they spoke of the world to come, as they frequently did, it was as the logical, necessary and desirable conclusion to the long saga of man's life in the present order.

It should also be explained that when Bible students in the seventeenth century spoke of 'the world to come' they did not always mean the same thing. To some, the term referred to the reign of Christ and the saints during the Millennium, while to others it referred to the earth as it was to be recreated after the Last Judgement, and in which state it would be the home of the redeemed for eternity. How these conclusions were reached, and how they might relate to each other, we shall attempt to survey in this chapter. In either case, of course, the emphasis is on the reward of the righteous, but inasmuch as all men would not be saved at last, our study would be incomplete without some consideration of the destiny of the unsaved. Most early Protestants accepted without question the mediaeval doctrine of eternal hell-fire, but, as Bible study became more critical, there appeared towards the middle of the seventeenth century an alternative doctrine which, its advocates claimed, was more consistent with the character of God and the system of biblical truth as a whole.

The Millennium

As prophetic interpretation assumed greater significance, claiming the attention of more and more scholars, it was inevitable that the Church would have to come to terms with Revelation xx and the Millennium, and that an explanation would be required of that fascinating but formidable chapter. David Pareus doubtless voiced the feelings of many when he confessed, 'The more I think upon it, the less I find how to untie the knot that hath troubled so many.'[2] Even Mede admitted that the Millennium was 'the most abstruse of all the prophetical scripture'.[3] These reservations should not be forgotten as we endeavour to bring together some of the interpretations which appeared in English religious thought between 1600 and 1700.

Revelation xx mentioned a period of one thousand years, during which Satan would be bound and the saints live and reign with Christ, a period which was to commence with a resurrection of the saints and close with a resurrection of the wicked. Although there is evidence that in the sixteenth century the Millennium was believed by some to be in the future,[4] the overwhelming consensus of opinion in early English Protestantism placed it firmly in the past. To mention only some of those whose works on prophecy were quoted in the previous chapter, Napier, Dent, Brightman, Bernard and Pareus, all maintained that the thousand-year period had already been fulfilled in the earlier history of the Church.[5] This view was a direct continuation of the theology of Augustine, who had

equated the Millennium with the whole period between Christ's first and
second comings, believing that the Last Judgement would take place in
the year A.D. 1000 or thereabouts. Coming five hundred years or more
after that date had passed, early Protestant expositors modified the
Augustinian view, explaining that the thousand years referred to a deter-
minable period of time, and dating them either from a point early in
Christian history, or from the conversion of Constantine at the beginning of
the fourth century. Pareus may be cited as an example of the former
group. He took the destruction of Jerusalem, which he placed in A.D. 73,
as the starting-point, thereby terminating the Millennium in A.D. 1073,
with the elevation of Gregory VII to the papal see.[6] Napier, Bernard and
Brightman, all took the later starting date, thus bringing the end of the
Millennium to c.1300.[7] Constantine's conversion to Christianity was
supposed to have paved the way for the Christian conquest of Europe, and
to have introduced an era during which the Christian faith had flourished
and Satan had been contained. To be fair, there was some debate as to
how effectively Satan had been bound, and Dent, for one, maintained that
his binding had been only partial. It was generally held to be the case,
nevertheless, that for the duration of the Millennium the Church had been
protected from the onslaughts of her enemies, and given the opportunity
for growth and establishment. With the effective appearance of the Turk in
European history (c.1300), however, an ideological and physical assault
had been launched on the Church which, together with the full growth and
activity of the Antichrist, marked the loosing of the Devil, and the end of the
millennial age. It is difficult to generalise, but those who contended for a
fulfilled Millennium held that it had been a literal period, that it related to the
Church's pilgrimage on earth, and that Satan's binding and loosing were to
be explained in terms of prevailing circumstances relating to the prosperity and adversity attending the proclamation of the Gospel. Although the
precise extent of Satan's binding was for some a debatable point, during
the Millennium the Church had enjoyed a degree of peace and prosperity
which she would not have done had Satan not been bound at all.

The more men thought about history, however, and the more they related
it to prophecy, the more they felt that the facts did not support this
interpretation. To begin with, there were too many qualifications and too
many disputed points between the various exponents of a past Millennium
for that view to have credibility. More important, no period in history that
even approximated a thousand years could be found during which the
Devil had been effectively bound and in which the Church had enjoyed an
era of peace and spiritual prosperity. Nathaniel Homes insisted that the
saints could not possibly already have reigned as the prophecy indicated,
since for the greater part of history error had prevailed in the Church and
persecution had prevailed against it, at least until the Reformation.[8]
Moreover, a chronological interpretation of the Revelation required the
Millennium to follow the reign of Antichrist, and if Antichrist was to rule for
1,260 years, and if the time of Antichrist's supremacy was to be marked by

error, blasphemy, idolatory and persecution, it was self-evident that the Millennium could only be placed in the future. Indeed, most expositors said that the 1,260 years must be fulfilled before the Millennium could begin. Homes, again, says that the Millennium must 'follow the times of the beast, and of the false prophet, and consequently the time of Antichrist'.[9]

The first known Englishman to reach this conclusion was Joseph Mede. He did so reluctantly, and only after the most careful consideration of the text and the relevant facts of history. Dr. William Twisse, Prolocutor of the Westminster Assembly, wrote in the preface to the 1643 edition of Mede's *Key of the Revelation* that Mede was not in any way indebted to previous interpreters in reaching his conclusions, an opinion which was later confirmed by Mede's biographer in 1672. It was Mede's concern for an objective exegesis of Scripture that led him to reject the traditional Augustinian interpretation and place the Millennium in the future, a conclusion which, as he later confessed to a friend, he had 'tried all ways imaginable' to avoid, since he had wanted to date it from Constantine. His critical study of the text, however, obliged him to revise this view and conclude instead that the Millennium could only occur at the end of world history, since it was inseparably bound up with the second advent, the resurrection of the righteous, and the destruction of the beast.[10] While extreme and unjustifiably subjective interpretations were to cause later advocates of a coming Millennium to bring the doctrine into much disrepute, Mede's motive for advocating that the thousand years of Revelation were still in the future was unquestionably his determination to arrive at an interpretation consistent with all the relevant statements of Scripture.

Mede believed that the Bible taught that the Millennium was bounded by two resurrections, both of which would be literal, as opposed to preceding interpretations which saw them as symbolic. The first resurrection would be that of the righteous, which according to I Thessalonians iv 15-17 would take place at Christ's second coming and would mark the beginning of the thousand-year period. This was the 'first resurrection' referred to in the text of Revelation xx. The general resurrection of the remaining dead would then take place at the end of the Millennium.[11] A similar view had been reached independently by the continental theologian Johannes Alsted, whose commentary on Revelation was translated into English in 1643. William Burton, who translated Alsted's work, maintained that it had been the general understanding of the early Church that there would be a resurrection of the faithful before the general resurrection to judgement at the Last Day, and that the Millennium would occur between them.[12] Most English expositors of any consequence who followed Mede and Alsted took the same stand on what was admittedly a difficult chapter. George Hammon explained:

> God showed John the state of the resurrection of the just to be a
> thousand years before the resurrection of the wicked, and when Christ

speaks of His coming, and raising the dead and changing the living (that live in Him), He saith that 'two shall be in one bed, the one taken and the other left'. And that this agreeth with Paul's words to the Thessalonians (which saith 'The dead in Christ shall rise first') is plain, because Christ adds this word also, 'Where the carcass is, thither, will the eagles be gathered.' All which showeth that the dead in Christ shall rise first. And John resolves the doubt, that is, how long the dead in Christ shall rise before the other dead men, and that is (saith he) a thousand years, (for the rest of the dead men lived not again until the thousand years are finished), this is the first resurrection. So then the resurrection spoken of by John is not to be understood of a resurrection from a state of sin to a state of grace, but it is to be understood a resurrection from the grave, and the soul is to be understood the body or the entire man.[13]

There were many students of prophecy in seventeenth-century England, like Hammon, who came to the understanding that the Millennium would begin with Christ's second advent and the resurrection of the righteous dead, and that it would end with the resurrection of the wicked and the Last Judgement.

The effects of the Millennium on the wicked, and the relationship of the wicked to the events of the millennial age in general, were of some importance in arriving at a thorough understanding of the whole prophecy. Mede had maintained that Antichrist, together with all the living enemies of Christ, would be destroyed at the second coming, and that the way would thus be cleared for the reign of Christ and the saints. Mede's view, of course, was that while Christ would be in heaven, the saints would reign on earth for the millennial period. The wicked who had died at Christ's coming would be resurrected at the end of the Millennium, together with the wicked of all ages, and then would follow a brief but intense period of renewed conflict between the forces of good and the forces of evil.[14] Alsted descriptively adds, 'not only the great Antichrist shall flourish again, but also pagan and barbarous people, and other monsters of the same batch'.[15] Thus Satan would be loosed at the end of the Millennium for a little season, until at the Last Judgement he and the host of the wicked would be cast into the lake of fire. Mede thus equated the Millennium with the Day of Judgement, 'A continued space of many years wherein Christ shall destroy all His enemies, and at length death itself, beginning with Antichrist, by His revelation from heaven in flaming fire, and ending with the universal resurrection, during which space of time shall be the kingdom of the saints in the New Jerusalem.'[16] Mede, then, if we may summarise his order of millennial events in a sentence, believed in Christ's second coming, the destruction of the wicked, the resurrection of the righteous, the thousand-year reign of the saints on earth when Christ would be in heaven, the resurrection of the wicked, and a brief period of renewed conflict terminating in the Last Judgement and the final destruction of Satan and the unredeemed.

While Mede's new interpretation of the Millennium was restrained in itself, and more in harmony with the Bible as a whole than previous interpretations had been, it was neither then nor at any later time universally accepted. There remained a sizeable body of opinion which continued to teach that the Millennium had been fulfilled in the past, and in retrospect it is not difficult to understand their feelings. The seventeenth century in English religious history was marked by intense millennarian excitement, largely the result of highly speculative and unrestrained interpretations of Revelation xx imposed against the socio-political background of the time. Many who followed Mede in placing the Millennium in the future came to predict a golden age of the Church on earth, and some, among them the Fifth Monarchy Men, confidently asserted that the saints were to be God's instruments in establishing the Kingdom, using the sword as an instrument of accomplishment if necessary. Many of those with a more cautious outlook feared that such millenarianism was but a short step from the licentious and sensual millenarian beliefs which were held to have broken out in some areas early in Christian history. Wishing to avoid a recurrence of that type of millenarianism, indeed of anything which could be interpreted to resemble it, they felt it safer to hold to the neo-Augustinian view, thereby avoiding the necessity for a future Millennium altogether. Such thoughts were clearly in John Seagar's mind when he wrote his *Discoverie of the World to Come* (1650), which argued the case for a fulfilled Millennium on the grounds that the Bible predicted that the condition of the world would grow progressively worse until the coming of Christ and the fires of the Last Day. It was an error, plainly contrary to Scripture, to think that there would be a universal conversion or a time of Church rule when the whole world would be subject to the spiritual government of Christ and the saints prior to the Last Judgement.[17] Thomas Hall felt that millenarianism had 'brought forth the malignant fruit of schism in the church and sedition in the state'.[18] This was a reference to the Fifth Monarchy faction, and Hall, an implacable opponent of millenarianism under any guise, called for its rejection as 'an old error new vamped, or an old harlot new painted'.[19] If the new doctrine of a coming Millennium was wrong anywhere, it was at this point where it taught or implied an age of latter-day glory for the saints on earth.

Despite these reservations, Mede's concept of a future Millennium and the pre-millennial second advent continued to gain ground, and in a hundred years or so it could number among its adherents some of the most illustrious names of the age: Isaac Newton, and William Whiston, Newton's successor as Lucasian Professor of Mathematics at Cambridge; Thomas Burnet, the Master of Charterhouse; Thomas Newton, Bishop of Bristol and Dean of St. Paul's, and Joseph Priestly. Of the theological writers who adopted Mede's interpretation, few gave it as much attention as did Nathaniel Homes, an Oxford Doctor of Divinity whose strong Puritan sympathies soon led him out of the Anglican Church and into the Independent fold, and whose facile pen produced several works on prophecy and the implications of millenarian belief. By some standards

Homes might well have been classified with the more extreme wing of millenarianism. Certainly he spoke strongly for a golden age of the Church on earth during the Millennium, thereby incurring the wrath of Thomas Hall, who described Homes' views as 'learned nonsense', and said that his arguments hung together 'like ropes of sand'.[20] For all that, Homes' order of events for the millennial age closely followed that of Mede, beginning with the second coming of Christ and the literal resurrection of the righteous dead, and ending with the resurrection of the wicked, the last conflict between good and evil, and the final destruction of Satan and the wicked. Homes explained that in purpose the Millennium corresponded to the weekly Sabbath, being the last age of the world and therefore a period of rest for the earth, 'a sabbatism', 'a sabbatical rest', 'the seventh thousand of years', 'a distinct, determinate time bounded with two resurrections'.[21] The Millennium was only the preface to eternity for the saints, and those who were raised in the first resurrection would never die again.[22] From a practical viewpoint perhaps the most important conclusion Homes drew from his study of the millennial age was that it would not offer a second chance of salvation to the unsaved. 'In all that time,' he says, 'there shall be no degenerating of any believers, so no more regenerating of any unbelievers.'[23] When the Millennium comes, the day of salvation is past. The destinies of all men are finally settled at the beginning of the Millennium, at the second coming of Christ, the resurrection of the just, and the destruction of the living wicked. Even those who might have opposed other aspects of millenarianism could have agreed with that. The present life was man's period of probation, his opportunity for accepting or rejecting the Gospel of grace.

Eternal Punishment

A recurring factor in the foregoing survey of millennial beliefs is the punishment which is to be meted out to the wicked. Most millenarians of the day believed that at the second coming those alive on the earth who for any reason were not counted among the righteous, would be slain at the appearance of Christ in glory. They would then be raised in the second resurrection at the end of the Millennium, together with the reprobate dead of all ages, to hear the verdict of the Last Judgement and to receive their just retribution. But precisely what would that retribution be? A similar question presented itself to those who did not believe in the Millennium at all. How would God deal ultimately with the unrighteous? To be more accurate, this question only occurred to those who thought into the matter, for most men of the time, theologians included, saw little reason to challenge the traditional answer inherited from the doctrines of the mediaeval Church. That answer, in a phrase, was eternal hellfire. Yet, as previously indicated, there were some in the seventeenth century who came to question the theological validity and the moral sufficiency of that reply, and who sought to discover the more acceptable alternative.

There were several objections to the conventional belief that the wicked would suffer the eternal torments of hell. For one thing, the origin of the doctrine and its associations were suspect. It was embodied with belief in natural immortality, which Thomas Hobbes described as a window giving entrance into the Church to the doctrines of eternal torment, purgatory, indulgences and invocations of the dead.[24] Hobbes reminds us that natural immortality is a pre-Christian Greek concept, which the theologians of the post-apostolic Church accepted to their embarrassment, being unable to decide consequently where the souls of the departed should reside between death and the resurrection. At first it was supposed that disembodied souls awaited the resurrection beneath the altars of churches, but later, Hobbes points out, 'the church of Rome found it more profitable to build for them this place of purgatory'.[25] It was a relatively short step from the cleansing torments of purgatory to the punitive torments of hell, and he who understood the origin of one also understood the origin of the other. Samuel Richardson held that the first mention of eternal torment in Christian history appeared in the teaching of the second-century heretic Marcion, who denied the existence of Christ and believed in two gods, one good and one evil, to mention but a few of his more basic deviations.[26] From that contaminated spring the seeds of eternal torment had been borne into the Church and had come to fruition at length in the syncretistic doctrines of the Antichrist.

The more serious objections to the doctrine of eternal torment were that it impugned the character of God, and that it was contrary to the true teachings of Scripture. Thomas Hobbes had exposed the weaknesses of eternal torment in his influential *Leviathan* (1651), a book which in turn had been criticised by John Bramhall, Bishop of Derry and later Archbishop of Armagh. Hobbes replied to Bramhall's criticism in a work which was published posthumously, and which is still little known, and hence infrequently cited. Hobbes defended his earlier views on eternal torment against the background of the intense Calvinism of his day which taught that all men were predestined either to eternal life or to everlasting punishment. The connection between natural immortality and eternal torment is again evident in Hobbes' argument:

> If God bestowed immortality on every man when He made him, and He made many to whom he never purposed to give His saving grace, what did his Lordship [Bramhall] think? That God gave any man immortality with purpose only to make him capable of immortal torments? 'Tis a hard saying and I think cannot piously be believed. I am sure it can never be proved by the canonical Scripture.[27]

It was this last point, as well as the moral and philosophical difficulties of believing in a God who had deliberately created some men to suffer eternal torment, which made that doctrine doubly unacceptable to Hobbes. Samuel Richardson further pointed out that according to Scripture the consequence of sin was death, which by definition is final, and not eternal suffering in hell, which could never rightly be construed as anything but a continuation of life.[28]

Just how many opponents there were in the seventeenth century to the prevailing doctrine of eternal torment it is difficult to assess. Probably there were not many. D.P. Walker has drawn attention to the fact that some who personally disbelieved in eternal torment were perhaps unprepared to say so in public. That may have been true of those whom Walker cites, including Sir Isaac Newton, Thomas Burnet, Bishop of Salisbury, and John Tillotson, Archbishop of Canterbury, all of whom appeared to have questioned the doctrine of hell.[29] It was not true, however, of others whose works have survived to demonstrate their opposition to the accepted doctrine. That opposition was based on Scripture, and on their understanding that Scripture rightly interpreted, taught that everlasting destruction was to be the fate of the wicked. Hobbes agrees that the fire prepared for the wicked is truly an everlasting fire which burns both body and mind, but says that it is unquenchable and eternal in the sense that its effects are everlasting. Hobbes then adds, 'But it cannot thence be inferred that he who shall be cast into that fire, or be tormented with those torments, shall endure and resist them so as to be eternally burnt and tormented, and yet never be destroyed nor die.'[30] It was the outcome of the punishment that was everlasting, not the process itself. John Biddle's Two-Fold Catechism (1654) listed several texts to support the argument that the Bible taught the final extinction of the wicked, among them II Thessalonians i 7-9, II Peter ii 12, Matthew iii 12, Hebrews x 26-27 and II Corinthians ii 15-16. Biddle explains that the wicked would 'be destroyed, punished with everlasting destruction, burnt up, devoured, pass away, perish'.[31] Hobbes' comment on Matthew x 28 was similar.[32]

The biblical teaching of death and punishment could only be seen in its wholeness as the various original words translated into English as hell were explained. The Hebrew word sheol appeared sixty-five times in the Old Testament, and was translated as 'hell' (thirty-one times), 'the grave' (thirty-one times) and 'pit' (three times). George Hammon pointed out that even the biblical usage of 'hell' gave that word different meanings. Scripture said that Jonah cried to the Lord 'out of the belly of hell' (sheol, Jonah ii 2), 'by which', says Hammon, 'is meant the sea or the whale, take it which way you please'.[33] Hugh Broughton, rabbinical scholar and linguist, in explaining that article in the Creed which refers to Christ's descent into hell, pointed out that where in the Old Testament most English translations used hell for sheol, more correctly by sheol 'the loss of this world only is meant'.[34] Broughton said that the Creed therefore, when it spoke of hell, should be understood as meaning 'the world to come', or 'separation from this world' rather than a place of torment. With reference to the Old Testament use of sheol, if any further sense was required it could only be derived from the use of the word in its context, and not from any inherent meaning in the word itself.[35] Samuel Richardson maintained that the primary meaning of sheol in the Old Testament was the grave,[36] a point which Broughton undoubtedly would have conceded, since it was in that sense that Job used sheol when speaking of his approaching death and future resurrection. Referring to Job vii 9, xiv 13-14 and xvii 13-16, Broughton says:

> Job speaketh of all men thus: That when we descend to *sheol*, we come not ever up hither and our place knoweth us no more. And he wished that God would lay him up in *sheol*, till his change (in the resurrection) should come. And he looked that *sheol* would be his house, and that all his hopes should descend with the bier into *sheol*. He that would overreach Job's style should need wisdom.[37]

On the strength of the linguistic evidence it was quite clear that hell in the Old Testament did not refer to a specific place of punishment or torment. It did not refer to a specific place at all, but rather, as Broughton says again, to 'the state after this life,[38] which for all men, good and evil alike, was the grave.

The New Testament equivalent of *sheol* is *hades*, and again it is Broughton who points out that *hades* does not signify a place of eternal torment. Not once in the New Testament, Broughton says, does *hades* have that meaning.[39] He was in fact in error here, for in the parable of Dives and Lazarus in Luke xvi 23, *hades* is used in association with the torments of hell. This instance, however, was irrelevant to the argument, which may have been the reason why Broughton chose to ignore it — it was generally agreed that one could not construct doctrine from parables. Therefore, as Samuel Richardson explained, the passage concerning Dives and Lazarus 'is not proof of any torments in hell, because it is a parable, not a history'. The story was no more proof of punishment immediately after death, or of eternal torment, than Judges ix 8 was a proof that trees could walk or speak.[40] Hobbes defines *hades* as 'the name of the place where all men remain till the resurrection,' that is all who were either buried according to custom or 'swallowed up of the earth', since *hades* literally signifies 'a place where men cannot see, and containeth as well the grave as any other deeper place'.[41] The most obvious meaning of *hades* as used in the New Testament was again the grave, the sense in which Paul used it in I Corinthians xv 55 in that triumphant exclamation, 'O grave (*hades*), where is thy victory?' Again, in Revelation xx, it is said that death and hell (*hades*) were to be cast into the lake of fire at the second death. Hobbes explains, 'That is to say, were abolished and destroyed, as if, after the day of judgement there shall be no more dying, no more going to hell, that is, no more going to hades, which is the same as no more dying.'[42] If hell itself was to be destroyed in the second death, how could it possibly be eternal?

Perhaps the most misunderstood word for hell in Scripture, and the one that gave the whole concept its connotation of punishment and torment, was the Greek word *gehenna*. The word appears in the original some twelve times, and is always translated as hell or hell-fire, as for example in Mark ix 47-48, 'It is better for thee to enter into the kingdom of God with one eye, than having two eyes to be cast into hell-fire (*gehenna*); where their worm dieth not and their fire is not quenched', or in Matthew x 28,

'Fear him which is able to destroy both soul and body in hell (*gehenna*)'. The inference from these and similar statements was that hell is a place of punishment where the wicked are recompensed for their evil deeds with unquenchable fire. Richardson explains the interesting origin of the word *gehenna*. It is not a true Greek word, but a composite of the Greek *ge*, meaning earth or ground, and a derivative of the Hebrew *hinnom*, the name of a valley to the south-west of Jerusalem in which the city waste was burned.[43] Hence *gehenna* literally means the burning ground or place of burning. To *gehenna* or the valley of Hinnom all the city refuse was taken for disposal, including putrefying flesh and the unburned carcasses of dead animals. On occasion Gehenna was even used to dispose of human bodies. Richardson cites a Jewish rabbinical authority as saying that sometimes the Sanhedrin decreed that the bodies of criminals should be cast unburied into the Valley and there burned with the other refuse. For some serious acts, it was said, offenders were even burned alive there.[44] *Gehenna*, therefore, derives its meaning from the valley of Hinnom, the place of burning and destruction, and inasmuch as the fires of Gehenna seldom went out the word acquired a sense of the unquenchable. Hobbes, therefore, says, 'From this abominable place, the Jews used ever after to call the place of the damned by the name of Gehenna, or the Valley of Hinnom. And this *gehenna* is that word which is usually now translated hell, and from the fires from time to time there burning, we have the notion of everlasting and unquenchable fire.'[45] Clearly the fires in the Valley of Hinnom were unquenchable only as long as there was sufficient material to feed them, and the use of *gehenna* as the synonym for Hell, as Hobbes realises, is purely metaphorical. The same must apply to the fires of destruction which will follow the Last Judgement — they will burn until there is nothing more to consume, and their effects will be eternal. *Gehenna*, then, as *sheol* and *hades* correctly understood, does not signify a place of everlasting punishment, or fire that can never be quenched. The linguistic evidence of Scripture in no way supports the doctrine of eternal torment in Hell, and Hobbes must be allowed to speak for all who considered the matter at any length, when he says of the wicked, 'Man at his resurrection shall be revived by God and raised to judgement, and afterwards body and soul destroyed in hell-fire.'[46]

The New Earth

Necessary as it might be to understand the destiny of the damned, it would be totally wrong to conclude that the English Church in the seventeenth century was obsessed by Hell, or that believers were motivated to godly living either by a fear of eternal torment or eternal extinction. Nathaniel Homes, who believed that the Millennium was but the introduction to eternity, 'the prelude to everlasting, infinite glory,' also urged his fellow-believers to recognise that a knowledge of such things must lead to a deeper experience, 'cleaving to Christ ... and to one another in love'.[47]

Arthur Dent looked forward to the future inheritance of the redeemed, and exclaimed, 'Let us spend many thoughts upon it, let us enter into deep meditations of the inestimable glory of it, let us long till we come to the ... possession of it.'[48] No, the eyes of English Christians in the seventeenth century were firmly focussed on the future reward of the saints — more so, in all probability, than at any other time in the history of the Church in these isles. Some, as we have already seen, pinned their hopes for the realisation of the promises on a millennial kingdom on earth. The weakness of that position, particularly if one followed Homes in looking for an eternity beyond the Millennium, was that the millennial glory detracted from the glory which was to follow. What could be better than the glorious, golden age on earth which some millenarians anticipated? There were many, however, including millenarians, who understood that when the Bible spoke of the world to come, as it often did, it referred specifically to the creation of a new earth which was to be the home of the redeemed for all eternity, and not merely to a period of a thousand years. In a general sense, the world to come might refer to the Millennium, it might include also that indefinite rest in the grave, but in substance it signified the ultimate realisation of God's purpose for man and the world, in the creation of a new heaven and a new earth. It was precisely that hope which led Dent to write of 'the infinite glory and endless felicity to which ... the elect of God shall be advanced'.[49]

The certainty of a new earth rested upon the most explicit statements of Scripture. A basic text was that at Isaiah xlv 18, which stated that God had not created the earth in vain, but that He had created it specifically to be inhabited. Thomas Burnet maintained that this text set forth the immutable purpose of God in respect of 'the present earth and the future'.[50] This is to say, in effect, that the eternal will of the Creator would be frustrated should a time ever come when the world no longer existed, or when it existed without inhabitants. John Napier believed in the literal new earth on the combined strength of Revelation xxi-xxii, II Peter iii 10, Isaiah lxv 17 and lxvi 22, and related the continuity of the earth to the perpetual 'motions of the spheres, planets, and stars'.[51] Napier's argument is that the known order of celestial movement requires the continuing existence of the present world as one of the heavenly spheres. Humphrey Hody, whom we met previously as a protagonist of the literal resurrection of the body, provides a similar argument. The place in which believers would live in the next life cannot simply be of an ethereal or immaterial nature, as was most commonly supposed. 'Perhaps after all, our heaven will be nothing but a heaven upon earth,' Hody says. 'It seems more natural to suppose that since we have solid and material bodies, we shall be placed, as we are in this life, on some solid and material orb.'[52] This is more in harmony with Scripture, scientific law and reason. Thomas Adams relates the ultimate purpose of God for man and the world to Christ's own promise that the meek would 'inherit the earth' (Matthew v 5),[53] and Arthur Dent maintains that the physical world will be restored to its pristine, Edenic condition.[54] This will mark the 'restitution of all things', anticipated by Peter and included as an important aspect of the first recorded proclamation of the early Church (Acts iii 21). It is, then, the divine purpose, as Dent says again, to 'restore the world to that excellent estate wherein it was before Adam's fall,'[55] and only as that is accomplished will the prophetic assurances of Isaiah, Peter and John, be fulfilled. Pareus adds, in a comment on II Peter iii 10, 'By which plainly we gather that a new heaven and new earth is to be looked for historically and properly.'[56] The consistent and reasonable testimony of Scripture is that, following the present evil world, God will create a new heaven and a new earth.

How that new earth would come into being was also outlined in Scripture. God had created the world in the beginning, and He would re-create the world after the cleansing fires of the Last Day. Dent correctly speaks of 'the renewed estate of heaven and earth', explaining that the present world will continue eternally in substance, although 'greatly altered and changed in condition and quality'.[57] We are clearly talking here of both continuity and change, as Thomas Adams further emphasises when he refers to 'the permutation of the world'. The end of the present order is 'certain' and 'determined', he says, but it will be a 'perfective' rather than a 'destructive' end.[58] A frequently cited passage in discussions of the new earth was II Peter iii, which places the end of the present order and the creation of the new earth in the context of the dissolution of the Noachian world by the Flood. As the earth had once been purified by water, so it will finally be purified by fire. The two events are inseparable historically and theologically. Burnet says of II Peter iii, that it is a 'true account of what hath been and what will be at the great day of the Lord'. In James Durham's view the fires which will purify the earth at the Last Day will act in a similar manner to a goldsmith's fire. It is a fire which melts the metal but does not consume it, even 'as a goldsmith doth with metal that he hath a mind to put a new form or mold upon'.[59] So from the fires of the Last Day there will emerge a 'new heaven and new earth, as a refined lump from which the dross is taken away'. Since no elemental change in the nature of the earth occurred as a result of the Flood, there will be no change in substance as a result of the last conflagration, only a change 'to the better'.[60] Nathaniel Homes sums up: 'As sure as the old earth was totally drowned, and after totally renewed, so this very earth, now grown old again in age and wickedness, shall be totally burnt, and after that totally renewed.'[61] When John saw in vision a new heaven[62] and a new earth, and the New Jerusalem prepared as a bride adorned for her husband, he witnessed nothing less than the very consummation of the divine purpose and the fulfilment of all prophetic hope.

And so when men in the Puritan tradition spoke or wrote of that new earth, they conceived of a physical world that was as real and as tangible as that in which they presently lived. Adam had been a real man with a real body, in a real world, and the children of the second Adam, to whom the promises belonged, must expect nothing less. This is what the spokesmen of Puritan hope meant when they used such words as 'restored', 'renovated', 'redintegrated', 'renewed', to describe the process by which the earth would be returned to that state in which originally it had been created for the habitation of man. Later generations might seek to spiritualise the assertions of Scripture regarding the final destiny of man and his world, but they were too clear and too numerous in the Bible for preachers in the Puritan tradition to dismiss them as poetic imagery or the uninspired yearnings of unsophisticated minds. Of course, Arthur Dent was quite right to point out that words could never adequately describe the re-created earth or convey what it would be like to live forever in Paradise,[63] and if in the event the streets of the city were not paved with gold or its foundations were not garnished with precious stones, the reality nonetheless would be equally as true and infinitely more glorious.

A real Adam in a real world in Eden, meant real men with real bodies in Eden restored, and nothing was more sure or more warmly anticipated in the Puritan vision of the future than the resurrection of the body. Only through the resurrection of the body and the creation of a new earth could all the promises relating to eternal life be brought together in a doctrine of immortality consistent with all the declarations of Scripture, and only the resurrection of the body could enable the promise of eternal life in the new earth to be a reality for each individual believer. It was a doctrine which Puritanism clearly understood, but which later Protestantism has tended to forget. So John Flavel can declare with utter conviction:

> Let my body lie where it will, in earth or sea, let my bones be scattered and my flesh devoured by worms or fish, I know thou canst and wilt reunite my scattered parts. And in this body I must stand before thy awful tribunal to receive according to what I have done therein.[64]

He who had made man from the dust of the ground in the beginning could equally well remake him at the end, from nothing if necessary, but certainly from the remains of the grave or the ocean. That might appear contrary to reason, but it was not contrary to revelation or to faith, and Christian hope in the last analysis was posited on God's revelations in Scripture and in Christ, and on man's faith in the inherent certainty of the promises. Men would experience eternal life, not as immaterial spirits flitting interminably and purposelessly through the broad ethereal sky, but as real people, with real being, in a real world.

The grounds for such hope were the resurrection of Christ Himself and the assurances of the New Testament that those who believed would at the Last Day be like Him, since at His appearing He would change the bodies of all who were His (I John iii 2, Philippians iii 21). The promises applied to the living and to the dead, and the change which they would undergo would not merely be to a different state, in which the bodies of believers would be recreated and made immortal, attractive as that might be in itself, but to the very condition which Christ Himself had experienced as a result of the resurrection. 'Christ's body was marvellously improved by the resurrection,' says Flavel, for 'it fell in weakness, but was raised in power, no more capable of sorrow, pain, and dishonour.'[65] It was a real body, but with different properties, as those who read the record carefully would observe. That body was the prototype of all believers' bodies in the resurrection. Hence Flavel continues, 'Our bodies are sown in weakness, but raised in strength, sown in dishonour, raised in glory, sown mortal bodies, raised spiritual bodies.'[66] The concept of the spiritual body need not detain us long, although there were probably those in Flavel's day, as there have been ever since, who found it difficult to conceive of a body being at the same time corporeal and spiritual. Flavel uses the word 'spiritual' in opposition to 'carnal', and not in opposition to 'material', and so the spiritual body is the body freed from the effects of sin, and re-created after the manner of Christ's resurrection body. Flavel can therefore say, 'There are no flaws, defects, or deformities in the children of the resurrection. What members are now defective or deformed will then be restored to their perfect being and beauty.'[67] John Seagar explains the nature of the resurrection body more precisely:

These bodies are corruptible, those shall be incorruptible. These bodies are mortal, those shall be immortal. These bodies are weak and frail, those shall be strong and able. These bodies are deformed and vile, those shall be well-formed. These bodies are natural, those shall be spiritual. These are, it may be, imperfect for stature or limbs, those shall be perfect in both respects.[68]

Thus the resurrection body is real and spiritual at the same time, real in substance, spiritual in quality, and above all immortal. It was with bodies of this kind that the meek would inherit the earth, and that the earth itself would be enabled to fulfil its role in the divine purpose.

A world restored to its pristine, Edenic state presupposes a world without sin and without any of the consequences of sin so evident in the world as it has degenerated since creation. It envisages a physical world fresh from the hand of the Creator, unblemished and unmarred by the selfishness and waywardness of man, and where all is peace and harmony. The men who wrote of that world in the seventeenth century were of one accord in asserting that it was indeed this kind of world which the Bible described as the ultimate home of man. 'A new earth wherein dwelleth righteousness,' declared the Word of God (II Peter iii 13). On that phrase from Peter, Thomas Adams remarked, 'that is, holiness, pureness, innocency, and the perfection of goodness'.[69] The present world is subject to corruption and decay. From the moment of birth, death rests upon the whole creation. But Adams describes the new earth as 'eternal spring' and says it will 'be new forever'.[70] James Durham holds that in the new earth there will be no more death, sickness, sorrow, crying, or pain, 'whether from external causes of violence, or inward infirmities of body or ... mind'.[71] Since the new earth is essentially a restoration of the Edenic state in which man is lord over the creation and sinless in mind and body, Durham concludes that there is no external threat to that renewed estate, 'neither any internal tendency to disease, but absolute freedom from all effects of sin'.[72] It all might have been difficult for the ordinary man to visualise, but Milton had told the story of a Paradise lost and a Paradise regained, and in so doing had touched the heart of Puritan hope. Paradise restored would be Paradise as it had been in the beginning, and Scripture declared that to the Creator Himself it had been very good.

But the most important question, perhaps, has yet to be answered. Did that righteousness which the Bible said would characterise the new earth, refer only to the physical world, to those conditions which would return as the Edenic harmony between man and nature was restored? Or did that righteousness have a deeper significance? The prophet Isaiah, in a passage which was widely taken to refer to the new earth, had stated quite clearly, 'Thy people also shall be righteous' (Isaiah lx 21). To be sure, the way of salvation for sinful man in the present world was through righteousness imputed and imparted. But how was the Bible to be understood when it asserted that righteousness would be established as the way of life for ever in the world to come? It was quite clear to Puritans and to those who accepted their theology on this point, that righteousness is not a quality or a condition which can describe inanimate objects or apply to brute creatures. 'It cannot hang upon trees or grow out of the ground,' as Burnet realistically points out. 'Righteousness cannot be without righteous persons,' he continues, ' 'tis the endowment of reasonable creatures.'[73] The righteousness which will prevail in the new earth, which will indeed be its most distinctive feature, is a righteousness which is manifest in the lives of the redeemed. It is a condition of people, as Isaiah had intimated, not of nature or natural beauty, however idyllic the new earth might be. Yet even that is not all. Thomas Adams points to the crowning glory of Paradise restored when he says simply, 'There dwelleth Christ, and He is righteousness.'[74] Scripture promises, 'They shall see His face, and His name shall be in their foreheads' (Revelation xxii 4). Those who in the present life had experienced by faith the righteousness of Christ, and whose lives had been changed by His Spirit, would, in the earth made new, see Him and live in His presence for evermore. Christ is the eternal source of righteousness, and His redeemed people the eternal consequence. It was, perhaps, in that sense that Arthur Dent, David Pareus and many others besides, interpreted the Tree of Life as a symbol of Christ, 'our never-failing physician which in this life healeth all our spiritual diseases and infirmities, and after this life will preserve us in perpetual health and happiness.'[75] Regardless of ecclesiastical leaning or denominational loyalty, of doctrinal position or prophetic interpretation, it was a place at which all believers, if they were truly Christ's, could meet, a point from which together they could look towards the world to come and know that in God's good time it would assuredly come to reality.

REFERENCES

INTRODUCTION

. The date from which Seventh-day Adventism takes its beginnings in the British Isles is open to some question. Ings and Loughborough, formally sent from America, arrived in Southampton on 30 December 1878, and commenced their work in 1879. Ings had previously spent some time in England during the summer of 1878, distributing literature on his own initiative. The first group of Seventh-day Adventists came together in 1879, as a result of the combined efforts of Ings and Loughborough, and the first converts were baptised in 1880. It would seem that either of these latter dates is more appropriate as marking the beginning of the Church's existence in the British Isles

. D. Mitchell *Seventh-day Adventists Faith in Action* (New York, 1958) p.9

. Between July 1976 and June 1977, the annual growth-rate was 5.13 percent. Between July 1977 and June 1978, the rate had increased to 5.21 percent. The rate for 1978 as a whole was 5.69 percent. Current growth rate is approximately 6 percent.

. cf. also A. Hoekema *The Four Major Cults* (The Paternoster Press, 1963) in which the Seventh-day Adventist Church is classified with Mormons, Christian Science, and Jehovah's Witnesses

. D. Edwards *Religion and Change* (London, 1970) p.262

. e.g. *Seventh-day Adventist Bible Commentary*, 7 vols.; *Adventist Review*, weekly general church paper; *Ministry*, monthly professional journal for Seventh-day Adventist ministers

. W. Haller *The Rise of Puritanism* (New York, 1957) p.5

. e.g. M. Powicke *The Reformation in England* (London, 1961) pp.1-3, W. Walker *A History of the Christian Church* (Edinburgh, 1959) pp.358-360

. Puritans in general followed the theological system of John Calvin, which required some measure of commitment to the doctrine of predestination. This is one point where Adventism diverges from Puritan theology

. Haller *The Rise of Puritanism* 49

. W.C. Abbott *The Writings and Speeches of Oliver Cromwell* (Cambridge Mass., 1937-47) III p.61

. Haller *The Rise of Puritanism* 235

. C.E. Whiting *Studies in English Puritanism, 1660-1688* (1931) p.20

. *The Western Martyrology or the Bloody Assizes* (1705) *passim*, cited in W.T. Whitley *A History of British Baptists* (1923) p.149

. see B.W. Ball *A Great Expectation, Eschatological Thought in English Protestantism to 1660* (Leiden, 1975) p.8, and C.H. and K. George *The Protestant Mind of the English Reformation 1570-1640* (Princeton, 1961) pp.71-2

CHAPTER 1

. Article Six of the Thirty-nine Articles (1571) referred to 'the sufficiency of Holy Scriptures for salvation'

. John Ball *A Treatise of Faith* (1632) p.198

. Thomas Adams *The Workes of Tho. Adams* (1630) p.903

. William Perkins *The Workes of that Famous and Worthy Minister of Christ . . . Mr. William Perkins* I (1626) p. 581

. see John Owen *Of the Divine Originall, Authority, Self-evidencing Light, and Power of the Scriptures* (Oxford, 1659) Ep. ded., sig. a4v

. see Richard Baxter *The Saints' Everlasting Rest* (1669) p.199

. James Ussher *A Body of Divinitie, or the Summe and Substance of Christian Religion* (1647) p.18

. *ibid*

. Henry Denne *Antichrist Unmasked in Two Treatises* (1645) p.52

. Baxter *Saints' Rest* 199

. George Lawson *Theo-Politica or, a Body of Divinity* (1659) p.7

. Perkins *Workes* I 484

. Baxter *Saints' Rest* 222

. *ibid* 226

. John Goodwin *The Divine Authority of the Scriptures Asserted* (1648) pp.251-2

. Owen *Divine Originall* 220

. Rabbinical scholars whose special task it was to ensure the accurate transmission of the Old Testament text

. Owen *Divine Originall* 175-178

. Baxter *Saints' Rest* 206

. Owen *Divine Originall* 34

. Perkins *Workes* I 582

. Ussher *Body of Divinitie* 9

. Goodwin *Divine Authority* 320

. Richard Baxter *The Reasons of the Christian Religion* (1667) p.263

25. William Perkins *The Whole Treatise of the Cases of Conscience* (1651) p.126
26. Goodwin *Divine Authority* 320
27. John Ball *A Short Treatise Containing all the Principal Grounds of Christian Religion* (1654) p.26
28. Perkins *Workes* I 484
29. Goodwin *Divine Authority* 148-9
30. John Flavel *The Whole Works of the Reverend Mr. John Flavel* (1716) I p.325
31. *ibid*
32. Goodwin *Divine Authority* 17
33. Baxter *Saints' Rest* 201
34. Goodwin *Divine Authority* 13
35. e.g. Ussher *Body of Divinitie* 8, Richard Baxter *More Reasons for the Christian Religion* (1672) p.56
36. Goodwin *Divine Authority* 13
37. Flavel *Works* II 39
38. *ibid*
39. Richard Baxter *A Call to the Unconverted* (1660) p.231
40. Flavel *Works* II 39
41. Flavel *Works* I 2
42. Adams *Workes* 1209
43. Perkins *Workes* I 484
44. Flavel *Works* I 626
45. Ball *Short Treatise* 7
46. Joseph Alleine *Remains of that Excellent Minister of Jesus Christ Mr. Joseph Alleine* (1674) p.76
47. Flavel *Works* II 185
48. Alleine *Remains* 76
49. Adams *Workes* 663
50. Daniel Featley *The Dippers Dipt* (1647) sig. B3r
51. John Owen *The Causes, Waies and Means of Understanding the Mind of God as Revealed in His Word* (1678) p.5
52. Flavel *Works* II 72
53. Richard Sibbes *A Fountaine Sealed* (1637) pp.98-9
54. Owen *Causes, Waies and Means* 10
55. Flavel *Works* I 613
56. Owen *Causes, Waies and Means* 10-11
57. Richard Sibbes *Christs Exaltation Purchast by Humiliation* (1639) pp.47-8
58. Flavel *Works* I 615
59. John White *A Way to the Tree of Life* (1647) Ep. ded., sigs. A3v, A4r
60. John Owen *An Exposition of the Two First Chapters of . . . Paul . . . unto the Hebrews* (1668) p.111
61. Humphrey Hody *The Resurrection of the (same) Body Asserted* (1694) p.210
62. Owen *Causes, Waies and Means* 146
63. Francis Bampfield *All in One* (1677) pp.59-61
64. John Goodwin *Imputatio Fidei, or a Treatise of Justification* (1642) sig. b3v
65. Goodwin *Divine Authority* 48, 51
66. Flavel *Works* I 2
67. *see* Nathaniel Homes *The Resurrection-Revealed* (1661) pp.278-9
68. Henry Danvers *Treatise of Baptism* (1674) sigs. A3v, A4r
69. Goodwin *Treatise of Justification* sigs. b4r, v
70. Flavel *Works* I 392

CHAPTER 2

1. Perkins *Workes* I 626
2. Goodwin *Treatise of Justification* 133
3. John Bunyan *The Work of Jesus Christ* (1688) p.151
4. *ibid* 167-8
5. Goodwin *Treatise of Justification* 133
6. Flavel *Works* I 288
7. Perkins *Workes* I 626
8. John Downame *A Guide to Godlynesse* (1622) Ep. ded., sig. A2v
9. Flavel *Works* I 95
10. *ibid*
11. *ibid* 169
12. Owen *Hebrews* I 203
13. Flavel *Works* I 380
14. Thomas Taylor *Christ Revealed, or The Old Testament Explained* (1635) p.5
15. A series of sermons by Samuel Mather on the same theme was published under the title *The Figures or Types of the Old Testament, by which Christ and the Heavenly Things of the Gospel were Preached and Shadowed to the People of God of old* (1683)
16. *see* Hebrews vii 3
17. Taylor *Christ Revealed* 18, 24, 70, 36, 43, 86
18. Andrew Willett *Hexapla in Leviticum* (1631) pp.6-7
19. John Owen *A Continuation of the Exposition of . . . Hebrews* (1680) p.325

20. Samuel Mather *The Figures or Types of the Old Testament* (1705) pp.137-142
21. Willett *Hexapla* 7
22. Mather *Figures or Types* 145-150
23. Perkins *Workes* I 217
24. Owen *Hebrews* III 141, 326
25. e.g. John Flavel who says, 'As Aaron laid the iniquities of the people upon the goat, so were ours laid on Christ,' *Works* I 27. The Adventist position on this point is that the scapegoat represents Satan
26. White, *Tree of Life* 179
27. Flavel *Works* I 288-9
28. Alleine *Remains* 185-6
29. Cited in *The Midnight Cry*, 10 August 1843
30. Adams *Workes* 1209
31. Flavel *Works* I *passim*
32. Christopher Love *The Penitent Pardoned* (1657) p.132
33. Adams *Workes* 1209
34. Nicholas Byfield *An Exposition upon the Epistle to the Colossians* (1615) pp.110, 112
35. Thomas Manton *Christs Eternal Existence, and the Dignity of His Person* (1685) p.31
36. George Hutcheson *An Exposition of the Gospel of Jesus Christ according to John* (1657) pp.12, 8
37. David Dickson *A Short Explanation of the Epistle . . . to the Hebrews* (Cambridge, 1649) p.6
38. *ibid* 6, 8
39. Baxter *Reasons* 266
40. *ibid*
41. George Lawson *An Exposition of the Epistle to the Hebrews* (1662) p.12
42. F. Bampfield *All in One* 77
43. *ibid* 70
44. Flavel *Works* I 33
45. Joseph Alleine *An Alarme to Unconverted Sinners* (1673) p.141
46. *ibid*
47. *ibid* 142
48. Flavel *Works* I 49
49. *ibid* 160
50. *ibid* 157
51. John Durant *The Salvation of the Saints by the Appearances of Christ* (1653) To the Reader, sig. A7r
52. Flavel *Works* I 158-9
53. Joseph Truman *The Great Propitiation* (1669) p.211
54. Flavel *Works* I 160
55. Sibbes *Christs Exaltation* 131
56. *ibid* 132
57. Truman *Great Propitiation* 209
58. Adams *Workes* 1095
59. Flavel *Works* I 175
60. Baxter *Saints' Rest* 73
61. Flavel *Works* I 88
62. Perkins *Workes* I 626
63. Flavel *Works* I 239
64. George Downham *A Treatise of Justification* (1633) pp.352-3
65. Perkins *Workes* I 201
66. Flavel *Works* I 249
67. Sibbes *Christs Exaltation* 183-4
68. *ibid*

CHAPTER 3

1. Truman *Great Propitiation* 201
2. Thomas Gataker *Sermons* (1637) p.76
3. Perkins *Workes* I 161
4. Ussher *Body of Divinitie* 142
5. Downham *Treatise of Justification* 229
6. *ibid*
7. Flavel *Works* I 414
8. Downham *Treatise of Justification* 230-1
9. Ussher *Body of Divinitie* 143
10. Flavel *Works* I 414
11. Perkins *Cases of Conscience* 9
12. Ussher *Body of Divinitie* 144
13. Perkins *Cases of Conscience* 8
14. Richard Baxter *Confession of His Faith* (1655) sig. A3v
15. *ibid*
16. *ibid*
17. Gataker *Sermons* 29

18. Owen *Hebrews* III 159 (the second so numbered)
19. *ibid*
20. Baxter *Saints' Rest* 17
21. Downham *Treatise of Justification* 18
22. *ibid* 24-5
23. Ussher *Body of Divinitie* 175
24. Flavel *Works* I 159
25. Ussher *Body of Divinitie* 194
26. *ibid* 195
27. Richard Baxter *A Treatise of Justifying Righteousness* (1676) p.65
28. Ussher *Body of Divinitie* 194-5
29. Adams *Workes* 1217
30. John Bunyan *Grace Abounding to the Chief of Sinners* (1697) pp.90-1
31. *ibid* 91
32. Downham *Treatise of Justification* 5-6
33. *ibid* 3-4
34. Ussher *Body of Divinitie* 194
35. *ibid* 193
36. Downham *Treatise of Justification* 2
37. Flavel *Works* I 253
38. Downham *Treatise of Justification* 265
39. *ibid* 50, 97, 126, 261, 313, 433, 547
40. *ibid* 7-8
41. Flavel *Works* I 675
42. *ibid*
43. Downham *Treatise of Justification* 52, 57
44. Flavel *Works* I 264
45. *ibid* 258
46. Downham *Treatise of Justification* 273
47. *ibid* 14
48. Ball *Treatise of Faith* 218
49. *ibid* 3
50. *ibid* 7
51. Downham *Treatise of Justification* 14
52. *ibid* 357
53. Baxter *Justifying Righteousness* 162
54. Flavel *Works* 254-5
55. Downham *Treatise of Justification* 434
56. Flavel *Works* II 22
57. Lawson *Theo-Politica* 313
58. Goodwin *Treatise of Justification* 116
59. Ball *Treatise of Faith* 218
60. Downham *Treatise of Justification* 4
61. Baxter *Confession of Faith* 101-2
62. Downham *Treatise of Justification* 252, Perkins *Works* I 368-9
63. Alleine *Alarm* 201
64. Downham *Treatise of Justification* 4
65. Ussher *Body of Divinitie* 200
66. Downham *Treatise of Justification* 242 (incorrectly numbered 240)
67. Truman *Great Propitiation* 133
68. Downham *Treatise of Justification* 79
69. Richard Sibbes *The Brides Longing for her Bridegroomes Second Coming* (1638) pp.82-3
70. Downham *Treatise of Justification* 234
71. Baxter *Confession of Faith* sig. a2v
72. *ibid* 41
73. Downham *Treatise of Justification* 434
74. *ibid* 6-7
75. Lawson *Theo-Politica* 316
76. *ibid* 313
77. *ibid*
78. Downham *Treatise of Justification* 3
79. Mather *Figures or Types* 501
80. Gataker *Sermons* 38
81. Flavel *Works* I 260

CHAPTER 4

1. Alleine *Alarm* 59
2. Adams *Workes* 721
3. *ibid* 1102

4. Gataker *Sermons* 11
5. Alleine *Alarm* 61
6. Taylor *Christ Revealed* 170-1
7. *ibid* 163
8. Alleine *Alarm* 72
9. Flavel *Works* I p.331
10. *ibid*
11. Baxter *Confession of Faith* 49
12. Haller *Rise of Puritanism* 151
13. Alleine *Alarm* 76
14. *ibid* 5, 59
15. Flavel *Works* II 728
16. *ibid* I 334
17. *ibid* 351
18. Alleine *Alarm* 9
19. Thomas Adams *Happiness of the Church* (1619) p.109
20. Flavel *Works* II 109
21. Gataker *Sermons* 295
22. Flavel *Works* I 334
23. Alleine *Alarm* 20
24. Flavel *Works* II 35
25. *ibid* I 242
26. *ibid* 241
27. Haller *Rise of Puritanism* 8
28. Flavel *Works* II 20
29. *ibid*
30. Perkins *Workes* I 637
31. Baxter *Call to the Unconverted* 39
32. Flavel *Works* I 345, Alleine *Alarm* 27
33. Bunyan *Grace Abounding* 2
34. Adams *Workes* 729
35. Alleine *Alarm* 27
36. *ibid* 39-40
37. Flavel *Works* I 329
38. *ibid* II 21
39. Sibbes *Christs Exaltation* 94
40. Alleine *Alarm* 46
41. Gataker *Sermons* 76
42. Alleine *Alarm* 46
43. *ibid* 50-1
44. Flavel *Works* I 346
45. Perkins *Workes* I p.716, Downham *Treatise of Justification* 506
46. F. Bampfield *All in One* 88
47. Flavel *Works* I 354
48. Ball *Treatise of Faith* 116-17
49. White *Tree of Life* 114
50. Perkins *Cases of Conscience* 12
51. *ibid*
52. *ibid* 16
53. Flavel *Works* I 282
54. Alleine *Alarm* 37
55. Ball *Treatise of Faith* 141-2
56. Flavel *Works* I 243
57. *ibid* 282
58. *ibid* 265
59. *ibid* 283
60. Lawson *Theo-Politica* 307
61. Gataker *Sermons* 215
62. Flavel *Works* II p.5 (the third so numbered)
63. *ibid*
64. Perkins *Workes* I 370
65. *ibid* 637
66. Flavel *Works* II 35
67. *ibid* I 242
68. *ibid* 355
69. Perkins *Workes* I 370
70. Gataker *Sermons* 215
71. Flavel *Works* I 282
72. Owen *Hebrews* III 41

73. Lawson *Theo-Politica* 290
74. Flavel *Works* I 329
75. *ibid* 218
76. White *Tree of Life* 80-2
77. Alleine *A Sure Guide to Heaven* (1705) 270-2

CHAPTER 5

1. John Penry *Treatise [of] Reformation* (1590) sig. B2v, 3r
2. *ibid* sig. B3v
3. Edward Dering *M. Derings Workes* (1614) sigs. L8r, A3v
4. Ussher *Body of Divinitie* 188
5. Lawson *Theo-Politica* 286
6. John Smyth, 'Principles and Inferences concerning the Visible Church' (1607), in *The Works of John Smyth*, ed. W.T. Whitley, (Cambridge, 1915) I p.251-2
7. John Robinson *Of Religious Communion, Private and Public* (1614) p.4
8. Hanserd Knollys *Christ Exalted* (1645) p.17
9. Thomas Grantham *Truth and Peace* (1689) p.45
10. Joseph Stennett *The Works of the late Reverend and learned Mr. Joseph Stennett* (1732) IV p.340
11. Thomas Helwys *A Short Declaration of the Mystery of Iniquity* (1612) p.125
12. *ibid* 127
13. *ibid* 157
14. Ball *Treatise of Faith* 411
15. Ussher *Body of Divinitie* 411
16. Christopher Blackwood *The Storming of Antichrist* (1644) p.7
17. Gossip: Originally a child's sponsor at baptism; from Old English *godsibb*, relation in God
18. Hercules Collins *Believers Baptism from Heaven and of Divine Institution* (1691) p.66
19. Blackwood *Storming of Antichrist* 9
20. Collins *Believers Baptism* 8
21. *ibid* 21
22. Henry Danvers *Treatise of Baptism* (1674) p.2
23. George Hammon *Syons Redemption and Original Sin Vindicated* (1658) p.37
24. cf. Hammon *ibid*
25. Collins *Believers Baptism* 26-7
26. Blackwood *Storming of Antichrist* 22
27. John Smyth *The Character of the Beast, or The False Constitution of the Church* (1609) sig. A3r
28. Flavel *Works* II 727
29. Grantham *Truth and Peace* 33
30. John Tombes *Two Treatises and an Appendix to Them Concerning Infant Baptism* (1645) p.132
31. Danvers *Treatise of Baptism* 24
32. Collins *Believers Baptism* 67
33. Tombes *Two Treatises* 27
34. Danvers *Treatise of Baptism* 36-7
35. Blackwood *Storming of Antichrist* 20
36. Grantham *Truth and Peace* 59
37. *The Confession of Faith of those Churches which are commonly (though falsely) called Anabaptists* (1644) sigs. C1v, C2r
38. Henry Jessey *Miscellanea Sacra, or Diverse Necessary Truths* (1665) p.128
39. Collins *Believers Baptism* 122
40. *ibid* 15
41. Jessey *Miscellanea Sacra* 128
42. Lawson *Theo-Politica* 238
43. Collins *Believers Baptism* 15
44. Danvers *Treatise of Baptism* 14
45. Blackwood *Storming of Antichrist* 2
46. Hammon *Syons Redemption* 16
47. *ibid* 17
48. Blackwood *Storming of Antichrist* 2
49. Collins *Believers Baptism* 18
50. Hammon *Syons Redemption* 16
51. Danvers *Treatise of Baptism* 89-90
52. *ibid* 181
53. *ibid* 182
54. Collins *Believers Baptism* 14
55. *ibid* 12
56. Hanserd Knollys *The World that Now Is, and The World that Is to Come* (1681) p.74
57. Blackwood *Storming of Antichrist* 2
58. William Cave *Primitive Christianity, or, The Religion of the Ancient Christians in the First Ages of the Gospel* (1673) Pt. I pp.320-2
59. Danvers *Treatise of Baptism* 101

60. Collins *Believers Baptism* 64, Tombes *Two Treatises* 29
61. Grantham *Truth and Peace* sig. A2r
62. *ibid*
63. Danvers *Treatise of Baptism* title-page
64. *ibid* sig. A2r
65. *ibid* sigs. Av, A2r
66. *ibid* sigs. A2v, A3r
67. Blackwood *Storming of Antichrist* 55
68. Tombes *Two Treatises* 26
69. *ibid* 110
70. Danvers *Treatise of Baptism* sig. A2v
71. Blackwood *Storming of Antichrist* pt. 2 p.59
72. *ibid* 15-16

CHAPTER 6

1. Love *The Penitent Pardoned* 122
2. Owen *Hebrews* III p.184, Lawson *Hebrews* 127
3. Owen *Hebrews* III pp.248-9
4. Mather *Figures or Types* 318
5. Flavel *Works* I 178
6. Flavel *Works* I 178, Owen *Hebrews* III 247
7. Durant *The Salvation of the Saints* 46
8. *ibid* 46, 48-9
9. *ibid* Ep.ded.
10. Lawson *Hebrews* 127
11. Love *Penitent Pardoned* 122
12. Bunyan *Work of Jesus Christ* 19
13. Flavel *Works* I 57
14. Dickson *Hebrews* 182
15. Flavel *Works* I 57
16. Bunyan *Work of Christ* 27
17. Flavel *Works* I 45
18. Love *Penitent Pardoned* 122
19. Taylor *Christ Revealed* 203
20. *ibid* 202
21. Mather *Figures or Types* 61
22. Thomas Hobbes *Leviathan, or the Matter, Form, and Power of a Commonwealth Ecclesiastical and Civil* (1651) p.261
23. Owen *Hebrews* III 309-10
24. *ibid* 325
25. *ibid* 310
26. Taylor *Christ Revealed* 146
27. *ibid* 117
28. *ibid* 121
29. Love *Penitent Pardoned* 213
30. Perkins *Workes* I 218
31. Love *Penitent Pardoned* 213, Flavel *Works* I 55, 45, Lawson *Theo-Politica* 96
32. Lawson *Theo-Politica* 133
33. Lawson *Hebrews* 137
34. [Thomas Lushington] *The Expiation of a Sinner: In a Commentary upon the Epistle to the Hebrews* (1646) pp.146-7; this work appears to be largely a translation from a Latin commentary on Hebrews by Johannes Crellius (1590-1633)
35. *ibid* 144
36. *ibid* 166
37. *ibid* 167
38. *ibid* 145, 147
39. Flavel *Works* I 169
40. Abraham Wright *A Practical Commentary or Exposition upon the Pentateuch* (1662) p.119
41. Taylor *Christ Revealed* 107-8
42. Gervase Babington *Comfortable Notes upon the Book of Leviticus* (1604) pp.9-10
43. *ibid* 39
44. Willett *Hexapla* 94
45. Taylor *Christ Revealed* 107-8
46. *ibid* 109
47. Flavel *Works* I 119
48. Owen *Hebrews* I 306
49. *ibid*
50. *ibid* III 247
51. *ibid* 330

52. *ibid* I 301
53. *ibid*
54. Lawson *Theo-Politica* 96
55. Mather *Figures or Types* 450
56. Lushington *Hebrews* 160, 165
57. *ibid* 166
58. Love *Penitent Pardoned* 213, Flavel *Works* I 55
59. Lawson *Hebrews* 166
60. Owen *Hebrews* III 315
61. *ibid* I p.303
62. Lushington *Hebrews* 165, Lawson *Hebrews* 127, Bunyan *Work of Jesus Christ* 19
63. Durant *Penitent Pardoned* 84
64. *ibid* 129
65. Mather *Figures and Types* 509
66. *ibid*
67. Flavel *Works* I 473
68. Mather *Figures and Types* 516
69. Lawson *Theo-Politica* 139
70. Dickson *Hebrews* 99
71. Flavel *Works* I 85
72. Lawson *Theo-Politica* 139
73. Dickson *Hebrews* 182
74. *ibid* 99
75. *ibid* 98
76. Henry Denne *The Man of Sin Discovered* (1645) pp.15-16
77. Love *Penitent Pardoned* 122 (the second so numbered)
78. David Pareus *A Commentary Upon the Divine Revelation*, trans. E. Arnold, (1644) p.15

CHAPTER 7

1. Baxter, *Saints' Rest* 15
2. Owen *Hebrews* I 275
3. Downham *Treatise of Justification* 465
4. *ibid*
5. Lawson *Theo-Politica* 149
6. Downame *Guide to Godlynesse* 420
7. Owen *Hebrews* I 275; cf. Downham *Treatise of Justification* 445
8. White *Tree of Life* 206
9. *ibid* 315, 321
10. Willett *Hexapla* 17
11. *ibid*
12. Theophilus Brabourne *Three Treatises in Defence of The Seventh-day Sabbath* (1660) 19
13. White *Tree of Life* 206
14. Adams *Workes* 762
15. Downham *Treatise of Justification* 478, Owen *Hebrews* I 275
16. Ball *Short Treatise* 37
17. Ralph Venning *Sin, the Plague of Plagues* (1669) p.3
18. John Dod and Robert Cleaver *A Plain and Familiar Exposition of the Ten Commandments* (1604) p.8
19. Anthony Burgess *Vindiciae Legis* (1646) p.4
20. Lawson *Hebrews* 152
21. F. Bampfield *All in One* 136
22. White *Tree of Life* 202
23. Ussher *Body of Divinitie* 124
24. *ibid*
25. White *Tree of Life* 200
26. Adams *Happiness of the Church* 111
27. Baxter *Confession of Faith* 105
28. Richard Byfield *The Doctrine of the Sabbath Vindicated* (1631) p.79
29. Ussher *Body of Divinitie* 134
30. Ball *Short Treatise* 254
31. Downham *Treatise of Justification* 525
32. Ball *Short Treatise* 253, White *Tree of Life* 301
33. Ussher *Body of Divinitie* 206
34. Perkins *Workes* I 460-1
35. *ibid*
36. Baxter *Saints' Rest* 390
37. Christopher Love *Englands Distemper* (1645) pp. 16-17
38. Thomas Taylor *Regulae Vitae, The Rule of the Law Under the Gospel* (1635) pp.65, 70
39. William Strong *A Discourse of the Two Covenants* (1678) pp.104, 158
40. Baxter *Justifying Righteousness* 45

1. F. Bampfield *All in One* 6
2. *ibid* 39
3. Goodwin *Treatise of Justification* pt. 1 183
4. Baxter *Confession of Faith* 105
5. Baxter *Reasons of the Christian Religion* 227
6. Lawson *Theo-Politica* 149
7. Daniel King *A Way to Sion Sought Out, and Found* (1650) p.135 (the second so numbered)
8. *ibid* 136 (the second so numbered)
9. Sibbes *Christs Exaltation* 147
10. Baxter *Justifying Righteousness* 184, Perkins *Cases of Conscience* 48
11. Francis Roberts *Of God's Covenants . . . The Mystery and Marrow of the Bible* (1657) p.729
12. Thomas Manton *A Practical Commentary . . . on The Epistle of James* (1651) p.275
13. John Seagar *A Discoverie of the World to Come* (1650) p.46
14. Richard Baxter *Aphorismes of Justification* (1649) pp.317-18
15. Flavel *Works* I 278
16. White *Tree of Life* 314
17. Downham *Treatise of Justification* 457
18. Owen *Hebrews* I 66
19. Flavel *Works* I 278, 48
20. Theophilus Brabourne *Of the Sabbath Day* (1660) p.17
21. Flavel *Works* I 320
22. *ibid* 278
23. Bunyan *Grace Abounding* 8
24. Downham *Treatise of Justification* 457
25. Ball *Short Treatise* 149
26. Ussher *Body of Divinitie* 205
27. E.F. Kevan *The Grace of Law* (1964) p.92
28. Flavel *Works* I 160
29. Ball *Short Treatise* 258
30. Ussher *Body of Divinitie* 203
31. Ball *Treatise of Faith* 379
32. Flavel *Works* I 313
33. Brabourne *Of the Sabbath Day* 7
34. Truman *Great Propitiation* 200
35. Ussher *Body of Divinitie* 201
36. Truman *Great Propitiation* 199
37. Ussher *Body of Divinitie* 205
38. Baxter *Confession of Faith* 162-3
39. Owen *Hebrews* III 227 (the second so numbered)
40. Edward Stennett *The Insnared Taken* (1677) pp.80-82
41. Ball *Treatise of Faith* 32
42. Baxter *Aphorismes of Justification* 156-7
43. *ibid* 157
44. *ibid* 301-2
45. Edward Stennett *The Seventh Day is the Sabbath of the Lord* (1664) p.27
46. Downham *Treatise of Justification* 434

CHAPTER 8

1. Ephraim Pagitt *Heresiography or a Description of the Heretics and Sectaries of these Latter Times* (1661) Ep.ded., sig. A3r
2. Thomas Bampfield *An Enquiry Whether the Lord Jesus Christ made the World, and be Jehovah, and gave the Moral Law? And Whether the Fourth Command be Repealed or Altered?* (1692) p.3
3. Stennett *The Insnared Taken* 13
4. White *Tree of Life* 299
5. *ibid*
6. Ussher *Body of Divinitie* 242-3
7. Richard Bernard *A Threefold Treatise of the Sabbath* (1641) p.58
8. John Owen *Exercitations Concerning the Name, Original, Nature, Use and Continuance of a Day of Sacred Rest* (1671) pp.57, 152
9. Brabourne *Of the Sabbath Day* 3-4
10. Theophilus Brabourne *A Discourse Upon the Sabbath Day* (1628) p.1
11. F. Bampfield *All in One* 10
12. *ibid* 51
13. Brabourne *Discourse* 68-9
14. Stennett *The Insnared Taken* 153
15. Joseph Davis *The Last Legacy of Mr. Joseph Davis* (1720) pp.41-2
16. Ussher *Body of Divinitie* 244
17. Francis White *An Examination and Confutation of a Lawless Pamphlet* (1637) p.51
18. F. Bampfield *All in One* 51-2

19. Brabourne *Discourse* 71
20. Theophilus Brabourne *An Answer to M. Cawdry's Two Books of the Sabbath* (1654) pp.64-5
21. *ibid* 33
22. *ibid* 65
23. Perkins *Workes* I 152
24. Henry Soursby and Mehatabel Smith *A Discourse of the Sabbath* (1683) p.93
25. Brabourne *Discourse* 101
26. *ibid* 101-2
27. Soursby and Smith *Discourse* 80
28. *ibid*
29. F. Bampfield *All in One* 22
30. *ibid* 65
31. *ibid*
32. *ibid*
33. *ibid* 45
34. *ibid*
35. *ibid* 137
36. Brabourne *Of the Sabbath Day* 27, *Three Treatises* 8
37. Brabourne *Of the Sabbath Day* 57
38. *ibid*
39. F. Bampfield *All in One* 80
40. *ibid* 8
41. Davis *Last Legacy* 32
42. T. Bampfield *An Enquiry* 39
43. Francis Bampfield *A Name, an After-One . . . in the Latter-day Glory* (1681) p.13
44. Thomas Bampfield *Reply to Dr. Wallis* (1693) p.6
45. F. Bampfield *All in One* 8
46. Owen *Sacred Rest* 399
47. Brabourne *Answer* 8
48. T. Bampfield *An Enquiry* 45
49. William Saller and John Spittlehouse *An Appeal to the Consciences of the Chief Magistrates of this Commonwealth, touching the Sabbath-day* (1679), p.5
50. [James Ockford] *The Morality of the Fourth Commandment* (1652) p.29
51. Stennett *The Insnared Taken* 113-14
52. Saller and Spittlehouse *An Appeal* 5
53. Brabourne *Discourse* 222-3
54. Cave *Primitive Christianity* 175
55. Brabourne *Answer* 56-7
56. Stennett *The Insnared Taken* 4-5
57. F. Bampfield *All in One* 109
58. *ibid*
59. *ibid* 8
60. Ockford *Fourth Commandment* 103
61. *ibid* 103-4
62. Jessey *Miscellanea Sacra* 70
63. *ibid*
64. Owen *Sacred Rest* 81-2
65. F. Bampfield *All in One* 96, 98
66. *ibid* 98-9
67. Brabourne *Answer* 72
68. F. Bampfield *All in One* 23
69. Stennett *The Insnared Taken* 148
70. T. Bampfield *Reply to Dr. Wallis* 17
71. Soursby and Smith *Discourse* 15
72. Brabourne *Answer* 62
73. Edward Elwall *The True and Sure Way* (1738) p.49
74. F. Bampfield *All in One* 75
75. *ibid*
76. *ibid* 64
77. *ibid* 101
78. Brabourne *Answer* 62
79. Brabourne *Of the Sabbath Day* 74
80. *ibid* 28
81. F. Bampfield *All in One* 14
82. Ockford *Fourth Commandment* 22, 26
83. Edward Elwall *A Declaration Against All the Kings and Temporal Powers Under Heaven* (1731) pp.62-3
84. Edward Fisher *A Christian Caveat to the Old and New Sabbatarians* (1653) p.11
85. Timothy Puller *The Moderation of the Church of England* (1679) pp.254-5
86. John Prideaux *The Doctrine of the Sabbath* (1634) sigs. cr, cv

87. Brabourne *Discourse* 61-2
88. *ibid* 225
89. *ibid* 226
90. *ibid* 224
91. John Ley *Sunday a Sabbath* (1641) pp.163-4, 166
92. Cave *Primitive Christianity* 173-4
93. Brabourne *Discourse* 61
94. White *Examination* 8
95. William Saller *An Examination of a late Book published by Dr. Owen* (1671) p.43
96. F. Bampfield *All in One* 129
97. *ibid*
98. Ockford *Fourth Commandment* 53-4
99. Elwall *A Declaration* 48-9
100. *ibid* 57

CHAPTER 9

1. R[ichard] O[verton] *Mans Mortalitie* (1644) p.1
2. [Henry Layton] *An Argument Concerning the Human Souls Separate Subsistence* [1699] p.10
3. Hobbes *Leviathan* 214
4. R[ichard] O[verton] *Man Wholly Mortal* (1655) pp.29-30
5. Layton *Argument* 15
6. Hobbes *Leviathan* 209
7. *ibid*
8. John Milton *A Treatise on Christian Doctrine*, trans. C.R. Sumner, (1825) p.189
9. Downham *Treatise of Justification* 274
10. Milton *Christian Doctrine* 189
11. *ibid* 130
12. Hobbes *Leviathan* 339, 238
13. *ibid* 238
14. *ibid* 339
15. Overton *Mans Mortalitie* 33
16. *ibid*
17. *ibid* 41-2
18. John Locke *The Reasonableness of Christianity* (1695) p.199
19. Hobbes *Leviathan* 339
20. *ibid* 340
21. Willett *Hexapla* 100
22. Overton *Mans Mortalitie* 18
23. cf. George Hammon *Truth and Innocency Prevailing against Error and Insolency* (1660) p.35
24. Overton *Mans Mortalitie* 18
25. Francis Blackburne *An Historical View of the Controversy Concerning An Intermediate State* (1772) p.liv
26. Milton *Christian Doctrine* 279
27. Overton *Mans Mortalitie* 3
28. Locke *Reasonableness of Christianity* 5
29. Milton *Christian Doctrine* 279
30. *ibid* 189
31. Hammon *Syons Redemption* 45
32. Overton *Man Wholly Mortal* 23
33. Hammon *Syons Redemption* 85-6
34. Milton *Christian Doctrine* 280-1
35. [Henry Layton] *A Search After Souls and Spiritual Operations in Man* (1692) p.21
36. Overton *Mans Mortalitie* 6-7
37. Adams *Workes* 768
38. Lushington *Hebrews* 228
39. Layton *Search After Souls* 184
40. Overton *Mans Mortalitie* 17
41. Layton *Search After Souls* 190
42. *ibid* 185
43. Milton *Christian Doctrine* 285
44. *ibid* 286
45. *ibid*
46. William Hodson *Credo Resurrectionem Carnis* (1636) pp.65-6
47. Hammon *Syons Redemption* 86
48. *ibid*
49. Layton *Search After Souls* 44ff
50. Hody *Resurrection* 137
51. Layton *Search After Souls* 16-17, Hody *Resurrection* 211
52. Hody *Resurrection* 178
53. *ibid* 138

54. *ibid* 164-5
55. *ibid* 165
56. Layton *Search After Souls* 17
57. Milton *Christian Doctrine* 279
58. Hobbes *Leviathan* 340
59. *ibid*
60. Layton *Search After Souls* 231
61. R[ichard] O[verton] *Mans Mortallitie* (1643) p.55
62. *ibid*
63. Overton *Mans Mortalitie* (1644) 43
64. F. Bampfield *All in One* 113
65. Symon Patrick *A Sermon Preached at the Funeral of Mr. Thomas Grigg* (1670) p.38
66. *The Great Evil of Health-Drinking* (1684) p.112
67. Thomas White *The State of the Future Life* (1654) pp.68-9
68. Alleine *Remains* 24-5
69. Baxter *Saints' Rest* 693
70. Alleine *Remains* 24
71. Baxter *Saints' Rest* 103
72. Adams *Workes* 329
73. Ball *Treatise of Faith* 366
74. Overton *Man Wholly Mortal* 111
75. Willett *Hexapla* 212, Mather *Figures or Types* 28
76. Perkins *Cases of Conscience* 316
77. Thomas Tryon *The Way to Health, Long-Life and Happiness: Or, A Discourse of Temperance* (1697) p.232
78. *ibid* 36
79. *ibid* 38
80. *ibid* 257
81. *ibid*
82. *ibid* 46
83. *ibid* 38
84. *ibid* 118
85. *ibid* 113
86. *ibid* 48
87. *ibid*
88. *ibid*
89. *Evil of Health Drinking* 118
90. Tryon *Way to Health* 34, 36

CHAPTER 10

1. Haller *Rise of Puritanism* 50
2. Joseph Alleine *A Sure Guide to Heaven* (1705) p.274
3. Love *Penitent Pardoned* 173-4
4. Seagar *World to Come* 77-8
5. Love *Penitent Pardoned* 175
6. Christopher Love *Heavens Glory Hells Terror* (1653) 32
7. Love *Penitent Pardoned* 176
8. Ussher *Body of Divinitie* 477
9. Robert Bolton *The Four Last Things* (1632) p.87
10. Owen *Hebrews* III 470
11. Thomas Taylor *A Commentary on . . . Titus* (1619) 480
12. Baxter *Saints' Rest* 791
13. *ibid* 776
14. Samuel Smith *The Great Assize or Day of Jubilee* (1628) 21
15. Love *Heavens Glory* 38
16. Thomas Hall *A Practical and Polemical Commentary . . . upon . . . the latter Epistle . . . to Timothy* (1658) p.7
17. *ibid*
18. Adams *Workes* 19
19. Henry Symons *The Lord Jesus His Commission* (1657) pp.35-6
20. Knollys *World to Come* 81
21. Thomas Adams *A Commentary or Exposition upon . . . Second . . . Peter* (1633) p.1130
22. Robert Maton *Israels Redemption Redeemed* (1646) p.64
23. Baxter *Saints' Rest* 254
24. John White *The Troubles of Jerusalems Restauration* (1646) p.1
25. Love *Penitent Pardoned* 115
26. Owen *Hebrews* III 471
27. Sibbes *The Brides Longing* 55-6
28. *ibid* 15
29. William Jenkyn *An Exposition of the Epistle of Jude* (1652) Pt. I p.537
30. Baxter *Saints' Rest* 92

1. Sibbes *The Brides Longing* 72
2. Durant *Salvation of the Saints* Epistle to the Reader, sig. A7r
3. *ibid* 221
4. Richard Sibbes *An Exposition of the Third Chapter of the Epistle ... to the Philippians* (1639) p.225, *Love Heavens Glory* 51
5. Haller *Rise of Puritanism* 93
6. John Milton *Complete Prose Works of John Milton* VI (1973) 614
7. Love *Heavens Glory* 4, 6
8. Thomas Brooks *The Glorious Day of the Saints Appearance* (1648) p.6
9. Sibbes *The Brides Longing* 50-1
10. Sibbes *Fountaine Sealed* 192-3
11. Richard Sibbes, 'The Churches Echo', p.107 in *Beams of Divine Light (1639)*
12. Love *Penitent Pardoned* 115
13. *ibid* 122
14. *ibid*
15. Durant *Salvation of the Saints* 48-9
16. Baxter *Saints' Rest* 47
17. This represents the usual understanding of death among Puritan theologians; but cf. the minority view examined in chapter 9
18. *ibid* 836
19. *ibid* 837-8
20. Love *Penitent Pardoned* 197
1. Durant *Salvation of the Saints* Ep.ded., sig. A4v
2. *ibid* 224-5
3. Dickson *Hebrews* 193
4. Bolton *Last Things* 129
5. Sibbes *Brides Longing* 73-4
6. Alexander Nisbet *A Brief Exposition of ... St. Peter* (1658) p.330
7. Sibbes *Brides Longing* 74
8. *ibid* 79
9. Ussher *Body of Divinitie* 451
10. Thomas Goodwin *The Works of Thomas Goodwin* V pt. 2 p.25
1. *ibid* II pt. 1 p.190
2. Durant *Salvation of the Saints* Ep.ded., sig. A5r
3. Joseph Hall *The Revelation Unrevealed* (1650) 233
4. Love *Heavens Glory* 4-5
5. Sibbes *Beams of Divine Light* 102
6. Sibbes *Brides Longing* 105-6
7. Goodwin *Works* I pt. 3 p.133
8. Thomas Brooks *Heaven on Earth* (1654) p.540
9. Love *Heavens Glory* 47
10. Homes *The Resurrection Revealed* 542
11. Sibbes *Philippians* 230
2. Taylor *Titus* 492
3. Brooks *Heaven on Earth* 606-7
4. Richard Sibbes *The Glorious Feast of the Gospel* (1650) Preface
5. *ibid*
6. Stephen Marshall *A Sermon ... The Unity of the Saints with Christ* (1653) pp.21, 37
7. William Strong *The Trust and Account of a Steward* (1647) p.29
8. Jeremiah Whitaker *The Christian's Hope Triumphing* (1645) Ep.ded.

CHAPTER 11

1. Joseph Mede, 'The Apostasy of the Latter Times', in *The Works of ... Joseph Mede, B.D.* (1672) p.654
2. T. Hall *Commentary* 5
3. [Edmund Hall] *Manus Testium Movens* (1651) Ep. to the Reader, sig. A2r
4. T. Hall *Commentary* 5
5. E. Hall *Manus Testium Movens* sig. A2r
6. Nathaniel Homes *The Resurrection — Revealed Raised Above Doubts and Difficulties* (1661) p.268
7. William Hicks *The Revelation Revealed* (1659) Preface, sig. c3r
8. Adams *Commentary* 354
9. *ibid* 335
10. Richard Bernard *A Key of Knowledge for the Opening of the Secret Mysteries of St. John's Mystical Revelation* (1617) p.93
11. Hammon *Syons Redemption* 189-90
12. Jenkyn *Jude* Pt. I p.537
13. Thomas Parker *The Visions and Prophecies of Daniel Expounded* (1646) p.128
14. Hicks *Revelation* Epistle to the Reader, sig. b1r
15. Nathaniel Stephens *A Plain and Easy Calculation of the Name, Mark, and Number of the Name of the Beast* (1656) p.13

16. E. Hall *Manus Testium Movens* sig. a2r
17. John Napier *A Plain Discovery of the Whole Revelation of St. John* (1593) p.18
18. Bernard *Key of Knowledge* 4
19. Joseph Mede, 'A Paraphrase and Exposition of the Prophecy of St. Peter', in *Works* 611
20. Stephens *Name of the Beast* 114
21. Adams *Workes* 392
22. *ibid*
23. Hicks *Revelation* sig. b1r
24. Arthur Dent *The Ruin of Rome: or An Exposition Upon the Whole Revelation* (1603) p.261
25. Edmund Calamy, Preface to the Reader, sigs. A4r, v, in Stephens *Name of the Beast*
26. Bernard *Key of Knowledge* 141
27. *ibid* 112
28. *ibid* 113
29. *ibid* 120
30. Hugh Broughton *A Revelation of the Holy Apocalypse* (1610) p.26
31. V.N. Olsen *John Foxe and the Elizabethan Church* (1973) p.25
32. Joseph Mede, 'Epistles', in *Works* 787
33. Bernard *Key of Knowledge* 130-1
34. Napier *Revelation* 2
35. Thomas Brightman *A Revelation of the Revelation* (1615) p.429
36. James Durham *A Commentary Upon the Book of Revelation* (1658) pp.542-547, John Cotton *An Exposition Up the Thirteenth Chapter of the Revelation* (1655) p.8
37. Joseph Mede *The Key of the Revelation* (1643) pt. 2 p.52
38. Pareus *Commentary* 337, John Cotton *The Pouring Out of the Seven Vials* (1642) p.3, William Strong *A Treat Shewing the Subordination of the Will of Man unto the Will of God* (1657) p.111
39. Pareus *Commentary* 338, 343, 351
40. Mede *Works* 654, 787
41. Bernard *Key of Knowledge* 4
42. Brightman *Revelation* 3-4
43. Hicks *Revelation* 7-8
44. Brightman *Revelation* 5
45. Durham *Commentary* 496
46. Jeremiah Burroughes *Jerusalem's Glory Breaking Forth into the World* (1675) p.87
47. Mede *Works* 654
48. Parker *Daniel* 21
49. Thomas Goodwin, 'An Exposition Upon the Revelation', in *The Works of Thomas Goodwin D.D.* II (168 pp.22-24
50. Hicks *Revelation* Preface, sig. c1v
51. *ibid*
52. Owen *Hebrews* I 186-193
53. Edward Haughton *The Rise, Growth and Fall of Antichrist* (1652) p.3
54. Pareus *Commentary*, p. 318
55. *ibid.*, pp. 277, 289
56. Durham, *Commentary*, pp. 443, 444
57. Pareus, *Commentary*, p. 288
58. Haughton, *Antichrist*, p. 13
59. *ibid.*, pp. 13-16
60. Mede, *Works*, pp. 643, 647
61. Denne, *Man of Sin*, pp. 29, 30
62. Goodwin, *Works*, II, p. 151

CHAPTER 12

1. H. Quistorp *Calvin's Doctrine of the Last Things* (1955) p.15
2. Pareus, *Commentary* 506
3. Mede, *Revelation* Pt. II, 121
4. The Forty-two Articles (1553) condemned 'heretics called millenarii', although it is unclear whether the reference to English or continental advocates of the millennium
5. e.g. Napier, *Revelation* 54
6. Pareus *Commentary* 508
7. e.g. Napier, *Revelation* 54
8. Homes *Resurrection Revealed* 456
9. *ibid* 434
10. Mede *Works* 603-4
11. Mede *Revelation* pt. 2 pp.122-3, *Works* 603-4
12. W. Burton, in J.H. Alsted *The Beloved City* (1643) Preface, p.iv
13. Hammon *Syons Redemption* 174-5
14. Mede *Revelation* pt. 2 p.123
15. Alsted *Beloved City* 20

26. Mede *Works* 603
27. Seagar *World to Come* p.31
28. Thomas Hall *Chiliasto-mastix redivivus: A Confutation of the Millenarian Opinion* (1657) Ep. to the Reader
29. *ibid* 98
30. *ibid* 13-14
31. Homes *Resurrection Revealed* 174-6
32. *ibid* 515, 532
33. *ibid* 510
34. Hobbes *Leviathan* 340
35. *ibid*
36. Samuel Richardson *Of the Torments of Hell* (1658) p.74
37. Thomas Hobbes *An Answer to a Book Published by Dr. Bramhall* (1682) p.93
38. Richardson *Torments* 140
39. D.P. Walker *The Decline of Hell* (1964) *passim*
40. Hobbes *Leviathan* 245
41. John Biddle *A Two-Fold Catechism* (1654) pp.135-138
42. Hobbes *Answer* 90
43. Hammon *Syons Redemption* 85
44. H. Broughton *An Explication of the Article . . . of our Lord's Soul Going from His Body to Paradise* (1605) sig. a4r
45. *ibid* 35. *ibid*
46. Richardson *Torments* 6
47. Broughton *Explication* 10-11
48. *ibid* sig. A4r
49. *ibid*
50. Richardson *Torments* 22
51. Hobbes *Leviathan* 242
52. *ibid* 243
53. Richardson *Torments* 12
54. *ibid* 15
55. Hobbes *Leviathan* 243
56. Hobbes *Answer* 91
57. Homes *Resurrection Revealed* 532, 542
58. Dent *Ruin of Rome* 296
59. *ibid* 283
60. Thomas Burnet *The Theory of the Earth* III (1690) 143
61. Napier *Revelation* 250
62. Hody *Resurrection* 206
63. Adams *Commentary* 1359
64. Dent *Ruin of Rome* 285
65. *ibid* 287
66. Pareus *Commentary* 550
67. Dent *Ruin of Rome* 284
68. Adams *Commentary* 1358-9
69. Durham *Commentary* 755
70. *ibid*
71. Nathaniel Homes *Miscellanea* (1666) p.35
72. The Bible speaks of a three-fold heaven: of the heaven of heavens where God dwells, of the ethereal heavens where the stars appear, and of the atmospheric heavens where birds fly and the winds blow. It was in the last sense that it spoke of 'a new heaven and a new earth', Mede *Works* 614-5
73. Dent *Ruin of Rome* 293
74. Flavel *Works* II 29
75. *ibid* I 183
76. *ibid*
77. *ibid* 67. *ibid*
78. Seagar *World to Come* 110-11
79. Adams *Commentary* 1377
80. *ibid* 1380
81. Durham *Commentary* 760
82. *ibid*
83. Burnet *Theory of the Earth* IV 144
84. Adams *Commentary* 1377
85. Dent *Ruin of Rome* 300

BIBLIOGRAPHY

BIBLIOGRAPHY

A short title, if used in the footnotes and if different from the first word(s) of the given title, is shown in parentheses at the end of an entry. The original date of publication, if known and if earlier than the edition cited, is also shown in parentheses. The place of publication, if not otherwise given, is London.

PRIMARY SOURCES

Adams, Thomas *A Commentary or Exposition upon the Divine Second Epistle General, written by the Blessed Apostle St. Peter* 1633
> *The Happiness of the Church, or a Description of those Spiritual Prerogatives wherewith Christ hath endowed her* 1619
> *The Workes of Tho. Adams, Being the Sum of his Sermons, Meditations and Moral Discourses* 1619
Alleine, Joseph *An Alarm to Unconverted Sinners* 1673 (1672)
> *Remains of that Excellent Minister of Jesus Christ, Mr Joseph Alleine* 1674
> *A Sure Guide to Heaven* 1705
Alsted, Johann *The Beloved City* (tr W. Burton) 1643
Babington, Gervase *Comfortable Notes upon the Book of Leviticus* 1604 (Leviticus)
Ball, John *A Short Treatise Containing all the Principal Grounds of the Christian Religion*, 1654 (1629)
> *A Treatise of Faith, divided into two Parts. The First Showing the Nature, the Second the Life of Faith* 1632 (1630)
Bampfield, Francis *All in One. All Useful Sciences and Profitable Arts in One Book of Jehovah Elohim . . Comprehended and Discovered in the Fulness and Perfection of Scripture-Knowledge* 1677
> *A Name, an After-One; or . . . A Name, a New One* 1681
Bampfield, Thomas *An Enquiry whether the Lord Jesus Christ made the World, and be Jehovah, and gave the Moral Law, and whether the Fourth Command be Repealed or Altered* 1692
> *A Reply to Doctor Wallis, his Discourse Concerning the Christian Sabbath* 1693
Baxter, Richard *Aphorismes of Justification, with their Explication Annexed* 1649
> *A Call to the Unconverted to Turn and Live* 1660
> *Confession of His Faith, especially Concerning the Interest of Repentance and Sincere Obedience to Christ, in our Justification and Salvation* 1655
> *More Reasons for the Christian Religion, and no Reason Against it* 1672
> *The Reasons of the Christian Religion* 1667
> *The Saints Everlasting Rest: Or a Treatise of the Blessed State of the Saints in their Enjoyment of God in Glory* 1669 (1649)
> *A Treatise of Justifying Righteousness* 1676 (Justifying Righteousness)
Bernard, Richard *A Key of Knowledge for the Opening of the Secret Mysteries of St. John's Mystical Revelation* 1617
> *A Threefold Treatise of the Sabbath* 1641 (Treatise of the Sabbath)
Biddle, John *A Twofold Catechism* 1654
Blackburne, Francis *An Historical View of the Controversy Concerning an Intermediate State and the Separate Existence of the Soul Between Death and the General Resurrection* 1772
Blackwood, Christopher *The Storming of Antichrist* 1644
Bolton, Robert *The Four Last Things* 1632
Brabourne, Theophilus *An Answer to M. Cawdrey's Two Books of the Sabbath* Norwich, 1654
> *A Discourse upon the Sabbath Day* 1628
> *Of the Sabbath Day, which is now The Highest Controversy in the Church of England* 1660
> *Three Treatises in Defence of the Seventh-Day Sabbath* 1660
Brightman, Thomas *A Revelation of the Revelation* 1615 (1611)
Brooks, Thomas *The Glorious Day of the Saints Appearance* 1648
> *Heaven on Earth* 1654
Broughton, Hugh *An Explication of the Article . . . of Our Lord's Soul Going from His Body to Paradise* 1605
Bunyan, John *Grace Abounding to the Chief of Sinners* 1697 (1666)
> *The Work of Jesus Christ as an Advocate Clearly Explained* 1688
Burgess, Anthony *Vindiciae Legis* 1646
Burnet, Thomas *The Theory of the Earth* 1690
Burroughes, Jeremiah *Jerusalem's Glory Breaking Forth into the World* 1675
Byfield, Nicholas *An Exposition Upon the Epistle to the Colossians* 1615
Byfield, Richard *The Doctrine of the Sabbath Vindicated* 1631
Cave, William *Primitive Christianity: or, The Religion of the Ancient Christians in the First Ages of the Gospel* 1673
Collins, Hercules *Believers Baptism from Heaven, and of Divine Institution* 1691
The Confession of Faith of those Churches which are commonly (though falsely) called Anabaptists 1644
Cotton, John *An Exposition Upon the Thirteenth Chapter of the Revelation* 1655
> *The Pouring Out of the Seven Vials: or an Exposition of the Sixteenth Chapter of the Revelation* 1642

Danvers, Henry *A Treatise of Baptism: Wherein that of Believers, and that of Infants, is Examined by the Scriptures* 1674

Davis, Joseph *The Last Legacy of Mr. Joseph Davis* 1720

Denne, Henry *Antichrist Unmasked in Two Treatises* 1645
    The Man of Sin Discovered 1645

Dent, Arthur *The Ruin of Rome, or an Exposition upon the Whole Revelation* 1603

Dering, Edward *M. Derings Workes* 1614

Dickson, David *A Short Explanation of the Epistle of Paul to the Hebrews* Cambridge, 1649 (1635) *(Hebrews)*

Dod, John (and Cleaver, Robert) *A Plain and Familiar Exposition of the Ten Commandments* 1604

Downame, John *A Guide to Godliness* 1622

Downham, George *A Treatise of Justification* 1633

Durant, John *The Salvation of the Saints by the Appearances of Christ, 1. Now in Heaven, 2. Hereafter from Heaven* 1653

Durham, James *A Commentary Upon the Book of Revelation* 1658

Elwall, Edward *A Declarartion Against All the Kings and Temporal Powers Under Heaven* 1731
    The True and Sure Way to Remove Hirelings out of the Church 1738

Featley, Daniel *The Dippers Dipt* 1647

Fisher, Edward *A Christian Caveat to the Old and New Sabbatarians* 1650

Flavel, John *The Whole Workes of the Reverend Mr. John Flavel* 2 vols, 1716

Gataker, Thomas *Certain Sermons, First Preached, and After Published at several times* 1637

Goodwin, John *The Divine Authority of the Scriptures Asserted* 1648
    Imputatio Fidei, or a Treatise of Justification 1642 *(Treatise of Justification)*

Goodwin, Thomas *The Works of Thomas Goodwin, D.D.* 5 vols, 1681-1704

Grantham, Thomas *Truth and Peace, or, The Last and most Friendly Debate Concerning Infant Baptism* 1689

The Great Evil of Health Drinking: Or A Discourse wherein the Original, Evil, and Mischief of Drinking of Healths are discovered and detected 1684

[Hall, Edmund] *Manus Testium Movens* 1651

[Hall, Joseph] *The Revelation Unrevealed* 1650

Hall, Thomas *Chiliasto-Mastix Redivivus: A Confutation of the Millenarian Opinion* 1657
    A Practical and Polemical Commentary or Exposition Upon the Third and Fourth Chapters of the latter Epistle of St Paul to Timothy 1658 *(Commentary)*

Hammon, George *Syons Redemption and Original Sin Vindicated* 1658
    Truth and Innocency Prevailing Against Error and Insolency 1660

Haughton, Edward *The Rise, Growth and Fall of Antichrist: Together with the Reign of Christ* 1652 *(Antichrist)*

Helwys, Thomas *A Short Declaration of the Mystery of Iniquity* 1612 *(Mystery of Iniquity)*

Hicks, William *The Revelation Revealed: Being a Practical Exposition on the Revelation of St. John* 1659

Hobbes, Thomas *An Answer to a Book Published by Dr. Bramhall, late Bishop of Derry* 1682
    Leviathan, or the Matter, Form, and Power of a Commonwealth Ecclesiastical and Civil 1651

Hodson, William *Credo Resurrectionem Carnis* 1636

Hody, Humphrey *The Resurrection of the (same) Body Asserted* 1694

Homes, Nathaniel *Miscellanea* 1666
    The Resurrection-Revealed, or the Dawning of the Day-Star about to rise 1653
    The Resurrection-Revealed Raised Above Doubts and Difficulties 1661

Hutcheson, George *An Exposition of the Gospel of Jesus Christ according to John* 1657

Jenkyn, William *An Exposition of the Epistle of Jude* 1652 *(Jude)*

Jessey, Henry *Miscellanea Sacra, or Divine Necessary Truths* 1665

King, Daniel *A Way to Sion Sought Out, and Found, For Believers to Walk in* 1650

Knollys, Hanserd *Christ Exalted* 1645
    The World That Now Is; and The World that is to Come, or The First and Second Coming of Jesus Christ 1681

Lawson, George *An Exposition of the Epistle to the Hebrews* 1662 *(Hebrews)*
    Theo-Politica, or, A Body of Divinity 1659

Layton, Henry *An Argument Concerning the Human Soul's Separate Subsistence* 1699
    A Search After Souls and Spiritual Operations in Man 1692

Leigh, Edward *Critica Sacra: or Philological and Theological Observations upon all the Greek words of the Old Testament* 1641
    Critica Sacra: Observations on all the Radices or Primitive Hebrew words of the Old Testament 1641

Ley, John *Sunday a Sabbath* 1641

Locke, John *The Reasonableness of Christianity as Delivered in the Scriptures* 1695

Love, Christopher *Englands Distemper, having Division and Error as its Causes; Wanting Peace and Truth as its Cure* 1645
    Heaven's Glory, Hell's Terror 1653
    The Penitent Pardoned ... Together with a Discourse of Christs Ascension into Heaven, and of His Coming again from Heaven 1657

[Lushington, Thomas] *The Expiation of a Sinner, In a Commentary upon the Epistle to the Hebrews* 1646 *(Hebrews)*

Manton, Thomas *Christs Eternal Existence, and the Dignity of His Person* 1685
    A Practical Commentary ... on the Epistle of James 1651

Marshall, Stephen *A Sermon ... wherein the Unity of the Saints with Christ, the Head, and especially with the Church, the Body; With the duties thence arising ...* 1653

Mather, Samuel *The Figures or Types of the Old Testament, By which Christ and the Heavenly Things of the Gospel* were *Preached and Shadowed to the People of God of Old* 1705

Maton, Robert *Israels Redemption Redeemed* 1646

Mede, Joseph *The Key of the Revelation* 1650 (*Revelation*)

    The Works of . . . Joseph Mede B.D. 1672

Milton, John *A Treatise on Christian Doctrine, Compiled from the Holy Scriptures Alone* Cambridge, 1825

Napier, John *A Plain Discovery of the Whole Revelation of St. John* 1593 (*Revelation*)

Nisbet, Alexander *A Brief Exposition of . . . St. Peter* 1658

[Ockford, James] *The Morality of the Fourth Commandment* 1652

O[verton], R[ichard] *Mans Mortality, or a Treatise wherein 'tis proved both Theologically and Phylosophically, that whole Man (as a rational creature) is a Compound wholly Mortal, contrary to that common distinction of Soul and Body: and that the present going of the Soul into Heaven or Hell is a mere Fiction: And that the Resurrection is the Beginning of our immortality, and then actual Condemnation and Salvation, and not before* Amsterdam, 1644 (1643)

    Man Wholly Mortal, or a Treatise wherein Tis Proved, both Theologically and Philosophically, that as Whole Man sinned, so whole man died 1655

Owen, John *The Causes, Ways, and Means of Understanding the Mind of God as Revealed in His Word* 1678

    Of the Divine Original, Authority, self-evidencing Light, and Power of the Scriptures Oxford 1659

    Exercitations Concerning the Name, Original, Nature, Use and Continuance of a Day of Sacred Rest 1671 (*Sacred Rest*)

    Exercitations on the Epistle to the Hebrews . . . An Exposition of the Two First Chapters of the Epistle . . . 1668 (*Hebrews I*)

    A Continuation of the Exposition of the Epistle of Paul the Apostle to the Hebrews . . . 1680, (*Hebrews III*)

Pagitt, Ephraim *Heresiography, or A Description of the Heretics and Sectaries of these Latter Times* 1661

Pareus, David *A Commentary Upon the Divine Revelation of the Apostle and Evangelist John,* trans. E. Arnold, 1645

Parker, Thomas *The Visions and Prophecies of Daniel Expounded* 1646 (*Daniel*)

Patrick, Symon *A Sermon Preached at the Funeral of Mr. Thomas Grigg, B.D.* 1670

Penry, John *A Treatise wherein is manifestly proved that Reformation and those that sincerely favour the same, are unjustly charged to be enemies unto her majesty and the state* n.p. 1590 (*Treatise [of] Reformation*)

Perkins, William *The Whole Treatise of the Cases of Conscience* 1651 (*Cases of Conscience*)

    The Workes of that Famous and Worthy Minister of Christ in the University of Cambridge, Mr. William Perkins, 3 vols., Cambridge 1626-1631

Prideaux, John *The Doctrine of the Sabbath* 1634

Puller, Timothy *The Moderation of the Church of England* 1679

Richardson, Samuel *Of the Torments of Hell . . . With many infallible proofs that there is not to be punishment after this life for any to endure that shall never end . . .* 1658

Roberts, Francis *Of God's Covenants . . . The Mystery and Marrow of the Bible* 1657

Robinson, John *Of Religious Communion, Private and Public* n.p. 1641

Saller, William *An Examination of a late book published by Doctor Owen, concerning a Sacred Day of Rest* 1671

    and Spittlehouse, John *An Appeal to the Consciences of the Chief Magistrates of this Commonwealth, touching the Sabbath Day* n.p. 1679

Seagar, John *A Discovery of the World to Come According to the Scriptures* 1650

Sibbes, Richard *Beams of Divine Light, Breaking Forth from several places of holy Scripture* 1639

    The Brides Longing for her Bridegroomes second Coming 1638

    Christs Exaltation Purchast by Humiliation 1639

    A Fountain Sealed: or, the Duty of the Sealed to the Spirit, and the Work of the Spirit in Sealing 1637

    The Glorious Feast of the Gospel 1650

Smith, Samuel *The Great Assize, or Day of Jubilee* 1628

Smyth, John *The Character of the Beast; Or the False Constitution of the Church* n.p., 1609

    The Works of John Smyth (ed. W.T. Whitley) 2 vols, Cambridge, 1915

Soursby, Henry and Smith, Mehetabel *A Discourse of the Sabbath; or The Controversies about the Sabbath stated and Examined, with reference unto the Law of Nature, the Law of Moses and the Law of Christ* 1683

Stennett, Edward *The Insnared Taken in the Work of his Hands* 1677

    The Seventh Day is the Sabbath of the Lord n.p., 1664

Stennett, Joseph *The Works of the late Reverend and learned Mr. Joseph Stennett* 4 vols, 1732

Stephens, Nathaniel *A Plain and Easy Calculation of the Name, Mark, and Number of the Name of the Beast* 1656

Strong, William *A Discourse of the Two Covenants* 1678

    A Treatise Shewing the Subordination of the Will of Man unto the Will of God 1657

    The Trust and Account of a Steward 1647

Symons, Henry *The Lord Jesus His Commission . . . to be the alone Judge of Life and Death, in the Great and General Assize of the World* 1657

Taylor, Thomas *Christ Revealed: Or The Old Testament Explained. A Treatise of the Types and Shadows of Our Saviour contained throughout the whole Scripture* 1635

    A Commentary on the Epistle of Saint Paul written to Titus Cambridge, 1619

    Regulae Vitae: The Rule of the Law Under the Gospel 1635

Tombes, John *Two Treatises . . . concerning Infant Baptism* 1645

Truman, Joseph *The Great Propitiation: or, Christs Satisfaction, and Mans Justification by it upon His Faith* 1669

Tryon, Thomas *The Way to Health, Long Life and Happiness: or, A Discourse of Temperance, and the Particular Nature of all things Requisite for the Life of Man* 1697

Ussher, James *A Body of Divinity, or The Sum and Substance of Christian Religion* 1647

BLIOGRAPHY

nning, Ralph *Sin, the Plague of Plagues, or Sinful Sin the Worst of Evils* 1669

itaker, Jeremiah *The Christians Hope Triumphing* 1645

ite, Francis *An Examination and Confutation of a Lawless Pamphlet intituled, A Brief Answer to a late Treatise of the Sabbath-Day* 1637

ite, John *The Troubles of Jerusalems Restauration, or The Churches Reformation* 1646
   A Way to the Tree of Life 1647

ite, Thomas *The State of the Future Life* 1657

lett, Andrew *Hexapla in Leviticum* 1631

ight, Abraham *A Practical Commentary or Exposition upon the Pentateuch* 1662, *(Pentateuch)*

HER WORKS

bott, W.C. *The Writings and Speeches of Oliver Cromwell*, 4 vols., Harvard University Press, Cambridge Mass., 1937-47

ll, B.W. *A Great Expectation: Eschatological Thought in English Protestantism to 1660*, E.J. Brill, Leiden, 1975

ach, W.R. *Dimensions in Salvation*, Review & Herald Publishing Association, Washington D.C., 1963

rns, N.T. *Christian Mortalism from Tyndale to Milton*, Harvard University Press, Cambridge Mass., 1972

wards, D. *Religion and Change*, Hodder & Stoughton, London, 1969

oom, L.E. *The Prophetic Faith of Our Fathers*, 4 vols., Review & Herald Publishing Association, Washington D.C., 1950-1954

orge, C.H. & K. *The Protestant Mind of the English Reformation, 1570-1640*, Princeton University Press, Princeton, N.J. 1961

ller, W. *The Rise of Puritanism, Or, The Way to the New Jerusalem as set forth in pulpit and press from Thomas Cartwright to John Milton, 1570-1643*, Harper & Brothers, New York, 1957

rdinge, L. *The Celtic Church in Britain*, S.P.C.K., London, 1972

ppenstall, E. *Our High Priest*, Review & Herald Publishing Association, Washington D.C., 1972

ekema, A. *The Four Major Cults*, The Paternoster Press, Exeter, 1963

mison, T.H. *Christian Beliefs*, Pacific Press Publishing Association, Mountain View Calif., 1959

van, E.F. *The Grace of Law: A Study in Puritan Theology*, The Carey Kingsgate Press, London, 1964
   Keep His Commandments, The Tyndale Press, London, 1964

wis, P. *The Genius of Puritanism*, Carey Publications, Haywards Heath, 1975

lton, J. *The Complete Prose Works of John Milton*, 6 vols., Yale University Press, New Haven & London, 1953-1973

tchell, D. *Seventh-day Adventists. Faith in Action*, Vantage Press, New York, 1958

ttall, G.F. *The Holy Spirit in Puritan Faith and Experience*, Blackwell, Oxford, 1946

dom, R.L. *Sabbath and Sunday in Early Christianity*, Review & Herald Publishing Association, Washington D.C., 1977

sen, V.N. *John Foxe and the Elizabethan Church*, University of California Press, Berkeley, Los Angeles & London, 1973

wicke, M. *The Reformation in England*, Oxford University Press, London, 1961

ice, G.M. *The Greatest of the Prophets*, Pacific Press Publishing Association, Mountain View Calif., 1955

uistorp, H. *Calvin's Doctrine of the Last Things*, Lutterworth Press, London, 1955

venth-day Adventists Answer Questions on Doctrine, Review & Herald Publishing Association, Washington D.C., 1957

venth-day Adventist Bible Commentary, 7 vols., Review & Herald Publishing Association, Washington D.C., 1953-1957

venth-day Adventist Bible Dictionary, Review & Herald Publishing Association, Washington D.C., 1960

rong, A.H. *The Great Poets and Their Theology*, Griffin & Rowland, Philadelphia, 1899

alker, D.P. *The Decline of Hell*, University of Chicago Press, Chicago, 1964

alker, W. *A History of the Christian Church*, T. & T. Clark, Edinburgh, 1959

arnes, J. *Baptism: Studies in the Original Christian Baptism*, Paternoster Press, London, 1957

hite, E.G. *The Desire of Ages*, Pacific Press Publishing Association, Mountain View Calif., 1898
   The Great Controversy Between Christ and Satan, Pacific Press Publishing Association, Mountain View Calif., 1911

hiting, C.E. *Studies in English Puritanism From the Restoration to the Revolution, 1660-1688*, Frank Cass, London, 1931

hitley, W.T. *A History of British Baptists*, Charles Griffin, London, 1923

rcher, J.R. *The Nature and Destiny of Man*, Philosophical Library, New York, 1969

INDEX OF BIBLICAL REFERENCES

Genesis
i: 1, 20 — 41, 163
ii: 1-3, 7 — 144, 160
iii: 15 — 37
viii: 21 — 163
ix: 3, 4, 22 — 125, 175
xii: 5 — 163
xxi: 9 — 126
xxxvii: 31 — 95
il: 10 — 37

Exodus
xx: 8-11 — 141, 144
xxi: 24 — 126
xxv: 40 — 110

Leviticus
iv: 1, 14-15 — 112, 163
vi: 2 — 163
vii: 19 — 163
xix: 32 — 126

Numbers
xiv: 34 — 202
xv: 39 — 163
xxx — 126

Deuteronomy
viii: 11 — 135
xii: 23 — 163
xviii: 15 — 37
xxii: 26 — 126
xxvi: 17 — 135
xxxiii: 24 — 95

Job
vii: 9 — 221
x: 10-12 — 162
xiv: 13, 14 — 201
xvii: 13-16 — 201
xxvii: 3 — 161

Psalms
vi: 5 — 165
xvi: 10 — 163
xxii-xxiv — 38
xxxix: 13 — 165
xl: 6-8 — 127
xlv: 13, 14 — 66
lxxii:1-7 — 53
lxxxv: 9-11 — 53
civ: 29, 30 — 165
cx — 38
cx: 3, 44 — 37
cxv: 17 — 166
cxlvi: 2 — 166

Proverbs
ix: 16 — 163
xii: 18 — 126
xxii: 28 — 126
xxvii: 4 — 163

Isaiah
vii: 14 — 37
ix: 6 — 37
xxxv: 4, 5 — 37
xl: 3 — 42
xlv: 18 — 213, 224
xlv: 23 — 42
liii — 38
liii: 5, 17 — 37, 163
lx: 15-21 — 53, 228
lxi:1, 2 — 37
lxv: 17 — 224
lxvi: 22 — 224

Jeremiah
vi: 2 — 202
xiii: 17, 3 — 72, 163
xiv: 17 — 163
xxiii: 6 — 66
xxxi: 33 — 134
xlviii: 10 — 126

Ezekiel
i: 20 — 161
ii: 2 — 161

Ezekiel
iv: 6 — 202
xviii: 7 — 126
xxxvi: 25, 26 — 72

Daniel
i: 8-16 — 176
ii — 201
ii: 31-45 — 206, 207
vii — 201-202, 206, 209
ix — 38, 202
ix: 24, 26 — 37
xii: 4 — 30

Matthew
iii: 2, 3, 12 — 42, 178, 221
v: 5, 17-23 — 126, 128, 147, 224
x: 28 — 222
xii: 1-13, 39-40 — 37, 147
xxii: — 222
xxii: 11, 36-40 — 126, 128
xxiv — 148
xxiv: 30 — 179
xxv: 31 — 179
xxvi: 34 — 179
xxviii: 19, 20 — 89

Mark
i: 9-10, 14-15 — 94, 178
ii: 23-28 — 146-147
ix: 47, 48 — 222
xvi: 16 — 89

Luke
iv: 16 — 147
vi: 1-12 — 147
xv: 22 — 63
xvi: 19, 23 — 126, 222
xxi: 37 — 179
xxiii: 43 — 169

John
i: 1-3 — 41, 146
i: 12 — 62
i: 14 — 41
i: 25, 26 — 95
iii: 6, 16, 23 — 39, 83, 94, 162
iv: 14 — 72
xii: 37-41 — 42
xiv: 2-3, 29 — 178, 179, 183, 195
xvi: 7 — 105

Acts
i: 11 — 179
ii: 41 — 163
iii: 21 — 224
iv: 19 — 125
vii: 14 — 163
viii — 94
viii: 36-39 — 83, 89
xiii: 14, 42, 44 — 148-149
xv — 149
xvi: 11-13 — 148
xvii: 2, 3 — 148
xviii: 4, 8 — 88, 149
xx: 10 — 163

Romans
i: 29-30 — 125, 126
iii: 19-27, 31 — 55, 61, 129, 132
iv: 5 — 60
v: 1, 10, 12-20 — 46, 49, 50-57, 131
vi — 83
vi: 3, 4, 7 — 79, 90, 93
vii: 8, 9, 12-14 — 123, 131, 141
viii: 24 — 195
xi: 10 — 126
xiii: 1 — 163
xiv: 9-11 — 42
xv: 13 — 195

I Corinthians
i: 30 — 55
vi: 19 — 173
x: 19, 31 — 38, 175

I Corinthians
xi: 28 —
xv —
xv: 19, 22, 55 — 50, 213

II Corinthians
ii: 15, 16 —
v: 17, 19-21 — 55, 6?

Galatians
iii: 24 — 130
iv: 29 —
v: 17, 20 — 77,

Ephesians
i: 5, 18 — 6?
iii: 9 —
iv: 31 —
vi: 9 —

Philippians
ii: 7, 10-11 — 4?
iii: 21 —

Colossians
1: 5, 15-17 — 39, 41, 146,
ii: —
ii: 3, 9 —
iii: 1, 4, 22 — 103, 125, 180,

I Thessalonians
iv: 13-17 — 168, 178-179, 188,

II Thessalonians
i: 7-9 —
ii: 4, 7 — 87,

I Timothy
ii: 5 —
ii: 2, 42 — 125?
iv: 1 —

II Timothy
iii: 1-2, 1-17 — 15, 125?
iv: 3, 4 —

Titus
ii: 13 — 178,
iii: 7 —

Hebrews
i: 2-3, 8-10 — 41, 103, 146,
iii: 4 —
iv: 10, 14-16 — 41,
vi: 18 —
vii: 3, 2-25 — 35, 44, 107,
viii: 1-2, 4 — 103,
ix: 2-12, 19, 21, 28 — 95, 114,
x: 16, 22, 26-27, 38 — 90, 134, 163,
xii: 2 —

James
ii: 10, 12 — 121,
iii: 14 —
iv: 1 —
v: 4, 7-9 — 126,

I Peter
i: 3, 20 — 182,
iii: 2, 22 — 103,

II Peter
i: 19-21 —
ii: 12 —
iii: 3, 10, 13 — 182, 224-225,

I John
iii: 2, 3, 1 — 126, 195,

Revelation
i: 1, 7 — 118,
iii: 18 —
ix —
xii —
xii: 9 —
xiii —
xiii: 1-3 —
xiv —
xvii —
xx — 203,
xx-xxii — 197, 214, 216, 218,
xxii: 4 — 205,

INDEX OF NAMES

Adams, Thomas 16, 23, 26, 38, 46, 55, 68, 71, 74, 76, 123, 124, 166, 174, 179, 181, 182, 195, 199, 224, 225, 227, 228
Alcasar, Luis de 205
Alexander, Archibald 31
Alleine, Joseph 1, 12, 24, 37, 43, 48, 62, 67-72, 74, 76, 77, 81, 174, 179
Alsted, Johannes 181, 216, 217
Anselm 32
Athanasius 149
Augustine 97, 181, 214
Babington, Gervase 111, 112
Bailey, Nathaniel 140
Bale, John 197
Ball, John 15, 20, 24, 59, 61, 76, 78, 88, 123, 124, 132, 135, 174, 175
Bampfield, Francis 28, 41, 42, 76, 124, 127, 139, 141, 143, 145-147, 150-153, 157, 173
Bampfield, Thomas 139, 147, 148, 152
Bancroft, Archbishop Richard 9
Barbones, Praise-God 8
Baxter, Richard 1, 12, 16-23, 40, 43, 45, 46, 48, 52-54, 59, 61, 63, 64, 69, 73, 83, 120, 127-130, 134, 136, 138, 174, 180, 182-184, 187
Bellarmine, Archbishop Roberto 35, 49, 205
Bernard, Richard 141, 195, 198, 200-202, 204, 214, 215
Biddle, John 221
Blackwood, Christopher 88-90, 92, 94, 95, 98, 100
Bolton, Robert 180
Brabourne, Theophilus 123, 131, 139-146, 148, 149, 151-153, 155, 156
Bramhall, Archbishop John 220
Brightman, Thomas 193, 194, 196, 198, 199, 202, 204, 205, 214, 215
Brooks, Thomas 185, 190, 191
Broughton, Hugh 201, 221, 222
Bullinger, Henry 193, 196, 197, 199, 209
Bunyan, John 12, 31, 32, 34, 43, 47, 55, 56, 74, 76, 83, 105, 107, 115, 132, 138
Burnet, Thomas 218, 221, 224, 225, 228
Burns, N. T. 165
Burroughes, Jeremiah 206
Burton, William 216
Byfield, Nicholas 39
Calamy, Edmund 191, 200
Calvin, John 6
Cartwright, Thomas 5, 6
Cave, William 95, 96, 149, 156
Charles I 7-9, 138, 142, 199
Clarendon, Earl of 12
Chamberlen, Peter 140
Cleaver, Richard 123
Collins, Hercules 88-91, 93-95, 97
Cotton, John 14
Constantine, Emperor 29, 156, 210, 215, 216
Cromwell, Oliver 7, 8, 11, 85, 199
Cyprian 96, 97, 181
Danvers, Henry 30, 89, 91, 92, 94, 95, 97-100
Davis, Joseph 140, 142, 147
Denne, Henry 17, 98, 118, 211, 212
Dent, Arthur 198, 200, 214, 215, 223-226, 228
Descartes, Rene 170
Dering, Edward 84
Dickens, A. G. 6
Dickson, David 40, 106, 117, 118, 188
Dod, John 123
Downame, John 34, 122
Downham, George 47, 50, 51, 53, 54, 56-65, 76, 121, 124, 129-132, 136, 161
Durant, John 44, 104, 105, 115, 116, 184, 186-189
Durham, James 202, 205, 210, 225, 227
Edwards, David 3
Edwards, Jonathan 31
Elwall, Edward 152, 157, 158
Fisher, Edward 155
Flavel, John 1, 12, 21-26, 29-35, 37, 42-48, 51, 57-60, 66, 67, 69-81, 83, 90, 104, 105, 107, 109, 111, 112, 116, 117, 130-132, 226, 227
Foxe, John 9, 87, 197, 201
Froom, L. E. 204
Gataker, Thomas 50, 53, 64, 66, 68, 72, 75, 79, 174, 207
Goodwin, John 18, 20, 21, 22, 28-30, 32, 34, 60, 62, 128
Goodwin, Thomas 189-191, 212
Grantham, Thomas 86, 90, 92, 97, 98, 215

Hall, Edmund 194, 198
Hall, Joseph 189
Hall, Thomas 159, 181, 194, 218
Haller, William 5, 7, 69, 72, 178, 185
Hammon, George 89, 90, 94, 165, 169, 196, 216, 217, 221
Hardinge, Leslie 2
Haughton, Edward 210, 211
Helwys, Thomas 87, 98
Henry VIII 6
Henry, Matthew 31, 66
Heylin, Peter 138
Hicks, William 195, 196, 199, 204, 208
Hobbes, Thomas 14, 108, 160-164, 172, 219-223
Hodson, William 168
Hody, Humphrey 27, 170, 171, 224
Homes, Nathaniel 215, 216, 218, 219, 223-225
Hutcheson, George 39
Ings, William 1
James I 7, 9, 176, 197
Jenkyn, William 184, 198
Jerome 97
Jessey, Henry 93, 151
Johnson, Samuel 140
Jonson, Ben 4
Kevan, E. F. 13, 121, 132
King, Daniel 129
Knollys, Hanserd 86, 95, 181
Laud, Archbishop William 7, 9-11
Lawson, George 18, 25, 41, 60, 64, 65, 79, 81, 85, 93, 103, 105, 109, 114, 117, 121, 123, 128
Layton, Henry 160, 161, 164, 166, 167, 169-172
Leigh, Edward 95
Ley, John 156
Locke, John 163, 164
Loughborough, John 1
Love, Christopher 38, 103, 105, 107, 109, 114, 127, 179, 180, 183-190
Lushington, Thomas 110, 114, 166
Luther, Martin 56, 65, 155, 203
Manton, Thomas 39, 129
Marcion 220
Marshall, Stephen 191
Mather, Samuel 65, 66, 104, 108, 114, 116, 175
Mede, Joseph 193, 194, 197-199, 201, 204, 206, 207, 211, 214, 216-219
Milton, John 160, 161, 164, 165, 166, 168, 171, 185, 227
Napier, John 181, 194, 197-200, 202, 214, 215, 224
Newton, Isaac 194, 209, 218, 221
Newton, Thomas 218
Nuttall, G. F. 13
Ockford, James 149, 150, 157
Olsen, V. N. 201
Origen 170, 171, 179
Overton, Richard 159, 160, 162-167, 172, 173, 175
Owen, John 16, 19, 26, 27, 35, 53, 81, 83, 103, 104, 108, 113, 115, 121, 122, 131, 135, 138, 141, 148, 151, 180, 183, 209
Pagitt, Ephraim 139
Pareus, David 95, 118, 119, 203, 210, 211, 214, 215, 225, 228
Parker, Thomas 196, 207
Patrick, Symon 173
Penry, John 84
Perkins, William 15, 18, 19-21, 23, 32-34, 47, 48, 50-52, 61, 73, 76, 77, 80, 81, 83, 109, 125, 126, 128, 129, 143, 144, 174, 175
Phocas 210
Plato 71, 170
Pooley, Christopher 140
Prideaux, John 155
Priestly, Joseph 218
Puller, Timothy 155
Quistorp, H. 213
Raleigh, Walter 176
Ribera, Francisco 205
Richardson, Samuel 220-223
Robinson, John 28, 86
Saller, William 148, 149, 156
Seagar, John 130, 179, 218, 227
Sibbes, Richard 25, 26, 34, 45, 48, 63, 75, 129, 183, 184, 186, 188, 190, 191
Smith, Mehatabel 144, 145, 152
Smith, Samuel 179, 180
Smyth, John 85-87, 90

Socrates 170
Soursby, Henry 144, 145, 152
Spittlehouse, John 148, 149
Stennett, Edward 135, 136, 139, 142, 149, 150, 151
Stennett, Joseph 86, 139
Stephens, Nathaniel 196, 199
Strong, William 127, 191
Symons, Henry 181, 182
Taylor, Thomas 34-36, 68, 107-109, 111, 112, 127, 180
Tertullian 181
Theodosius, Emperor 156
Tillotson, , Archbishop John 221
Tombes, John 91, 97, 99, 100
Traske, John 139
Truman, Joseph 34, 44, 50, 62, 133
Tryon, Thomas 175-177
Twisse, William 216
Tyndale, William 159, 160
Ussher, Archbishop James 14, 16, 17, 20, 50-52, 54, 55, 57, 62, 85, 88, 124, 132, 134, 140, 142, 180

Valentinian, Emperor 156
Venning, Ralph 123
Walker, D. P. 220, 221
Wallis, John 138, 152
Warnes, Johannes 97
Watts, Isaac 119
Wesley, Charles 34, 102
Wesley, John 2
Whiston, William 218
Whitaker, Jeremiah 191
White, Ellen 1
White, Francis 138, 142, 156
White, John 23, 26, 37, 77, 81, 122-124, 130, 140, 183
White, Thomas 173
Whitefield, George 31
Whiting, C. E. 11
Willett, Andrew 35, 36, 112, 122, 163, 175
Williams, Daniel 140
Wright, Abraham 111
Wycliffe, John 2, 6, 160, 203

GENERAL INDEX

Act of Uniformity 11, 139
Adoption 62, 184
Affusion 92, 97
Alcohol 177
Angels 44, 70, 118, 128, 154, 180, 188, 203, 211
Anglican(ism) 8-12, 14, 84, 85, 95, 97, 110, 139, 155, 193, 218, see also Church of England
Antichrist 6, 9, 10, 87, 90, 98-100, 118, 157, 189, 193, 203, 205, 209-212, 215-217, 220, see also Little Horn, Papacy
Antinomian(ism) 127, 133
Ark of the Covenant 36, 111, 123
Apocalyptic Prophecy 88, 189, 193, 197, 201, 208, see also Prophetic interpretation
Appetite 173, 174
Assurance 116
Atonement 46, 69, 90, 92, 102, 113, 115, 185, 199
Authority 6, 16, 17, 22, 27, 48, 100, 129, 143, 148, 153, 155, 156, 183, 211
Babylon 30, 87, 209
Babylonian Empire 207, 208
Baptism, believers Chapter 5 passim, 3, 71
Baptism, immersion 83, 84, 92-96
Baptism, infant 87, 89-100
Baptismal Regeneration 71, 88, 90
Baptist(s) 10, 17, 84, 86-100, 197, see also Church, Baptist
Behmenists 10
Believer(s) 6, 16, 17, 22, 25, 30, 32-34, 45, 47, 60, 62-65, 67, 70, 74-81, 85, 87, 88, 90, 92-95, 99, 103, 106, 107, 116, 117, 119, 128, 130, 133, 136, 168, 181, 183-192, 226
Bible Chapter 1 passim, 5, 13-14, 32-33, 41, 48, 56, 76, 88, 90, 92, 94, 127, 134, 147, 153, 159-161, 163, 165, 171, 175, 182-183, 188, 194-195, 198, 200, 203, 205-207, 214, 216-218, 221, 224, 226-228, see also Scripture, Word of God
Bible, Authorised Version 14, 35, 42, 131, 161, 163, 169
Bible, authority of 6, 13, 15-18, 24-25, 28, 59, 148, 183, 211
Biblical interpretation 25-28, 143, 146, 171
Biblical languages 25, 39, 90, 91, 94, 95, 129, 131, 153, 161, 163-164, 205, 221-223
Bibliolatry 21
Body 107, 159-161, 164-165, 168, 170-174, 184, 186-188, 190, 221, 225-227
Book of Common Prayer 11
Burnt Offering 111, 112
Calvinism 7, 73, 99, 185, 213, 220
Cambridge University 5, 11, 15, 35, 83, 85, 95, 140, 218
Canon Law 16, 98, 99, 156
Canterbury 104, Archbishop of 7, 10, 221
Catholic(ism) 6, 16-17, 27, 38, 53, 58, 69, 85, 99, 157, 172, 205, 211-212, see also Anglicanism, Papacy, Rome
Christ, Ascension of 20, 37, 44, 48, 55, 103, 105, 110, 154, 169, 180, 182, 186, 207, Baptism of 35, 88, 94, 209, Birth of 20, 32, 35, 37, 55, 186, 196, 207, Death of 20, 31-33, 35, 37, 43-49, 54, 55, 59, 69, 93, 96, 103-105, 112, 114, 115, 121,

134, 148, 168, 186, 196, 207, 209, 213, Deity of 29, 34, 39-41, 192, 199, Example of 148, First advent 178, 182, 184, 186, 189, 196, Incarnation 32, 41, 42, 48, 123, 149, 180, 184, 190, Kingdom of 29, 107, 184, 207, (see also Kingdom of God), Life of 20, 31, 32, 35-37, 39, 40, 43, 44, 54, 55, 109, 146, 150, 186, 189, 196, Nature of 5, 32, 36, 39, 40, 42, 48, 54, 109, Parables of 55, 63, 71, 222, Pre-existence of 35, 39, 41, 127, Priesthood of, Chapter 6, passim, 35, 37, 44, 48, 59, 129, 134, 186, 187, 211, Resurrection of 20, 32, 35, 37, 44, 48, 55, 59, 93, 96, 103, 104, 110, 118, 142, 146, 148, 154, 168, 169, 213, 226, Second Coming (see Second Advent)
Christian Life 5, 6, 9, 24, 33, 47, 53, 60, 64, 81, 88, 90, 102, 103, 105, 106, 120, 121, 132, 133, 195, 213
Christology 23, 24, 29, 31, 32, 39, 44, 107, 127, 146
Chronology 38, 189, 193, 194, 200, 207, 208, 210, 215
Church 6, 8-10, 13, 16-19, 22-30, 39, 48, 70, 71, 74, 77, 78, 81, 83-89, 92, 93, 97, 99-102, 105, 108, 109, 112, 113, 116, 117, 120, 121, 129, 135, 137, 143, 147-149, 153, 155, 156, 158, 170-173, 178, 179, 183, 184, 186, 188-192, 195-199, 203, 205, 207-215, 218, 219, and State 84, 85, 99, 191, 218, Anglican 5, 7, 9, 12, 84, 155, 218, (see also Anglicanism, Church of England), Church, Baptist 14, 84, 86-89, 92, 165, Celtic 2, 98, Congregational 44, 88, 104, Early Christian 55, 83, 88, 95-98, 149, 152, 155, 156, 170, 171, 181, 182, 189, 204, 210, 211, 216, 220, 224, English 7, 17, 84, 92, 97, 130, 197, 223, History of 23, 39, 95, 214, 215, 218, 220, 224, Lutheran 99, Mediaeval 16, 85, 98, 155, 158, 171, 172, 210, 219, National 5, 6, 9, 10, 156, Nature of 5, 84, 86, of England 5, 10, 155, 171, (see also Anglicanism), Organization 5, 6, 9, 84, 86, 87, 99, Reformed 5, 99, Roman 99, 155, 157, 171, 205, 220, (see also Catholicism, Papacy), Seventh-day Adventist 2-4, 13, Unity of 192, Visible 85-87
Church Membership 10, 71, 77, 87, 92, 93, 100
Civil War, English 7, 8, 85
Clarendon Code 12
Clergy 7, 10, 11, 84, 85, 105, 139, 154, 178, (see also Ministers), Ejected 11, 12, 179
Communion 92, see also Lord's Supper
Conditional Immortality Chapter 10 passim, 162
Confirmation 89
Congregationalists 10, 44, 86 see also Separatists
Conscience 7, 21, 23, 24, 46, 56, 61, 69, 73, 74, 77, 90, 91, 107, 123, 128, 132
Conventicle Act 12
Conversion 22, 23, 47, 67, 70, 72, 74-77, 80, 81, 133
Corporation Act 12
Council of Laodicea 156

Covenant(s) 36, 88, 89, 91, 100, 127, 134-136,
    146, 150
Creation 39, 41, 61, 62, 124, 136, 140, 144-148,
    150, 151, 160, 163, 165, 213, 227
Creed(s) 17, 92, 221
Daily Sacrifice 112, 115
Damnation see Punishment of Wicked
Day of Atonement 37, 113-116
Day-Year Principle 202, 208
Death 36, 51, 57, 59, 62, 77, 97, 159, 162-170,
    177, 187, 188, 191, 192, 220-222
Decalogue 14, 120-130, 137, 138, 140, 142, 144,
    146, 150, 157, 158, see also Law, Moral
Declaration of Indulgence 12, 86
Devil see Satan
Diet 174-176
Diggers 10, 24
Discipleship 89, 90, 92
Disestablishment 85
Dissent(ers) 11-13, 83, 86
Doctrine 2-6, 8, 9, 12-19, 21-30, 34, 39, 41, 44, 46,
    49, 53, 55, 56, 58-62, 66-70, 78, 79, 83, 85,
    87-89, 92, 94, 97, 99-105, 107, 117-121, 140,
    145, 155, 156, 159, 161, 164, 166, 169-173,
    178, 179, 181, 183, 185-189, 195, 198, 211,
    213, 214, 216, 219-222, 226, 228
Dualism 159, 170, 171
Egypt 36
Election 34, 55, 92, 185
Elizabethan Settlement 6
End of the Age 3, 30, 44, 103, 130, 157, 181, see
    also Last Days
England 1, 2, 4, 5-7, 11, 13, 14, 38, 47, 73, 84, 86,
    87, 92, 98, 102, 118, 127, 138, 140, 152, 153,
    159, 171, 172, 176, 179, 182, 184, 188, 191,
    192, 194, 197, 198, 210, 217 see also Church of
    England Protestants, English
Episcopal(ian), Episcopacy 5, 9, 84, 87, 88, 197
Eschatology 9, 63, 87, 107, 130, 178, 182, 189,
    191
Eternal Life 16, 25, 45, 47, 62, 63, 69, 102, 159,
    162, 164, 167, 169, 177, 187, 188, 192, 220, 226
Ethiopia 156
Evil 32, 50-53, 68, 72, 75, 77, 106, 170, 175
Faith 16-18, 22, 24, 28, 32, 36, 56, 58-61, 63-66,
    69, 78, 79, 81, 86, 88-93, 102, 104-107, 120,
    135, 136, 183, 189, 190, 195, 199, 211, 226
Fall, The 50, 124, 171
Family of Love 10
Fifth Monarchy Men 10, 24, 140, 200, 218
Five Mile Act 12
Flood, The 163, 175, 225
Forgiveness 61, 64, 97, 102, 107, 112, 113, 117,
    134
Forty-Two Articles of Religion 159
Future 1, 9, 20, 28-30, 53, 61, 102, 107, 130, 168,
    173, 182-185, 189, 190, 192, 193, 195, 205-208,
    212, 214, 216, 226
Futurism 204, 205
Geneva 5, 6
Glorification 78, 185, 188
Godhead, The 34, 40
Goths 207
Grace 32, 49, 57, 64, 71-73, 77, 92, 106, 117, 120,
    121, 132-136, 147, 150, 188, 190, 191, 219, 220
Great Advent Awakening 2
Great Ejection 11, 68
Health 122, 174, 176, 228
Heaven 36, 41, 42, 55, 56, 62, 63, 69, 70, 74, 76,
    102, 103-107, 109, 111, 114, 116-119, 159, 163,
    166-169, 172, 186, 188, 190, 192, 217, see also
    New Earth
Heidelberg 203
Hell 164, 172, 214, 219-223
Heresy 11, 24, 26, 32, 78, 139, 150, 159, 172, 211
Historicism 204-206, 208, 210
History 1-3, 7, 8, 10, 11, 19, 24, 29, 33, 38, 39, 43,
    48, 60, 76, 96, 98, 108, 132, 134, 135, 148, 151,
    154, 157, 168, 178, 181, 182, 189, 190,
    193-195, 197, 203-207, 215, 216, 218
Holiness 5, 52, 54, 64, 74, 77, 78, 80, 81, 106, 130,
    133, 136, 185, 188-190, 227
Holland 7, 86
Holy Spirit 15, 20, 22, 25, 26, 30, 35, 42, 61, 65, 67,
    69, 72, 77, 80-83, 86, 89, 90, 93, 96, 105, 131,
    141, 173, 174, 176, 185, 195, 228
Hope 9, 29, 63, 81, 102, 104, 130, 159, 167-169,
    178, 187-192, 195, 199, 213, 225, 226, 228

House of Commons 8, 139
Illuminaton 25, 26, 59, 81
Image of God 51, 52, 79
Immortality 159, 161-166, 169, 171-173, 219, 220,
    226
Imputation 51, 52-57, 58, 60, 61, 63-66, 78, 79,
    111
Independent(s) 9, 10, 86, 142, 197, 218
Indulgences 172, 220
Inspiration 15, 18-22, 25, 38, 199. see also Verbal
    Inspiration
Jehovah's Witnesses 3
Jerusalem, Destruction of 148, 215
Jews 19, 38, 40, 122, 123, 127, 143, 146, 147, 152,
    200, 205, 209, 223
John, Gospel of 34
Judaism 27, 113, 139, 142, 149, 152, 156, 205
Judgement 21, 74, 115, 116, 130, 167, 178, 180,
    185, 192, 203, 207, 216
Judgement, Day of 85, 214, 217-219, 222, 223,
    see also Last Day
Justification Chapter 3 passim, 29, 31, 33, 44, 67,
    69, 78-80, 86, 90, 91, 103, 107, 133, 136, 150,
    185
Kingdom of God 8-10, 29, 47, 63, 69, 85, 93, 154,
    178, 189, 195, 201, 206, 207, 218, 222, see also
    Christ, Kingdom of
Last Day 63, 71, 78, 85, 118, 159, 167, 168, 172,
    179, 180, 182, 185, 187, 188, 190, 195, 196,
    199, 216, 218, 225, 226, see also Judgement,
    Day of
Last days 29, 30, 181, 190
Law, Ceremonial 109, 122, 123, 127, 139, 141,
    143, 144, 146, 149, Civil 122, Moral Chapter 7
    passim, 76, 140-144, 146, 147, 150, 151,
    Natural 35, 124, 163, of God Chapter 7 passim,
    32, 36, 44, 46, 51, 52, 54, 57, 60, 76, 81, 90, 115,
    141
Legalism 60, 120, 133, 139
Levellers 24
Life 18, 33, 57, 62, 73-76, 79-81, 90, 93, 96, 100,
    106, 119, 120, 159, 161, 163-167, 173, 185,
    188, 190-192, 213, 219, 228
Limbo 172
Literature, Puritan theological 4, 6, 7, 11, 33, 48,
    67, 70, 149, 183
Little Horn 199, 208, 209 see also Antichrist,
    Papacy
Liturgy 5, 6, 12, 119, 211 see also Worship
Lollards 2, 6, 98
London 7, 11, 14, 87, 140
Lord's Day 132, 153, 155, see also Sunday
Lord's Supper 91, 92, see also Sacraments
Man, Nature of Chapter 9 passim, 20, 49, 50, 56,
    64, 68, 72, 73, 76-78, 106, 120, 123
Marriage 91, 122, 124, 184, 190
Masoretes 19
Mass 118, 119, 211
Medo-Persian Empire 207
Messiah 35, 37, 38, 111, 114, 129, 192, 194, 196,
    208, 209
Messianic prophecy 20, 35, 37, 38, 42, 53
Methodist 5
Middle Ages 30, 206
Millennium 8, 9, 189, 197, 214-219, 223, 224
Millenarianism 218, 224
Ministry (Ministers) 12, 23, 25, 28, 47, 67, 71, 74,
    84, 89, 99, 105, 132, 139, 140, 142, 155, see
    also Clergy
Miracles 36, 40, 48
Monasticism 173
Monism 159
Mortalism(ists) 159-173
Moslems 152
Muggletonians 10, 24
New Earth 213, 214, 223-225, 227, 228
New England 14, 176
New Jerusalem 217, 225
New Testament 16, 21, 23, 34, 39, 41, 42, 55, 67,
    81, 85, 88, 89, 92, 94, 106, 118, 121, 122,
    127-129, 135, 140, 146-149, 154, 161, 164, 167,
    181, 182, 189, 191, 195, 199, 222, 226
Nominated Parliament 8
Nonconformity(ist) 11, 12, 86, 140
North America 2, 8, 13
Obedience 21, 24, 51, 54, 60, 62, 64, 79, 86, 90,
    120, 122, 127, 129, 130, 133, 134, 136, 149,
    162, 190

Old Testament 16, 19-21, 23, 34-39, 41, 42, 45, 53, 55, 95, 102, 105, 107, 108, 121, 127, 135, 146, 166, 187, 194, 196, 208, 213, 221, 222
Original Sin 51, 52, 64, 90, 162
Orthodoxy 169, 171, 179, 198, 199
Oxford University 11, 27, 35, 68, 83, 138, 148, 155, 170, 207, 218
Paganism 28, 170, 171, 205, 211
Papacy 9, 87, 155, 210-212, 215, see also Antichrist, Little Horn
Paradise 53, 124, 144, 147, 162, 169, 226-228
Parliament 7, 9, 11, 149, 191
Passover 36
Perfection(ism) 64, 78
Persecution 7, 12, 18, 86, 87, 209, 215
Philosophy 27, 28, 71, 108, 160, 162, 163, 170-173, 181, 205, 220
Pilgrim Fathers 28, 86
Platonism 151, 152
Poland 38
Pope(s) 16, 100, 157, 211, 212, see also Papacy
Pray(er) 47, 74, 80, 108, 117, 134, 190
Preacher(s) 9, 11, 15, 17, 24-26, 28, 33, 34, 39, 43-48, 55, 66, 68-70, 72, 82, 84, 85, 104, 107, 132, 168, 173, 178, 182, 185, 191, 195
Preaching 7, 20, 22, 23, 25, 28, 29, 33, 67, 69, 155, 210
Predestination 185, 220
Presbyterian(ism) 5, 7-10, 87, 142, 197
Press, The 7, 9, 11
Preterism 204, 205
Priest(hood) 22, 99, 118, 211
Priesthood, Levitical 37, 108, 111-114, 116, 118
Prophecy Chapter 11, passim, 10, 19, 20, 23, 30, 34, 38, 42, 87, 88, 98, 127, 181-183, 215, 217, 218,
Prophetic Interpretation Chapter 11 passim, 14, 88, 182, 189, 214, 216, 218, 228
Protectorate 7, 8, 85
Protestant(ism) 1, 3, 4, 6, 9, 12, 13, 16-18, 27, 32, 49, 53, 70, 83, 92, 98-100, 117-119, 138, 155, 172, 194, 198, 200-202, 204, 205, 209-212, 214, 215, 226, English 8, 15, 18, 21, 22, 84, 87, 98, 103, 118, 130, 157, 197, 208, 214
Punishment of Wicked 97, 172, 217, 219-223
Purgatory 172, 219, 220

Quaker(s) 5
Ransom 45
Ranters 10, 24
Reason 17, 25, 26, 32, 48, 55, 56, 73, 74, 78, 81, 91, 143, 224, 226
Reconciliation 32, 45, 46, 62, 114, 185
Redemption 29, 31, 32, 35, 39, 43-46, 53, 62, 69, 103-105, 110, 115, 116, 124, 136, 150, 159, 160, 167, 168, 177, 183-186, 213
Reformation, the 3, 13, 16, 27, 29, 49, 66, 69, 84, 87, 88, 99, 100, 155, 157, 169, 171, 181, 197, 202, 204, 215, English 5, 6, 9, 13, 17, 155, 157
Regeneration Chapter 4 passim, 22, 62, 65, 88, 90, 93, 106, 120, 133, 184, 189
Repentance 62, 63, 79, 88, 90, 93
Resurrection, general 107, 159, 164, 167-170, 172, 177, 185-188, 191, 213, 214, 216, 217, 219-224, 226, 227
Restoration, the 7, 9, 11, 24, 28, 179
Revelation 3, 16, 17, 18, 24, 28, 29, 38, 81, 103, 119, 127, 162, 178, 194, 196, 199, 205, 206, 208, 226
Rhode Island 14
Righteousness Chapter 3 passim, 31, 47, 67, 78-80, 91, 102, 109, 116, 131, 150, 227, 228
Roman Empire 170, 207-209
Rome 6, 10, 16, 17, 87, 90, 98, 99, 118, 156-158, 170-172, 200, 209, 220, see also Catholicism, Church of Rome, Papacy
Sabbatarians 138-142, 151-153, 155-158
Sabbath Chapter 8 passim, 14, 109, 124, 132, 169, 219
Sacraments 12, 71, 84, 118, 156

Sacrificial System, Levitical 111-114, 122, 187
Saints, Invocation of 118, 172, 211
Saints (Living) 8, 23, 24, 69, 70, 73, 76, 85, 86, 105, 107, 119, 180, 181, 186, 187, 189-191, 205, 209, 214, 215, 217-219, 224
Salvation 9, 16, 17, 21-25, 28, 29, 32-34, 36, 38, 43, 44, 48-51, 53-56, 58-60, 62-67, 69, 70, 78, 81, 84, 90, 91, 102-105, 111, 113-115, 119, 120, 122, 128, 130-136, 149, 150, 168, 178, 179, 183, 185, 187, 188, 195, 211, 219, 228
Sanctification 21, 58, 60, 63-66, 78-81, 90, 91, 106, 133, 143, 150, 185, 188
Sanctuary, Heavenly 102, 109, 110, 114, 115, 119
Sanctuary, Mosaic 36, 104, 108, 109, 110, 111, 113, 114, 119, 122, 123, 187
Satan 32, 36, 69, 74, 78, 80, 117, 123, 174, 186, 190, 191, 203, 205, 213-215, 217, 219
Scapegoat 37
Scripture Chapter 1 passim, 3, 6, 10, 13, 31-35, 39, 40, 42, 45, 47, 49, 55, 59, 64, 67, 69, 70, 79, 81, 88-92, 94, 96, 98-100, 103, 105, 107, 110, 117, 118, 120-122, 133-135, 137-139, 141, 143, 146, 149, 153-158, 160-163, 167, 169, 171, 175, 178, 179, 182-184, 189, 193-199, 201, 202, 205, 209-211, 216, 218, 220-224, 225, 226, 228, see also Bible
Second Advent Chapter 10 passim, 3, 9, 14, 44, 103, 104, 118, 119, 130, 167, 168, 193, 199, 204, 207, 216-219
Sectarianism 3, 10, 120, 139, 191, 192, 198, 199
Seekers 24
Separatists 7, 9, 10, 86, 87
Sermon on the Mount 128
Sermons 6, 67, 132
Seventh day Adventists(ism) 1-44, 13, 14, 116
Seventh-Day Baptist(s) 14, 86, 135, 139
Sin 20, 33, 37, 39, 40, 43, 45-47, 50-54, 56-58, 60-62, 64, 67, 68, 73-78, 80, 88, 90, 93, 96, 102, 106, 107, 112, 113, 115, 123, 125, 131-136, 162, 163, 171, 175, 185-187, 190, 213, 220, 227
Sin Offering 111, 112, 115
Smoking 176, 177
Sola Scriptura 88
Soul 159, 160, 161, 163-173, 187, 220, 222
Spirit 160, 161, 165, 166
Stuarts 7, 178, 197
Sunday 138, 139, 142-144, 149, 151-153, 155, 156, 158
Symbolism 15, 36, 37, 90, 91, 93, 104, 108, 109, 111, 112, 115, 119, 193, 197, 201-204, 206, 216
Temperance 174, 177
Temple 111
Ten Commandments see Decalogue
Test Act 12
Thirty-nine Articles 40
Tobacco 176, 177
Toleration Act 12
Torment, eternal see Hell
Tree of Life 228
Tradition 16, 17, 27, 100, 155, 158, 210, 211
Transubstantiation 118
Traskites 139
Tudors 7, 178
Turks 215
Typology 23, 34-37, 42, 127
Utopia 6
Vegetarianism 175, 176
Verbal Inspiration 21
Week, Origin of 151
West Indies 12
Westminster Assembly 7, 8, 9, 183, 191, 199, 216
Westminster Confession of Faith 8, 92
Will, the 20, 58, 59, 67, 68, 73, 74, 77, 79, 80, 164
Word of God Chapter 1 passim, 1, 6, 33, 62, 68, 73, 80, 81, 83, 85, 98, 100, 130, 141, 194, see also Bible, Scripture
Works 32, 58-60, 64, 65, 117, 119, 134, 135, 150, 211, see also Obedience
Worship 6-8, 10, 12, 16, 39, 84, 86, 100, 111, 114, 145, 149, 155, 210, 211 see also Liturgy